The al-Ghazali Engima and Why Shari'a is not Islamic Law

The al-Ghazali Engima and Why Shari'a is not Islamic Law

Haifaa G. Khalafallah

equinox

SHEFFIELD UK BRISTOL CT

Published by Equinox Publishing Ltd.
UK: Office 415, The Workstation, 15 Paternoster Row, Sheffield, South Yorkshire S1 2BX
USA: ISD, 70 Enterprise Drive, Bristol, CT 06010

www.equinoxpub.com

First published 2017

British Library Cataloguing-in-Publication Data

A catalogue record for this book is available from the British Library.

ISBN-13 978 1 78179 295 7 (hardback)

Library of Congress Cataloging-in-Publication Data
Names: Khalafallah, Haifaa G., author.
Title: The al-Ghazali engima and why shariʿa is not Islamic law / Haifaa G. Khalafallah.
Description: Bristol, CT : Equinox Publishing Ltd, 2016. | Includes bibliographical references and index.
Identifiers: LCCN 2016009238 (print) | LCCN 2016011735 (ebook) | ISBN 9781781792957 (hb) | ISBN 9781781794661 (e-PDF) | ISBN 9781781794678 (e-epub)
Subjects: LCSH: Ghazālī, Muḥammad, 1917-1996. | Islamic law.
Classification: LCC BP80.G284 K43 2016 (print) | LCC BP80.G284 (ebook) | DDC 297.1/4092--dc23
LC record available at http://lccn.loc.gov/2016009238

Typeset by BBR, Sheffield
Printed and bound by Lightning Source Inc. (La Vergne, TN), Lightning Source UK Ltd. (Milton Keynes), Lightning Source AU Pty. (Scoresby, Victoria).

Contents

Acknowledgements

Many contributed to Mohammed al-Ghazali's Shari'a story in this book.

From Bani Suwayf to Istanbul, from Sharjah to Chicago, from Cairo to Kayseri, from sitting rooms from Washington, DC to Primrose Hill, and to circles in East London and Berlin, a great number of people, institutions, students, friends, family, and, indeed, Muslim communities across the Middle East, Europe, and the United States all informed its substance over the years. I owe so many so much. Whatever value is found in this book belongs to this multitude; the shortcomings are my own.

I am especially indebted to the many prominent scholars of Islam in Egypt who opened their doors and libraries to me. When they continued to invite me into their midst despite my open critiques of their scholarly world, they provided a first-hand glimpse of the excellent old mettle of *fiqh* as a varied, energetic intellectual enterprise. Although I openly differed with their views, some of al-Azhar's famous names tutored me over the years in *usul al-fiqh* and Hadith, and let me into their concerns as well as their homes.

This was also so with exceptional professors at other universities, and experts at religious and media institutions in Egypt, but I must single out the executive manager of the IIIT branch in Cairo, Khaled abd al-Mun'im, because I have no words with which to thank him and his colleagues. Throughout the years their generosity and dedication kept this work on track. I must also name the departed; scholars who always took my calls, welcomed my visits, and answered my painful questions: Shaykh Taha Jabir al-Alwani and Hasan al-Banna's brother, *ustadh* Gamal al-Banna.

Besides access to many of the great and the good of Islam's contemporary scholars in Egypt, I also reaped the bounty of one of Western academia's outstanding institutions: Georgetown University ensured that I had a space in which to differ and bolstered my research in every imaginable way, as a student, then as a professor in its exceptional history department at more than one of the university's world campuses. Even long after I left their official fold, this excellent department's administrators magnanimously provided help with my research. In particular, I continued to draw on the varied expertise of some of academia's best historians including the amazing Andrzej Kaminski as well as the late professors Richard Stites, Barbara Stowasser, and my first advisor, Hisham Sharabi. Why specialists including James Shedel and Roland Johnson took interest in my work, I will never know but I am certain that their insights and backing greatly enriched this research. For this I am very grateful.

From the start, the endearing John Voll saw to it that my investigation pushed ahead against the odds. But, to Judith Tucker I owe much of what I learned and loved about the treasures of Middle East and Islamic historiography. Amira Sonbol set a shining example of academic tutorship. Too many to count are the intellectual and logistical doors she opened for this research, not to mention the actual doors of her homes. No expressions of thanks can repay her. Also enormous is the debt I owe to Jo Ann Moran Cruz, who patiently led me through the riches and rigours of the brilliant world of comparative history. Over the years, this inspiring professor of medieval European history challenged me every step of the way, commenting on drafts of this book and sometimes even editing the English.

The former Saudi oil minister Shaykh Ahmed Zaki Yamani and his Furqan Education Foundation provided the much-needed early financial support that allowed me to study English common law and pass the Common Professional Examination, without ever laying claim to, or questioning the substance of, any of my research. The grant by the American Research Center in Egypt (ARCE) and its stimulating Cairo setting were equally valuable and much appreciated.

Mention must also single out friends who never expected to nurture a book on Shari'a but still propelled this effort forward with their professionalism and sound advice. They include the former editor of *Africa Analysis*, Ahmed Rajab; the novelist Fatima al-Nahed; Carol Madison-Graham, former Executive Director of Fulbright UK; Anne Walmsley, a Caribbean art specialist and former Africa editor of *Index on Censorship*; the writer and accomplished author Patricia Crisafulli; Loubna Yusuf, vice-dean of Cairo University's Faculty of Arts; and Selda Kapan, a professor at Erciyes University, Turkey.

Equally priceless were the contributions of my students in the United States, Britain, Egypt, and elsewhere. Volunteers at the Sinai Centre for Islamic Mediterranean Studies especially helped shape this book with their backing, candid comments, and infectious enthusiasm.

Most of all, I owe all my family an apology for years of unintended inattentiveness along with deep gratitude for their never-ending help. However, it was my departed parents who inspired the essence of this book.

INTRODUCTION

Studying Shari'a and al-Ghazali

When did "Shari'a" become "Islamic law"? All attempts to reconfigure Shari'a from a methodology into a code of law have in fact floundered—from Ibn al-Muqaffa's effort in the eighth century CE[1] to the Majallah project of the Ottomans in the nineteenth century.[2] In some cases, those who made the attempt wanted to bring lawmaking under political control (as is found in many societies), but often the driving force has been the desire to achieve the clarity that a set of precise rules offers judges who apply the law and all to whom it is applied. But no matter how well intentioned, assembling Shari'a into a code misunderstands its quintessence: such attempts have always failed, because codifying Shari'a means taking an essentially rule-deducing process—a living methodology that relies on changing human choices as much as eternal, divine principles—and squeezing it into a predetermined mould. The legislative jurisdiction of Shari'a has thus managed to stay beyond the reach of rulers and powerful groups, at least officially. Even when bad choices produced bad rules, all framed in God's name, the process continued to defy attempts to fully own it. Such insubordination to executive power made Shari'a a political menace that every government over Muslim societies has had to address; and when it defied the authority of the European nation states that had occupied most Muslim lands by the nineteenth century it posed the single greatest obstacle to European colonization projects. Muslim subjects continued to resort to the rulemaking process of Shari'a as the foundation of legitimacy, frustrating the paradigm of modernization that sets Western standards as the only yardstick for advancement. Therefore, in order to grasp this pervasive yet elusive phenomenon, the scholars who arrived via the colonizers' ships recast Shari'a according to European templates. They renamed it "Islamic law", explaining Shari'a in terms of their Western experiences as a canon law, but one with the audacity to interfere in almost every secular matter. Removed from its multi-layered context, Shari'a appeared to these occupiers as both an exotic enigma and as a threat to European ways; as such, the Europeans concluded that what they saw as an obstructive medieval system of law would undoubtedly give way to modern Western laws.

The newly constructed term "Islamic law" also found support among some Muslims. As a way of resisting their colonizers' attempts to impose European laws, nineteenth and early twentieth-century Muslims who conversed in European languages, most significantly in India, unwittingly helped entrench the construct by adopting the term to argue that they had no need for new, imported laws. In time, this convenient but misleading template came to predominate, and "Islamic law" is now the lens through which the modern world—including academia—sees all things Islamic. But does it really matter that Shari'a is understood or merely labelled as "Islamic law"? Perhaps not, if it were not for the detrimental outcome of such a misnomer. Misrepresenting the active process of Shari'a rulemaking as law has blurred our understanding of how Muslims have actually conceptualized lawfulness, making it harder to see their past or contemporary experiences as they really were or are. Every substantial new development in these societies has taken academic expertise by surprise. More seriously, however, is the question of how Islamic law affects Muslims wherever it encompasses them. Whether through heavy-handed colonization or through being raised or trained within the Western educational terrain, Muslims find themselves in a difficult, solitary space. Unable to bridge the gap between their implicit understanding of Shari'a rulemaking and Islamic law, their responses to modernity have often struggled intellectually. Some have opted for embracing suspended worldviews divorced from reality, while others live in isolated extremes. Distorting Shari'a has thus had catastrophic consequences, as contemporary events continue to show.[3]

My encounter with the conundrum of Islamic law began in the late 1990s, when I started investigating Shari'a rulemaking.[4] As I searched the enormous wealth of resources available in Egyptian archives and at the centres of Sunni Muslim scholarship—examining the collections at al-Azhar Mosque-University, interviewing al-Azhar's *fuqaha*, and attending Azhari lectures and mosque sermons across Cairo—I came to a dead end. I just could not find "Islamic law". Harder still was to encounter such a "law" in the everyday lives of Egyptians, whether in urban centres besides Cairo or elsewhere. There was no trace of it in Upper Egypt, from where my father originated. Yet, at the time, many in the country believed themselves devotees of Shari'a, which raised questions about the connection between their Shari'a rulemaking and Islamic law. For like an optical illusion, the closer one comes to "Islamic law" the quicker it unravels into other things. Unless observation was bent to fit predetermined assumptions, "Islamic law" did not make sense. In order to grasp Shari'a, at least in this setting, the sacred conjectures that fill the mountain of Western academic literature on Islamic law had to be questioned, and even abandoned.

However, it became just as necessary to interrogate the predominant Muslim narrative, starting with several questions: Why do these Egyptians subscribe to particular rules that some of their scholars advance as being of Shari'a, while they reject others? How do people in contemporary Egypt understand these Shari'a rules/laws? What should one make of their fluid landscape of rulemaking, which they call Shari'a? What had changed, if anything, in this understanding from earlier centuries, and what has stayed the same?

Shaykh Mohammed al-Ghazali (1917–1996) offered a good starting point for investigating these queries. The seeming paradoxes surrounding him came into full view the day he died in March 1996. In the last years of his life, this leader of mainstream Muslim orthodoxy had declared an open—some would even say reckless—all-out war on the "orthodox" Saudi religious and political establishments; yet the same authorities disrupted regular radio and TV broadcasting to announce as a "loss to the Muslim world" his sudden death in their capital. Why did the Saudi establishment accord al-Ghazali in death the decorum that befits a great Muslim scholar? When the time came, they laid to rest this Egyptian, who publicly censured their approaches to Shari'a, at Islam's most revered burial place, Baqi'i, in Medina, in the company of the Prophet's companions.[5] Why such reverence for someone whose enemies dismissed as a mere loud-mouthed preacher?

Shaykh Ali Goma (b. 1952), one of the leading modern scholars of *usul al-fiqh* (Shari'a lawmaking) and a former mufti of Egypt,[6] judges that Mohammed al-Ghazali's influence over Egyptians will eventually prove to be far greater than that of their most famous modern *'alim* and mufti, Shaykh Mohammed Abduh (d. 1905).[7] Another world authority on Muslim lawmaking, Shaykh Yusuf al-Qaradawi (b. 1926), has frequently described al-Ghazali as one of Islam's most sincere and candid experts in contemporary times.[8] Privately, both Shaykhs Goma and al-Qaradawi could not digest some of al-Ghazali's views, especially on Muslim history,[9] but in public they eagerly joined the circle of scholars that assembled under the umbrella of this maverick shaykh. Egypt's most dynamic Islamic intelligentsia trailed Shaykh Mohammed al-Ghazali wherever he went in the last two decades of his life, ever-present in the wings of his lectures or travels as disciples or as admirers.[10] However, like many in this senior circle of *fuqaha* after the 2011 revolution which ousted President Hosni Mubarak, Shaykhs Goma and al-Qaradawi then became enemies, describing lawfulness in opposing terms; and in contrast to al-Ghazali, their reputations as the most important *usul al-fiqh* scholars suffered immensely when they ventured into controversial subjects, especially Shari'a rules about government.

Al-Ghazali's strength and influence mainly derived from the way he was viewed by ordinary men and women: the many Arabic-speaking Muslims from diverse backgrounds who saw—and continue to see—Ghazali as speaking for them makes him especially relevant, highlighting the connection between Shari'a and communal memories. Al-Ghazali appears to have triggered in the minds of the people in his region images of the original *fuqaha*, the early "learned"-activists who placed Muslim rulemaking at the centre of socio-political resistance as well as of erudition. Their initial project left lasting impressions that have resonated through the centuries, despite the fact that many of these *fuqaha*-activists in time became a part of the establishment that they were supposed to be resisting. Consequently, scholars whose careers resemble these early activists' stir in the minds of the people in the region agreeable memories tied to loyalty to a particular method of rulemaking; they are often seen as the true representatives of Islam and lawfulness, but they are equally seen as the genuine voices of their communities, expressing their identities and mundane worldly concerns. This is how many in his community perceived al-Ghazali: a deputy-president of al-Azhar—the pre-eminent centre of Sunni learning—mirroring a common sentiment of Egypt's streets, described al-Ghazali as "the imam of *mujadiddin* in modern times [...] of whom the Prophet had informed us."[11] Even those who openly criticized al-Ghazali nevertheless regarded him as a contemporary authority on their faith, or "*hojat* al-Islam in our time", as Ahmed Shawqi al-Fangari, a medical doctor and Islamic campaigner, described him.[12] Whether Shari'a experts or laypersons, the majority of Egyptians regarded al-Ghazali as their leader, and his ideas as authoritative expressions of Islam—including instances when he controversially overturned well-known rules that had long been held as constituting Shari'a.[13] The question is: why?

Best of times, worst of times

The paradoxes surrounding Shaykh Mohammed al-Ghazali do not end there. Al-Ghazali exemplified the contemporary Muslim spirit of defiant intransigence, as well as becoming its most influential critic, whose words were heeded by a majority of Arabic-speaking Muslims. He first emerged as a spokesman for mainstream Islam in the struggle against Western colonialism in the 1940s, but by the late 1980s he seemed to be raining on the Muslim parade of which he was supposed to be a flag-bearer. The timing of al-Ghazali's censure of his people here is especially significant: at the height of the Islamists' political and economic influence, when even Western governments indulged their strident voices, al-Ghazali stood in their midst to scorn them, and warning of the dangers they posed to the world.[14] He also broke ranks with his colleagues, the contemporary grand *fuqaha* of Islam: unlike them, he publicly considered subjects deemed too sensitive or too controversial to discuss outside their elite circles. The authenticity of particular Hadith reports (describing the words and deeds of the Prophet) is one such issue; another was his description of many entrenched rules that were regarded as part of the Shari'a—including laws on women and governance—as reflecting a corrupt worldview.

Al-Ghazali's continuing significance is also related to the world events of the last years of his life, and what has followed since. In the late 1970s and early 1980s, Muslim men poured into the rugged Afghani landscape in support of their brethren in an unequal war against a world power. Hoping to harness this energy to weaken communism, Western governments backed these *mujahideen* in the name of freedom. The strategy worked, for a time: fighting from mountain caves, the Muslim guerrillas appeared to be draining the Soviet Union's economic and military might; but soon after the collapse of the USSR, the same fighters instead directed their fury against the United States and Europe—also in the name of freedom, angry with Western governments' continuing meddling in Muslim affairs. Islam became a preoccupation of the whole world—some even argue, a threat to it.

After the destruction of the World Trade Center in New York in 2001, and the bombing of ordinary men and women on their way to work in Madrid in 2004 and then London in 2005, instead of a faith, Islam became headline news, a byword for terror.[15] It appeared as if suddenly everyone in the world had acquired an expert opinion on Muslim lawmaking. In a 2014 radio interview, Northern Ireland's first minister publicly announced that he would not trust Muslims who were "fully devoted to Shari'a law".[16] This senior British official articulated a contemporary reality: early in the twenty-first century, Shari'a had become a "radioactive" word,[17] as Noah Feldman, an American law professor, put it, leading him to ask: "How is it that what so many Westerners see as the most unappealing and pre-modern aspect of Islam is, to many Muslims, the vibrant, attractive core of a global movement of Islamic revival?" Feldman concluded that "the explanation surely must go beyond the oversimplified assumption that Muslims want to use Shari'ah to reverse feminism and control women."[18] Although it seemingly threatened the world, neither he nor many other experts like him really attended to basic questions about Shari'a. These include:

- Is Shari'a really a law?[19] Or is it a method of making laws and other rules? Does this distinction matter?
- How do the *'ulama*, Muslim scholars like al-Ghazali, actually derive Shari'a's rules/laws? In other words, what is the trajectory of rulemaking? How are these rules translated into real life?
- What role does the Muslim street (or powerful sections in society) have in deciding the shape and outcome of these divine rules?
- Which Shari'a laws/rules are absolute? What are those that researchers can examine independently from a particular context?
- Why are the predominant tools with which we study how Islam makes its rulemaking so hard to grasp, and why do they almost always lead to the

"oversimplified assumption that Muslims want to use Shari'ah to reverse feminism and control women"?[20]

- What impact does the lens through which a Muslim community sees its past have on Shari'a lawmaking? (The least discussed question of all.)
- What does Shari'a and all the above questions have to do with momentous events, such as the Arab Spring?

Al-Ghazali's career provides a good case for probing how and why Muslim communities read both written and oral texts within actual, not abstract, contexts and how their scholars have approached Qur'anic content to produce a variety of Shari'a rules and legal arguments. Here, the key questions are: what was it in his approach to Muslim rule-/lawmaking that guaranteed al-Ghazali his immense following among common people and senior scholars alike? And how does that throw light on the "attractive core" of Shari'a, at least as many Arabic speakers see it in our times?

Consequently, this is not only an overdue intellectual biography of al-Ghazali. It is a slice of the story of Shari'a rulemaking and of modern Egypt. The story has a beginning, and many twists and turns, and it has an end—but only a tentative one. For al-Ghazali is to be found at the epicentre of this Shari'a "radioactivity"; and, in contrast with Egyptians' apprehension of both Islamists and self-described progressive Muslims, he enjoyed widespread trust as an expert on Shari'a, even after he revised his opinions about some of its best-known rules/laws. Does his influence on his fellow Egyptians—reformers, traditionalists, and dissidents alike—enhance our understanding of Shari'a?

The academic study of al-Ghazali and Muslim lawmaking

Despite his prominence at a critical time, al-Ghazali has been mostly overlooked in Western scholarship. That is not to say that Mohammed al-Ghazali has gone unnoticed. During most of his life, Western experts viewed him as a spokesman for Muslim orthodoxy, a rigid and fervent enemy of all things Western (see Chapter 7 for examples). There has been little interest in delving into his world, in order to explore the evolution of his views or how he influenced people in the ways and to the extent that he did. Fanaticism—inherent in Islam, or in Egyptian and Arab societies—presumably explained it all. Static phraseology, such as "extremism" or "traditionalism", which experts assumed summed up al-Ghazali's thought, only reflected their perceptions of "Muslim orthodoxy" as a strain of thought that obstructed the brave champions of "modernization" and "progress".[21]

By the 1990s, some experts in the West began to describe al-Ghazali in contrasting terms, as a voice of reform and moderation. Professor Khaled Abu El Fadl, of the UCLA School of Law, led the way here.[22] Today, a few more scholars see al-Ghazali as the flag-bearer of moderation in Egypt, while others regard him as a conventional preacher swayed by the West.[23] Rarely do these three scholarly camps—those who see him as either extremist or conventional, or as a moderate reformer—ever consider the al-Ghazali of a different perspective, or seek to synthesize contrasting perspectives. However, the experts all agree on the extent of al-Ghazali's influence over Muslims, although they also find him a poor candidate for the study of Shari'a rulemaking—because he does not "merit engagement at a doctrinal level", as even his biggest admirer in Western academia once put it.[24] This demonstrates the opinion that, although al-Ghazali was important, there is nothing in the predominant academic lens through which they view Shari'a and Muslim societies that warrants a closer look. In that, al-Ghazali's fate is not his alone. He joins other influential Egyptians of modern times, such as the self-taught 'Abbas Mahmoud al-'Aqqad (d. 1964), Shaykhs Mustafa al-Maraghi (d. 1945) and Ahmed Hasan al-Baquri (d. 1985), or a poet such as Mahmoud Bayram al-Tunsi (d. 1961).[25] In spite of their great impact on modern Egyptian perceptions of faith and community, such figures are not extensively examined, because they too do not fit Western academic templates and tools for studying this society's experiences.

Despite this, it must be allowed that the early European orientalists raised awareness that historical settings mattered. Most importantly, they diligently collected, preserved, and published many Muslim records, amassing a significant, accessible legacy. Yet when these orientalists investigated the texts they collected, they did not really take account of real-life circumstances to understand how Muslim rule-/lawmaking evolved. Not only did they freeze Muslim societies' experiences in a number of standard frames, they also quarantined them into separate boxes—in the case of Egypt: pharaohs, Greeks, Romans, Islamic Egypt, modern Egypt, and so on—which were almost always disconnected from each other. Continuities were often read as Muslim lack of originality, or missed altogether. Realities in Egypt fracture this myopic lens and insular perspective. In the case of Shari'a, this dominant academic template has imprisoned the Muslim past and present in predetermined formats sustained by static, anachronistic terms. This approach also ignores the tension generated whenever a *faqih*, or community, attends to Islam's scriptural content, thereby missing the single most potent feature that has generated Muslim legal ideas. Many modern researchers of Shari'a rule-/lawmaking regularly neglect the Qur'an, albeit quietly, truncating its contents into whatever *fiqh* products are under examination, and imagining doctrinal content and the line of reasoning to be one and the same. As such, modern academia has created a template for the study of Shari'a rulemaking that ignores both context and doctrinal content, paying disproportionate attention to a single or a few texts from which are derived universal statements on Islam and its many cultures. To presume that any two Muslim legal texts share identical contexts and dynamics in relation to Qur'anic doctrine is untenable, because it posits one motionless, unthinking Muslim society at every historical moment. The study of Shari'a requires new templates.

The case of al-Ghazali reveals the painful mismatch between actual Muslim rulemaking and the modern study of Islam. Academic experts use the terms "Islamic law", "*fiqh*", and "Shari'a" interchangeably, in a slipshod and crude way. Little attention is paid to changes and continuities in the works of influential *fuqaha* on Shari'a; instead, academia concentrates on reinterpreting ancient *fiqh* texts according to its assumptions about Islamic law. Perhaps that is why the *fuqaha* at the centre of Shari'a rulemaking have not found much to attract them to modern Western study of Islam. Islam's own Shari'a experts rarely encounter the phrase "Islamic law", and when such a misnomer or one of its premises is put before them, do not know what to make of it: "I have an objection to [your] phrase: 'the fixed Islamic Shari'a'", was how Shaykh Mohammed al-Ghazali interrupted what he viewed as an oddly formulated question. "There is stability in [Shari'a's] principles, but its applications change", he explained.[26] Al-Ghazali then challenged his interviewer, in order to underline the point: "Could applications of justice in a seventh-century Bedouin primitive environment possibly remain the same as those in a twentieth-century urban, industrialized society?"[27]

Although he stands at the opposite end from al-Ghazali's thought, the *usul al-fiqh* expert Goma has also expressed unease about perceiving the corpus of *fiqh* rules, arguments, maxims, and array of other legal products as "Islamic law". A law must be specific as to time, place, and geographic area to be a valid legal code, Goma explained,[28] and because these vary, the *fuqaha* have understood that any law which invokes Islamic principles must be modified every so often to meet changing circumstances. This recognition has generated streams of new rules, further adding to the assortment of legal codes. However, "none of these codes can be described as Shari'a; they do not make an Islamic Law either." Describing the corpus of *fiqh* as Islamic law belittled the nature and purpose of Shari'a lawmaking, according to Goma; it also misrepresented *fiqh*, he concluded (this is further explained in Chapter 7).

All about a method

Through the lens of Islamic law, al-Ghazali puzzles many. They interpret adjustments in his thinking in the same way that early European orientalists regarded all things Muslim: as being inherently irrational and erratic. However, such assumptions ignore context as well as the evolution of his thought. Al-Ghazali's view of gender is an example here. From the 1950s to the 1970s, al-Ghazali spearheaded the fight against employing women in any public posts; but in the 1990s he declared to an audience in the Arabian Peninsula (UAE) that he would support a qualified woman as president of Egypt. The thought of a female leading the most populous and culturally significant Arab country shocked his people at the time. Yet, somehow, he eventually persuaded many among the devout in Egypt to adjust long-held views on women and Shari'a. Why did he succeed in persuading people in his country to change their minds on such an important issue when so many others of his contemporaries, both traditionalists and progressives, had failed? Discussing Islamic law in relation to labels such as "moderate", "fundamentalist", or "extremist" does not help us to answer this question. Instead, the key factor is that al-Ghazali had managed to evoke agreeable communal memories in the minds of his countrymen and, in the process, he proved his absolute loyalty to the Shari'a method of rulemaking. In other words, whereas those guided by an idea of "Islamic law" saw in al-Ghazali fickleness, many Muslims rather saw constancy.

For at the heart of the Muslim legal universe reigns a basic methodology that, for both historical and inherent technical reasons, has never developed into a law or formed a single code. Loyalty to and mastery of this schema of rulemaking—but not to any particular law or norm—propels a *faqih* to lasting influence. That has meant, in practice, that far from condemning scholars who dare challenge accepted rules, Muslims trust *fuqaha* who show the fortitude to break free from internal shackles and external pressures in order to clarify or defend from misuse what they believe to be a fit-for-all-times "way" of deducing sound rules (discussed further in Chapters 1, 3, and 7). The influence of these scholars, as defenders of the integrity of Shari'a, originated in challenging—not defending—long-standing "Islamic laws"; this is clear from a seminar that al-Ghazali held in Cairo in the 1990s that was attended by some of the most senior Muslim scholars of the time, and which is summarized in Appendix 1.

However, it would be wrong to regard this ancient rule-deducing process in essentialist or reductionist terms: it has had a history as long and as varied as the societies which embraced it, and while there are some continuities from different periods, the processes of Shari'a have undergone significant changes or even reversals. Until today the ebb and tide of adjustment has carried on uninterrupted. Consequently, every Shari'a-linked rule, or *fiqh* argument, related to how, at a given time, a given community—or scholar—approached the components of this rulemaking process. The history of Shari'a rule-/lawmaking includes thousands of stories; and somewhere along his intellectual journey, al-Ghazali came to believe that not just the story itself, but also how it is told, is of immense importance. In this, he started a new chapter in his career and in his country's approaches to Islam.

Shari'a: An outline for study

This investigation of Shari'a starts from the following premise: that the "Islamic" in any legal experience consists of three inter-related spheres that create a constant exchange between Qur'anic contents and the world in which Muslims live: (1) the layers of specific contexts, in contrast to the generic understanding constructed by modern academia as a standard reference;[29] (2) the contents of the scriptures, especially those that Muslims view as expressing the Qur'an's permanent principles and injunctions; and (3) the innumerable results of this dynamic between ever-changing, multiple contexts and Qur'anic directives: the *fiqh* texts in which scholars have explained how they discerned particular rules and elaborated legal ideas. What is Islamic about a particular law, rule, or legal argument is embedded in the place where it manages the tension generated from attempts to relate its setting, or an ever-changing set of circumstances, to the unchanging tenets of the Qur'an—and also often in reference to an ever-increasing variety of *fiqh* precedents. Put another way, lawfulness in Islam does not reside in a law, but in a rulemaking trajectory that consists of a ceaseless flow between context, Qur'anic content, and outcome, the last of these usually as collected in *fiqh* records. How correct or otherwise a rule is perceived depends on how well it is argued within this process, which generates long-lasting directives that effectively supersede the jurisdiction of any executive authority.

Book structure

In line with the outline above, the discussion of al-Ghazali here starts with his contexts, after which key texts in his legacy are examined in relation to their settings and the questions to which he was responding when he authored his works. However, written documents do not and cannot tell the whole story of Muslim legal mores. From an early point in Islamic history, Muslims also turned to more elusive texts to assess the validity of their experts on rulemaking: such tacit manuals, generated by various crises, can be seen as "texts of tension". How a *faqih* responds to challenges has long served as the yardstick against which Muslims have found evidence of the true worth of Shari'a experts, with these controversies defining which issues were significant. Researchers can also find in them valuable texts that situate the original purpose of a rule or legal argument, and clarify the continuities or breaks in Shari'a rule-/lawmaking. Accordingly, Chapters 3 and 4 in the current study explore the controversies that al-Ghazali either created or was a central figure in; many in his country used such points of stress to assess his status as an expert on Shari'a.

In order to illustrate how this rulemaking method works in practice, in Chapter 5 special attention is given to rules for women, especially whether or not Shari'a allows them to hold public office (*wilaya*). It is true that in modern times the topic of women and Shari'a has become fashionable to the point of crudeness, but the discussion here serves other purposes: it provides an important indication of how al-Ghazali understood reality at different times, while the circumstances surrounding the changes in his thinking throw light on the trajectory of Shari'a rule-/lawmaking as an unceasing flow between divine instructions, how to interpret the world, and the precedents that the community has established for reading the scriptures.

The following chapter investigates the role of revelation in Shari'a rule-/lawmaking, beginning with how the Qur'an approached women and how Muslim (men) approached the Qur'an to prohibit women from public leadership and spaces. The discussion then considers the difficult evolution and make-up of what Muslims came to regard as divinely-guided precedent, the Sunna. Al-Ghazali, in the late twentieth century, found himself standing at a juncture between two conflicting traditions: one path leading to a scholarly legacy preoccupied with the absolute integrity of reports about the examples that the Prophet and his community had set, and the other leading into a vast landscape populated by an army of petty clerics who dispense God's instructions mostly by means of Hadith reports and *fiqh* anecdotes embedded in a training which has been meticulously designed to fend off questioning the past—especially where there are political implications. Mohammed al-Ghazali belonged simultaneously to both traditions. When troubled by certain features that had long sustained the omnipotence of Hadith in Muslim societies, he recorded the incidents that provoked him. Managing relationships of power, especially between the state and religion, often figures in these episodes, leading him to rethink his community's approaches to rulemaking. Here, he turned to the basic Shari'a method to which all Muslims subscribe (discussed in Chapter 7) as his measure. And when he discovered faultlines in their historical narratives, al-Ghazali put sound understanding of the past at the centre of Shari'a rulemaking, which gave his arguments an extra dimension.

History? No, it's how to tell it

Al-Ghazali's most important, but least noted, contribution was extending critiques of Muslim history into Egypt's streets. Criticism of particular historical episodes is not uncommon among Muslim scholars and preachers. In al-Ghazali's lifetime, leading Azhari academics famously attempted critiques of mainstream Muslim historical narratives, such as Shaykh Ali abd al-Raziq (d. 1966) in 1925 and Shaykh Khaled Mohammed Khaled (d. 1996) in 1950.[30] They failed, sometimes spectacularly. More successful were preachers without significant training in Shari'a rulemaking, such as Abu al-'Ala al-Mawdudi (d. 1979) and Sayyid Qutb (d. 1966). They too condemned aspects of Muslim history, but their insular critiques usually remain confined to marginalized and militant sections of society. In contrast to eminent Azhari scholars and populist preachers, al-Ghazali managed to persuade a diverse and significant cross-section in his country that their common narrative of the past contained dangerous delusions. With his new emphasis on a critical assessment of their heritage, he shifted the political discourse, having discovered that the integrity of Shari'a depended on a clearer understanding of the past. However, no one expected the impact of the final battle: when al-Ghazali campaigned to question the past he also sowed the seeds of a new, albeit still embryonic, Muslim political discourse of the common man and woman in his country, the vernacular of which came into the full view of the world when it found a public platform in early 2011, in Tahrir Square. This novel discourse was not Islamist, and consequently found diverse subscribers. How al-Ghazali convinced Egyptians from different backgrounds to see the cracks in the historical story, and that this left them with a corrupt view of the world, is equally important. The last chapter of the present study discusses the means by which he injected into the everyday Arabic-speaking Sunni landscape a narrative linked to Shari'a that was later to give the Arab Spring its grassroots support. That al-Ghazali may have prepared the common person in his country for democracy protests may be difficult to comprehend, or may even be an unwelcome discovery for many who circle in the orbit of "Islamic law". Here too, the lens used to investigate Islam predetermines the conclusions, restricting views of reality.

The dilemma of unwelcome findings

The story of al-Ghazali creates an "interesting dilemma" for liberal Western intelligentsia, wrote an American historian commenting on an early version of this work. What he said is true: "The last thing the [American] East Coast reader wants is an argument that can play into the hands of the religious and political right about living religion."[31] But that is not the same as accepting that political expediency dictates the parameters of our scholarship. Political purposes, which continue to haunt the study of Islam, do not reflect liberal values, nor do they help our comprehension of contemporary or past Muslim experiences. They blur them. The "dilemma" that a close scrutiny of someone like al-Ghazali presents cannot be ignored; its unfashionable suggestions must be considered. One implication is that rule-/lawmaking in Islam may not, after all, be parallel to canon (church) law in Christianity. And, as discussed earlier, Shari'a may not even be a law at all, in the Western understanding of the term, technically or historically, but rather predominately a method that different people, at different times, and with different resources, have used very differently. Similarly unfashionable is the suggestion that Islam's legal experience may not be threatening, nor bizarre, nor exotic. But perhaps the most unfashionable question that a close investigation of this legal experience raises is this: could Shari'a lawmaking be one of the oldest surviving self-governance rulemaking modes, albeit one that never developed clear mechanisms by which to implement its inbuilt allowances for collective choices other than mob pressure?

The dilemma of unwelcome findings confronts Muslims, too, and al-Ghazali's case and that of many others can throw light on this. That technically and in practice Shari'a rulemaking depends on choices—individual and communal—has also meant that many *fiqh* rules and arguments primarily reflect the preferences of their authors and societies. Many senior *fuqaha* know it—and have known it throughout the centuries. This decisive but rarely noted feature of their rulemaking seldom figures in discussions of Shari'a; senior *fuqaha* dare not impose into spaces where public sentiments forbid. In April 2009 al-Qaradawi revealed that he did not always report some Shari'a rules, for fear of incurring the displeasure of the mob.[32] Similarly, Shaykh Mohammed Abu Zahra (d. 1974), a most illustrious expert on *usul al-fiqh*, confided to colleagues in 1972, towards the end of his life, that he did not dare disclose that the stoning of adulterers was not a punishment prescribed by Shari'a, also out of fear. Such anxiety prevails among the *'ulama*, according to al-Qaradawi.[33] Findings that disentangle flawed perceptions of the Muslim rulemaking process could prove ultimately worthwhile in this case.

The systematic examination of Shari'a rulemaking: Who is qualified?

Finally, there is the small matter of who really is qualified to describe Shari'a systematically. At one conference on British higher education, one of its Western organizers urged sensitivity to Muslim university students and researchers. At face value, an excellent, well-meaning sentiment—but the explanation of how to exhibit such sensitivity was alarming. Effectively, it was argued, there should be two tiers of scholarship, one of which would allow Muslim students and researchers to avoid critical investigation of subjects such as Hadith and not challenge their predominant narrative of the past. In the other, presumably non-Muslims would look thoroughly at all Islamic topics. Bizarre as it sounds, this view reflected a modern truism: Muslims are not capable of robustly examining subjects pertaining to their faith, unless they first reject Islam's tenets. Only those who do not really follow Islam observe rigorous standards of investigation and reporting. Consequently, also former Muslims and "Islam bashers" are celebrated as experts on Muslims in the Western media and the most prestigious academic institutions, whether or not they know much about Islamic scholarship, legal history, or its sources. So entrenched is this conviction that many devout Muslims unconsciously subscribe to it. As one such British university student put it, "non-Muslim scholars studied Islam more objectively" than those who shared his faith. Although far from accurate, his perception mirrors the troubling yet predominant academic narrative on Islam.[34] As with other stereotypes, there are some genuine reasons for these prevailing views, but all of them are accidental and circumstantial. The story of al-Ghazali highlights where some such reasons have come from.

This book speaks in the voice of a Muslim, Egyptian historian living in the early twenty-first century, which hopefully adds to its value, not diminishes it. And despite its academic origins, the current work seeks out informed non-specialists who today find themselves unintentionally preoccupied with Islam. To these, it brings a figure whose contemporary pronouncements on Shari'a have mattered, and still matter, to many Muslims, if not yet to Western experts. Its subject is only one case of how and why various Shari'a rules are deduced, with hopefully many more such investigations to come. Perceptions of Muslims as irrational aside, what truly matters is to describe Shari'a rulemaking for what it is, instead of obscuring it with what it is not by labelling it with faulty terms and politically inspired assumptions. For, however politically useful it may be to some, the mismatch between the actual trajectory of Shari'a rule-/lawmaking and Islamic law has proved universally unhelpful.

Notes

1. Ibn al-Muqaffa (Abu Mohammed Abd Allah Ruzbih Ibn Dadya, d. 756 CE) was a literary figure whose writings included works on statecraft. In his epistle "Risala fi al-sahaba" he urged the founder of the Abbasid dynasty, Abu Ja'far al-Mansour, to systemize and promulgate a Muslim law code to replace the rampant rulemaking by the *fuqaha* in the culturally diverse Muslim state. This and other extracts from Ibn al-Mqafaa's epistles can be found in Mohammed Kurd Ali, *Rasa'el al-Bulagha* (Cairo: Dar al-Kutub al-'Arabiya, 1913), 1–138. A fuller collection of his works can be found in *Athar Ibn al-Mqaffa* (Beirut: Dar Maktabat al-Haya, 1978). On the orientalist treatment of this document, see Joseph Lowry, "The First Islamic Legal Theory: Ibn al-Muqaffa' on Interpretation, Authority, and the Structure of the Law", *Journal of American Oriental Society* 128/1 (2008): 25–40.
2. *Majallah al-Ahkam i-Adlia*, or the *Mecelle*, was a nineteenth-century Ottoman attempt to codify Shari'a rules by proclaiming a civil code based on Hanafi *fiqh* as practised at the time. Reflecting the internal contradictions that plagued this project, the *Mecelle*

exempted family Shari'a law from the jurisdiction of this would-be Islamic law code. Its 1851 articles became the law of most of the Empire in 1877, but it did not take root. Less than 40 years later, and following the dissolution of the Ottoman Empire, all signs of it had disappeared from the Muslim world. Nevertheless, the idea of the *Mecelle* continues to inspire modernist Muslims, who still aspire to organize their choices of *fiqh* into concise European/Western-like law formats. Such a vision has at one time or another attracted even the likes of Shaykh Yusuf al-Qaradawi and the government of Saudi Arabia, although all such projects have eventually failed.

3. See Chapters 7 and 8 and the Epilogue for discussions on the impact of Islamic law on modern Muslims.
4. This was as a doctoral student, researching for my dissertation: Haifaa G. Khalafallah, *Rethinking Islamic Law: Genesis and Evolution in the Islamic Legal Method and Structures: The Case of a 20th Century 'Alim's Journey into his Legal Traditions; Muhammad al-Ghazali* (PhD diss., Georgetown University, 1999).
5. Al-Ghazali's opponents responded by publishing reports that it was al-Ghazali who had requested burial in Medina, and that the Saudi authorities had simply obliged the request of a man who had died in their midst. Harder to contest, however, is the deference that the Saudi authorities showed at the time of al-Ghazali's death. This included unequivocal official statements such as that made by the secretary-general of the Saudi cabinet, Shaykh abd al-Aziz al-Salem. In an article published in Riyadh, he described al-Ghazali as a Muslim warrior scholar, "a *mujahid* who, in the way of God, feared no one [...] in his fight against all deviation. He confronted his mighty enemies that possessed every means of power, while without any power, he stood up to them fortified with his faith as his only armour." Quoted in Abd al-Halim 'Awais, "Al-Shaykh al-Ghazali, Imam al-Dawah al-Islamiya fi al-'Asr al-Hadith", *Al-Sha'b*, 19 April, 1996.
6. Author interview with Shaykh Ali Goma, al-Azhar, Cairo, December 1999. At the time of this interview Goma, an Egyptian Shafi'i professor of *usul al-fiqh* at al-Azhar University-Mosque, also headed the International Institute of Islamic Thought (IIIT) office in Cairo. Four year later, in 2003, the state appointed Shaykh Goma as Egypt's grand mufti, a post that he occupied until 2013. Until the 2011 Revolution, Egyptians generally celebrated Shaykh Goma as a key authority on Muslim rule-/lawmaking. For discussions on the connection between politics and Shari'a's spokesmen see Chapter 8.
7. Shaykh Mohammed Abduh al-Turkomani served as Egypt's grand mufti from 1899–1905. Egyptians credit him with effecting great changes in Muslim practices and perceptions of their faith in the nineteenth and early twentieth centuries. His continuing influence is discussed in Chapters 1 and 7.
8. Shaykh Yusuf al-Qaradawi, "Nazarat fi turath al-Shaykh Mohammed al-Ghazali", *Islamyiat al-Ma'rifa* 7 (1997): 17–47. Shaykh al-Qaradawi joined the Muslim Brotherhood as a young Azhari student and he has remained loyal to the organization ever since, rarely criticizing its actions. He was jailed by the state in 1949, along with other members of the Brotherhood (including al-Ghazali), and then again in 1961. He founded Qatar University's Faculty of Shari'a in the 1970s and served for a while as its dean. In the early 1990s, the Algerian state appointed him chairman of their Scientific Council of Islamic University and Higher Institutions. Back in Qatar, at the time when a commotion had begun in Egypt over the nature of the Sunna, Shaykh al-Qaradawi founded a new body in the university, which he named the Centre for the Seerah and Sunnah (referring to history and to precedents set by Mohammed). By the end of the twentieth century, al-Qaradawi had become an internationally renowned *usul al-fiqh* expert, but it was his adoption of the latest digital technology that guaranteed his views on Shari'a immediate and wide global exposure. Besides presenting a regular programme on Shari'a on Qatar's global Al-Jazeera TV channel, he started *Islamonline*, an internet forum for publishing his thought, in the late

1990s. In Europe, too, he served for a time as a trustee of the Oxford Centre for Islamic Studies and headed the European Council for Fatwa and Research. At the time of writing, al-Qaradawi is also chair of the International Union of Muslim Scholars.

9. Shaykh Yusuf al-Qaradawi's open criticism of Mohammed al-Ghazali's views on history is discussed in Chapter 8.
10. Chapters 7 and 8 have further discussion of the Islamic reformers' circle that attached itself to Mohammed al-Ghazali in the 1980s–1990s.
11. *Mujadiddin* (sing. *mujaddid*), literarily "revivers of the faith", refers to a common Muslim belief that there will always be scholars who appear every hundred years to renew the energy of Islam, usually by correcting flawed Muslim practices and approaches to the faith. This conviction is deposited in a Hadith in which Mohammed tells Muslims that "at the head of every century, God shall raise for this community a man who shall revive anew its religion" (*Sunnan Abu Dawud* 37: 4278).
12. Following al-Ghazali's testimony, al-Fangari wrote that he "consider[ed] such [testimony] by a senior shaykh [...] a grave mistake", and that "[W]e ask him to correct it even if he has to withdraw what he said." Quoted in Gamal al-Banna, *Kala thuma Kala* (Cairo: Dar al-Fikr al-Islami, 1994), 41.
13. For examples of Shari'a rules about women that al-Ghazali overturned see Chapters 5–7.
14. Mohammed al-Ghazali, *Al-Islam wa al-Mar'a* (Cairo: IIIT, 1990), 21. This was a lecture moderated by Tariq al-Bishri on 2 December, 1990.
15. Also significant were further atrocities committed in the name of Shari'a by Boko Haram, al-Qa'ida, *Dae'sh* (the self-declared Islamic State of Iraq and Syria, ISIS), and others.
16. Henry McDonald, "Northern Ireland First Minister Defends Pastor who Described Islam as 'Satanic'", *Guardian*, 28 May, 2014 (online: http://www.theguardian.com/uk-news/2014/may/28/northern-ireland-peter-robinson-defends-pastor-james-mcconnell-islam-satanic).
17. During an interview on 4 August, 2013, the British Channel 4 News, which is usually accepting of difference, derided the UK Independence Party leader, Nigel Farage, who usually rejects multiculturalism, for merely suggesting that Shari'a might not be all bad.
18. Noah Feldman, "Why Shariah?", *New York Times*, 16 March, 2008 (online: http://www.nytimes.com/2008/03/16/magazine/16Shariah-t.html). More detailed arguments by this author can found in *After Jihad: America and the Struggle for Islamic Democracy* (New York: Farrar, Straus and Giroux, 2003) and *The Fall and Rise of the Islamic State* (Princeton, NJ: Princeton University Press, 2008).
19. Feldman does note the more usual panoramic Muslim description of Shari'a as "not just a set of legal rules", explaining that "[t]o believing Muslims, it is something deeper and higher, infused with moral and metaphysical purpose. At its core, Shariah represents the idea that all human beings—and all human governments—are subject to justice under the law" (Feldman, "Why Shariah?").
20. Ibid.
21. These are prominent early descriptions that set the tone for framing the study of al-Ghazali. This can be seen from two reviews of an English translation of al-Ghazali's *Min Huna Nalam* (*Our Beginning in Wisdom*): that of Franz Rosenthal (in the *Journal of the American Oriental Society* 74/2 [1954]: 100–103) and that of Gustave E. von Grunebaum (in the *Journal of Near Eastern Studies* 14/3 [1955]: 200–202).
22. Professor Khaled Abou el Fadl, who knew al-Ghazali at the time of the shaykh's late twentieth-century campaign against Salafi groups, has mainly focused on responding to Islamists or finding parallels between his adopted country (the United States) and Islam. His works include *And God Knows the Soldiers: The Authoritative and Authoritarian in Islamic Discourses* (Lanham, MD: Rowman and Littlefield, 2001); *Speaking in God's Name: Islamic law, Authority and Women* (Oxford: Oneworld, 2001); *Islam and the Challenge of Democracy*

(Princeton, NJ: Princeton University Press, 2004); *The Great Theft: Wrestling Islam from the Extremists* (San Francisco: HarperCollins, 2005); and *Reasoning with God: Reclaiming Shari'ah in the Modern Age* (Lanham, MD: Rowman and Littlefield, 2014). For differences between Abou el Fadl's and al-Ghazali's approaches to Shari'a rulemaking, see Chapter 7.

23. Raymond Baker, *Islam without Fear: Egypt and the New Islamists* (Cambridge, MA: Harvard University Press, 2003), 190. Similarly of note is Ibrahim M. Abu-Rabi, *Contemporary Arab Thought: Studies in Post-1967 Arab Intellectual History* (London: Pluto Press, 2004). In one of the earliest English discussions of al-Ghazali's critiques of Hadith, Daniel Brown described him as "a spokesman of moderate Islamic revivalism"; idem, *Rethinking Tradition in Modern Islamic Thought* (Cambridge: Cambridge University Press, 1996), 108.
24. Khaled Abou El Fadl, *Speaking in God's Name: Islamic Law, Authority and Women* (Oxford: Oneworld, 2003), 172.
25. Al-Aqqad was a towering literary figure of his period who also influenced modern Egyptian perceptions of early Muslim history through his work *Al-Abqariyiat al-Islamiyia*, 3 vols (Beirut: Dar al-Kitab al-Lubnani, 1974); al-Tunsi (d. 1961), a poet who articulated and helped chart Egyptians' perceptions of their modern collective identity, is similarly neglected. There is so far a single academic monograph in English that focuses on this key figure: Marilyn Booth, *Bayram al-Tunisi's Egypt: Social Criticism and Narrative Strategies* (Exeter, UK: Ithaca Press, 1990).
26. Al-Ghazali, videotape interview (#IQTS-1).
27. Ibid.
28. Shaykh Ali Goma, author interview, Doki, Cairo, March 2007.
29. Chapters 3, 7, and 8 explain the inapplicability of phrases such as "progressive", "orthodox", "traditionalist", or "moderate" Islam.
30. Such Azhari works also include those of Shaykh Ahmed Amin, such as *Fajr al-Islam* (Cairo: Dar al-Shorouk, 1999); idem, *Dhuha al-Islam* (Cairo: Hindawi, 2012).
31. Peter Gran (professor of history, specializing in Egypt, the modern Middle East, and political economy, at Temple University, PA).
32. "Ya'tarif: Katamtu ba'dhu al-Fatawa Tajanuban li-Hiyaj al-'Ama wa Tashwish al-Jamidin", *Islamonline* (online in 2008, archived at http://web.archive.org/web/*/www.islamonline.net/Arabic/karadawy/part3/14.SHTML); also published in *Al-Dostor*, 23 April, 2009 and on *Shrouknews.com* and *Al-naba.com*.
33. Ibid. Elsewhere, al-Qaradawi indicated that al-Ghazali might have been exceptional among his *fuqaha* colleagues in that he could not be intimidated: "Al-Shaykh al-Ghazali refused to submit to popular whims or rulers' sway in pronouncing Shari'a rule" (*Al-'Alam al-Islami*, 8 April, 1996).
34. Guided by nineteenth-century European discourse, many Muslims still embrace the vision of a "scientific" and "objective" history. As late as the 1980s, Western scholars suggested that only non-Muslims are able to "scientifically" or "objectively" write Muslim history. See, e.g., Derek Hopwood, "An Approach to Islamic History", *Bulletin of the British Society for Middle East Studies* 7/1 (1980): 24–32.

PART ONE

PORTRAITS FROM A MUSLIM JOURNEY INTO THE TWENTIETH CENTURY

ONE

Contexts: Al-Ghazali and His Worlds (1917–1996)

"Context" is an expansive term. Many of its aspects may be straightforward and commonplace, but their details mould a lens as individual and as intricate as fingerprints: the fingerprints of Shari'a rules. Adaptations to movement, to challenge, to grades of light and darkness have determined how Muslims deduce, amend, and even reverse rules, all in the name of Shari'a. In practice, those who deduced the rules/laws, how, and under what circumstances have counted just as much as the rules themselves; none of the *fuqaha* (Muslim scholars) who have left their mark on Muslim rulemaking have done so independently of their immediate settings. So it was with Mohammed al-Ghazali. He had an immense influence on ordinary Muslims in Egypt and among other Arabic-speaking Muslims in the region, but he also had bitter enemies in positions of intellectual, religious, and political power. Who applauded him and who censured him is a good place to start his Shari'a story.

Those who cry and those who clap

It was a cold Ramadan night. The audience and its reactions to the recorded words of the late Shaykh Mohammed al-Ghazali both seemed somewhat surreal in the the crowded venue of the hall at the Cairo Opera House.[1] When the lights went out to show a short film in which al-Ghazali discussed Islam, from the front rows one could hear muted sounds of weeping from among the stylishly dressed, some in Italian and German clothes and others in the flowing brown and grey robes of the senior *fuqaha*. Filling the rows behind them, in shabby garments and worn-out shoes, the hard-pressed men and women of Cairo applauded rowdily. Could those who cried and those who cheered—on the one hand, the educated and the celebrities, and on the other, the deprived and uneducated—really understand the videotaped words of al-Ghazali in similar ways? And more broadly, outside the opera house, do the many Muslims who admire al-Ghazali—conservatives and traditionalists, or Salafis and liberals and reformers—all see this Egyptian *alim* (Muslim scholar) through the same lens? Do they revere him for the same reasons?

Al-Ghazali's admirers in Egypt fall broadly into two groups. One is the intelligentsia, with influence over the cultural and economic life of Egypt and beyond its borders, and including professionals, graduates of Western universities, and religious scholars, many with links to the media, the arts, and the religious establishment. The other, and far more numerous, group consists of millions of ordinary Egyptians, both in the countryside and in poor urban centres. With limited opportunity for making their views heard, they saw in al-Ghazali not only a scholar articulating their understanding of Islam, but also a community spokesman for their day-to-day concerns. A traveller in Egypt encounters Mohammed al-Ghazali everywhere: on the bookshelves in private homes, in offices and modern boutiques, and even on the bookstands of "rest houses" (service centres with restaurants and gift shops) on the road between Cairo and Alexandria. Twenty years after his death, Muslims continue to see in al-Ghazali a spokesman for their faith and for genuine Shari'a.

Similar sentiments can be found in the Arabic-speaking world outside Egypt. One Algerian admirer who I interviewed in London in 2008 remembered how al-Ghazali's weekly programme had ranked as the most popular on his country's television, with football matches trailing a distant second place.[2] When al-Ghazali died, Fu'ad al-Hashim, a sharp-tongued Kuwaiti columnist usually unsympathetic to religious expressions, published a lamentation in *Al-Watan*, gushing that al-Ghazali "will forever remain" in their midst.[3] Al-Hashim quoted a Kuwaiti woman doctor who wrote in memory of "the departed star [...Ghazali] who taught us that integrity is the foundation of faith, that standing up for what was right was a sacred obligation." Even in Saudi Arabia, despite a bitter public confrontation between al-Ghazali and the religious authorities towards the end of his life, many of the country's learned, including key religious figures, have now openly or implicitly embraced some of his views on Shari'a.[4] Egypt's religious establishment has also put to use the overwhelming public reception given this seemingly maverick shaykh: as discussed in Chapter 8, when al-Azhar University-Mosque sought to demonstrate its social and political credentials at critical moments, it openly adopted al-Ghazali's articulation of Shari'a rulemaking—rulemaking that had once shocked some Muslim scholars.[5]

Those who object

Despite his overwhelming popularity, there are also some who dislike and even abhor al-Ghazali, and these opponents will be discussed in the course of this book. Among the self-described secularists, leftists, and modernists of the intelligentsia—*al-muthaqafin* in Egypt—some believed that al-Ghazali nurtured intellectual terrorism. Critics included Ghali Shukri (d. 1998), a modernist literary critic, university professor, and translator; Salah Jahin (d. 1986), a nationalist and multi-talented lyricist, cartoonist, and playwright; and the equally popular novelist and poet Abd al-Rahaman al-Sharqawi (d. 1987), who sought to reconcile Islam and Marxism.[6] Chapter 4 examines the circumstances that led to the murder of Farag Foda (d. 1992), a gifted writer, which al-Ghazali justified and became identified with.

Some Arabic-speaking modernists outside Egypt also saw him as a dangerous man, and not just a backward figure. In 2000, I interviewed an Algerian from this modernist class who was troubled by the excessive hold al-Ghazali seemed to have had over his countrymen, and who believed that al-Ghazali had been behind the violent civil unrest that had plagued Algeria since the early 1990s.[7] Religious and secular governments have both often regarded al-Ghazali as a menace,[8] and his various conflicts here illustrate aspects of the curious relationship between state and scholar in Sunni Islam. Two conflicts between al-Ghazali and the Egyptian state are examined in this book. However, experience taught Arab authorities that clashing publicly with al-Ghazali cost dearly, and so many preferred to be seen to be honouring him rather than opposing him.[9] Many in the higher echelons of the Sunni religious establishment were equally circumspect in their disapproval of his public questioning of the Muslim literary heritage. These senior clerics, mindful of the widespread support for al-Ghazali in the street and among an important section of the intelligentsia, often couched their condemnations in roundabout terms. They began by praising al-Ghazali as a treasured *da'yia*, a missionary—after which they would claim that he had not been trained in *usul al-fiqh*, the discipline of rule-/lawmaking that had developed by the fourth century AH (tenth century CE),[10] and that, strictly speaking, he had not been a scholar, a *faqih*, and therefore his arguments had no weight. Such representations fail to address the incongruity of why, then, for the largest part of his career Shaykh al-Ghazali had held senior academic posts in key Islamic institutions of learning—not only in Egypt, but also in Saudi Arabia, Qatar, and Algeria—and had served on the boards of the highest *fiqh* councils in which a number of these critics also served, but often in less senior posts.

In his home country, overt Muslim disparagement of al-Ghazali is instead found among the less distinguished figures of the religious establishment and also among self-declared spokesmen of Islam who had no formal training in *fiqh*.[11] At al-Azhar, one such critic exploded in anger at a comparison between al-Ghazali and Imam Ahmed Ibn Hanbal (780–855 CE), the eponym of the Hanbali *madhhab*, who, like al-Ghazali, had challenged the official establishment of his time and who had also been regarded by the scholars of his day as a man with limited or no *fiqh*.[12] Al-Ghazali eventually incurred the wrath of the full gamut of the Islamist movements of his times; however, most of the quarrels in which he became involved did not revolve around theology. His experience with Egypt's Muslim Brotherhood (*al-Ikhwan al-Muslmeen*) provides an early example. Doctrinally, he belonged to the Ikhwan, but influential members saw him as unruly and disobedient and he was expelled from the organization following a factional dispute in the 1950s. Al-Ghazali's late-twentieth century disputes with Salafi groups provides further illustrations. For decades, al-Ghazali was seen as a defender of Salafi causes, but late in his life some Salafis waged a ferocious war against him after he reconsidered how they used Shari'a to make laws/rules, including rules about women.[13] In the eyes of these Salafis, al-Ghazali appeared to be a weak figure, and a secret agent of the West and of other enemies of Islam, to use the terms of an Algerian asylum seeker I interviewed in London.[14] Despite the seriousness of the accusations levelled against him from many directions, to this day the devout who belittle Mohammed al-Ghazali constitute a minority of disparate, often warring groups.

The covert disparagements of some senior scholars and the loud condemnations of Islamist groups often did not matter in the end. In Egypt and in its Arabic-speaking neighbourhood, there is a common conviction that al-Ghazali was, and continues to be, a man who articulates their understanding of Islam and its correct laws. An Azhari professor echoed a familiar sentiment in Egypt when he asked: "If al-Ghazali is not the leading *'alim* [of our age], who could possibly be?"[15] Even when enraged by some of his positions, many still regarded him in terms such as those expressed by an Egyptian leftist: "I can only say that what [al-Ghazali] said must be correct. Who can possibly claim that al-Ghazali does not know the rules of Islam? No one can."[16] The following sections explore the combination of Egypt's ancient riches and contemporary afflictions, and the confluence of circumstances that helped him to acquire his great influence.

The beginning

Mohammed al-Ghazali's story starts well before his birth in the lower Nile Delta village of Nakhla al-'inab in 1917. His father Ahmed al-Saqa, while himself a teenager, had a vision in a dream in which his hero, the eleventh-century *faqih* Abu Hamid Mohammed al-Ghazali (1058–1111 CE), appeared to him to request that he name his son after him.[17] Years later, not only did al-Saqa name his firstborn Mohammed al-Ghazali after Abu Hamid, but he also resolved to prepare his son for a career of Islamic learning. Most of al-Saqa's meagre income was henceforth dedicated to preparing the young Mohammed al-Ghazali to follow in the footsteps of his eleventh-century namesake. When the time came, al-Saqa uprooted the whole family to Alexandria so that Mohammed, then only a child of ten, could join the Azhar-affiliated primary school in the city.

Dreams of dead figures communicating with the living are common among villagers, but Ahmed al-Saqa's story deserves closer attention, not as a tale of mythical devotion, but for the embedded undercurrents in the Muslim eastern Mediterranean world which it underlines. At first glance, al-Saqa's religious choices appear naïve and inconsistent: on the one hand, this early twentieth-century Egyptian villager rearranged his life and that of his family according to a message—uttered in a dream—from an eleventh- to twelfth-century Persian Shafi'i *faqih*. However, when the young al-Ghazali actually began his *fiqh* lessons at an Azhar school in Alexandria, al-Saqa chose the Hanafi *fiqh* school of thought (*madhhab*) for his son to study, not Abu Hamid's Shafi'i *fiqh* school.[18] Al-Saqa continued to revere Imam Abu Hamid al-Ghazali, but he also felt free to contradict him. His bond with Abu Hamid, combined with his choice not to educate his son in Abu Hamid's school, underscores the multi-cultural day-to-day realities in his Muslim landscape, and it demonstrates the ways in which the society of this part of the eastern Mediterranean has embraced diversity since the early centuries of Islam. To examine an influential *faqih* like Mohammed al-Ghazali or Abu Hamid al-Ghazali in terms of an imagined concept of orthodoxy is likely to blur their legacies, especially when it comes to their approaches to Shari'a; without taking their settings into account, a central question becomes hard to even conceptualize: What is the one certain factor that transforms a person into a *faqih* permitted by his society to guide—and often adjust—Shari'a rulemaking?

Communal memories

To answer the question posed above one must first leave behind, or at least query, seeing the most influential of the *fuqaha* as representatives of "classical" or "traditional" Islam. One should also leave behind their portrayal as men of intense religious fervour, comparable to the powerful figures of medieval Christianity.[19] Despite fanciful suppositions and an abundance of tall stories that pepper later narratives, the *fuqaha* with the greatest influence on Muslim rulemaking all have two things in common: they challenged their societies' accepted approaches to the methodology of Shari'a; and in one way or another, they resisted what they regarded as the injustices of their times, especially governmental control over Shari'a. What started in the second half of the seventh century CE as an effort to curb the influence of a usurper government developed into a convention of learning whose intelligentsia quickly became significant agents of change. Their project, which rivalled the legislative authority of the state, revolved around a process from which they derived lawful rules. These early scholar-activists came to be known as the *fuqaha* (singular *faqih*). Muslims saw them as the courageous, knowledgeable voices of their community, and as defenders of its interests against the various injustices they experienced. In time, the word *faqih* would acquire new meanings, and many members of this intelligentsia would attach themselves to government circles and became part of the state's bureaucracy—in some cases even providing intellectual and legal justifications for the excesses of ruling dynasties. Yet, the model of the early *faqih* endured, and its memories continue to occupy a central place in legitimizing Muslim communal lives; to appear too close to the executive authorities has often cost even the most erudite of the *fuqaha* their scholarly standing.

A central aspect of the story and evolution of Shari'a rulemaking is intellectual and political resistance, and how these conflicts are remembered. Over the centuries, the most outstanding *fuqaha* attained distinction by daring to question the Islamic scholarly traditions of their times, not by confirming them. Principal names in *fiqh* (including the eponyms of its main Sunni schools, Abu Hanifa [d. 767 CE], Malik Ibn Anas [d. 795 CE], Shafi'i [d. 820 CE], and Ibn Hanbal) achieved prominence by contesting, then readjusting, the method by which their contemporaries deduced Shari'a rules. Even scholars with links to the authorities, such as Abu Hamid al-Ghazali, maintained a tradition of distrusting political offices, effectively hoping to separate Shari'a and themselves from the influence of governments.[20] In modern times, key *fuqaha* have also had to reconsider the legacy of *fiqh* too, and the famous examples of al-Afghani and Abduh are discussed in the section on al-Azhar that follows. Again, there were clashes with the state in one way or another, and al-Ghazali's career followed this path. It can be said that al-Ghazali benefitted from the most important factor in transforming a person learned in Islamic subjects into a powerful agent of change: appearing to tread an old course that combines political activism with a specific rule-/lawmaking methodology, which Muslims regard as the fountain of legitimacy. Al-Ghazali thus invoked memories in his society, and these memories were underlined with meanings; and it is through the prism of such memories that his people usually assessed the credibility of *fuqaha*, even if outsiders did not, or could not. Portraits from his life throughout this book illustrate how al-Ghazali came to be seen in terms of these early learned-activists.

Institutions: al-Azhar

Among the factors that helped to propel Mohammed al-Ghazali into being a trusted authority on Islam, his affiliations with al-Azhar must take the first place. As the main centre of Muslim Sunni scholarship since the thirteenth century CE, the people of Egypt have learned to treasure al-Azhar as a priceless institution without equal. Certainly, it has played an important role in lifting the masses in the Egyptian countryside out of the poverty, serfdom, and general brutality that their secular masters would otherwise have continued to impose on them. In al-Ghazali's case, al-Azhar provided a free education from childhood until he joined the university to specialize in what Muslims call the science of the foundations of the faith, *'ilm usul al-din*.[21] Al-Ghazali remembered how his dire financial circumstances meant that he did not possess a single book throughout most of his student years.[22] Al-Azhar also rescued the young al-Ghazali from other bleak fortunes. It was only in 1928, as a young pupil, that al-Ghazali "realize[d] that urinating blood was unusual", and there, at the Azhar elementary school in Alexandria, he was finally treated for the bilharzia worms that ravage the Egyptian countryside.[23] Along with receiving education and basic healthcare, al-Ghazali's student years also saw the birth of his political consciousness and even activism, as he joined his fellow Azharis in demonstrations against the British occupation. His punishment for peaceful protest was prison and a one-year expulsion from school, which left a long-lasting mark.[24] Later, and again thanks to al-Azhar, al-Ghazali gained access to Cairo's cultural riches and elite political circles. With these connections, he would never think or work in isolation. His educational cultural community—teachers, colleagues, and students—extended beyond the borders of his country, and the world of this simple villager acquired regional and international dimensions.

Membership in his country's quintessential institution is not a small matter. For centuries, al-Azhar has served as an intellectual hub, bringing together Sunni Muslims from great distances to learn or teach in its *riwaqs*. But it has also come to mirror Egypt's mental inertia: besides serving as a gateway to the world's cultures, in the modern period al-Azhar has acted as the fortress from which the country resisted foreign assaults. When Bonaparte conquered Egypt late in the eighteenth century, the country's rulers, the Mamluk chiefs, fled, leaving Egyptians to their fate,[25] and al-Azhar functioned as the voice of Egypt as well as headquarters of opposition to the invading French. Nevertheless, however, al-Azhar also served as one of the most significant (perhaps even the foremost) factors responsible for introducing Egyptians to modernity. When Napoleon created a council to administer Egypt, the senior *'ulama* served as their country's representatives in this *diwan*. Daily negotiations with the general and his army of scientists unexpectedly turned this centre of Sunni learning into a public forum where Muslims and revolutionaries from Western Europe worked side by side for almost two astonishing years. Senior scholars of Islam and experts from the French avant-garde daily observed one another and made notes,[26] and these remarkable close encounters would change Muslim and Europeans lives in many ways. But it also made al-Azhar, the custodian of religious conformity, into the leading institution from where new ideas were successfully introduced to Egyptians.[27] Not much attention has been given to the story of how this religious institution became the place where a modern Egyptian identity was skilfully crafted; this is a subject that requires thorough examination, without the presuppositions of the predominant neo-orientalist narrative on Islam. By the early twentieth century, al-Azhar would also be a hub of Egyptian (Muslim and Christian) resistance against the British occupation of their country, which had begun in 1882.[28]

In the late nineteenth century, two *'ulama*, Shaykh Gamal al-Din al-Afghani (d. 1897) and his student Mohammed Abduh, used the institutional shelter of al-Azhar to inject a new dose of tension into contemporary Muslim thinking. They not only accepted the validity of the triumphant modern Western emphasis on reason; they also appropriated it, declaring it the backbone of their faith. They argued that embracing reason, rather than traditions, would awaken Islam's genius and protect its peoples. This was not a new approach: for centuries, the *fuqaha* had deliberated the ideas of the age in which they lived and, in times of uncertainty, they had often adopted arguments that drew on a variety of sources rather than just Islamic tenets, including their cultural background.[29] However, the new emphasis on reason came as European armies were installing themselves as the masters of most Muslim lands. Further, Western cultural products appeared antagonistic to the ways of Islam, and both factors led many Muslims to associate systematic critical thinking with their enemies. The teachings of al-Afghani and Abduh were opposed by groups who defended the *status quo*, and who denied that Islamic traditions, as they understood them at the time, could ever admit foreign (Western) ideas. However, despite al-Afghani's and Abduh's outspokenness, and fears about how the enemy's culture was sweeping the country, supporters of the primacy of reason won the battle for the Muslim mind in Egypt. In the first decades of the twentieth century, Shaykh Mustafa al-Maraghi (d. 1945), the head of al-Azhar and a former student of Abduh, assumed that his people would know the answer to the rhetorical question with which he challenged a European visitor: "How could Islam, which is based on requirements of human nature and reason; which requires its followers to seek and augment their knowledge [...]—how could such a faith be unfit, or inconsistent with, the needs of our modern age of science and culture?"[30]

At the root of the arguments deployed by al-Afghani and Abduh was a call to return to the original, fundamental sources of Muslim faith: the Qur'an, and the earliest historical precedents. In this regard, Abduh, al-Afghani, and their many students were Muslim fundamentalists and self-described Salafis. By the end of the twentieth century and following the declaration of the War on Terror, the label "Salafi" had become a much-maligned term, associated with an obstructive and violent outlook; yet it was because of his distinct Salafi outlook that Abduh's emphasis on reason, promoted through al-Azhar, was successful in changing Muslims' discourse on Islam. The Salafi circle around al-Afghani and Abduh did not dismiss the vast literary heritage of *fiqh*; instead, it demonstrated to Muslims how they ought to deal with what they regarded as an important but chequered inheritance. These scholars did not only publicly examine extant Muslim practices; they also reconsidered well-established disciplines of Shari'a rule-/lawmaking, which included *tafsir*, Qur'anic exegeses, and the legacy of Hadith.[31]

Instead of treating *fiqh* as a monolith, Abduh and his Azhari company paid skilled attention to its variety, examined through a broader prism. With the help of his student Shaykh Rashid Ridha (d. 1935), Abduh delved expertly into the large and varied Muslim legal legacy, bringing to attention treatises that expressed sentiments corresponding to some modern values, but which the predominant Sunni narrative had long buried. Thanks largely to their efforts, works such as those of the fourteenth-century Abu Ishaq al-Shatibi (d. 1388 CE)[32] and, to a lesser extent, Najim al-Din al-Tufi (d. 1316 CE),[33] two scholars whose ideas the religious establishment had long ignored, were transformed into *fiqh* references in the present.[34] Discussions of al-Shatibi's work on *maqasid* as representative of Sunni rulemaking are devoid of context, and pay little attention to the greater number of *fuqaha* who actually deduced Shari'a rules over many centuries. Such academic neglect of Muslim social and legal history means that Islamic law presentations of Shari'a do not often correspond to reality. Even today, most *usul al-fiqh* professors at al-Azhar refuse to recognize al-Shatibi as a *faqih*. They dismiss his works, including the now-famous *al-Muawafqat*, as nothing more than amateur commentaries which have had no relevance to *usul al-fiqh*, legal discourse.[35] Al-Shatibi's emphasis on *maqasid al-Shari'a*, highlighting the ultimate objective of Muslim lawmaking, is in particular rejected as banal, on the grounds that a "real" *faqih*, Abu Hamid al-Ghazali, had treated the same idea of *maqasid* earlier (in the late tenth and early eleventh century CE) and in a specialized way.[36] Al-Tufi is more generally spurned as a heretic who had disguised himself as a Hanbali scholar. Concerned with his contemporaries' stilted readings of sacred texts, al-Tufi identified valid personal or communal interests and the common good as the most important sources of Shari'a rule-/lawmaking.[37] Notwithstanding the accusations against these earlier scholars, Abduh and his Azhari students not only brought these neglected works to the forefront of the discourse on Shari'a; by the early twentieth century they had redefined Muslim orthodoxy, at least in

Egypt.[38] Again and again, a historical lens, rather than doctrine, turns out to be what separates the various Salafi groups in modern times.[39]

What al-Afghani and Abduh started as a highly specialized critique of interest to the *'ulama* soon spread to Egypt's literary and artistic circles, encouraging significant figures from outside al-Azhar to explore Islam and its history in fresh terms.[40] Much of the intelligentsia at this time found in these Salafi assessments a revolutionary-evolutionary roadmap for reform.[41] Thanks mainly to Hasan al-Banna (d. 1949), the man who would offer al-Ghazali inspiration as well as his other institutional membership, the efforts of Abduh and his disciples did not stop at the doors of the learned. Nor did the ideas that al-Afghani and Abduh introduced to al-Azhar remain unchanged, as is discussed later in this chapter.[42]

Al-Ghazali's daring critiques—and many of his inconsistencies—originated in this modern Azhari legacy.[43] However, despite appearances, it is not quite correct to see in this legacy two "modernist" and "traditionalist" camps consisting of Abduh and his disciples and their opponents. At times of crisis many of those who embraced the primacy of reason have reverted to familiar customs or old *fiqh* arguments that they might have previously criticized or even rejected as inconsistent with Islamic doctrine. Similarly, those who championed what they saw as tradition, and who fiercely condemned any critical assessment of the extant *fiqh* discourse, often took refuge in Abduh's arguments about Islam's rationality in order to justify embracing Western products or values, especially the fruits of modern technology or changing practices regarding women. By the mid-1970s, as some of the portraits below show, it was increasingly difficult to establish where clinging to traditions and the rejection of fresh ideas ended, and where attitudes that embrace change began. The battle is not over, and the borders remain in continuous flux, assuming different positions as new realities meet communal memory. Additionally, Abduh's fundamentalist thought was to undergo significant modification, as would al-Banna's own vision, at the hands of al-Banna's grassroots people's movement. The blurred lines that separate the Muslim camp of reason from that of tradition do not only reveal the constant tension that lurks below the surface; they also show continuous changes.

Thus key shifts in Muslim approaches to orthodoxy from the eighteenth century did not originate in modernity's paradigms: they actually started in senior Azhari circles, and their shaykhs, not modern critics of Islam, led the way. True, the *fuqaha* that al-Afghani and Abduh trained had immersed themselves in the world around them, where cultural and political expressions of the West predominated, but when it came to adjusting the discourse on their faith they carefully embedded reforms in doctrine and the past and the immediate socio-political reality of their communities; that is, in Qur'anic content and contemporary contexts. Some of these figures taught al-Ghazali, including Shaykh Mahmoud Shaltut (d. 1963) and Shaykh Mohammed Abd al-Azim al-Zarqani

(d. 1948),[44] and with this in mind his description of the school of thought to which he belonged becomes that much clearer:

> [A school] based on the full use of all intellectual [human] achievements as well as of all *fiqh* schools. It believes in using [modern] discoveries in the disciplines of psychology, sociology, politics, economics and history. It combines them with the correct comprehension [*fiqh*] of the Book [the Qur'an] and the Sunna [Prophetic precedent].[45]

Al-Ghazali recognized how al-Azhar empowered his country and Muslims everywhere, what the institution had meant for him personally, and much more. He passionately defended its independence, as an essential organizational structure under which Muslim thought could gather. But he equally understood the harm that al-Azhar's out-dated syllabi and archaic system of education had inflicted on his people.[46] Soon after his graduation, he discovered that his Azhari degree could not academically sustain him for more than a month, and that this supposedly specialized Islamic learning imparted little of value for his society as regards faith or anything else, he once wrote.[47] As al-Ghazali saw it, learning in this centre of Muslim education consisted of a sad jumble of subjects and texts, amassed haphazardly over the years, many of which he found worthless, even suffocating. He recalled how, as a boy at the Azharite institute in Alexandria, he had been put off by titles "such as *Nour al-Idhah* and *Matn al-Qadhuri* and exegeses like the *tafaseer* of al-Nasfi and Abu al-Saud." He found such works mostly irrelevant.[48] Even the Arabic language, which al-Ghazali loved with a passion, was badly presented in the Azhar curricula, he thought, leading him to question the wisdom of "holding on to outdated texts" which rendered Arabic awkward and impractical to use, especially in understanding the Qur'an.[49] Fortunately, al-Ghazali found a special guide to unlock the treasures that this ancient university preserved.

The mentor: Hasan al-Banna

The story of influential Egyptian *'ulama* in modern times has often included a mentor who has helped to bridge Islam and the ever-changing world. Abduh recorded his own seminal experience of this: his first mentor, an inspiring villager, sparked his transformation from a young malcontent, hoping to escape the tedious mantras of religious texts, into a keen but critical student of Muslim thought. Thus stirred, he strove to rediscover Islam in terms relevant to the world of his contemporaries, Abduh remembered.[50] Besides inspiration, al-Ghazali's mentor also furnished his young disciple with another institutional framework, parallel to but at the same time livelier than al-Azhar.

Al-Banna's career offers another early twentieth-century portrait of the quintessential *faqih*, a key agent of change in formative Muslim history, which communal memories in that part of the world continue to celebrate. With these predecessors, al-Banna shared an absolute loyalty to the Shari'a, and an animosity to the injustices of the social and political order of his day. European nationals' supremacy over the people of his country and the humiliating collapse of the Ottoman Caliphate in 1923 both accentuated the wrongs from which Hasan al-Banna hoped to rescue his people. With a handful of like-minded friends, all living close to the camps of the British occupying forces at Ismailiya (by the Suez Canal), this young primary-school teacher organized a Muslim fraternity in 1928. As brothers, the Ismailiyia group promised to fully give themselves to the service of God by preserving genuine Islamic instructions, looking after one another, and creating the society which their faith commended. This goal of providing a communal self-service that safeguarded Muslim dignity, both socially and politically, became the fuel that would sustain their movement over the decades; it would also remain dismally unfulfilled, for the most part.

The founder of the Ikhwan found his intellectual energy in the Salafi approach of Abduh's Azhari circle, and his street movement would introduce the essence of these scholarly assessments of Muslim "orthodoxy" into urban working-class slums as well as villages across the country. The Muslim Brotherhood also protected Abduh's legacy in other ways, such as in continuing to publish *Al-Manar*, the periodical that Abduh's student Shaykh Ridha had started in 1898 to keep alive his teacher's ideas.[51]

In common with the practices of the learned-activists of Islam throughout the centuries, al-Banna was willing to use any ideas that he judged not to contradict Islam's principles, including contemporary ones. Some of his adaptations appear now to have been wise and open-minded, and others to have been rash and dangerous. For his 1930–1940s fraternity, al-Banna drew up a constitution, formed a governing council of representatives,[52] established various specialized committees, and even founded sections for "Muslim Sisters".[53] Without hesitation in trying novel approaches, he led his brethren into what were then unconventional settings, such as the bustling coffee houses, taking the call for a relevant Islam to his fellow Egyptians as they played backgammon, sipped cups of tea and coffee, or smoked their shishas. Al-Banna shrugged off the anger of those who rose in defence of the then-Muslim orthodoxy, preferring to focus instead on how his group made their rounds in ancient Cairo's centre, starting "in Salah al-Din's circle [...] into al-Sayyida 'Aisha [district ...] then to the neighbourhoods around [Ibn] Tulun [Mosque] until we reached [the coffee houses of] Salama Street and al-Sayyida Zaynab [district], up to al-Jabal Road [neighbourhood]."[54] Furthermore, despite the general illiteracy in their midst, the Ikhwan energetically produced their own periodicals and pamphlets and also organized athletic activities and Boy Scouts corps, all along Western models. When it came to education, al-Banna equally welcomed working with both their ancient centre of learning, al-Azhar, and the newly imported, secular-oriented university that became Cairo University.[55]

Despite this communal flurry of activities, it was mainly al-Banna's sheer energy and seemingly good nature which transformed his group of working-class discontents into an influential national grassroots movement within less than 20 years.[56] Al-Ghazali's encounter with al-Banna provides glimpses of this. In 1937 the young al-Ghazali had been preparing to move from Alexandria to Cairo to begin his higher education. In his memoirs, he identifies his first, chance meeting with the founder of the Muslim Brotherhood as the turning point in his life. Al-Ghazali recalled how he intended to rush out of the Bin Hurmuz mosque, at Ras al-Teen suburb, Alexandria, after praying the *maghreb* [sunset prayers] when, suddenly, "a man stood up [...] and gave an impromptu lesson." In contrast to the mayhem and oftentimes frivolity of his Azhari studies, al-Ghazali found al-Banna's improvised lesson "clear, effective, and truthful". According to al-Ghazali, Hasan al-Banna introduced him to a faith which is connected to the real lives of those who embraced it, in contrast to the disengaged muddle of out-of-date learning such as that al-Azhar had to offer.[57] "That very day", on an Alexandria evening, the young al-Ghazali found his life's purpose, having "decided to follow the man [al-Banna], to walk with him wherever he went in the service of Islam and Muslims."[58]

He did just that, at one point becoming one of al-Banna's secretaries.[59] In such close proximity, al-Banna taught al-Ghazali the ways of the early learned-activists of Islam. One important lesson was that a reformer had to be daring, but could never afford to lose sight of realities. In the words of al-Banna's brother Gamal, "*al-Ustath* [Hasan al-Banna] recognized that if a leader moved too fast, much faster than those whom he leads, he would soon find himself charging alone, with no one behind him."[60] This would prove a valuable strategy in difficult times, when al-Ghazali challenged the popular *fiqh* narratives. Al-Banna also appears not to have minded al-Ghazali's outspoken nature, often encouraging his young protégé to express views that contradicted the official stance of the movement.[61] One example concerns Islam's principles of government. When al-Banna refused to support the Egyptian Constitution, al-Ghazali and another young Azhari member of the Ikhwan, Khalid Mohammed Khalid (d. 1996), held a meeting with their leader to protest his position. According to al-Ghazali, al-Banna explained to the young men that the Qur'an was Muslims' only constitution. Unfazed, al-Ghazali boldly challenged his hero: If so, why did he, al-Banna, adopt a constitution for the Muslim Brotherhood? If a group needed a charter to organize rights and duties among its members, al-Ghazali asked, what diminished this need for a whole country?[62] However, although al-Banna tolerated such exchanges, after his death in February 1949 influential factions among the Ikhwan did not. Like his bonds with al-Azhar, al-Ghazali's link to the Ikhwan had many aspects, and these continuously unfolded into newer phases. Nevertheless, from the time he met al-Banna, and despite bitter hostilities between him and some influential elements in the Ikhwan, al-Ghazali saw himself, and continued to be seen by others, as epitomizing the Muslim Brethren, even after they officially severed their ties with him.[63]

Institutions: The Muslim Brotherhood (Ikhwan)

Contemporary Egyptians often confuse al-Banna with the organization that he left behind, and which has had various roles in modern Egyptian society. Despite the Brotherhood's goals as regards creating an ideal community, the actual day-to-day practices of the Ikhwan mirrored Egyptian society's usual approaches to authority, and despite his great loyalty to al-Banna, al-Ghazali thought that the rot in the Muslim Brotherhood had started early, during the lifetime of their founder. Difficult circumstances had led al-Banna to give leadership positions to individuals with little or nothing to offer in terms of morality or intellect, as al-Ghazali saw it.[64] Many Brotherhood members would never consider challenging al-Banna's views, and his departure would lay bare a political culture that would in time divide Egyptian society. Here, al-Ghazali's experience provides an eyewitness account from within that community.

Al-Ghazali appreciated the significance of what he considered to be a practical grassroots Muslim group, but he rejected how it mirrored what he saw as his society's noxious approaches to power relations and governance. Even as the Ikhwan's leader after al-Banna's assassination, when members of the Ikhwan including al-Ghazali were incarcerated in Sinai's al-Tor prison, al-Ghazali found his brothers narrow-minded and incapable of tolerating any view that differed from theirs.[65] As such, al-Ghazali lectured them about where Islam stood in relation to freedom and tyranny. His audience in the jail was unreceptive, and so he instead published his talks as a book.[66] Al-Ghazali found that the Muslim Brothers remained neutral in any fight for democracy, and had little concern when the state fabricated election results.[67] Worse, Muslim Brotherhood members were immersed in leader-worship and a culture of unquestioned obedience (*al-sam'e wa al-ta'a*).[68]

Conflicts always revolved around power-relations rather than theological disagreement, but in Muslim societies religious terminology has long served as the sole language for disputes, especially about governance. Al-Ghazali thus denounced the ways of the Ikhwan and other Islamists' "political paganism",[69] and he spared no one.[70] Al-Banna's son-in-law Sa'id Ramadan (d. 1995), who became a key voice for Islam in Europe and died in Geneva, sought "to make religion into an opium for the masses"; similarly, al-Ghazali regarded the Brotherhood's new leader, Hasan al-Hudaybi (d. 1973), as dictatorial and, more seriously, as conniving with the palace against the will of the nation. Al-Ghazali joined like-minded members of the Ikhwan in an attempt to oust him,[71] but al-Hudaybi's faction consolidated their position and al-Ghazali, along with other dissenters, was swiftly expelled from the organization at the end of 1953, to his deep regret.[72]

What infuriated al-Ghazali about many of his Muslim brethren may have helped ripen his thought. He looked inwards to understand his people's troubles, and he charted his own activism separate from the Brotherhood[73] while remaining loyal to al-Banna's vision. He did not hesitate to participate in state-led initiatives after the Brotherhood was banned and forced underground following an assassination attempt on President Gamal abd al-Nasser. Al-Ghazali declared that in Islam, just as there was no place for compromise in the battle between right and wrong, there was no place for secret fraternities.[74] Later, instead of his criticism of some of the Muslim Brothers' leaders, he concentrated on the political traditions to which great numbers of the devout subscribed, not only his Ikhwan brethren.[75] These long-entrenched traditions, according to al-Ghazali, turned Muslims into tyranny's allies and supporters, and reform had to start by dismantling their conception of power relations. By the first decades of the twenty-first century, many Egyptians had come to agree, and to regard the most revered *'ulama* as speaking a political language that horrified them.

In conclusion: with his links both to Abduh's academic school at al-Azhar and to the populist Muslim Brotherhood, al-Ghazali inherited the tensions between these two contemporary movements. However, it also gave him an advantage as a spokesman on Islam.

The career path of a twentieth-century *faqih*

With the steady rise of the nation state in the Middle East from the late nineteenth century, rulers acquired an almost complete monopoly over all aspects of their people's lives, including religion. States mostly manage Islam through *awqaf*, a department of government. This originally referred to independent pious trusts set up to generate income to provide for students, teachers, hospitals, and other charitable purposes, and in the contemporary Arabic-speaking world *awqaf* effectively joins the religious establishment to the state bureaucracy. This meant that in early twentieth-century Egypt, those with Azhari education, like al-Ghazali, depended primarily on the state for work. Indeed, an opportunity for employment at the Ministry of *Awqaf* soon after he graduated was much welcomed. In his first post, in which he led prayers and delivered the Friday sermon as *khatib* and imam of an 'Ataba mosque, al-Ghazali quickly discovered the dearth of his Azhari education: "Only one month into [preaching at the mosque]", he wrote, "I realized that I was utterly ignorant, that I had used up all I knew in a matter of weeks, that if I did not renew myself and seek diverse sources of knowledge, I would soon be shamed."[76] Keen interest in the world around him paid off, and his well-received sermons at a busy part of Cairo eventually led him back to al-Azhar University, where he delivered the weekly Friday sermons from its world-famous mosque and where he also occasionally taught.[77] More promotions laid in store, leading to his appointment to the position of director of Egypt's mosques. Al-Ghazali reached the pinnacle of his "official" career during Anwar al-Sadat's first years as president—when Sadat was wooing religious sentiments as a means to neutralize the left—as undersecretary of state at the Ministry of *Awqaf*, overseeing Egypt's "Religious Instruction and Preaching". However, such alliances never lasted, as shown by the often awkward relationship between the *'ulama* and the state.

Exodus

In Egypt, conflict between a despotic ruler and a religious patriarch is as old as Biblical accounts, and it was inevitable that al-Ghazali, an outspoken activist, would have found himself confronting his employer, the state. Whether Nasser, Sadat, or Mubarak, whoever ruled Egypt came to regard the now well-established Shaykh al-Ghazali as a menace, and from time to time their wrath forced him to seek sanctuary abroad. Relocating outside Egypt under adverse circumstances caused him great distress, but it also brought opportunities: work abroad greatly increased his income but, more significantly, it set him on a journey of intellectual discovery. He experienced first hand how the world—and indeed Islam—was broader than just Egypt.

Al-Ghazali's first major clash was with the socialist and anti-Western government of Nasser. Consequently, the beleaguered shaykh headed east into the Arabian Peninsula, where young states had begun to reap considerable wealth from oil exports.[78] His short trip, organized by supporters in the Gulf for him to give a series of Ramadan lectures in Kuwait, shored up his finances and, more importantly, his morale.[79] He later similarly clashed with the pro-capitalist, pro-Western government of President Sadat and his wife, Jihan, but this time he was forced into exile.[80] Again, he headed east, and his Salafi supporters found a post for him as a professor at Umm al-Qura University in Mecca. After six years, following the death of his beloved wife in June 1980 and disagreements with the Saudi religious establishment, he returned home dispirited. However, he could not stay for long: friends advised him not to return from a short visit abroad during which Sadat had ordered widespread arrests of the country's intelligentsia and religious figures, including the Coptic pope. Al-Ghazali first sought refuge in Kuwait, in the autumn of 1981, followed by a short stint in Qatar as a professor in its university. Then he headed west to North Africa, close to his treasured Mediterranean shore, at the invitation of Algeria's President Chadli Bendjedid. In partnership with Algeria's government, al-Ghazali established the country's first institution of higher Islamic education in modern times, Abd al-Qadir University. However, new cultures led to new conflicts, this time with some of the religious figures who had previously hailed al-Ghazali as a hero.

Away from Egypt's economic and political limitations, but also its relaxed social settings, al-Ghazali began to compare and contrast Muslim societies in which he had lived. He observed that supposedly pre-colonial Islamic traditions were not uniform across Egypt, the Arabian Peninsula, and North Africa, and that they did not necessarily reflect the tenets of Islam—indeed, in some cases they were antithetical to Islam. To historians, all this may seem a truism, but it was not how al-Ghazali understood it. Islam, he had been taught, was always one and indivisible. Distance from Azhari and Egyptian customs persuaded him to consider the inconsistencies between this idea of a uniform model of Islam and the reality. He thus gained new insights, which led him to understand how adjustments to rules were deduced from the same Shari'a method. "He himself realized it", explained Shaykh Ali Goma, adding, "Shaykh Mohammed al-Ghazali often noted that had he not moved to live in other countries, his world would have remained limited; he would have had different emphases."[81] Later chapters in this book discuss some of this tension in some detail. First, however, we must complete the outline of the combination of circumstances that introduced the shades of light and darkness that were sculpted onto al-Ghazali's Shari'a rulemaking lens.

Consequently, what had begun in al-Ghazali's mind years earlier as trepidation about the Ikhwan's modus operandi in time developed into a review of approaches to Shari'a itself.[82] Living—or perhaps teaching—in Mecca and Medina forced al-Ghazali to readjust his Islamic perspective. This may be surprising: Professor Peter Gran has commented that "I would have thought that [...] going to Saudi Arabia for a man of Mohammed al-Ghazali's generation would not be transformative",[83] and it is true that life in Saudi Arabia would be likely to confirm rather than transform the affiliations of an aging champion of Hanbali ideas. After all, intellectually and personally, al-Ghazali truly admired Ibn Taymiya (d. 1328 CE) and his student, Ibn al-Qayyim al-Jawzyia (d. 1350 CE), the same *fuqaha* that contemporary Salafis venerated. According to al-Qaradawi, al-Ghazali believed that in deducing Shari'a rules, these two Hanbali scholars adopted a sensible approach of constant re-assessment that used Islam's tenets as yardsticks. Their rulemaking was dynamic and supported by accurate, convincing legal evidence, al-Ghazali thought,[84] and he called their school *madrassat al-muwazana wa al-tarjih*.[85] Accordingly, when he taught at al-Azhar, in his class syllabi he substituted Ibn al-Qayyim's works for those of al-Ghazali's namesake, Abu Hamid al-Ghazali.[86] Not just the usual Sunni voices who wished to preserve the *fiqh status quo*, but also the Salafis counted al-Ghazali as a leader during the 1960s and early 1970s.[87] On a personal level too, al-Ghazali felt close connections to Ibn Taymiya. Like al-Ghazali, Ibn Taymiya lived in the worst of times, when Muslim power had crumbled, yet he had never wavered in his fight against evil, al-Ghazali thought.[88] However, when circumstances forced al-Ghazali to relocate to Saudi Arabia, the strict confines of the single Hanbali school of thought began to disturb him. He yearned for his Azhari world, which embraced several schools of thought, and where he could substitute works most admired by academic religious circles in Egypt with works much less popular. He also missed Egypt's freedoms when compared with Saudi Arabia. Eventually, al-Ghazali openly clashed with his students and fellow faculty members. The quarrels were often over what he judged as his hosts' exaggerated adulation of these Hanbali scholars, which prevented Muslims from truly benefiting from their thought. Al-Ghazali's daily confrontations in Mecca and Medina centred on correct Islamic rulemaking norms—not on Western modernity. They led al-Ghazali to reconsider the ideas to which his Saudi hosts clung, and that he had also once championed as Islamic.[89] When he subsequently moved to the new setting of Algeria, his concerns only deepened: not only in the Arabian Peninsula, but also in the Muslim Mediterranean, around which he grew up, al-Ghazali discovered indefensible "Islamic" norms. However, what he missed about his country also helped him recognize the limitations of modern Egypt, and his comparisons highlighted the extent of the chaos, methodological and cultural, that dominated his fellow Muslims' use of Shari'a rules. All was not well in the perfect world of Islam after all. As a *faqih*, he had to attend to this disorder. The following chapters will often revisit these experiences in investigating al-Ghazali's texts, the uproar he triggered in the Arabic-speaking Sunni universe, and his readings of Shari'a texts. How and where he sought answers to what he regarded as chaos while remaining loyal to Shari'a gives his story notable dimensions.

Disturbed by the different outlooks in the countries in which he had lived, al-Ghazali set out to determine what really established a practice or a rule as Islamic. But had not the time-honoured method of making Shari'a rules accomplished just that? Again and again, at the heart of every argument that al-Ghazali found disturbing he encountered reports that claimed the Prophet as their originator (Hadith). Morally untenable instructions or impractical regulations were thus turned into Islamic rules. Even worse, al-Ghazali concluded, these reports had become the main source of Shari'a lawmaking, regardless of what Muslims claimed. These observations both troubled him but at the same time gave comfort: the fault which he found was not in Shari'a methodology, as he saw it, but in the Muslim failure to follow it correctly. From there on, al-Ghazali's attention shifted to probing the meaning of the Sunna, or Prophetic examples and instructions, the precedents from which Muslims learn with certainty the correct applications of Islam's general principles.

Accordingly, by the late 1980s al-Ghazali had reversed his perspective. Muslim misuse of precedent replaced the Western cultural and physical onslaught against his people as his main enemy. His public investigation of these precedents took many by surprise and created tension in Sunni religious circles. Al-Ghazali's open probing to determine a Hadith's exact place within the Sunna triggered ferocious reactions from groups representing every Sunni tradition, all of whom had been weaned on the common story of *fiqh*. Advocates of *madhahib* that referred to themselves as *ahl al-Sunna wa al-Jama'a*, along with their neo-Salafis foes and even Sufis, all rose against al-Ghazali, as they saw it in defence of Islam. An eclectic collection of Salafi groups were the best-financed, with the backing of powerful states. Subscribing to the view of Hadith as an uncontested, divine source of Shari'a, these new Salafi adversaries sponsored a barrage of books, articles, and mosque sermons, and even held a seminar for the sole purpose of denouncing what they saw as the errors of the fallen shaykh.[90] However, instead of weakening his stature, the controversy over the Sunna of the Prophet, between al-Ghazali and those who rejected his conclusions on how the Sunna had been misused, seemed to enhance rather than diminish his credibility. Paradoxically, most of the Muslim attacks on al-Ghazali coincided with most of the awards and honours showered on him by Sunni institutions, newspapers, and scholars.[91] They also originated in the same neighbourhood: in the Sunni Arabic-speaking world in and around the Mediterranean, mainly in Egypt, Saudi Arabia, the Gulf States, and their close neighbours. The fact that al-Ghazali was able to persuade many observant Muslims to consider a review of the Sunna at all was his real accomplishment, and despite the exile and commotion, or because of them, al-Ghazali's career can be described as a success. The real surprise is that although deprived of any official religious post, the Salafi-inclined al-Ghazali in the end emerged as a leader of a seemingly liberal camp who also carried with him millions in Islam's historically central lands.

And where to run from oneself?

The single most-mentioned personal trait that comes to the minds of those who remember al-Ghazali is either candour or recklessness, depending on perspective. He is described as passionate, with a fiery temper. For those who belittled him, al-Ghazali remained an unpolished and uncouth Egyptian villager, a *fallah*; for those who admired him, he embodied the traditions of independence and candid scholarship of the "genuine" *fiqh*. For the researcher, his unguarded disposition throughout a long career provides an open text, because unlike many Azhari scholars at the time, his evolving approach to Shari'a tended to be more transparent. When he did not spell out his concerns in books, newspaper articles, or his mosque sermons, al-Ghazali spoke out in senior *fiqh* circles. A fellow member in the Higher Council for Muslim (*fiqh*) Affairs, Amna Nosseir, speaks of how, during their deliberations, al-Ghazali light-heartedly often reminded them that it was the *fuqaha* who truly destroyed Islam.[92]

Two brief incidents best capture this forthrightness, much appreciated by his admirers, or demonstrating an imprudence not befitting of an *'alim*, according to his detractors. Shortly before he died, al-Ghazali described what he saw as a general contemporary Muslim distaste for serious considerations of their faith. Following a lecture he had given to a crowded hall, he "waited to hear inquires about the burning issues that I had just raised." Instead, al-Ghazali wrote, his audience had a set of farcical questions that preoccupied them, that it was impossible for him to ignore: "Do spirits know what we are up to? Do our dead relatives watch us? Do they intercede for us to be forgiven?" These were the problems that preoccupied these good Muslims, not the muddle in which they were living, he added. Worse was to come when a "chubby, self-possessed, bearded shaykh stood up" to contradict al-Ghazali's answer, using a Hadith; "once again, I was dragged into futile arguments of the kind that I detest", al-Ghazali lamented.[93]

In the second incident, a university student, while visiting al-Ghazali's home in Saudi Arabia, snapped at the old shaykh for humming the tune of a song he had been listening to, before his young visitor demanded that he turn off the radio. "Islam forbade music; it was *haram*", the student reminded al-Ghazali. There was no such Shari'a rule; God could not have possibly forbidden something so innate and beautiful as music, the incensed al-Ghazali explained. Music could only be bad when it inspired vice, he added. To deduce this rule/fatwa on music, al-Ghazali did not turn to earlier *fiqh* arguments. Instead, he used his own experiences, noting that "I am naturally inclined to humor [...] I would, if I could, live all my life cheerful and smiling." He wondered how "it came to be expected that we [Islam's scholars] should display a countenance of gloom and melancholy."[94]

The final years

Exhausted by his daily confrontations in Algeria, the aging al-Ghazali resigned his position there. Influential scholars who regarded him as the leading Muslim reformer of their times then sought to find him a fitting post in Egypt.[95] The Muslim Brotherhood turned down the suggestion that he should be appointed as the

Ikhwan's new leader to rejuvenate the movement, while the Egyptian government rejected a proposal to appoint such a troublemaker as head of al-Azhar.[96] With the roads to these two key Muslim institutions in Egypt blocked, a new organization stepped in: the International Institute of Islamic Thought (IIIT). The IIIT had been established in 1981 by a group of well-funded Arab intellectuals in the hope that an independent think-tank would energize Muslim thought and counter the ever-increasing management of Islam by nation-states. To this end they founded branches worldwide but chose Herndon, a quiet town near Washington, DC, as Islam's new intellectual headquarters. How practical or wise was it to organize their project in this way remains unstudied; but for the first decade, their plan succeeded, with some help from al-Ghazali. They saw in his daring journey of discovery their model for contemporary times: the IIIT founder prodded al-Ghazali to write his most controversial book, which broke the silence of many *'ulama* about the popular approaches to Hadith.[97] With conventional gateways to influence closed, leaders of the IIIT invited al-Ghazali to preside over their Council of Scholars, *Majlis al-Ulama*, at their Cairo office. This institution organized and financially sponsored many of his lectures, books, and trips worldwide. The move served both parties very well. It gave the IIIT immediate credibility inside the largest Muslim Arab country, where people are usually wary of Western-based Islamic initiatives; but more importantly, it also transformed al-Ghazali's last years into the most effective and richest of his long career. At last, al-Ghazali appeared to have overcome the weaknesses of both al-Azhar and the Muslim Brotherhood. In the late twentieth century, Azhar scholarship remained constrained and the logic of the Muslim Brotherhood appeared fractured. Their attempts to catch up with the times were shallow, with little rationale behind them. In contrast, the modern IIIT setting was energetic, affluent, and ready to embrace critical ideas. It offered al-Ghazali a large canvas and a vibrant brush with which to draw the conclusion of his long journey, and he fully embraced the opportunity: while al-Azhar and the Muslim Brotherhood were struggling as they faced the novelties of the modern world, the IIIT Cairo Council of Scholars headed by al-Ghazali brought together the most energetic Islamic figures of the 1980s–1990s from within the religious establishment and outside. Its members included a woman, Zahira Abdin,[98] as well as much hailed legal experts such as Tariq al-Bishri,[99] Ahmed Kamal abu al-Magd,[100] and the-then rising star of *usul al-fiqh*, Ali Goma.[101] Thus, despite having no official post in the religious establishment, al-Ghazali found himself at the summit of the Sunni establishment in Egypt and elsewhere.

Al-Ghazali had come full circle. In the late 1930s, al-Azhar and the Muslim Brotherhood had given him ready platforms as a young scholar of Islam. In the late 1980s, a latter-day Sunni institution, the IIIT, had given him a new, more contemporary structure, with financial and other resources that established him as the Muslim reformer of his time at the end of his life's journey.

Al-Ghazali died suddenly in March 1996 in the Saudi capital, Riyadh. He suffered a heart attack during a conference while passionately responding to a comment that he interpreted as misrepresenting Islam. The Saudi government treated al-Ghazali's death as an event of the utmost significance, describing it as an immense loss to the *umma* (the Muslim community worldwide). The irony of it all did not escape his admirers. In the 1980s, al-Ghazali had responded in the most public way to the furious Saudi attacks on his deductions on Shari'a rulemaking, and years of bitter hostility had followed. However, despite their immense weight, the Saudi authorities eventually recognized that they could not afford to appear to be Mohammed al-Ghazali's enemies and they had sought to end his boycott of their country.[102] With much persuasion, the outspoken shaykh reluctantly agreed to attend the Riyadh conference from whence he never returned home.[103] Amid displays of much respect, al-Ghazali's Salafi enemies laid him to rest in Baqi', the most revered Muslim burial ground, next to the Prophet's companions—in the eyes of his supporters, the final vindication of Mohammed al-Ghazali's efforts to correct how Muslims deduced rules from Shari'a.

Notes

1. Part of a series on contemporary Muslim scholars, *'Alam al-Ulama'* (moderated by Mohammed Salem, Opera House, Zamalek, Cairo, 12 January 1999).
2. Author interview with Algerian national, Regent's Park Mosque, July 2008.
3. Fu'ad al-Hashim, "Alamat Ratha", *Al-Watan* (Kuwait City), 18 March, 1996.
4. See Epilogue.
5. Published in 2011 as *Wathiqat al-Azhar*; "Shahed al-Tayyib, Shaykh al-Azhar Yasdiru Wathiqat al-Dawla al-Madaniya wa Yarfudhu al-Dawla al-Dinyya", *Al-Masry al-Youm*, 21 June, 2011 (online: http://www.masralyoumnews.com/2011/06/video-sheikh-al-azhar-declares-support.html); also "Dr Ahmed al-Tayyib Yu'linu Wathiqata al-Azhar al-lati Tuda'imu Tas'sis al-Dawla al-Madaniyya al-Dimokratiya", *Al-Masry al-Youm*, 20 June, 2011 (online: http://www.masralyoumnews.com/2011/06/dr-ahmed-al-tayeb-al-azhar-declares.html). The document along with other illustrations are discussed in the Epilogue.
6. Al-Sharqawi was a recipient of the Lenin Prize in 1979. Al-Sharqawi's presentations of Muslim history especially irritated al-Ghazali, such as in "Al-Amana fi Naql al-Turath", in his book *'Ilal wa Adwiya* (Cairo: Maktabat Akhbar al-Tum al-Islamiya, 1992 [1984]), 2: 117–143.
7. Author interview with Algerian national, Washington, DC, October, 2000. These views are shared by Ghali Shukri, who argued in a chapter entitled "Who Does Not Fear al-Ghazali?" that al-Ghazali was behind the rise of Algeria's Islamist violence. See Ghali Shukri, *Thaqafat al-Nizam al-'Ashwa'i: Takfir al-'Aql wa 'Aql al-Takfir* (Cairo: Kitab al-Ahali, 1994), 231–239.
8. Some Arab governments showed him great deference. In Algeria, it was reported that President Chadli Bendjedid met al-Ghazali at the airport when he moved to Algeria in the 1980s (*Al-Sha'b*, 17/18 May, 1996).
9. His confrontations with Presidents Nasser and Sadat are discussed in Chapter 3.

10. Among other things, dismissing al-Ghazali as a *da'yia* overlooks the historical evolution of the *faqih* and *fiqh* which preceded the discipline of *'usul al-fiqh* and continued to change thereafter.
11. See Chapter 8.
12. For an erudite modern-day account of Ibn Hanbal, albeit heavily wrapped in the now-predominant Sunni narrative, see Shaykh Mohammed Abu Zahra, *Ibn Hanbal, Hayatuh, wa 'Asruhu, wa Ara'auhu* (Cairo: Dar al-Fikr al-'Arabi, n.d. [1947]).
13. Attacks on al-Ghazali by the Saudi religious establishment in the late 1980s and early 1990s include Rabi' bin Hadi al-Madkhali, *Kashf Mawqif al-Ghazali min al-Sunna wa Ahliha*, 3rd edn (Medina: Maktabat Ibn al-Qayyim, 1410/1989 AH/CE); Salman al-Odah, *Hiwar Hadi' ma' al-Shaykh al-Ghazali* (Riyadh: [the Saudi state's] al-Ri'asa al-'Ama li'Idarat al-Bohouth al-'Ilmiyya wa al-Ifta wa al-Da'wa wa al-Irshad, 1989); Salih bin 'Abd al-'Aziz bin Mohammed al-Shaykh, *Al-Mi'yar li-'Ilm al-Ghazali fi Kitabih al-Sunna al-Nabawiya bayn Ahl al-Fiqh wa-Ahl al-Hadith* (no location or publisher, 1410/1989 AH/CE); and Abu Bakr al-Jaza'iri, *Al-Qawl al-Karim al-Ghali fi al-Difa' 'an al-Da'iya al-Ghazali* (Mecca: Maktabat Umm al-Qura, 1991); Examples of critiques from within Egypt include Ashraf 'Abd al-Maqsud bin 'Abd al-Rahim, *Jinayat al-Shaykh Mohammed al-Ghazali 'ala Mohammed al-Hadith wa-Ahlih* (Cairo: Maktabat al-Imam Bukhari, 1989); Mohammed Galal Kishk, *Al-Shaykh Mohammed al-Ghazali bayn al-Naqd al-'Atib wa-l-Madh al-Shamit* (Cairo: Maktabat al-Turath al-Islami, 1990); Gamal Sultan, *Azmat al-Hiwar al-Dini: Naqd Kitab al-Sunna al-Nabawiya bayn Ahl al-Fiqh wa-Ahl al-Hadith* (Cairo: Dar al-Safa, 1990).
14. Author interview with Algerian asylum seeker in Britain, The Strand, London, June, 1997 (anonymous by request of subject).
15. Ahmed Hijazi al-Saqa, *Dafu' al-Shubuhat 'an al-Shaykh Mohammed al-Ghazali* (Cairo: Maktabat al-Kuliya al-Azhariyya, 1990), 84, 134.
16. Even when uncomfortable with some of his positions, such as al-Ghazali's court testimony in the case of the assassination of Farag Foda, Farid abd al-Karim, an Egyptian leftist, wrote: "How can I ever claim to know half or even one tenth of what al-Ghazali knows about Islam? [...] therefore, I can only say that what [Ghazali] says must be correct. Who can ever claim that al-Ghazali does not know Islamic rules? No one can ever claim this"; quoted in *Majalat al-Ahali*, 4 August 1993, 7; Gamal al-Banna, *Kalla Thuma Kalla* (Cairo: Dar al-Fikr al-Islami, 1994), 55.
17. Mohammed al-Ghazali, "Qissat Haya", *Islamiyat al-Ma'rifa* 2/3 (2007): 157. More on Ghazali's reflections on his own life and education csn be found in a series of two interviews, "Sirat Haya" (interviewer: Mohammed Kamal Imam. Two parts: #S-1, #S-2).
18. Ibid., 158–160.
19. "Piety minded", a phrase coined by Marshal Hodgson, *The Venture of Islam*, vol. 1: *The Classical Age of Islam* (Chicago: Chicago University Press, 1977), 247–256, 263, 316–322.
20. Abu Hamid al-Ghazali, "Risalat Ayuha al-Walad", in Wadad al-Qadi, *Mukhtarat Min al-Nathr al-Arabi* (Beirut: no publisher, 1959), 45–59. For an English translation see *Ayyuha 'L-Wald, Lettre au Disciple*, 2nd edn (Beirut: Catholic Press, 1951 [Collection UNESCO D'oeuvre representatives]).
21. Al-Ghazali, videotape interview (#U-1). On *'ilm usul al-din*, which translates as "the science of the origins/bases of the faith", and for another reference to *'ilm al-kalam*, see Louis Gardet, "Ilm al-Kalam", *Encyclopaedia of Islam*, 2nd edn (Leiden: Brill, 1999).
22. Al-Ghazali, "Qissat Haya", 173, 174.
23. Ibid., 163.
24. The British occupation of Egypt left a permanent impression on al-Ghazali. Towards the end of his life, he remembered the British regiment camped in front of a mosque in his village despite the fact that at the time "I may have been only three, a mere toddler carried on his mother's shoulder." He wrote how on the day his village of Nakhla al-Inab

"joined the uprising against the English by cutting off telephone lines, declaring its mutiny [*tamarrud*], and when a villager did not abide by the occupiers' imposed curfew, he was shot." Ibid., 15.

25. Al-Ghazali, "Qissat Haya", 159, 165. As he saw it, al-Azhar was exceptional among religious institutions because it taught various schools of thought, not just one. In a videotape interview (#U-1), al-Ghazali proudly spoke of al-Azhar's "excellent Maliki *faqih*, Shaykh Mohammed al-Madani", who taught a variety of *fiqh* views that included those of Ibn Taymiya, Ibn al-Qayyim, Ibn Hazm, and many more. He also noted how the same shaykh encouraged his Azhari students to research treatises on the forgotten *fiqh* of 'Aisha, the wife of the Prophet.
26. For an English translation of eyewitness accounts, see *Napoleon on Napoleon: The Autobiography of the Emperor*, ed. Somerset de Chair (London: Sterling Publishers, 1992); *Napoleon in Egypt: Al-Jabarti's Chronicle of the French Occupation, 1798*, trans. S. Moreh (Princeton, NJ: Markus Wiener, 1993); for an academic reading of these events, Juan Cole, *Napoleon's Egypt: Invading the Middle East* (New York: Palgrave Macmillan, 2007).
27. The long list of *'ulama* who introduced modern Egyptians to new ideas include Shaykhs Rifa'a al-Tahtawi (d. 1873), the above-mentioned Mohammed Abduh and Rashid Ridha, Mustafa al-Maraghi (d. 1945), and Mahmoud Shaltut (d. 1963).
28. One early twentieth-century Egyptian patriot was Father Sergius, a Coptic priest who famously used al-Azhar's pulpit to preach against the British occupation. He gathered both Muslims and Christians to hear his sermons around the Abbasid Quarter of this ancient mosque during the uprisings of March and April 1919. Sergius is reported to have described how he instinctively turned to this centre of Sunni Islam to deliver his message. As he left the home of family members he had been visiting, he heard demonstrators chanting for Egypt's freedom, and "I [...] found my feet taking me straight to al-Azhar", he said; Vivian Ibrahim, *The Copts of Egypt: The Challenges of Modernisation and Identity* (London: I.B.Tauris, 2010), 64; Vivian Fuad, "Al-Azhar and Egypt's Copts: From Defensive Relations to Constructive Dialogue", January 18, 2015 (online: http://mesbar.org/paper/al-azhar-egypts-copts-defensive-relations-constructive-dialogue/).
29. For an accessible outline of these early developments, see Majid Fakhry, *A Short Introduction to Islamic Philosophy, Theology and Mysticism* (Oxford: Oneword, 1997).
30. Paul Brunton, "An Interview with the Spiritual Head of the Muhammedans", in *A Search in Secret Egypt* (London: Arrow Books, 1965 [1935]), 142–152.
31. See Rashid Ridha, *Tafsir al-Manar, al-Ustadh Muohammad Abduh*, 12 vols (Cairo: al-Hay'a al-Misriya al-'Ama li al-Kitab, 1990); idem, *Yusr al-Islam wa Usul al-Tashri' al-'Am* (Cairo: Maktabat al-Salam al-Alamiya, n.d.).
32. Al-Shatibi was a Maliki scholar, born in Granada, Andalusia. Like Abu Hamid al-Ghazali, his works discussed *maqasid al-Sharia* (the intentions of Shari'a) as the principle of Shari'a rule-/lawmaking. Al-Shatibi deployed his arguments against the *fiqh* "orthodoxy" of his contemporaries; idem, *Al-Muwafaqat*, ed. Abu Ubaida al-Hasan Ibn Salam (Cairo: Dar Ibn 'Affan, 1997).
33. Al-Tufi was a Hanbali scholar. He was born in Iraq and moved in the scholarly circles of Syria and Egypt. Besides al-Shatibi's works, Abduh and Ridha also resuscitated al-Tufi's work, in which he stressed benefit and the common good (*al-maslaha*) as key principles of Shari'a rule-/lawmaking. Other scholars quickly followed Abduh's lead, such as the Syrian Gamal al-Din al-Qasimi (d. 1914), who published al-Tufi's epistle "Risalat al-Tufi fi ri'ayiat al-maslaha" in *Masadir al-tashri' al-Islami fi ma lais fihi Nas* in support of the move in *fiqh* circles against the common practice of resorting to established old *fiqh* rules and arguments when deciding pertinent Shari'a rules. The *Encyclopaedia of Islam* article on al-Tufi suggests that his radical-sounding thought should be placed within the context of his times, when circumstances were leading some scholars to reconsider predominant "orthodox"

approaches to Muslim rulemaking. See Wolfhart Heinrichs, "Al-Tufi", *Encyclopaedia of Islam*, 2nd edn (Leiden: Brill, 1999).

34. Inverview with Shaykh Ali Goma, April 1998. For an English discussion that notes this modern shift in *usul al-fiqh*, albeit from a different lens, see David Johnston, "A Turn in the Epistemology and Hermeneutics of Twentieth Century *Usul al-Fiqh*", *Islamic Law and Society* 11/2 (2004): 233–282.
35. Besides dismissing it as unscholarly and mediocre, until the late twentieth century many *usul al-fiqh* professors at al-Azhar thought his work did not not lend itself to instruction purposes, "*ghaira qabil li-al-tadriss*" (author interview with Ali Goma, who was speaking as Egypt's grand mufti, 15 February, 2006). See also Mohammed al-Ghazali, *Nadwat Tadris al-'Ulum al-Shar'iya, Fadilat al-Shaykh Muhamad al-Ghazali: Taqdim wa Idarat Dr Gamal Eldin Attia* (Cairo: IIIT, n.d.), Appendix I. However, it is also worth noting that al-Azhar's newly devised *usul al-fiqh* syllabus in the English language includes works by al-Shatibi, while their Arabic-language curricula continue to omit his titles.
36. The place of valid personal or communal interests and the common good in Shari'a rulemaking is discussed further in Chapter 7. Illustrations of Abu Hamid al-Ghazali's most popular works in the Muslim library are listed in the Selected Bibliography.
37. Najim al-Din al-Tufi, "Risalat al-Tufi fi Ri'ayiat al-Maslaha", in Abd al-Wahab Khallaf, ed., *Masadir al-tashr'i al-Islami fi ma Lais Fihi Nass* (Kuwait City: Dar al-Qalam, 1993).
38. Most notable in such changes is how by the mid-twentieth century a majority of learned Egyptians did not subscribe to a particular *madhhab* or to the previously popular Sufi *tariqas*. According to the reformed "orthodox" beliefs, affiliation to a *madhhab* is meaningless for a common person, and should be reserved for expert *fuqaha* who could discuss the details of different schools of rulemaking. As for Sufi *tariqas*, these were old cultural practices, some of which might be antithetical to Islam. Notwithstanding, Sufi practices endured in urban slums and were later revived by some Egyptians living in the West as antidotes to the spread of Wahabi ideas among their fellow countrymen who worked in the Gulf States following the oil price boom. The same fears of Wahabi practices, or rather, subscription to Hanbali ideas, helped revive interest in other schools, *madhahib*, and new alternative approaches to their faith.
39. See Chapters 7 and 8 and the Epilogue for discussions of some such differences and their impact on Shari'a rulemaking.
40. Hourani's work remains a standard reference guide to the thought of some of Abduh's key students, and the impact they have had. Albert Hourani, *Arabic Thought in the Liberal Age, 1798–1939* (Cambridge: Cambridge University Press, 1983), 161–192, 222–244, 324–340. For an example of the impact of an adjusted Muslim narrative, by the 1960s Aqqad's *Al-'Abqariyaat al-Islamiyah* or his *Al-Tafkir 'Aqqida Islamiyya* (*Thinking is an Islamic Tenet*) became the prism through which many Egyptians understood Islam and its past. In the 1960s, the Egyptian state included *Abqqariyat* in the national school curriculum. More illustations of Aqqad's other titles that influenced modern Egyptian perceptions of Islam can be found in the Selected Bibliography.
41. Such as those discussed in Hourani, *Arabic Thought*, 193–340.
42. That was how al-Ghazali also saw it: "Hasan al-Banna was the heir to Mohammed Abduh and Afghani", he wrote, adding that the founder of the Muslim Brotherhood could not be blamed for the follies of members of the Ikhwan, especially after his death (Mohammed al-Ghazali, "Hadha Dinuna", *Al-Sh'ab* [Cairo], 22 September, 1992).
43. Throughout his life, al-Ghazali remained staunchly loyal to this al-Afghani-Abduh school. When a reporter likened the career and role of their contemporary Omar abd al-Rahman to that of al-Afghani, al-Ghazali interrupted: "How can you equate a chicken with lions? [...] I will not allow such comparisons." Al-Ghazali, who objected to the former's detention, explained that, however one looked at it, Shaykh abd al-Rahman was not a leader of

Muslims, adding that, "the ill and the good cannot be compared" (*Al-Watan* [Kuwait City], 24 January, 1992); earlier, al-Ghazali penned a long article to defend Abduh and al-Afghani from contemporary Islamists' accusations. Al-Ghazali, "Lima'dha al-hugom 'ala Mohammed Abduh wa al-Afghani?", *Majalat al-Doha* (Qatar) 91, July 1983.

44. Although he even visited his teacher Shaykh Mahmoud Shaltut at home, al-Ghazali said in a videotape interview (#S-1) that it was Shaltut's students who had the greatest influence on him, including Shaykhs Mohammed al-Madani and Mohammed Abd Allah Diraz.
45. Al-Ghazali, quoted in Abd Allah al-Masri, *Al-Da'yia al-Shaheed al-Shaykh Mohammed al-Ghazali* (Cairo: Al-Rawafid al-Thaqafyia, 1996), 17.
46. Al-Ghazali, "Qissat Haya", 157–159, 164–165.
47. Ibid., 178.
48. Ibid., 162, 168; al-Ghazali, videotape interview (#U-2).
49. Al-Ghazali, "Qissat Haya", 164.
50. Mohammed Abduh, *Mudhakirat al-Imam Mohammed Abduh*, ed. T. Al-Tanahi (Cairo: Dar al-Hilal, n.d.), 29–35.
51. Hasan al-Banna, *Mudhakirat al-Da'wa wa-l-Da'iya bi-Qalam al-Imam al-Shahid Hasan al-Banna* (Cairo: Dar al-Shihab, 1979), 139–140.
52. Al-Banna, *Mudhakirat*, 150, 180–196.
53. Ibid., 150, 164.
54. Hasan al-Banna, *Mudhakirat al-Da'wa wa-l-Da'iya bi-Qalam al-Imam al-Shahid Hasan al-Banna* (Cairo: Dar al-Shihab, 1979), 50–51, 66–67:
ولما طال بنا الجدل حول هذا الموضوع قلت لهم: ولم لا تكون التجربة هي الحد الفاصل في الامر؟ فقبلوا ذلك وخرجنا فبدأنا بالقهاوي الواقعة بميدان صلاح الدين واول السيدة عائشة ومنها الى القهاوي المنتشرة في احياء طولون الى ان وصلنا من طريق الجبل الى شارع سلامة والسيدة زينب. وأظنني القيت في هذه الليلة أكثر من عشرين خطبة تستغرق الواحدة منها ما بين خمس دقائق الى عشرة. وقد كان شعور السامعين عجيبا، وكانوا يصنتون في اصغاء ويستمعون في شوق...لقد نجحت التجربة مائة في المائة...
55. Ibid., 164.
56. For works of Hasan al-Banna popular among his countrymen in Egypt, see Selected Bibliography.
57. Al-Ghazali, "Qissat Haya", 164.
58. Ibid., 139–202.
59. As the secretary in charge of requests for fatwas, al-Ghazali would look into their subject matter and then discuss with al-Banna (videotape interview #J-1).
60. Author interview with Gamal al-Banna, Mu'asasat Fawziya wa-Gamal al-Banna, Shari' al-Jaysh, Cairo, 23 February, 1999. On the younger al-Banna's views on religious practices and the Muslim Brothers, see Gamal al-Banna, *Jinayat Qabilat "Hadathuna"* (Cairo: Dar al-Fikr al-Islami, 2008); idem, *Kala thuma Kala* (Cairo: Dar al-Fikr al-Islami, 1994); idem, *Ma Ba'd al-Ikhwan al-Muslimin* (Cairo: Dar al-Fikr al-Islami, 1996).
61. Al-Ghazali, videotape interviews (#TAYR-1, #IKH-1).
62. Ibid.
63. A year after al-Ghazali's expulsion from the Brotherhood, Professor Gustave E. von Grunebaum described him as "a spokesman for the Muslim Brotherhood" when he reviewed the first English translation of *Min Huna Na'lam*, in the *Journal of Near Eastern Studies* 14/3 [1955]: 200–202.
64. Mohammed al-Ghazali, *Min Ma'alim al-Haqq fi Kifahina al-Islami al-Hadith*, 2nd edn (Cairo: Dar al-Kutub al-Haditha, 1963), 262–263.
65. Al-Ghazali, "Qissat Haya", 188; Yusuf al-Qaradawi, "Al-Ghazali Rajul al-Dawa", in Fathi Hasan Malkawi, ed., *Al-'Ata al-Fikry li-l-Shaykh Mohammed al-Ghazali* (Amman: IIIT, 1996), 208–209.

66. Al-Qaradawi, "*Al-Ghazali*", 208–209; Mohammed al-Ghazali, *Al-Islam wa al-Istibdad al-Siyasi* (Cairo: Dar al-Kutub al-Islamiya, 1984 [c. 1951]).
67. Al-Ghazali, videotape interview (#IKH-2).
68. Al-Ghazali, *Min Ma'alim al-Haqq*, 239–240, 272; idem, videotape interview (#IKH-2).
69. Al-Ghazali, *Min Ma'alim al-Haqq*, 249 ff.
70. Al-Ghazali thoroughly disparaged the Muslim Brotherhood's political culture in *Min Ma'alim al-Haqq*, 235 ff.
71. Ibid., 267.
72. In an interview, al-Ghazali told Gamal 'Attia, "In truth, I lived some of my worst days when the Ikhwan expelled me amid bitter feelings of reciprocal hostility." However, he added that when the state disbanded them and imprisoned many of their leaders, "I said to myself: I may not be part of the Brotherhood but the Brotherhood is part of me" (videotape interview #IKH-2).
73. When the Muslim Brothers criticised al-Ghazali for taking part in President Nasser's Socialist Union, for example, he spoke about how working within the system helped him to spread the message of Islam openly and to a wider audience, and that even when Nasser and his media attacked him for it, he always found supporters (including one of the original Free Officers, Kamal al-din Hussein) (Mohammed Shalabi, *Al-Shaykh al-Ghazali wa Ma'rakat al-Mushaf fi al-'Alam al-Islami* [Cairo: Dar al-Sahwa 1987], 129).
74. Al-Ghazali, videotape interview (#IKH-2); idem, "Qissat Haya", 203–204, 208.
75. Many years later, al-Ghazali made peace with the groups' leaders, and he concluded that al-Hudaybi had never been a traitor, as he had earlier thought. By the 1990s al-Ghazali had moderated his language against the Ikhwan significantly, even praising figures he still criticized, such as Sayyid Qutb (videotape interview #IKH-2). He also made amends in other ways, such as when he shocked mourners at a funeral by kneeling down to kiss the feet of Hasan al-Hudaybi and asking for forgivness for doubting his sincerity in the past, an eyewitness recalled. For, although al-Hudaybi might have made mistakes, time demonstrated his integrity, al-Ghazali thought (author's telephone interview with Fahmy Huwaidi, April 2004).
76. Al-Ghazali, "Qissat Haya", 178.
77. Thanks also to a government appointment, al-Ghazali escaped his troubles with the Muslim Brotherhood leadership early in the 1950s by heading the government-run Egyptian mission (*tikyyia*) in Medina (videotape interview #IKH-1; author's telephone interview with Dhi'a al-Ghazali [Shaykh al-Ghazali's son], 30 April, 2009).
78. See in Chapter 3, section "*Portrait*: State versus *'alim*: Nasser and Islamic dress".
79. Al-Ghazali, "Qissat Haya", 213.
80. See section on "Sadat and Family Laws" in Chapter 3.
81. Author interviews with Shaykh Ali Goma, 16–22 February, 2006.
82. Al-Ghazali, videotape interview (#IKH-2).
83. Professor Peter Gran's comments on the author's dissertation on al-Ghazali, 19 March, 2000.
84. Yusuf al-Qaradawi, "Nazarat fi Tarikh al-Shaykh", *Islamiyat al-Ma'rifa*, 25.
85. Ibid. For Ibn Taymiya's popular works on Shari'a among the modern Salafis see *Al-'Aqida al-Wasittiya* (Riyadh: Adhwa' al-Salaf, 1999); idem, *Majmu'at al-Rasa'el wa al-Masa'el*, ed. with commentary by Rashid Ridha (Beirut: Lajnat al-Turath al-'Arabi, n.d.); Ibn al-Qayyim al-Jawziya, *Jami' al-Fiqh*, ed. Yusri al-Sayyid. 7 vols (Al-Mansoura, Egypt: Dar al-Wafa, 2001); idem, *Ighathat al-Lahfan Min Mas'aid al-Shaytan* (Mecca: Dar 'Alam al-Fawa'ed, 1432 AH).
86. Such as Ibn al-Qayyim's *Madarik al-Salikin* (al-Ghazali, videotape interview #TJD-1).
87. Mohammed al-Ghazali, *Humum Da'iya* (Cairo: Dar al-Bashir, n.d.), 8–10.
88. Al-Ghazali, videotape interview (#S-1).

89. Mohammed Al-Ghazali, *Al-Sunna al-Nabawiya Bayna Ahl al-Fiqh wa ahl al-Hadith*, 5th edn (no location: Sahara, 1989), 75.
90. Fathi Hasan Malkawi, ed., *Al-'Ata al-Fikri li-l-Shaykh Mohammed al-Ghazali* (Amman: IIIT, 1996), 127.
91. Al-Ghazali was awarded the King Faisal Award in 1989, which coincided with the same year he published *Al-Sunna al-Nabawiya*. Consequently, many Saudi publications condemned this last book. At the same time, al-Ghazali also received awards from Algeria, Malaysia, Pakistan, and Mauritania. Official honours came late in Egypt, however. He had to wait until 1991 to receive the Egyptian state's Award for Social Sciences. In the same year, al-Ghazali's fame had reached a hard-to-ignore peak, which perhaps explains the Saudi international daily *Al-Sharq al-Awsat*'s selection of al-Ghazali as its writer of the year for "his exceptional intellectual energy".
92. Author interview with Amna Nosseir, Madinat Nasir, Cairo, 29 March, 1999. At the time, Nosseir was the dean of the Alexandria Faculty of Islamic and Arabic Studies (for Women) at al-Azhar. She served alongside al-Ghazali as a member of the Cairo-based Higher Council for Muslim (*fiqh*) Affairs.
93. Mohammed al-Ghazali, "Hadha Dinuna", *Al-Sh'ab* (Cairo), 2 July, 1991.
94. Ala' al-Ghazali, "Al-Sira al-Dhatia li al-Shaykh Mohammed al-Ghazali", in Fathi Hassan Malkawi, ed., *Al-'Ata al-Fikry li-al-Shaykh Mohammed al-Ghazali* (Amman: IIIT, 1996), 204. Al-Ghazali discussed the reported ban on music elsewhere in his books and in an interview with Gamal Eldin Attia devoted to the arts (videotape interview #FN-1).
95. Taha Jabir al-Alwani, "Shaykhuna Mohammed al-Ghazali wa Safahat min Hayatuh", *Islamiyat al-Ma'rifa* 2/3 (2007): 7–10. Al-Alwani, a senior Azhari *usul al-fiqh* scholar, also founded and chaired the Fiqh Council of North America and helped to found the IIIT, serving as its president until he left the United States.
96. Ibid., 8–9.
97. Introduction to the fifth edition of al-Ghazali's *Al-Sunna al-Nabawiya*, 6. Notwithstanding, al-Ghazali refused the IIIT's offer to print the first edition of *Al-Sunna al-Nabawiya* in the United States and to have its Virginia headquarters distribute it worldwide. He insisted that such a book on Sunna must first be published in Egypt, where one of the country's larger publishers, Dar al-Shorouk, accepted the task.
98. Zahira 'Abdin (d. 2002) studied medicine. Her father, a member of Parliament at the time of the monarchy, seems to have encouraged her to pursue Islamic and modern education. Zahira eventually taught at Cairo University's Faculty of Medicine and later, in the UAE, she set up various charitable projects for medicine and education. Her own equally accomplished daughter, Mona abu el-Fadl, who became a recognized professor of political science, married Shaykh Taha Jabir al Alwani.
99. Tariq Salim al-Bishri (b. 1933) studied law in Egypt. He too came from a prominent family in modern Egypt's religious and legal establishments. His grandfather served as head of al-Azhar and his father served as president of Egypt's Court of Appeals. Al-Bishri too held some of the country's highest legal posts, becoming deputy of the council of state (*majlis al-dawla*) and chairing the Legislative and Fatwa General Assembly. Following his country's humiliating defeat in 1967, he started to shed his leftist, Arab nationalist convictions in favour of Islamic ideas. He authored books on modern Egyptian history and Islam, by the 1980s emerging as a celebrated Islamic figure in his country. His connection to the establishment as well as to the Muslim street was demonstrated immediately after Mubarak's fall in the 2011, when the Supreme Council of the Armed Forces (SCAF) chose him to chair a committee to propose the shape of constitutional changes in the country. The appointment was met with widespread Egyptian approval at the time.
100. Ahmed Kamal Abu al-Magd (b. 1930) is another former Arab nationalist. He studied law in Egypt and the United States, and he appears to have had many leanings. He organized

Nasser's Socialist Youth Movement, after which the President sent him to Washington, DC as Egypt's cultural attaché. Abu al-Magd also joined Sadat's government as secretary of information, and later held posts at the World Bank, and then as legal consultant to Kuwait's crown prince. Besides his close ties to governments, Abu al-Magd served as a member of the Arab Human Rights Organization and an Arab League cultural group, and taught law at Cairo and Kuwait Universities.

101. Ali Goma (b. 1952) studied trade and commerce before he moved on to study Shafi'i *fiqh* at al-Azhar University, where he later became professor of *usul al-fiqh*. From 2003–2013 Goma served as Egypt's grand mufti.
102. Fahmy Huwaidi, *Al-Watan* (Kuwait City), 26 March, 1996; author interview with Afaf al-Ghazali, Zamalek, Cairo, April 1999.
103. Author interview with Afaf al-Ghazali.

TWO

The Texts: On the Shelves

Mohammed al-Ghazali's bountiful legacy on Islam and on how to deduce its rules is to be found in books, newspaper articles, transcripts of his Friday sermons, videotaped interviews, and television appearances over a forty-year period. Those who describe al-Ghazali as either an extremist or modernizer both draw on this documentation, although they focus on particular periods; and unaware of the changes and continuities in al-Ghazali's overall legacy, many researchers fail to connect his arguments with the ever-evolving context in which he wrote or spoke, and thereby miss the import of his ideas. To see al-Ghazali through records of a particular phase only is to commit what David Brooks has called "the fundamental attribution error": the assigning of permanent attributes to arguments with "qualities that are actually determined by context".[1] The current chapter thus places context at the heart of its consideration of al-Ghazali's legacy.

The books

Al-Ghazali wrote nearly 60 books, covering topics ranging from Islam's core beliefs to contemporary economic and political concerns and other subjects.[2] He also published a book of poems and a book of devotional invocations.[3] Like the quintessential learned-activists of early Muslim history, the *faqih*, al-Ghazali thought of his role mainly in terms of interpreting the world through the lens of his faith. He sought to explain every novel development in ways which were compatible with Islam and, if he could not reconcile new challenges with the principles of their faith, he considered them threats and campaigned against them. His first book provides an illustration of this. In 1947, before the oil price boom in his region, al-Ghazali published *Al-Islam wa 'al-Awda' al-Iqtisadiyia* (*Islam and Economic Conditions*), in which he deplored the economic insignificance of modern Muslim societies,[4] while his second book, *Al-Islam wa al-Manahij al-Ishtirakiya* (*Islam and Socialist Systems*), identified parallels between modern socialist principles and ancient Islamic values.[5] However, he revised the views he expressed here in the light of later developments, telling an interviewer in the 1990s that over the years he had come to realize that "all who advocated socialism craved material goods for themselves only."[6] In his third book, *Al-Islam wa al-Istibdad al-Siyasi* (*Islam and Political Despotism*), he contended that Islam could not coexist alongside tyranny.[7] This work included lectures al-Ghazali delivered while incarcerated at al-Tor, in the hope of changing what he regarded as the worrying attitudes of his fellow Ikhwan prisoners. However, it was his fifth book, *Min Huna Na'lam* (*From Here We Know*), that caught the attention of fellow Muslims worldwide.[8] It was one of many works produced in the region that rebutted, whether in the name of Islam or custom, suggestions that Muslims copy the ways of the occupying European armies and governors in their countries. However, al-Ghazali's arguments struck a special chord, propelling him into a new position as a key spokesman for the Sunni majority inside and outside his country.

Al-Ghazali described his books as streams of thought that he usually committed to writing following the *fajr* (dawn prayers).[9] Some of these early titles are not high calibre works; some may even be described as limp and weak. However, al-Ghazali excelled where it mattered most: in attending to the Qur'an, as regarded by Muslims to be the literal words of God. Al-Ghazali wrote to elaborate the Qur'an's principles and methods, and later, to highlight how Muslims had used or misused the Qur'an throughout the centuries. In these commentaries, he often examined Muslim realities and experiences in light of Qur'anic content, using common-sense reasoning and, more importantly, writing in a way that his fellow Arabic-speaking Muslims understood, in order to present evidence for the new Shari'a rules that he discerned in his critiques of *fiqh*. His Qur'anic considerations put him on firm ground when he called for the reform of well-entrenched approaches to Shari'a that he regarded as improper. In response, some vocal Sunni circles frequently attacked him for being, in their view, not a real scholar, a *faqih*, but merely a preacher, *da'yia*, albeit an energetic one.[10] Nevertheless, al-Ghazali's devotion and the sharp observation of his Qur'anic discussions impressed fellow Muslims, and in later years scholarly bodies celebrated what they described as his special contribution "to the understanding and disciplines of the Qur'an", as the Islamic Organization for Education, Sciences, and Culture put it when it nominated al-Ghazali for the Sultan of Brunei Award.[11] Four works published towards the end of his career formed the main basis for this scholarly renown, and their Arabic titles can be translated as *Considerations on the Qur'an*, *The Five Orbits of the Qur'an*, *Towards a Thematic Commentary of the Qur'an*, and *How to Deal with the Qur'an*.[12]

Translating Islam into real life: Three sign posts

Three titles in particular are signposts in al-Ghazali's long career. As stated earlier, extensive fame first came in the early 1950s, following the publication of *Min Huna Na'lam* (*From Here We Know*). At first glance this book could be easily dismissed as another diatribe against the West and all things modern.[13] In this work, al-Ghazali explained that it was clever packaging, not substance, which made flawed Western ideas and institutions attractive. In contrast to Western standards, he argued, the far superior Islamic values were also compatible with human nature, and would lead to prosperity for those who embraced them. The book mirrors the apprehensive mindset of British-occupied Egypt in the late 1940s. At this time, the Muslim intelligentsia were increasingly adopting the paradigm of modernity and proposing the expunging of Islam from secular spheres; al-Ghazali thus identified importing political, economic, or social models from the West as embodying the most serious danger facing Muslim societies.

From Here We Know was written in response to Shaykh Khaled Mohammed Khaled's *Min Huna Nabda'* (*From Here We Start*), which had just been published.[14] Shaykh Khaled, a close friend of al-Ghazali, was a scholar at al-Azhar and a member of the Muslim Brotherhood, but he shared the modernist intelligentsia's view that that the only way Muslims could advance was to turn their backs on their own past practices and to follow the successful examples of the West. Al-Ghazali saw the tests that Muslims faced differently: not from *where* to begin reform, but *how* to reach it. His *From Here We Know* stressed an epistemological position that many of his fellow Muslims recognized as expressing their understanding of Shari'a. For al-Ghazali the key question had to be: From what sources and by what processes should Muslims improve their lives? Islam did not allow off-the-rack solutions when it comes to deducing correct rules; Muslims ought not just to import modernity wholesale, he argued. To determine correct values, Muslims had to abide by the *how* that Shari'a offered them. A majority of Sunnis who read or were aware of the contents of both books in the 1950s overwhelmingly identified with al-Ghazali's vision rather than Khaled's.[15]

Shaykh Khaled's target was a "Muslim Church", which he did not clearly define. This Church, he argued, obstructed scientific and socio-political advancement in Muslim societies, in the same way that the medieval Catholic Church had stood against progress in the West.[16] Al-Ghazali took special exception to this contention, and turned to the fundamental tenets of their shared faith. Islam, al-Ghazali reminded his readers, liberated humanity when it rejected the idea that some individuals had spiritual authority over fellow humans. With this, Islam actually demolished all Church-like structures. However, although that might have been true in theory, it did not reflect actual experience, and al-Ghazali addressed the incongruity. He wrote that he too disapproved of some past and present Muslim practices, including the erroneous references to Muslim scholars, like himself, as "men of religion" (*rijal al-din*).[17] Islam had no place for clergy, he insisted. As al-Ghazali saw the past in the 1950s, all historical instances where this had occurred were exceptions to the rule and aberrations. As such, he dismissed the Umayyad caliph Yazid Ibn Mu'awyyia (d. 683 CE) as an "idiot", and described the Umayyad general Hajjaj Ibn Yusuf (d. 714 CE) as a criminal.[18] Their practices did not represent the norms of Muslim government, al-Ghazali argued, allowing him to cast them aside; but he also attacked Western political institutions and Khaled's praise of them. He described the West's institutions as shams, and his book is peppered with examples that show the West's claims of respect for human dignity and freedom to be bogus,[19] and that reveal the brutality and oppression of the Western democracies in practice.[20] At a time when many Arabic-speakers equated all things Western with colonialist schemes to subjugate them, al-Ghazali led the way from the 1940s to the 1980s. Despite this, however, he too fervently subscribed to Western political practices. Constitutionalism is one example of this, albeit at the time he regarded such contracts between the rulers and the ruled as essentially Islamic. Throughout his life, al-Ghazali unequivocally pronounced constitutional life to be the cornerstone of a healthy society and an ancient principle of Islamic government.[21]

Al-Ghazali followed *Min Huna Na'lam* with more titles that reflected widespread fears about the West. And he warned against the deluge of foreign poisons that were polluting his society. He argued against Arab nationalism (particularly as expressed by President Abd al-Nasser and the Ba'ath Parties of Syria and Iraq), communist parties, and what he regarded as the hidden toxins encased in orientalist scholarship, the Western study of Islam.[22] Decades later, Khaled retracted the modernist views he had presented in *From Here we Start*, expressing regret that he had ever advocated them.[23] Al-Ghazali's thought also underwent significant change, albeit in a different direction.

Reflections of the Holy Cities

Al-Ghazali's trepidation about Muslim societies began to shift inward as he spent time in Mecca and Medina. The first spark was in the early 1950s, when he took a position at the Egyptian religious commission (*tikkyia*) in Medina as a refuge from his bitter fight with the new leadership of the Ikhwan.[24] As he reflected on his misfortunes, he wrote two further books:[25] *Khulq al-Muslim* (*The Character of Muslims*), in which he described correct Muslim conduct,[26] and *Fiqh al-Sira* (*In-depth Comprehension of the Prophet's Life Story*), in which he pursued the theme of Muslim conduct further by exploring the example of Mohammed.[27] In this way, al-Ghazali sought to heal the wounds that his Muslim brothers' bad behaviour had inflicted on him, and both books have had a remarkable trajectory. By the twenty-first century, the former work had found considerable favour among

Muslims in the West;[28] and while the early edition of the latter did not attract much attention, his later revision of this work, following another period of refuge and reflection in Islam's Holy Cities, led to it acquiring greater fame.

This second period in Saudi Arabia was necessitated by al-Ghazali's unrelenting opposition to President Sadat's divorce-law reform. This infuriated the President, and in the spring of 1974 various restrictions were imposed on al-Ghazali, including banning him from delivering the Friday sermon in Ibn al-'As, the mosque that al-Ghazali put at the centre of Egypt's religious life. Like the Saudi religious establishment that al-Ghazali joined at this time, he fought attempts to grant wives desperately needed rights. By that time, however, al-Ghazali's concerns appeared to have altered with the changes in the world around him. In Arabia he increasingly complained about the idleness and lack of self-discipline and hygiene among many who flocked to worship in Mecca and Medina.[29] Frequent academic confrontations with colleagues and students at Mecca's Umm al-Qura University further added to al-Ghazali's woes, and he linked what he saw as the failure of the modern Muslim intellect to general Muslim misconduct.[30] Thus preoccupied with Muslim ill temper inside scholarly circles and bad manners in the streets, al-Ghazali had to accept that the ideals of his faith generally clashed with Muslim realities. In search of remedies, he revisited *Fiqh al-Sira.* As he reviewed the sources on the history of the Prophet, Mohammed al-Ghazali embarked on the second great phase in his intellectual journey.

How to trace the Prophet's footsteps?

When al-Ghazali initially attempted to trace the Prophet's footsteps in *Fiqh al-Sira* he resorted to Hadith reports about the Prophet's sayings and actions. However, in due course he came to realise that many of these reports were doubtful, despite being commonly cited in the most scholarly Muslim works. His namesake Abu Hamid al-Ghazali had been criticized throughout the centuries for frequently turning to forged Hadith, even in his masterpieces;[31] but as the modern al-Ghazali continued to ponder the examples set by the Prophet, years after he first published *Fiqh al-Sira*, he took an uncommon step among the *fuqaha*. Before sending his revised edition to the printers, he invited independent assessment of the Hadiths he had used in telling the story of the Messenger of God.[32] Shaykh Mohammed Nasir al-din al-Albani, the renowned *isnad* expert who evaluated the authenticity of the Hadiths in *Fiqh al Sira*, judged a good number of them to be doubtful or forged. Al-Ghazali did not exclude either the suspicious Hadith reports or al-Albani's comments in his new edition; instead, he reprinted the work with al-Albani's not-so-approving assessment as footnotes, along with a new introduction.[33] What was the aim behind this uncommon move? Naturally, al-Ghazali did not intend to undermine his scholarship by showing that he used forged Hadith in explaining the Prophet's practices; indeed, he even defended some of his Hadith choices in the new introduction. But what did he calculate would be the long-term impact of publishing al-Albani's damaging appraisal of many well-circulated Hadith? Perhaps he supposed that combining al-Albani's expertise with his own would spark interest in better approaches to the Prophet's legacy, which he knew to be a highly sensitive subject.[34] In the introduction to the eighth edition of the book, Mohammed al-Ghazali expressed concern that the memory of the Prophet suffered because of inadequate assessment of the accuracy of Hadith. Even *Sahih al-Bukhari* and *Sahih Muslim*, the two canonical collections of Hadith, contained some dubious accounts about Mohammed, at least if taken at face value, al-Ghazali noted.[35] The best way to defend the Sunna, therefore, was to address the confusion in its sources and ideas.[36] This call to the Arab street was significant. Steps to place the Prophet's real legacy on a firmer basis are not merely a matter of scholarly or moral propriety; Muslims have designated the precedents provided by their Prophet's life to be the second foundational source of Shari'a. Reconsidering these records, as al-Ghazali now counselled, could lead to substantial changes in Muslim rule-/lawmaking.

Al-Ghazali described *Fiqh al-Sira* as his favourite book.[37] Although its discussions did not amount to a systematic investigation of the past, his frequent return to the concerns of this book triggered troubling questions in his mind and led him to ponder the reliability of Hadith as a source of the Prophet's Sunna, especially as a valid legal principle. For if he, al-Ghazali, a conscientious Azhari scholar, could be so misinformed about authenticity, as evident from al-Albani's appraisal of the Hadiths used in *Fiqh al-Sira*, would not the average Muslim be likely to make the same or even more errors? Al-Albani also worried him for another reason: al-Ghazali later observed that this *isnad* expert had judged a number of disturbing Hadiths to be genuine, thereby embedding moral indifference in the Muslim midst. For example, as a result of neglecting to examine their contents (*matn*) against Islam's principles, al-Albani declared as reliable reports in which the Prophet commanded striking unsuspecting people without prior warning.[38] Such unethical conduct would not have been the Prophet's way, according to al-Ghazali.[39] Moreover, if al-Albani, an eminent Hadith specialist, could pass such reports as reliable, although they clearly contradicted Qur'anic tenets, did that not indicate a larger problem in how Muslims approached the Sunna?

Fiqh al-Sira raised urgent questions in al-Ghazali's mind: how discerning had the *fuqaha* and the *muhaditheen* been when considering precedents derived from accounts of the Prophet's life? How often had those who spoke in the name of Islam misused Hadith to champion what were essentially human (cultural, political, or economic) preferences, by claiming them as divine instructions? What led Muslims to keep quiet about false claims about their Prophet? In his pursuit of answers, al-Ghazali began to reconsider what he previously took for granted: the outline of the Muslim story and its sources. Probing the past sharpened al-Ghazali's critical eye and led to him becoming a renowned commentator on contemporary Muslim societies. He had a new cause: tackling what he saw as his people's representations of Islam in terms of a corrupt bequest that had grown over the centuries.

A final sign post

From this period, the Sunna continuously preoccupied al-Ghazali, and in the late 1980s he published his conclusions in *Al-Sunna al-Nabawiya Bayna ahl al-Fiqh wa ahl al-Hadith* (*The Prophet's Precedent between Champions of Hadith and Champions of Fiqh*). This work represents another shift in al-Ghazali's approach to Hadith, and it heralded the third and last phase in his intellectual journey. It also took Arabic-speaking Muslims and their religious circles by storm. Most Western experts on "Islamic law" ignored *Al-Sunna al-Nabawiya* or underappreciated the furore that followed its publication and that remains to be settled.[40] The concept of "Islamic law" found in academia was insufficient for evaluating this book. In contrast, many Sunni Arabic-speakers were captivated by the way al-Ghazali argued his case, and found that they could not turn away from the questions he posed or the painful answers his book thrust on them.

Al-Ghazali's book and the events surrounding its publication marked the beginning of a new, broad-based and organic chapter of self-critique in Islam's Arabic-speaking settings. Al-Ghazali, a mainstream Islamic leader, deconstructed common uses of Hadith, leading him to criticize some Hadith reports as false and to censure canonical collections and early Hadith scholars, including central figures whom Sunnis usually view as forming a *golden chain* of transmitters, such as Naf'i (d. ca. 737 CE), a servant of 'Abd Allah (d. 693 CE), the son of the second caliph, Umar Ibn al-Khatab.[41] Al-Ghazali unearthed an exchange between a grandson of this second caliph, Umar, and a grandson of the fourth caliph, Ali Ibn Abi Taleb, about a particular Hadith that Naf'i had narrated, whereby Umar's grandson concluded that "the slave [Nafi'] lied and made an error."[42] Other accounts that justified similarly reprehensible behaviour claimed as their sources Abu Hurayra and Abd Allah Ibn Masud, two of the most revered early Hadith reporters.[43] Al-Ghazali pressed further: not only these accounts, but also the early figures associated with them had to be questioned. Famous Hadith scholars he criticized included al-Nawawi (d. 1277 CE), who, instead of investigating a problematic narration, instead attempted to reconcile its contradictions.[44] According to al-Ghazali, when Muslims adopted approaches such as those of al-Nawawi they shaped whole sets of authoritative but unjust precedents that, in one instance, turned what was essentially murder into a rule of Shari'a.[45]

Al-Ghazali also found al-Mundhiri (d. ca. 1258 CE) wanting, when he reported at least 16 Hadiths that praised living in Syria as recommendations of the Prophet, transforming what might have been later instruments to encourage defending particular regions into foundational religious ideas.[46] Key Hadith collections, such as those of al-Tirmidhi, Abū Dāwūd, and Ibn Mājah, also contained flawed reports, al-Ghazali noted.[47] As noted above, even the two canonical Hadith collections of *Sahih al-Bukhari* and *Sahih Muslim* included unacceptable accounts about the Prophet, Mohammed al-Ghazali told the common Muslim.[48]

Changing boundaries

Al-Ghazali's book on the Prophet's Sunna crossed boundaries that popular Muslim narratives of history and *fiqh* had long marked as off-limits, yet its arguments were also grounded within the boundaries of Islam's tenets. Like other Sunnis, al-Ghazali held Umar Ibn al-Khatab, the second caliph and disciple of the Prophet, in the highest esteem, yet he posed a question the Sunni answer to which al-Ghazali knew well: where in Islam's tenets does it say that Umar, or any of Mohammed's disciples, could not make mistakes of memory or judgement?[49] Sunni memory celebrates traditions that show how they regarded the esteemed leaders of Medina and the excellent *fuqaha* that followed in their footsteps as men only, possessing no divine authority.[50] In theory, therefore, Muslims (at least Sunnis) were free to assess legacies of the past in light of Qur'anic tenets and sound reasoning. Nothing was novel in al-Ghazali's ideas: he merely brought back to the forefront of discussions a key Sunni principle: If no man was infallible, according to their faith, then why would accounts reported by early Muslims be infallible? Ironically, however, in his Arabic-speaking settings these sentiments continued to thrive side by side with a narrative that sanctified the past. The reasons behind the controversy that *Al-Sunna al-Nabawiya* set off are also the reasons behind its success: in a time of uncertainties, al-Ghazali merely threw the spotlight on a discrepancy between theory and practice.

On contemporary Muslims

As with his other books, al-Ghazali penned *Al-Sunna al-Nabawiya* in response to immediate challenges;[51] consequently, he reserved his harshest words for his contemporaries, targeting what he viewed as the recklessness and vulgarity of some contemporary Muslims. In the early 1990s, al-Ghazali warned in a lecture in Cairo that some modern Muslims "could very well destroy civilization on earth, for the meaning of humanity eludes us as a result of piles of superstition and ignorance that the boorish [in our midst] introduced" into Islam.[52] The intransigence of many of the self-styled Salafis of his time especially angered him:

they dismissed early legal scholarship (*fiqh*) in favour of Hadith reports, when in fact they toed the line of only one school, the Hanbali.[53] In reality, those who subscribed to this approach had little grasp of Islam's sources or method of rule-/lawmaking, al-Ghazali believed. Whereas the highly trained *fuqaha* of the past approached the Hadith legacy in a nuanced manner, these modern, noisy mobs suffered from an anaemic intellect, he contended. He further explained that their dearth of knowledge and limited aptitude for learning meant that such defenders of Hadith could not evaluate either the historicity (*isnad*) or meanings (*matn*) of the reports from which they deduced absurd rules.

Al-Ghazali filled *Al-Sunna al-Nabawiya* with illustrations. Obsession with appearances and cultural absurdities, or calls for war against non-Muslims and anyone who disagreed with their views, turned some of his fellow Muslims into tormentors of their societies. Such was the case of an Indian imam who instructed his community to eat only on the floor or to wear specific garments that included turbans.[54] Others misspent their energies on campaigns that championed women's face-coverings (*niqab*) or opposed modern toilets as "un-Islamic" because these facilities forced males to urinate standing up and not sitting down.[55] Al-Ghazali described these contemporaries as "'half-wits" and "juveniles" who often employed false or misconstrued Hadith reports to twist Qur'anic verses in order to promote a worldview hostile to reason, common decency, and prosperity.[56] Why did these Muslims not champion Shari'a's principles that upheld the dignity of humans or campaign for practices to advance social and political rights instead?, al-Ghazali asked.[57] He saw in these loutish representatives of Islam a continuation of an old phenomenon, but now with a modern and especially dangerous dimension, and their unprecedented economic muscle and global reach worried him at a time when the United States and other Western governments were treating them as valuable. Towards the end of his life, he openly expressed fears about what he saw as the combination of arrogance and ignorance that enveloped these supposed defenders of the "traditions" of his faith. They could eventually push the world towards a perilous brink, he warned.[58] The central question to which his society required an answer was this: Where did the faultline between use and abuse in the name of Islam lie, both in the past and in the present? And where did Shari'a fit in?

To deduce a Shari'a Rule: Past and present precedent

In modern times, Muslims have continuously sought a contemporary statement on Shari'a rule-/lawmaking, hoping to steer the process which sits at the centre of their faith into an orderly and functional reality. But how could this be achieved? Attempts to codify some existing *fiqh* rules into a law, as in the Ottoman *al-Majallah*, did not succeed. Nor did government attempts to impose *fiqh* rules show much promise either, as in twentieth-century examples that included Iran, Sudan, or Afghanistan. Shari'a applications of self-described Salafi groups in Egypt, Algeria, the West, and elsewhere have not fared any better, either. What practical solutions did *Al-Sunna al-Nabawiya* offer towards that end?

Al-Ghazali certainly believed Shari'a to be capable of organizing dynamic societies. As the title indicates, al-Ghazali was considering whether his contemporaries should copy the old schools of legal thought (*madhahib*) or directly deduce Shari'a rules from the corpus of Hadith, without reference to this old scholarship. At first glance, in this book al-Ghazali appears to favour a return to the accumulated *fiqh* legacy. For centuries, the *fuqaha* have been the intellectual leaders of Muslim society; they studied the Qur'an in detail, relied on sound reasoning, and understood the complexities of real-life situations, and al-Ghazali reiterated this long-established view. It was obvious: training combined with aptitude qualified the *fuqaha* to deduce rules, including from the mixed bag of genuine and false Hadith reports, al-Ghazali explained. Why squander this enormous inherited knowledge? A reasonable solution, therefore, was for Muslims, especially Hadith-oriented groups with limited competence and little training, to defer to the rules that the ancient and modern *fuqaha* deduced, a practice known as *taqlid*.[59]

But, as it turned out, it was not exactly the legacy of *fiqh* that al-Ghazali wanted Muslims to embrace when he wrote his book. Here one observes a clearly changed al-Ghazali, even a newly invented scholar. Whether in the old centres of Islamic learning or in Western academia, many modern scholars find the yardsticks with which to determine Shari'a's legal concepts in what they designate as "classical" *fiqh*. Al-Ghazali appears to have deserted their ranks. Conceiving *fiqh* as identical to Shari'a demonstrated carelessness or scholarly incompetence, he explained. The term *fiqh*, he further clarified in several occasions, did not indicate a single experience; it referred to numerous legal and cultural episodes, each with their own set of circumstances and merits.[60] Al-Ghazali thus warned Muslims against following *fiqh* ideas unquestioningly; he wanted them to discover, like he did, the many redefinitions that had been introduced to Shari'a throughout the centuries.

True, confronting Hadith-oriented groups of his time was a central and urgent purpose in writing his work. Less noted, however, is how al-Ghazali used this seemingly pro-*fiqh* book to censure key *fiqh* claims, albeit in subtler tones than those he reserved for Shari'a claims based solely on Hadith. Far from advocating a return to *madhahib*, the established schools' rules, al-Ghazali brought *fiqh*'s imperfections to fellow Muslims' attention. Even if the *fuqaha* possessed extensive training and nuanced views, many of them had lost their way when they neglected the sound process of Shari'a rule-/lawmaking, al-Ghazali concluded. Many *fiqh* rules now appeared to him as inevitably humiliating the vulnerable in society, whether women, non-Muslims, or any other group open to exploitation.[61] Further, many *fiqh* errors originated in misrepresentations of the Sunna, in ways not dissimilar to those of their Hadith-only contemporaries, as al-Ghazali explained it.[62] *Al-Sunna al-Nabawiya* ultimately made clear that both Hadith and *fiqh* misrepresented the Prophet's Sunna, and in so doing both legacies have debilitated Muslim intellect and weakened Muslim societies.

A thornier issue than critiquing the earlier *fuqaha* and ancient, divine-like rules, perhaps, was how *Al-Sunna al-Nabawiya* criticized contemporary Hadith scholars and other religious leaders. To demonstrate the sorry depths to which Muslim intellectual endeavour had declined, al-Ghazali noted media reports celebrating how the foremost Saudi religious authority at the time, Shaykh abd al-Aziz bin Baz (d. 1999), had rid a bedouin in the Arabian desert of a Buddhist devil.[63] Al-Albani, who had previously assessed the Hadith reports in *Fiqh al-Sira*, showed a similar disregard for both reason and Islam's tenets, according to al-Ghazali. It appeared that as long as an account met al-Albani's own *isnad* criteria of authenticity, this renowned Hadith expert overlooked its contents, no matter how outrageous or contrary to Muslim tenets these might be.[64] Al-Ghazali challenged fellow Muslims: What did it say about their collective mindset when contemporary senior spokesmen of Islam held ideas such as these? With the exception of al-Ghazali, no one at the time could have openly and relentlessly criticized the likes of Shaykhs Bin Baz and al-Albani without damaging his stature in the Sunni street or among its scholarly circles.[65] So, why did many Muslims accept al-Ghazali's criticisms?

Why did they listen?

When it comes to questioning Hadith, a number of explanations occur as to why Arabic-speakers accepted, or at least considered, al-Ghazali's book. First, he was not alone, as the reaction of Egypt's religious establishment to al-Ghazali's controversial book indicates. When no condemnations of *Al-Sunna al-Nabawiya* poured forth from al-Azhar, it appeared that this premier Sunni institution tacitly approved the book's sensitive contents, signalling that nothing in its pages threatened the tenets of Islam. His book rather signalled a break in the silence of the Azhari *'ulama* on this popular legacy. In deferring to al-Ghazali as the most credible voice to make such a challenge, these Sunni scholars both revealed their trepidations and conceded his greater weight. Why he used this influence towards the end of his life and how he did so are discussed in the chapters that follow.

Al-Ghazali thus merely pushed ajar a gate that had been closed to the public for centuries. When this door was unbolted, even if not fully opened, Azharis became able to air their critiques of Hadith as a source of rulemaking, if they so wished, albeit within certain parameters. Soon after the publication of *Al-Sunna al-Nabawiya*, some rushed to express bold views on Hadith. Shaykh

Yusuf al-Qaradawi, a world authority on *usul al-fiqh*, declared in 1996 that "we live in a Sunna crisis". In a front-page interview published in Kuwait's *Al-Watan al-Islami*, al-Qaradawi described Hadith reports as the ignorant mobs' instrument of choice: misrepresentation of the Sunna, al-Qaradawi explained, originated in fanaticism, "since wrongdoers could not falsify the Qur'an [...] they inserted into the honorable Prophetic way that which is alien to it."[66] Critics of popular approaches to Hadith also included the mufti of al-Azhar Mosque-University, Shaykh Abd Allah al-Mashad (d. 1991).[67] In a fatwa, he ruled that the rejection of Hadith reports had no consequences on the faith of a Muslim.[68] Islamic tenets were based only on certainty, whereas the bulk of Hadith was only provisional, as many *'ulama* had long indicated, he explained. However, fearful of the general reaction to this fatwa, al-Azhar did not publish it; it quietly buried the text in that year's fatwa records. In this, al-Ghazali's stature and role in leading this new broad-based chapter of self-critique in Islam's Arabic-speaking settings becomes clearer, for it was he who stepped in to publicize the official, undisclosed fatwa in one of his books.[69]

Perhaps more significant than any Azhari scholar was the then-imam of *al-Jam'iya al-Shar'iya li Ta'awun al-'Amilin bi al-Kitab wa al-Sunna*, a Hadith, Salafi group. Shaykh Abd al-Latif Mushtahiri (d. 1995) issued a statement in support of new efforts to re-examine the accuracy of Hadith, which was published in Egypt's largest circulation daily, *Al-Akhbar*.[70] Telephone conversations and correspondence reveal that this devotee of the Prophet's legacy apparently came around to the need to re-evaluate the legacy of Hadith and *fiqh* in part because his son Mohammed had taken up this task of criticism.[71] In a letter to al-Ghazali, Mushtahiri praised al-Ghazali's courage in publicizing the Azhar fatwa.[72]

Before *Al-Sunna al-Nabawiya* placed questions about Hadith into the Egyptian street, it would have been unthinkable that a woman dean at al-Azhar's college for girls in Alexandria and a member of the Higher Council for Muslim (*fiqh*) Affairs, Professor Amna Nosseir, could tell a Cairene weekly that *Sahih al-Bukhari* needed sifting.[73] Calling for *Al-Bukhari* and *Sahih Muslim* to be scrutinized for errors, and stating that she had often expressed the need to do this, as Nosseir did, was not something that Azhari professors commonly boasted about—at least not openly, and not without public uproar or serious consequences to their positions in religious institutions. However, no such pandemonium followed in Nosseir's case. Without attention to context, it is impossible to appreciate how unthinkable it would have been for a general Arabic newspaper to publish an appeal to re-assess *Al-Bukhari* or the magnitude of al-Ghazali's critique of Hadith origins, as opposed to other critiques. In the same interview, when Nosseir needed a modern authority to justify her call to sift the most revered Hadith collections, like many others she invoked the example of Shaykh Mohammed al-Ghazali.[74] Naturally, some in the Sunni establishment found Mohammed al-Ghazali's new approach to Hadith highly objectionable. The most vocal criticism came from *'ulama* in the Salafi establishment,[75] the lower echelons of religious education, and those without formal Azhari training. Their religious curricula discourage critical questions. From an early age they learn to locate Islam in a particular narrative of the past, especially in Hadith collections and ancient *fiqh* arguments. This meant that al-Ghazali's enemies did not speak with one voice, but represented a wide range of Sunni groups. The most ferocious attacks on him, however, came from the self-styled Salafis of the late twentieth century, whom he thoroughly disparaged in his book. They mainly used Hadith reports to derive Shari'a rules and rejected the bulk of the Muslim legal heritage, with the exception of that of the ninth-century CE Ibn Hanbal and his followers. Previously, these modern Salafis had long held al-Ghazali in great esteem, as a brave upholder of the Sunna. He often championed the Shari'a rulemaking methodologies of their key scholars, Ibn Taymiya and Ibn al-Qayyim, against famous figures such as Abu Hamid al-Ghazali.[76] So, when al-Ghazali published his adjusted approach to the Sunna in which he now derided their worldview, the same Salafi groups found themselves in the midst of an internal crisis that left them exposed. They responded by declaring an all-out open war on al-Ghazali, in which they were joined by powerful allies. Customarily at the time, Arabic-speaking Gulf governments subscribed to the Salafi approach to Shari'a, and in a move that added another grave dimension to the responses to *Al-Sunna al-Nabawiya*, the Saudi state and its religious establishment put their financial weight behind the groups that sought to tear down al-Ghazali's latest explanations of the Shari'a with a flurry of books, newspaper articles, and seminars that claimed to expose his errors.[77] This commotion is far from over yet, and it remains an open question who will prevail. However, there are abundant indications of change to Sunni approaches to Hadith. Shortly before al-Ghazali's death in 1996, the Saudi state appeared desperate to restore its damaged relations with him; in the 1990s al-Ghazali appeared to have won the support of many Muslims against the might of the richest states and groups in his region, just as he had previously won against Khaled Mohammed Khaled's thesis in support of the then-vogue modernization paradigm in the 1950s. Within a decade of publishing *Al-Sunna al-Nabawiya*, a quiet adjustment in Arabic-speaking discourse about Shari'a rulemaking had taken place, especially in Egypt.[78] Illustrations of these shifts, and of intensified responses against them, are discussed in Chapters 5–8.

Remarkable as it is in many ways, al-Ghazali's *Al-Sunna al-Nabawiya* is in some places weak and even contradictory. Its author sometimes relies on certain Hadith reports to argue against the reliability of others, but without providing sufficient grounds for why it is appropriate to employ the particular Hadiths of which he approves.[79] In other words, he casually uses Hadiths as an authority to dismiss other Hadiths as an authority; and despite berating what he believed to be the common practice of misquoting the Prophet, al-Ghazali did not really call for the many weak or false Hadith reports that riddle Muslim literature to be abandoned. Instead, he merely warned against using these reports in deducing Shari'a rules/ laws or in defining the tenets of Islam.[80] But that ambivalent positioning is a well-established Sunni practice too.[81] Accordingly, many point out that al-Ghazali provided no original perspective on Hadith criticism, which is of course true;[82] but that does not mean that it is a work of limited scope, and its significance to Muslim discourse should be understood. Al-Ghazali did not set out to find a new methodology for assessing Hadith or to provide an academic review of its history or historiography. He simply wanted to draw to the general attention of his fellow Muslims the danger that false Hadith reports destroy the Sunna of the Prophet, instead of preserving it; and that this consequently destroyed their communities.[83] In that, al-Ghazali succeeded, reconfiguring the popular understanding of Hadith at a careful, steady pace. An enthusiastic young man who assisted him in probing Hadith collections remembered how al-Ghazali advised him to slow down. In a recorded telephone conversation, the old Shaykh is heard reminding his younger acquaintance that "this ailing edifice [improper ideas about the Prophet] had been created over many centuries; it could not be pulled down in a day."[84] However, al-Ghazali openly expressed similar sentiments in a public seminar. He cautioned some of Egypt's top Islamic scholars that although much-needed, the deconstruction of Muslim approaches to Hadith and *fiqh* ought to be carried out with the greatest care, or else their reforming efforts were likely to be confused with, or end up as, attacks on Islam itself.[85]

There is also a personal dimension. After the publication of *Al-Sunna al-Nabawiya*, when al-Ghazali first heard how some fellow Muslims had accused him of disparaging the Prophet's Sunna, he is reported to have cried.[86] He explained, in his own defence, that his love of the Prophet had led him to stand up for the Sunna's accuracy against a wall of lies, and he expressed hope that such a stand on Hadith would prove to be among his most worthy deeds on Judgement Day.[87] More books followed in which al-Ghazali elaborated on what he saw as corrupt practices that passed as instructions of the Prophet, and that poisoned Muslim lives and minds.

Academic experts who refer to Mohammed al-Ghazali as modern or moderate usually look at these titles to the exclusion of the rest of his legacy; even today, many Arabic-speakers find inspiration in these books, which have become symbols of Muslim self-critique and form the basis for another modern reform movement. Al-Ghazali discussed what he saw as the entrapment of women between stagnant medieval ways and abusive modern practices,[88] deliberated his community's heritage in light of both Qur'anic tenets and common-sense reasoning,[89] and reflected critically on community approaches to the Qur'an through history.[90] He also further summarized the problem of Hadith for the ordinary person.[91]

A final book appeared after al-Ghazali's death, under the title *Kunuz min al-Sunna* (*Treasures from the Sunna*). Al-Ghazali's candid reviews are conspicuously absent from this posthumous work.[92] Although its editor insists that he only collated writings that the deceased shaykh intended to publish, *Kunuz min al-Sunna* appears to be a stranger in al-Ghazali's library. Its apologetic, unquestioning tenor justifies doubts that it may even be an attempt to recast the departed *'alim* as a devotee of Hadith. Among his admirers, some remained attached to the populist approach to the Prophet's legacy, regarding Hadith as not-to-be questioned divine instructions, despite their conviction that al-Ghazali accurately presented Shari'a. They did not see a need for a critical study of the past.[93] The accusations of disparaging the Sunna levelled against al-Ghazali and, by implication, also levelled at them too, embarrass some such admirers. This final book may tell us little about al-Ghazali's last thoughts on the Sunna, although it does underline the tensions in al-Ghazali's camp as well as the conflicting traditions that guide modern Sunni thought, including a quest for corrections and, simultaneously, the constant rebuff of the critical appraisal of pre-colonial ideas.[94] In that sense *Kunuz min al-Sunna* could also be a valuable text.

Other media, old sermons

Muslims have enthusiastically embraced modern Western media to spread their message. The careers of Shaykhs Gamal al-Din al-Afghani and Mohammed Abduh showed how keenly these two used print. By the 1970s, Muslim preachers also turned to audio recordings, and the pocket-sized cassette tape allowed them to hit two birds with one stone: preachers could bypass censorship at a time when governments had a media monopoly, while reaching even greater numbers of ordinary Muslims in a region afflicted by pervasive illiteracy.[95] Ayatollah Khomeini and Shaykh Galal Kishk are famous examples here, but numerous others also delivered their messages to far-flung listeners by means of cassette-tapes. After this came the age of television preachers, followed by videos, and, later, the world wide web. Today, Twitter, Facebook, and other social media have become associated with all sorts of contemporary Muslim movements.[96] Mohammed al-Ghazali did not follow this-all-too familiar pattern, and he did not take up the new media available during his lifetime.[97] It is not certain why this was, but he seemed to prefer print. Even so, though, audio- and videocassettes of al-Ghazali's recordings can be found.[98] Most important among these is a video series he recorded towards the end of his life. In each of these recordings, a prominent member of Egypt's Islamist intelligentsia interviewed him about topics that concerned them at the time.[99] Despite the fame of the shaykh and his interviewers, they have never been broadcast to this day, and a carefully sanitized version was published only in 2012.[100] Among various reasons for restricting access for such a long time, according to a source that helped to commission the recordings, was their "sensitive nature". Indeed, al-Ghazali seemed to have used the opportunity they offered, towards the end of his life, to freely articulate his conclusions on women, government, education, and contemporary Islamist movements and figures, as well as his personal life. The valuable texts that these video recordings provide also tell important aspects of Islam's and Egypt's stories during al-Ghazali's lifetime.

In addition to penning numerous books, al-Ghazali conveyed his Islamic instruction in interviews and regular columns that he wrote in newspapers and periodicals, which included international dailies, women's magazines, and religious journals. Thanks to this presence, many women and men who may never have known of his books came to know and like al-Ghazali. The captivating headlines and easy-to-read style of his press contributions ensured that by the late 1980s al-Ghazali's ideas had reached Muslims who did not share his village values or share the social background of the Muslim Brotherhood. Many of these readers found in his newspaper presentations of Islam a faith relevant to their day-to-day concerns. In short columns al-Ghazali stressed hard work, good education, and economic prosperity as requisite proactive expressions of Islam's essence. He explained to them that their faith did not separate the spiritual from the worldly, including the scientific or mundane. Equally, he clarified what he considered to be correct Shari'a rulemaking. That al-Ghazali pulled no punches often made readers smile, even laugh, bringing his points home in a memorable, plainspoken style. Stupidity and refusing to use common-sense reasoning, he instructed Muslims, were sins that God had forewarned about in the Qur'an, and were, therefore, punishable on the Day of Judgement. He especially ridiculed widespread obsessions with jinn, magic, and superstitions. Other un-Islamic practices that he warned against included indifference to economic and political justice or progress. The Arabic-press readership found in this steady flow of articles topical and contemporary answers about their ancient faith.

Al-Ghazali had access to the pulpits of mosques, including some of the most famous in Cairo. Although the numbers that the mosques accommodated were insignificant compared to those that al-Ghazali reached through newspapers, immediate contact through this well-established platform created a special bond between al-Ghazali and the worshippers who heard his Friday sermons.[101] From the ranks of such worshippers emerged what can be described as al-Ghazali's army, a legion that rose to defy whatever powers there were in the land whenever these troops deemed it necessary to defend al-Ghazali. When in the 1960s the state-owned media ridiculed al-Ghazali for his call for women to adopt an

Islamic dress code, this crowd took to the streets of Cairo to express its indignation.[102] Mosque attendees rose again in the 1970s to support al-Ghazali against a government that sought to punish his opposition to Sadat's intended reforms of family law.[103] It was not only with their feet that such mosque assemblies voted for al-Ghazali: they supported him with their labour, as when volunteers that included his students helped him to clear the ruins of Ibn al-'As mosque and, later, when their dedicated attendance helped al-Ghazali turn its derelict site into a central place of worship in Egypt.[104] His sermons that have been collected and published thus provide another source on Egypt's social history at the time.

Unexplored texts

What led increasing numbers of Arabic speakers to see in al-Ghazali a representative of Islam transcends the above-discussed legacy readily available on their shelves. Muslims in Egypt determined with certainty his expertise in Shari'a from another ancient source that they trusted best: crises. The intangible texts that crises offered the devout allowed al-Ghazali to harshly censure them, their key religious figures, and even their forefathers, as time and again modern Muslims withdrew their support from those whom they had previously backed when these spokespersons of their faith suddenly appeared too critical of Muslim society or when they changed their positions on Shari'a rules. Crises, as a source of Muslim rulemaking, remain poorly explored. The next chapter highlights their place—that is, when tension becomes the indispensable Shari'a text.

Notes

1. David Brooks, "Huntington's Clash Revisited", *New York Times*, 4 March, 2011 (online: http://www.nytimes.com/2011/03/04/opinion/04brooks.html).
2. A full list of al-Ghazali's texts that are known to the author and which the author of the book consulted can be found in the Selected Bibliography.
3. Mohammed al-Ghazali, *'Al-Hayah al-'Ula: Diwan Shir* (Cairo: Dar al-Shorouk, 1998); idem, *Fann al-Dhikr wa al-Du'a* (Cairo: Dar al-'Itisam, n.d.), translated into English as *Remembrance and Prayer: The Way of the Prophet Muhammad* (Leicester, UK: Islamic Foundation, 1986).
4. Mohammed al-Ghazali, *Al-Islam wa al-'Awda'al-Iqtisadiya*, 7th edn (Cairo: Dar al-Sahwa, 1987 [1947]); idem, videotape interview (#S-1).
5. Mohammed al-Ghazali, *Al-Islam wa al-Manahij al-Ishtirakiya* (Cairo: Nahdat Misr, 2007 [1951]).
6. Al-Ghazali, videotape interview (#MUL-1). At the time, al-Ghazali was not alone among Azharis to embrace socialism. Other "socialist" *faqihs* included his close friend, as he often described Shaykh Khaled Mohammed Khaled, and their great teacher, Shaykh Mahmoud Shaltut.
7. Mohammed Al-Ghazali, *Al-Islam wa al-Istibdad al-Siyasi* (Cairo: Dar al-Kutub al-Islamiya, 1984 [c. 1951]). On the circumstances behind writing this book, see idem, "Qissat Haya", *Islamiyat al-Ma'rifa* 2/3 (2007): 187–189. On his leadership of the Ikhwan while in prison

in Sinai, see Yusuf al-Qaradawi, "Al-Ghazali Rajul al-Dawa", in Fathi Hassan Malkawi, ed., *Al-'Ata al-Fikry li-al-Shaykh Mohammed al-Ghazali* (Amman: IIIT, 1996), 208–209.

8. Mohammed al-Ghazali, *Min Huna Na'lam* (Cairo: Dar al-Kutub al-Haditha, n.d.). This is the first of al-Ghazali's books to be translated into English (by the late Ismail El-Faruqi). It was published under the title *Our Beginning in Wisdom* for the Near Eastern Translation Program of the American Council of Learned Societies (ACLS) (Washington, DC, 1953).
9. Mohammed al-Ghazali, *Khutab al-Shaykh Mohammed al-Ghazali fi Sh'oun al-Haya wa al-Din* (Cairo: Dar al-Itissam, 1988), 18.
10. These attacks are discussed further in Chapters 6 and 7.
11. The awards included the Saudi King Faisal's Award in 1989, and honours from Algeria, Pakistan, and Malaysia, among other countries. In the same year, the Saudi international daily *Al-Sharq al-Awsat* declared al-Ghazali the writer of the year for what it described as his exceptional intellectual activity. Soon after, a body representing the Muslim *'ulama* also selected him as the most distinguished religious figure of 1991, according to the Kuwait daily *Al-Watan* (24 January, 1992, 11). As mentioned previously, al-Ghazali finally received the Egyptian State's Social Sciences Award in 1991.
12. Respectively, these are: Mohammed al-Ghazali, *Kaifa Nat'amal ma' al-Qur'an*, ed. Umar Ubaid Hassana (Herndon, VA: IIIT, 1992); idem, *Nazarat fi al-Qur'an* (Cairo: Dar al-Kutub al-Haditha, n.d.); idem, *Al-Mahawir al-Khamsa li al-Qur'an* (Cairo: Dar al-Sa'hwa, 1989); idem, *Nahwa Tafsir Mawdui li Suwar al-Qur'an al Karim* (Cairo: Dar al-Shorouk, 1992).
13. Most are still in print: Mohammed al-Ghazali, *Al-Isti'mar Ahqad wa Atma'* (Cairo: Dar al-Kutub al-Islamyia, 1983); idem, *Difa'a 'An al-'Aqida wa-al-Sharia Dhidd Mata'in al-Mustashriqin* (Cairo: Dar al-Kutub al-Islamiyah 1988); idem, *Al Ghazaw al-Thaqafi Yamtadu fi Faraghina* (Cairo: Dar al-Sahwa, 1987); idem, *Dhalam Min al-Gharb* (Cairo: Nahdat Misr, 2005).
14. Khaled Mohammed Khaled, *Min Huna Nabda'* (Cairo: al-Maktaba al-Anglo Misriya, 1969 [1950]).
15. Al-Ghazali nevertheless noted his close friendship with Shaykh Khaled; see videotape interview #MUL-2. On this close relationship between the two men, see Midhat al-Bassyoni, *Al-Haqiqa al-Gha'iba bayna Khaled Mohammed Khaled wa Mohammed al-Ghazali* (Cairo: no publisher, 1979).
16. Khaled, *Min Huna Nabda'*, 41–84. Al-Ghazali rejected Khaled's claim that there was ever a Church as in the Christian experience, in *Min Huna Na'lam*, 27, 131, 132 [English: *Our Beginning in Wisdom*, 75–77].
17. Al-Ghazali, *Min Huna Na'lam*, 7, 23, 27.
18. Ibid., 37.
19. Ibid., 69, 94, 100, 103, 198.
20. Ibid., 69, 93.
21. Ibid., 20–30.
22. Mohammed Al-Ghazali, *Al-Islam fi Wajih al-Zahf al-Ahmar* (Kuwait City: Maktabat al-Amal, 1966); idem, *Difa'a 'An al-'Aqida wa-al-Shari* (Cairo: Dar al-Kutub al-Islamiyah, 1988); idem, *Haqiqat al-Qawmiya al-'Arabiya wa Usturat al-Ba'th* (Cairo: al-Rawda li al-Nashr wa al-Tawzi', 1993).
23. Khalid Mohammed Khalid, *Al-Dawla fi al-Islam* (Cairo: Dar al-Thabit, 1981); idem, *Rijal Hawla al-Rasul Sala Allah 'alayhi wa Sallem* (Cairo: Dar al-Fikr li al-Tiba'a wa al-Nashir, 2006 [1999]).
24. Al-Ghazali, videotape interview (#IKH-2).
25. Ibid.
26. Mohammed al-Ghazali, *Khuluq al-Muslim* (Cairo: Akhbar al-Youm, n.d.).
27. Mohammed al-Ghazali, *Fiqh al-Sira*, 8th edn (Cairo: Dar al-Kutub al-Islamyia, 1988 [1965]), 4–8.

28. This book was one of the small number of his titles that were translated into English, as Mohammed al-Ghazali, *Muslim Character: An American-English Translation of Muhammad al-Ghazali's Khuluq al-Muslim* (Chicago: Kazi Publications, 2004).
29. Al-Ghazali, *Fiqh al-Sira*, 4, 8, 47, 57, 145.
30. Al-Ghazali, "Hadha Dinuna", *Al-Sha'b*, Cairo, 6 August, 1991.
31. Across the centuries some *'ulama* have levelled criticism against Imam Abu Hamid al-Ghazali for what they judged as his careless, limp use of Hadith. For a discussion of this censure, see Yusuf al-Qaradawi, *Al-Imam [Abu Hamid] al-Ghazali bayna Madihih wa Naqidhih* (Cairo: Dar al-Wafa', 1988), 140–142; Amna Nosseir, *Abu al-Faraj Ibn al-Jawzi* (Cairo: Dar al-Shorouk, 1987), 244–245.
32. For a brief discussion in English of Shaykh Mohammed Nasir al-din al-Albani (d. 1999), see Stéphane Lacroix, "Al-Albani's Revolutionary Approach to Hadith", *ISIM Review*, 21 (2008): 6–7.
33. Al-Ghazali, "Hawla Ahadith Hadha al-Kitab", in *Fiqh al-Sira*, 9–13.
34. Ibid., 9.
35. Ibid., 10, 12.
36. Ibid., 11–12.
37. Al-Ghazali, videotape interview (#MUL-1).
38. Mohammed al-Ghazali, *Al-Sunna al-Nabawiya Bayna Ahl al-Fiqh wa ahl al-Hadith*, 5th edn (no location: Sahara, 1989), 104.
39. Mohammed al-Ghazali, *Nadwat Tadris al-'Ulum al-Shar'iya, Fadilat al-Shaykh Muhamad al-Ghazali: Taqdim wa Idarat Dr Gamal Eldin Attia* (Cairo: IIIT, n.d.), 44.
40. Although Daniel Brown was one of the earliest in Western academia to note that in Egypt al-Ghazali's views were being described as "Islamic Perestroika" and "a true revolution", he did not explore this seeming revolution or its impact on his people's perceptions of Hadith or its place in Shari'a rulemaking, beyond placing al-Ghazali in a "modern revivalist" category; Daniel Brown, *Rethinking Tradition in Modern Islamic Thought* (Cambridge: Cambridge University Press, 1996), 108, 134.
41. Nafi' served abd Allah Ibn Umar Ibn al-Khattab. The *Encyclopaedia of Islam* article on Nafi' questions whether he really existed, on the basis that "there is no trace of him in Ibn Sa'd's Tabaqat, in which one would expect his name to be included among the mawali of Madina." See G.H.A. Juynboll, "Nafi", *Encyclopaedia of Islam*, 2nd edn (Leiden: Brill, 1999). Another informative article on the same figure is idem, "Nafi, The Mawla of Ibn Umar and his Position in Muslim Hadith Literature", in idem, *Studies on the Origins and Uses of Islamic Hadith* (Brookfield, VT: Variorum, 1996 [1993]); see also idem, "Some Notes on Islam's First Fuqaha Distilled from Early Hadith Literature", *Arabica* 39 (1992), 287–314.
42. Al-Ghazali, *Al-Sunna al-Nabawiya*, 103–104, 145.
43. Ibid., 26–27, 30.
44. Ibid., 29, 145.
45. Ibid.
46. Ibid., 30.
47. Ibid., 56, 114, 146–147, 158–159.
48. Ibid., 69, 103, 128, 145–146.
49. Ibid., 17.
50. This includes "*hum rijal wa nahnu rijal*" (they were but men and we are men too), a famous quote that Muslims report Abu Hanifa as having said as advice against the blind copying of rulings deduced by Mohammed's disciples or the revered *fuqaha* of early Muslim generations. However, although reported by Ibn Hazm, this quote is the subject of many refutations today; such warnings are often not about the quote's content, but its misuse by the "ignorant and arrogant", as in Salafi examples such as found online on *Islamweb* (online: http://articles.

islamweb.net/media/index.php?page=article&lang=A&id=44541) and *Islamport* (online: http://islamport.com/w/amm/Web/1583/188.htm).

51. Mohammed al-Ghazali, *'Ilal wa Adwiya* (Cairo: Akhbar al-Youm, 1992 [1984]); idem, *Humum da'yia*, 3 vols (Cairo: Dar al-Bashir, 1984); idem, *Mi'at Su'al 'an al-Islam* (Cairo: Dar Thabit, 1984); *Sirr Ta'akhur al-'Arab wa al-Muslimeen* (Cairo: Dar al-Sahwah, 1985); idem, *Ma' Allah* (Cairo: Akhbar al-Youm, 1992).
52. Mohammed al-Ghazali, *Al-Islam wa al-Mar'a* (Cairo: IIIT Publications), 21.
53. Al-Ghazali, videotape interview (#TAYR-2).
54. He also went after the source from which this imam concluded the ruling on turbans, a Hadith reported by al-Bayhaqi; al-Ghazali, *Al-Sunna al-Nabawiya*, 82, 85.
55. Ibid., 89.
56. Al-Ghazali, *Fiqh al-Sira*, 57, 145; idem, *Fi Shu'un al-Din wa al-Haya*, vol. 2 (Cairo: Dar al-'Itisam, 1988), 21; idem, *Al-Da'wa al-Islamiya Tastaqbilu Qarnaha al-Khamis 'Ashir* (no location: Dar al-Salasil, 1980), 70.
57. Among misguided priorities that disturbed him was the preoccupation over whether or not touching a woman invalidates ablution, rather than whether or not the elections in their country were rigged (al-Ghazali, *Al-Sunna al-Nabawiya*, 9).
58. "I swear by the One God, who has no other partner, that should we [Muslims] possess the atomic bomb, we would bomb the world and destroy civilization on earth because we do not comprehend the meaning of humanity, thanks to the piles of superstition, which the ignorant attached to our faith" (al-Ghazali, *Al-Islam wa al-Mar'a*, 11).
59. "I hate blind adherence to a *madhahib*, but copying a *madhhab*, *taqlid*, is less harmful than childish efforts" in Shari'a rulemaking, he qualified in advocating *taqlid* (al-Ghazali, *Al-Sunna al-Nabawiya*, 10). As there was "no Sunna without *fiqh*", he explained, the *fuqaha* are needed to judge the parameters of any report, describing them as the Hadith "verifiers of the community", to which he too turned for proofs; ibid., 15, 18, 24, 129.
60. Al-Ghazali, videotape interview (#UNV-1).
61. Al-Ghazali, *Al-Sunna al-Nabawiya*, 43, 46–47, 54–55.
62. Many *fuqaha*, al-Ghazali concluded, had let go of the actual Sunna and neglected explicit Qur'anic instructions because these benefitted women; Ibid., 46. See Chapter 6 for Ghazali's examples of how *fiqh*, and not just Hadith scholars, neglected the Sunna and misrepresented Islam.
63. Ibid., 95.
64. Ibid., 104.
65. An irate appendix to the fifth edition of *Al-Sunna al-Nabawiya* by an anonymous scholar suggested that al-Ghazali had not gone far enough in criticizing the self-styled Salafi spokesmen at the time. To underline the need for further censure, the author of the appendix included a story which the Saudi media reported as Islamic. The papers celebrated the news of how the highest Saudi religious authority at the time, Shaykh Bin Baz, had debated with a devil that possessed a Bedouin, and, "through irrefutable scientific evidence", according to the same reports, had finally convinced the devil to convert to Islam. Al-Ghazali also alluded to this story in *Al-Sunna al-Nabawiya*, 95.
66. "Shaykh Yusuf al-Qaradawi: Na'ish fi Azmat al-Sunna", *Al-Watan* (Kuwait City), 22 March, 1996, 1.
67. The official position of the "mufti of al-Azhar" is separate from that of the "mufti of Egypt".
68. The fatwa is dated 1 February, 1990. An English translation can be found in Appendix 2 of this book.
69. Mohammed al-Ghazali, *Turathuna al-Fikri fi Mizan al-Shar'i wa al-'Aql*, 2nd edn (Cairo: Dar al-Shuruk, 1991), 176–179.
70. *Al-Akhbar* (Cairo) 4 April, 1988.

71. Author interviews with Mohammed Mushtahiri, 23 March and 15 April, 1999. His father, abd al-Latif, was the fourth imam of al-Jam'iya al-Shar'iya li Ta'awun al-'Amilin bi al-Kitab wa al-Sunna until he died in 1995. In 2009 al-Jam'iya al-Shar'iya was awarded the King Faisal Award for its "long services to Islam". It is worth noting here that without al-Ghazali's book *Al-Sunna al-Nabawiya* unlocking this door, the older Mushtahiri might have not been able to issue such a statement publically. See his letter to al-Ghazali in Appendix 3.
72. See Appendix 1.
73. *Al-Geel* (Cairo), "Amidat al-Dirasat al-Islamiya fi Hiwar Khatir: Ahadith al-Bukhari wa Muslim Tahtaj ila Gharbala wa 'Ardaha 'ala al-Qur'an, Falisa Kulaha Sahiha", 14 March, 1999 (20): 1, 10.
74. Ibid.
75. For example, Abu Bakr al-Jaza'iri, *Al-Qawl al-Karim al-Ghali fi al-Difa' 'an al-Da'iya al-Ghazali* (Mecca: Maktabat Umm al-Qura, 1991); Rabi' bin Hadi al-Madkhali, *Kashf Mawqif al-Ghazali min al-Sunna wa Ahliha* (Medina: Maktabat Ibn al-Qayyim, 1410/1989 AH/CE); Salman al-Odah, *Hiwar Hadi' ma' al-Shaykh al-Ghazali* (Riyadh: [the Saudi state's] al-Ri'asa al-'Ama li'Idarat al-Bohouth al-'Ilmiyya wa al-Ifta wa al-Da'wa wa al-Irshad, 1989). This last book was also circulated in audiotape to rebut al-Ghazali's arguments. Despite al-Odah's apparent change of mind, those hostile to al-Ghazali continue to find in this particular book an outstanding response to al-Ghazali's arguments, such as in this Salafi site (accessed December 2015): http://ar.islamway.net/collection/1605/حوار-هادئ-مع-الشيخ-الغزالي
76. Al-Ghazali replaced Abu Hamid's al-Azhar's assigned texts with Ibn al-Qayyim's, such as *Madarik al-Salikin* (videotape interview #Univ-1).
77. Taha Jabir's al-Alwani's introduction to the fifth edition of al-Ghazali's *Al-Sunna al-Nabawiya*. One such Salafi leader, 'Ayidh al-Qur'ani, put the number of published refutations of al-Ghazali's *Al-Sunna al-Nabawiya* at 14. See video of al-Shaykh 'Ayidh al-Qur'ani yatahdathu an al-Shaykh Bin Baz and al-Ghazali at https://www.youtube.com/watch?v=O78rghy6Avw.
78. For some such adjustments, see the Epilogue.
79. Al-Ghazali, *Al-Sunna al-Nabawiya*, 85.
80. Ibid., 64, 83.
81. Ibid., 97. For modern illustrations of this view, see *Kaifiyat al-Tawfiq bayna al-Hadithin al-Mut'aridhiyn*, Fatwa 101452 (19 November, 2007), at *Markz al-Fatwa*, http://fatwa.islamweb.net/fatwa/index.php?page=showfatwa&Option=FatwaId&Id=101452 (accessed November 2015).
82. Such as Brown, *Rethinking Tradition*, 108.
83. As mentioned elsewhere, al-Ghazali insisted that *Al-Sunna al-Nabawiya* must first originate from inside Egypt, refusing an offer by IIIT to publish its first edition in the United States. See his Introduction to the fifth edition of *Al-Sunna al-Nabawiya*, 6.
84. Al-Ghazali talking to the then young Mohammed Mushtahiri; this recording of his private telephone conversation was made available to the author by Dr Mohammed Mushtahiri who, unlike al-Ghazali, finds a majority of Arabic-speaking Muslims less perceptive to his critiques of the Hadith legacy. The younger Mushrahiri is one among his contemporaries from every walk of life who attempted Hadith criticism with limited or no impact on the Egyptian street. It is worth noting that among them is Ismail Mansour, a doctor of veterinary medicine who gained fame in the 1970s as an inspiring Salalfi preacher but eventually found he could not reconcile the contents of the Hadith legacy with his faith as a devout Muslim. He authored a number of works to document his journey and research as well as warn his fellow Muslims regarding Hadith, such as Ismail Mansour, *Tabseer al-Umma bi Haqiqat al-Sunna* (Cairo: al-Nisr al-Dhahabi, 1995). As a result of his critical views on Hadith Mansour lost his status as a popular preacher.
85. Al-Ghazali, *Nadwat Tadris al-Ulum al-Shar'iya*.

86. Yusuf al-Qaradawi, "Al-Ghazali Rajul al-Dawa", *Al-'Ata al-Fikry li-l-Shaykh Mohammed al-Ghazali* (Amman: IIIT, 1996), 218.
87. Al-Ghazali said that he hoped his critique of Hadith had earned him God's rewards because "I made public the hidden disgrace [*'awrat*] of those who fight Islam [...] from within", thinking that they were Islam's friends (al-Ghazali, *Al-Islam wa al-Mar'a*, 19).
88. Mohammed al-Ghazali, *Qadhayia al-Ma'ra bayna al-Taqaleed al-Rakida wa al-Wafida* (Cairo: Dar al-Shuruk, 1991).
89. Mohammed al-Ghazali, *Turathuna al-Fikri fi Mizan al-Shar'i wa al-'Aql*, 2nd edn (Cairo: Dar al-Shuruk, 1991).
90. Mohammed al-Ghazali, *Kayfa Nata'amalu ma al-Qur'an, Mudarasah Ajraha 'Umar 'Ubaid Hassana*, 3rd edn (Cairo and Herndon, VA: IIIT, 1992), published in the format of a dialogue with Hassana, a respected Syrian Islamic scholar.
91. As in al-Ghazali, *Turathuna al-Fikri*, 143–182.
92. Mohammed al-Ghazali, *Kunuz min al-Sunna*, ed. Mohammed Khaled Fuad, 4th edn (Cairo and Giza: Nahdat Misr, 2003).
93. Including Shaykh Yusuf al-Qaradawi, *Tarikhuna al-Muftara 'Alayh* (Cairo: Dar al-Mashriq, 2006), 6. Notwithstanding, in other places al-Qaradawi even elaborated on how al-Ghazali hoped to improve Muslim study of history (al-Qaradawi, "Nazarat fi Tarikh al-Shaykh", 41).
94. See "Tenacity of a Historical Lens" in Chapter 8.
95. "Unofficial Cassette Culture in the Middle East", *Index On Censorship* 11/5 (1982): 10–11.
96. The first prominent example here is Shaykh Mutawalli al-Sha'rawi's *tafsir* lessons, some of which are transcribed and published under the title *Tafsir al-Sharawi: Khawatir Fadilat al-Shaykh Mohammed Mutawalli al-Sharawi hawla al-Qur'an al-Karim* (Cairo: Akhbar al-Yawm, 1991). For short English discussions on al-Sha'rawi (d. 1998), see J.J.G. Jansen, "Shaikh al-Sha'rawi's Interpretation of the Qur'an", in *International Congress for the Study of the Qur'an*, Series 1 (Canberra: Australian National University, 1980); Barbara Stowasser, "Religious Ideology, Women and the Family", in idem, ed., *The Islamic Impulse* (London: Croom Helm in association with the Center for Contemporary Arab Studies, Georgetown University, 1987).
97. Exceptions include al-Ghazali's tenure in Algeria. President Chadli Bendjedid not only invited al-Ghazali to help organize Islamic higher education in his country, but also gave him a regular slot on its small screen. Whether they liked or loathed him, interviewed Algerians remember how their country came to a virtual standstill when al-Ghazali's weekly programme was broadcast.
98. These exist mostly as privately recorded cassettes of conversations or public lectures.
99. A list of these video recordings, with names of interviewers, can be found in the Selected Bibliography.
100. Gamal Eldin Attia, ed., *Hiwarat al-Shaykh al-Ghazali: al-Sira wa al-Mu'asira* (Cairo: Dar al-Salam, 2012).
101. Some of these sermons were collected and published in al-Ghazali, *Fi Shu'un al-Din wa al-Haya*.
102. See in Chapter 3, section "*Portrait*: State versus *'alim*: Nasser and Islamic dress".
103. See ibid., section "*Portrait*: State versus *'alim*: Sadat and family law".
104. See ibid., section "*Portrait*: Amnesia and Agency".

THREE

Elusive Texts: The Book of Tension

If texts refer to records—reservoirs, if you will—from which one reads human experiences and their meanings, they must encompass a wider range of material than just written documents or inscriptions on relics. This is especially true in the world of Muslim rule-/lawmaking. Textual analysis alone, attempting to squeeze meanings from distant words in available *fiqh* manuscripts, cannot tell the story of Islam's legal experiences. Here, challenging times and the conflicts that a *faqih* faced or provoked themselves act as essential texts and contexts. Probing these times of disruption makes it possible to situate the original purpose of a law, rule, or a legal argument, and to identify what continuities or breaks it represents. From Islam's earliest times, in the part of the world where the faith first established itself, Muslims invested legitimacy in a basic process of deducing valid rules and deciding which of these would endure and which would not. Most often it was crises that helped the community to decide who to trust as an authority here, thereby shaping the direction of Shari'a rules. That meant that *who did what* during challenging times thrust a scholar into a position of influence, which included representing their communities' worldly interests. It also meant that Muslim communities acquired an undeclared form of self-rule, often amorphous and sometimes chaotic. In this chapter three portraits from al-Ghazali's life capture moments of crises that he either stumbled into or triggered. In two instances, al-Ghazali clashed with the state, or rather, with presidents: first the Arab nationalist, left-leaning president Gamal Abd al-Nasser and, a decade later, the Islamist, Western-leaning President Anwar al-Sadat. The third example is an altogether different kind of a crisis, in which al-Ghazali made an unexpected discovery about himself and his community: that, contrary to their claims, contemporary Muslims were neglecting the sound examination of the past and oftentimes showed contempt for its legacies. They knew even less about the history of other societies, he concluded. His increasing interest in Muslim uses and misuses of history would leave its deepest impact in the Shari'a rules that al-Ghazali later deduced.

Chapter 4 considers the theme of crises further, by considering al-Ghazali's role in the events surrounding the assassination of Farag Foda in June 1992 and the trial of Foda's assassins. A word of caution, however: although these four portraits appear to be a chronicle of disconnected, disparate stories, they are more than this. Al-Ghazali's responses in crisis after crisis allow a researcher to trace how and why the authority of this particular Azhari grew among his people, as well as why and when it sometimes shrank or was even sometimes lost altogether. It also reveals important patterns in Shari'a rulemaking that textual analysis alone cannot readily access.

From the commotion album

Portrait: State versus 'alim: Nasser and Islamic dress

The ways in which women in Egypt, Turkey, and Iran stood up for themselves in the early twentieth century have many similarities, but their stories also show crucial differences. Women activists in these three predominantly Muslim countries fought for their rights as part of an anti-colonial struggle: women hoped to free everyone, men and women, from humiliation and foreign dominance. In this quest for freedom, many of these Muslims gave up their then-traditional attire in favour of modern Western dress. However, unlike in Iran and Turkey, neither state nor society helped enforce this decision in Egypt. At these formative times, Egyptian women conceived of their liberation in markedly different terms from their Turkish and Iranian sisters.[1] Egyptians had been the first to publicly relinquish the *hijab*, their hair- and face-covers, but they did not revolt against or criticize Islam. As these women saw it then, embracing Western garments marked yet another way of championing their faith and country. At the time, many in al-Azhar accidently helped in constructing these perceptions. Accordingly, up to the 1950s, the younger female relatives of prominent Egyptian *'ulama* and religious figures—including relatives of Hasan al-Banna, Shaykhs Mahmoud Shaltut, Amin al-Kholi, Ahmed Amin, and al-Ghazali—appeared to have willingly abandoned their hair- and face-covers.[2] Put another way, the early feminist Egyptian project actively placed faith—Islam as well as Christianity—as the cornerstone of their modern dream.[3] Communal memories thus preserved the call to prayer (*adhan*) mingling with church bells, women chanting in street protests, and the falling *hijab* as the sounds and symbols of patriotism and modern Egyptian identity.

With changing contexts came new attitudes. By the early 1960s, Egyptians were living in a very different country from the Egypt of the 1920s when women first rose to claim their own voices and abandoned the *hijab*. Now, President Gamal abd al-Nasser had turned to the Soviet Union and Eastern European

Bloc for models of how to improve life for the long-suffering masses. One such step included setting up a state-run body, the Socialist Union, to which all the productive forces in society were supposed to belong. The Union organized its National Conference of the Popular Forces to discuss *al-'Mithaq'*, Nasser's blueprint of how to build a stronger Egypt. Many in the secular-leaning intelligentsia celebrated this event as a defining moment in Egypt's long history. At the time, the government was cracking down on the Muslim Brotherhood after its attempt to assassinate the President in 1954; accordingly, the willing participation of figures associated with the Muslim Brotherhood, such as Shaykhs Ahmed Hasan al-Baquri, Khaled Mohammed Khaled, and al-Ghazali in Nasser's leftist gathering enraged the Ikhwan.[4] Unrepentant, however, al-Ghazali lashed out at the group's unhealthy preference for working outside the system. He insisted that by participating in the Conference, a secular-sounding project, he was achieving what the clandestine Muslim Brotherhood could not: "I was able to erase a wrong and confirm a right; never was I without honourable supporters at every turn."[5] The incident marked another low point in his relationship with the leaders of the Ikhwan.

If the Ikhwan found al-Ghazali troublesome, their foes, including the President, discovered how disruptive he could really be. He used the Conference to promote his vision for Egypt, triggering a countrywide debate. As he saw it in the 1960s, what his community needed the most to rebuild a stronger Egypt was a return to its Islamic values, including dress codes, especially for women. As the country watched, al-Ghazali ascended the podium. He assailed the chaos that afflicted society and manifested in the Egyptian street. The solution he offered was to impose Islamic dress, which would protect the country against moral decay and against the erosion of its character by invading Western values. Al-Ghazali's call to return to dated attires, which Egyptian women had willingly abandoned decades earlier, dumbfounded much of Egypt's intelligentsia;[6] in the prevailing cultural atmosphere of the 1960s, they conceived of Egypt as a vanguard socialist state. Al-Ghazali's vision of imposing ancient ways of dress left them wondering: from where did this call for a restriction on appearances come? How did it ever find its way to the podium of a progressive gathering at a time when the whole country was looking on?

Nasser responded to al-Ghazali's unexpected call by explaining that he could not dictate to parents how to dress their daughters, but luminaries in the state-owned media were less circumspect. As products of the new nation-states in the region, which split education into exclusively Islamic or exclusively modern, many of Egypt's journalists, writers, and artists believed that progress resided in all things Western. Islamic attire appeared to them trivial, and al-Ghazali backward. To raise this proposal at the time and place that al-Ghazali did, they worried, would ruin a-once-in-a-lifetime gathering to put Egypt in control of its destiny as a leading nation. Accordingly, they expressed their contempt. The renowned cartoonist-lyricist Salah Jahin led the media offensive, ridiculing the obscurantist futility of al-Ghazali's views through a series of cartoons accompanied by verses, "On The al-Ghazalian Issue", which he published daily in the semi-official *Al-Ahram.*[7] These cartoon-verses record an outlook common among Egypt's post-colonial intelligentsia who subscribed to the paradigm of modernity, albeit with leftist leanings. They also demonstrate the dangerous communication gap in modern Muslim societies, between self-declared modernists and self-appointed keepers of tradition, who oftentimes shared common purposes such as improving the lot of their fellow countrymen, but no common discourse. As products of two separate educational systems, Jahin and al-Ghazali might as well have spoken different languages. Both wanted a better life and dignity for Egyptians, especially the poor, but thought the other's aspirations lay elsewhere, in narrow, self-serving, and meaningless ambitions. *Al-Ahram*'s cartoon of 31 May, 1962 provides an illustration here. It depicted al-Ghazali as a fashion czar, portraying nearly naked poverty-stricken boys carrying a sign that read "Where is our clothing? Do only women's garments interest you?" Similarly, Jahin's verses that accompanied the previous day's cartoon (30 May, 1962) read:

> And in the heat of the eventful conference
> While discussing how to provide for our children,
> Generation after generation
> His eminence, al-Ghazali, interrupted:
> The sleeves of the harem; these must be long.[8]

The scornful reference to al-Ghazali as "his eminence" meant to depict the shaykh as a high priest, ignorant of Egyptians' needs.[9] As it turned out, in this instance, "his eminence" recognized what Jahin, *Al-Ahram*, and Nasser had not: that the majority of Egyptians had a different perspective. In the now-independent Egypt, a sense of cultural alienation had swept across millions: feelings of estrangement not only haunted the villagers who migrated from the countryside in search of a livelihood in hostile urban slums; increasing numbers of well-to-do city residents felt equally lost in their 1960s surroundings, in which miniskirts and a visit by the existentialist French philosopher Jean-Paul Sartre and the writer Simone de Beauvoir appeared to be the intelligentsia's priority.[10] The prospect of cultural marginalization inside their own land terrified the people of Egypt. Al-Ghazali—not their revolutionary government or the country's modernist thinkers, such as Jahin—grasped their anxieties. Without a political voice, some such Egyptians proceeded to vote on "the al-Ghazalian Issue" with their feet. On 1 June, 1962, after al-Ghazali led the Friday prayers at al-Azhar, worshippers in the mosque began a spontaneous protest against Salah Jahin's cartoons scorning al-Ghazali.[11] By implication, such public anger appeared also to express defiance of the government. At the height of Nasser's popularity, al-Ghazali's power to mobilize dissent in the Egyptian street took all by surprise, including al-Ghazali himself. He hurried to explain it the following day in a statement sent to *Al-Ahram*:

> After the Friday service some of the worshippers tried to carry me on their shoulders. I found protection [from them] in the pulpit, shielded behind a wall of friends. When, under the pressure of the crowd, the [sheltering human] wall broke off, some of the [mosque's worshippers] were able to [forcefully] carry me. I clutched on tightly to the doors of al-Azhar, resisting all attempt to leave, [eventually rushing to] find refuge inside the Azhar administration [offices].[12]

Had the matter in question not been so grave, that day's events would have been comical: the sight of the modest figure of al-Ghazali, clad in his *faqih*'s attire and grasping a gate of an ancient Cairrene mosque while worshippers fervently attempted to break his grip in expression of their support, causing al-Ghazali to dash into nearby offices, where he locked himself in with his supporters in pursuit. Running away from the faithful who espoused his cause did not calm matters down: the protestors took to the streets, heading to *Al-Ahram*'s building to express their anger.[13] Al-Ghazali's call for restrictions on dress not only disrupted the Conference; it also turned into a national and international incident, to the dismay of all parties. It was no longer just a religious versus secular confrontation; the commotion caused by his call for Islamic dress triggered a crisis, in which the battlelines did not necessarily reflect al-Ghazali's loyalties or his intentions.

At the time, Nasser's enemies outside Egypt were watching for a chance to weaken him. In particular, France, Britain, and Israel had been seeking to redeem their battered images after their unsuccessful joint invasion of Egypt in 1956, while the United States and its Arab Muslim allies disliked Nasser's growing political and economic association with the Soviet Union and the Eastern Bloc. The disturbances in Cairo's streets, which had started due to al-Ghazali's call to enforce an Islamic dress code, were quickly seized upon. Nasser's enemies publicized the protests, each according to their own purposes. For example, Radio Mecca presented al-Ghazali as a beleaguered, outstanding *faqih* who was bravely defending Islam against an atheist government, which, among other things, sought to repeal divine principles that safeguarded man's superiority over woman.[14] In contrast, France's Arabic service described the same events in terms of a people's uprising against the dictatorial rule of Nasser.[15] Al-Ghazali was thus simultaneously cast as a staunch defender of the old ways as well as leader of civic freedoms. However, his own view of the world was different from that of the French or even the Saudis. Al-Ghazali disliked the Saudi political structure, which he had described a decade earlier as outdated and corrupt.[16] He disliked the French even more. The brutality of their forces against his Algerian brethren, who were struggling for their freedom, had prompted him to ridicule the hypocrisy of French proclamations of equality and liberty.[17] However, al-Ghazali's own intentions scarcely interested the parties involved in this political contest, of which he found himself at the centre; the unrest that his call had triggered was the only thing that mattered to governments in the West and in the Arab world.

Providing ammunition for the president's enemies in this way led to al-Ghazali being censured by the state, which reduced his rank from director of Egypt's mosques to a mere supervisor in the same department.[18] The demotion may have crushed al-Ghazali's spirits at the time, but the crisis he generated brought religious attire as a way of rejecting the wholesale westernization of Muslim societies to the attention of large numbers of Egyptians who would not otherwise have considered particular garments as a central aspect of Islam. He was not the first to sound such call in the twentieth century, but the crisis between al-Ghazali and the state helped to establish the significance of the issue, paving the way for widespread change: in the 1970s millions of politically voiceless Egyptians expressed themselves again on the issue of dress, with large numbers of women from all social and educational backgrounds taking up the veil or *hijab*, as well as other attires regarded as Islamic. Many of these women (as well as men) argued that adopting traditional garments protected society from moral decay and the erosion of cultural identity. Just like al-Ghazali's call in the 1960s, this mass adoption of the *hijab* also took modernists by surprise; the Western paradigms that they embraced had not forewarned these thinkers of a time when young, even highly-trained professional women, would willingly veil themselves. The reverse was supposed to happen. In June 1987, Yahyia Haqi, a litterateur, lawyer, and former diplomat captured this dreadful disconnect between Egypt's intelligentsia and the vast majority:

> What perplexes me the most is the sight of the *hijab* in Cairo's streets. I ask myself: What on earth could have happened? What came over the minds of these young women to change them in such a way [...]? My surprise is total.[19]

Within a decade, al-Ghazali's confrontation with the state and the intelligentsia that cheered it on had promoted a text about dress rules to the top of the political agenda—a text which many Muslims in Egypt read fluently. Far from weakening his standing, the crisis that followed his call for a change in dress propelled al-Ghazali to greater influence.

Veiling and sovereignty

Much has been written (and remains to be written) about aspects of Muslim women opting since the 1970s to wear the veil or *hijab*. In Egypt's case, one feature deserves reflection here: the *en masse* abandonment of the *hijab* early in the twentieth century, and the equally *en masse* return to the *hijab* late in the same century, was not the result of state intervention, as in other societies in the region. Egyptian women used dress as a language of resistance to express yearnings for liberation and for cultural and political sovereignty both when they abandoned the hair-cover and when they opted again to cover their hair. In the absence of a political or even a cultural voice, personal dress marked a free space for declaring new visions of the collective that the Egyptian state could not reach. The large numbers of women in the *hijab* appeared as a massive daily demonstration asserting some form of independence. Veiling as a form of liberation may seem paradoxical, yet their dress choice was the ultimate cultural mutiny, a longing to find an alternative vocabulary of how to live in modern times. The adoption of either old or new dress modes also reveals cultural chaos, which turned out to be a main concern of al-Ghazali and others like him. How do such yearnings, which are expressed in garments, relate to Shari'a?

It appears that context, rather than a Shari'a imperative, tipped the scale in favour of hair covering in this instance. After Israel crushed the Egyptian army in 1967, many in the country sought change and a remedy. With little access to power, altering their mode of dress became a practical solution for salvaging their seemingly crumbling world. Besides the quest to end the Israeli occupation of their country in Sinai, abandoning Western perceptions of womanhood also provided a remedy for painful cultural marginalization, the increasing estrangement Egyptians felt inside their country. Imposing symbols of themselves on their landscape appeared the ultimate triumph to a humiliated people.

That is why al-Ghazali's story did not end there, in his call to re-clothe the country in its pre-colonial garb. Later, he revisited Shari'a rules on proper Muslim dress, and he continued to believe in the righteousness of head-covering for women. However, he launched a scathing war against face-covering—the *niqab* or *burqu*—which he had previously declared to be a symbol of ignorance and impotence,[20] and he also attacked the rising trend to define Islam by appearances, what he denounced as a shallow Muslim obsession with beards and particular modes of dress for women and men.[21] In the late twentieth century, al-Ghazali expressed regret that he had once given high priority to the question of clothing. It had been the growing chaos in Egyptians' appearance that had prompted his call to re-adopt traditional dress in the 1960s, he further clarified. Besides tackling this unruliness in the Egyptian street, "homogeneity [of dress] would have [also] eliminated the great expense [wasted] on appearance", and, therefore, class differences among Egyptians—at least outwardly.[22] That al-Ghazali meant to defend the egalitarian principles of Islam, and not a particular Shari'a dress rule, is significant.[23] At stake here were grievances about sovereignty, identity, and social justice that threatened the message of the faith. Many years later he did not hesitate to raise the issue of clothing again, explaining that when it came to dress, all that Islam required was genuine decency for both men and women alike. When asked now if Islam prescribed specific garments, al-Ghazali's answer was unequivocal: "No".[24]

Portrait: Amnesia and agency

> Our study of Islamic history is shallow, of [the rest of] humanity is all but non-existent.[25]

'Amr Ibn al-'As was a contemporary of the Prophet and a member of Quraysh's wealthiest clan. The Sunni majority call these early Muslims the *sahaba*, venerating them all as disciples of their Prophet. After Mohammed's death, Ibn al-'As played a significant role in shaping the course of Muslim history: as commander of a military expedition, Ibn al-'As initiated the conquest of Egypt in 639 CE, but apparently without first referring to the caliph in Medina. Victorious, in 640/641 CE, Ibn al-'As became Egypt's first Muslim governor. The early Muslims chose to live in garrison towns, not among the people they had conquered. Fustat was their garrison town in Egypt, which they founded on the outskirts of a Byzantine fortress that they had captured near revered Christian and Jewish religious sites. In time, this extraordinary Jewish, Christian, and Muslim historical site had greatly deteriorated through inattention; experts at the Department of Antiquities and other scholars had failed to note that the first place of Muslim worship in their country—the mosque that Ibn al-'As built in Fustat—had become "a vacant plot, surrounded by falling walls, and often flooded with sewage", and was becoming a garbage dump.[26] One Egyptian who every now and then would agonize powerlessly over the dilapidation of this heritage site was Shaykh Abd al-Halim Mahmoud, and in the 1970s, having become minister of *awqaf*, he at last had the authority to address some of this. He began by instructing al-Ghazali to deliver the weekly Friday sermon at Ibn al-'As mosque.

Al-Ghazali was dumbfounded.[27] He knew the shambles of Misr al-Qadima, as the old *fustat* is now called. It was crumbling, neglected, and in one of modern Cairo's poor quarters. Washing hanging on lines crisscrossed the tightly-packed slums; garbage lined its dust-filled streets. The presence of ancient sites only added to the mood of wreckage. When he first heard that he had been assigned to lead the Friday prayers in such a pile of rubble, al-Ghazali felt insulted, as he later recalled. He protested that for all practical purposes Ibn al-'As was "not a mosque", and pressed the minister of *awqaf* as to why he would not allow him to return to al-Azhar's pulpit instead.[28]

However, resentment gave way to reflection. Al-Ghazali contemplated the fate of the ancient mosque: Why was it that a location that could be regarded as the most important, and was certainly the oldest, Muslim site in Egypt had been allowed to become a repulsive place, packed with refuse and sewage?, he wondered. More questions followed: What other civilized community would have allowed such neglect of their faith's monuments? It dawned on him that his people had fallen into a collective historical amnesia without realizing it. Now believing that Mahmoud's instructions showed foresight, al-Ghazali mobilized his students to clear the waste in and around the debilitated mosque.[29] Another attentive Egyptian official who also recognized the importance of the site, Hamdi 'Ashur, the Governor of Cairo, undertook the structural repairs to the building and its surrounding area.[30] With 'Ashour attending to the physical reconstruction of the site, al-Ghazali set out to reassemble the spiritual and intellectual foundations. He sought to revive the lost sense of historical interest, starting with the founder of the mosque, 'Amr Ibn al-'As.

From the pulpit at which the Prophet's companions had first assembled in Egypt, al-Ghazali focused on what he regarded as the disappointing political culture that 'Amr had helped bring about when he assisted Mu'awyyia, a fellow Umayyad clan member, to take control of the state, transforming Muslim government from a seeming republic into a despotic monarchy.[31] He also introduced his preferred Qur'anic commentary, the newer approach of Shaykh Abd Allah Diraz.[32] With these sermons, he wanted his fellow countrymen to reflect on their present, too. Worshippers now flocked to the old mosque of 'Amr Ibn al-'As in the thousands; they liked what they heard, many travelling great distances to heed the pertinent instruction which al-Ghazali offered. Soon, al-Ghazali transformed the Ibn al-'As Mosque from a neglected wasteland into a one-man platform for social and political activism, albeit wrapped in the religious idiom of the long tradition of Muslim societies.[33] There, at the pulpit of this mosque, al-Ghazali's words held sway in a way that few could match anywhere else in Egypt at the time.

However, al-Ghazali also encountered what he would later come to regard as the most difficult obstacle of all: the predominant historical narrative, which rejected critical or even methodological analysis of the past in favour of a politically approved version. To question early events did not rest comfortably with the constructs of this narrative, which had been entrenched for centuries under dynastic direction with the help of *fuqaha* working in and around the ruling courts. The boundaries between historical precedent and *fiqh* rulemaking are indistinguishable. Indeed, for centuries the greatest Muslim historians have been great *fuqaha*, some even with their own schools of rulemaking, or renowned *mujtahids* within their own schools of thought. The tenth-century al-Tabari, the eleventh-century Ibn Hazm, the thirteenth-century Ibn al-Jawzi, the fifteenth-century Ibn Khaldun, and the early sixteenth-century al-Suyuti are merely famous examples of a wider phenomenon. This was only to be expected: as discussed later in this book, sound (and especially early) precedent serves as a main source for deducing Shari'a rules/laws, and so it is natural that such Shari'a experts also presented themselves as keepers of and experts on Muslim records.

How the now-predominant Muslim narrative defended its version of history illustrates some of the means by which historical inquiry receded in Muslim societies. Shaykh Ahmed Hasan al-Baquri, the minister of *awqaf* in Nasser's government and general manager of the its new University of al-Azhar from 1964–1969, and al-Ghazali's fellow associate in the Muslim Brotherhood, intervened. Summoning al-Ghazali to his house, the esteemed al-Baquri looked distressed. A companion of the Prophet, 'Amr Ibn al-'As himself, has visited al-Baquri in a dream and asked him to relay a private message to al-Ghazali, the religious official explained. 'Amr Ibn al-'As wanted al-Ghazali to know that he forgave him for disparaging his character every Friday. After all, al-Ghazali had revived the mosque that he (Ibn al-'As) had first built for the Egyptians. Hearing this missive from the other world, al-Ghazali wept. That night he promised Shaykh al-Baquri and himself that "all companions of the Prophet must be left only to God and his Prophet to judge them [...] We should not pass the responsibility of our failures and backwardness onto them."[34]

However, al-Baquri's intervention may have come too late; al-Ghazali had already acquired a sharper sense of history. Instead of criticizing individuals from Egypt's past, he began to question the common narrative. Questions which the neglected ancient mosque had started in al-Ghazali's mind were pushed into unexpected terrain by a doctoral dissertation at Dar al-'Olum by Ibrahim al-Deek in the late 1980s. His investigation found case after case of women Hadith scholars in the twelfth century CE, revealing learned Muslim women who moved freely, both physically and intellectually.[35] As if belonging to an altogether different religious landscape, famous *fuqaha* who studied with them often praised the erudition of their women teachers. Once again, al-Ghazali felt remorse, for neither he nor his colleagues from among the contemporary *fuqaha* knew of such details of their past. As his attention to old records heightened, al-Ghazali publicized a critique of the common Sunni account of the Mongol destruction of Baghdad, which was that the Abbasid caliphate had been a victim of conspiracies against Islam.[36] Al-Ghazali also established that it had not been Christian missionaries or colonialist scholars who had concocted some of the most serious fabrications that stained the Prophet; rather, it was Muslim sources.[37] Delusional assumptions about the past corrupted essential areas of knowledge, he concluded,[38] and without the systematic study of history, Muslims would therefore continue to suffer from an intellectual lacuna that not only distorted the way they viewed the world, but also distorted Shari'a: "Islamic culture and [...] literary sources [...] are full of poisons and drugs; there is an urgent need to sift them", al-Ghazali warned.[39] He also wrote to elaborate on this point, as various chapters in this book show.

Al-Ghazali now saw illustrations of Egyptians' neglect of every aspect of history everywhere, and these filled him with an immense sense of shame. Even the *fuqaha* had meagre knowledge of the historical sources that they continuously invoked, starting with himself. Although he found Ignaz Goldziher (d. 1921) dishonest, al-Ghazali nevertheless conceded this famous orientalist's superior expertise, which very few Azharis matched. Goldziher "referred to around 300 books [...] while as a [*faqih* ...] I cannot say that I have actually read all these sources [...] As for manuscripts, these I know nothing about. Take for example my readings of Baladuri and others, these are imperfect", al-Ghazali remarked.[40] Worse still, al-Ghazali judged that careless investigation of the past meant that it was not orientalists who truly threatened Islam; famous works in the Muslim library did that. He noted accounts such as that of the Prophet's infatuation with Zaynab bint Jahsh "were not stories invented by a mendacious enemy [...] but by our own supposed scholars."[41] By the start of what was the fifteenth Muslim century (1980 CE), al-Ghazali had no doubt that, for some time now, rational investigation of the past had eluded his people: "I discovered that our study of Islamic history is shallow, while that of [the rest of] humanity's is all but non-existent", he judged.[42] He had no illusions: sound understanding of history required systematic investigation and long hours of tedious work, and Egypt's current culture did not support these habits of mind. In order to better archive, interpret, and publish the vast amount of material that their societies left behind, Muslim approaches to education had first to change; and to attend to Egypt's Muslim past required collective efforts, "teams [of scholars] with excellent and meticulous learning". Alas, "today, the world of the Muslims is physically and intellectually worn to shreds", al-Ghazali lamented towards the end of his life, leading him to wonder: would it ever be possible for contemporary Muslims to "acquire such a gift" of collective sound historical inquiry?[43]

Portrait: State versus 'alim—Sadat and family law

Anwar al-Sadat explained Islam in terms of "a civilized East", which he contrasted with the uncivilized West: "Western culture and its heritage, for which Europe and America fear so much, live only on the debris of the East and would not flourish if they had not sucked its blood", he wrote in 1957.[44] His words mattered because, at the time, this member of the Free Officers who ruled Egypt served as the secretary general of the Islamic Conference.[45] He believed that the destiny of the East, to which all Muslims belonged, was to conquer the shallow and avaricious ways of the West. In such a long-drawn *clash of civilizations*, the "struggle will continue until the genuine [Eastern] civilization triumphs over the false" one of the West, he predicted.[46]

But that was then: as president, Sadat reversed his position. Late in the 1970s he declared his wish to transform Egypt along the same Western lines that he had earlier thought to have "shame[d] the spirit and letter of Christianity".[47] Although, like with al-Ghazali, the changes in Sadat's views had not been linear, his approaches to and reasons for change differed from those of al-Ghazali.[48] Eager to raise women's position in society, Sadat's animated wife, Jihan, took a leading role in proposing legislation (Law 44/1979) that would restrict a man's right to unilaterally divorce his wife or marry more than one woman, and would protect a wife's rights. Despite the manifest injustices in their country's divorce laws, many Egyptians did not welcome the proposal, which imposed restrictions on men's legal privileges. They dubbed it "Jihan's Law". Shaykhs al-Ghazali and Abu Zahara spearheaded the opposition to these much-needed reforms, or at least to this particular suggested change in legislation. As a punishment, al-Ghazali was removed from the now-famous pulpit of Ibn al-'As Mosque, where his words reigned supreme at the time. Commotion ensued in Egypt's streets.

On a late spring afternoon in 1974, another demonstration in support of al-Ghazali erupted in Cairo, and the crowds who gathered at Ibn al-'As Mosque headed to the Parliament building.[49] To westernizers inside and outside Egypt, al-Ghazali's unrelenting campaign against much-needed amendments in family law appeared outrageous and out of tune with the times. It confirmed to some his image as an upholder of repugnant medieval practices and as a dangerous figurehead of Islamic fundamentalism. However, al-Ghazali's reaction against reforms to family laws (or personal laws) must also be examined against its multi-layered context. Outwardly, the contest revolved around women's rights, but the objections that al-Ghazali and Abu Zahra raised against Jihan's Law also underlined that an ancient conflict in Muslim societies remained unresolved. This was the conflict between *fuqaha* and the state, in which important *fuqaha* resisted state intervention in legislating laws as a matter of principle. They appear to have largely lost the battle, preserving only jurisdiction over family matters—or so they believed. In other words, legislation regarding the family marked the *fuqaha*'s last sphere of influence against the executive incursions on lawmaking. It also marked the average man's last sphere of power in a society where its members had few or no civil rights.

Years later, al-Ghazali gave clues to why he fought against Sadat's proposed changes to family laws. "I fear[ed ...] that [this can give] a ruler [license to] interfere in marital relations", he later reflected on the events.[50] In the same interview, he also remarked that he could not have possibly agreed to allow a spouse of a despot to dictate laws to Muslims. Al-Ghazali primarily saw it as a question of jurisdiction. Neither Sadat nor his wife had the mandate or tools to legislate for society. *How* Muslims made rules appeared to have been his main preoccupation in this case, not society's dire need to reform its laws on women. According to the legal standards that mattered so much to al-Ghazali, no ruler, least of all a dictator, could be allowed to meddle in family life: "What happened to the sanctity of oath [between husband and wife]? Where was trust [between them]?" Al-Ghazali quoted Umar Ibn al-Khattab, the second caliph whose rulings form an authoritative part of Shari'a case law: homes are not built merely on romance, Umar is reported to have told a man who had fallen out of love with his wife.[51]

Historical battles and precedents, therefore, dictated some of the reactions to Jihan's Law. Contemporary fears dictated others. In the 1970s, powerless ordinary men, who possessed neither political nor economic rights, did not welcome the prospect of their last vestige of real authority, at home, over their women, being demolished. Al-Ghazali appeared to them as their representative and a hero, and in both rural and urban centres, where patriarchal traditions reigned supreme, many Egyptians sided with him. However, there was no uniform Muslim voice in this case, and al-Ghazali's fierce opposition to law reforms did trouble some of his admirers. They wondered: if al-Ghazali's objection to the new laws was dictated by concern for Egyptian families, as he claimed at the time, then why the silence regarding the most unjust family law of all, the *Qanun Bait al-Ta'a* (House of Obedience Law)? Under this barbaric law the police dragged women against their will back to where their husbands lived. Marriage in Egypt resembled a sanctioned system of female incarceration enforced by the state apparatus. Such personal laws in twentieth century Egypt accentuated women's second-class status, providing little justice for the most vulnerable among them. That al-Ghazali created the conditions that led to the collapse of much-needed reforms to these legal codes appeared to some of his usual supporters callous and unmindful of woman's welfare.

There was no uniform voice of modernizers either. Some supported the President's initiative, while others opposed the proposed law, but not on religious grounds. They regarded it as coercive and, therefore, judged that it could prove counterproductive. Sadat was thus able to pass Law 44/1979 only through an emergency decree. Soon after his death, in response to negative perceptions of this forced legislation, Egypt's Constitutional Court repealed "Jihan's Law", albeit on procedural grounds.

Law 44/1979 did not accomplish the intended improvement in Egyptian women's lot, but it changed al-Ghazali's life in unforeseen ways. When the government banned him from giving public sermons in 'Amr Ibn al-As Mosque, or any other mosque in Egypt, al-Ghazali found refuge in Saudi Arabia again, where this time he worked from 1974–1988. The battle of agency over society between *'alim* and President did not stop there. When Sadat publicly scorned him for abandoning Egypt in pursuit of Saudi petrodollars, al-Ghazali responded with an open letter to Sadat that was published in *Al-Ahram*: "*Actually*, I get paid a great deal more money than what you have mentioned. I am ready to give up such high salary if I could only return to 'Amr Ibn al-As Mosque as its imam and *khatib* [...] I demand to work in Egypt. And I will not be silenced whenever I witness a wrong."[52] This open defiance only helped to confirm his punishment. The forced move from his familiar world in Egypt eventually started al-Ghazali on a new phase of his career, as various chapters in this book show.

Which Egypt? Which Shari'a?

Was this merely a story of a confrontation between a far-sighted reforming leader and a stubborn and short-sighted, ultra-conservative cleric? Not in this case—not in the 1970s, nor at any other time. As early as the 1940s, when both Sadat and al-Ghazali were young and devout activists seeking to liberate their country from British occupation, their dissimilar approaches make it hard to determine which of them was far-sighted and which was dangerously unwise. Like many other impressionable youths in the region, Sadat found inspiration in European fascist groups of the time.[53] His attempt to join Rommel in the Nazi regime's fight against Britain during World War II resulted in a prison sentence, which Sadat and his admirers later recorded in heroic patriotic terms.[54] In contrast, and perhaps inspired by 'Abbas Mahmoud al-'Aqqad, one of his favourite writers, al-Ghazali found pro-Nazi sentiments misguided. The British occupation of their country blinded those who cheered Rommel, al-Ghazali wrote, exposing the "utter and dangerous vacuum" in culture and education from which Egyptian society suffered.[55]

Even much later, at the time when Western governments celebrated him as a visionary reformer, Sadat strove to join religion and state under his command, charting dangerous directions. Consider the following proposed piece of legislation: on 8 June, 1977 *Al-Ahram* reported that the "State Council approved a proposed law [to punish] the crime of apostasy [*al-rida*]." The penalties that Sadat's government hoped to introduce included

> the death penalty for those who desert Islam by explicit language or clear acts; and a ten-year imprisonment for one who relapses into apostasy [having recanted the first time ...] Under the same law, which also [...] provides strict penalties for under-age persons, apostasy is determined by either confession [of the accused] or the testimony of two men.[56]

Under this proposed law, the judge would rebuke an apostate between the ages of seven and nine, or confine such a child to the care of a public institution. Apostates between ten and fifteen years of age would be subject to a beating with a cane of between ten and fifty lashes. A new class of Islamists commended

Sadat's administration for such zeal. But on the whole, the bulk of Egyptians did not. Their discomfort reflected the void between what most of these Muslims regarded as dictates of their faith and what a political narrative on Islam regarded as dictates of the same faith. The bulk of senior Azhari *'ulama* ignored the proposal, while other scholars spoke out against it. Gamal al-Banna, the younger brother of the founder of the Muslim Brotherhood, challenged the State Council:

> Have you gone insane? Do you want to disfigure the gentleness of Islam and bring about a Papal-like inquisition, one whose judges wear turbans? Do you want to [forcibly] guide he whom God did not wish to guide?[57]

Similarly, many Egyptians did not see this proposed law as particularly representing Shari'a. By the early 1980s it became clear: instead of piety, Sadat had unleashed a loutish tendency, effectively creating a state-sanctioned social-religious intransigence. The age of boorish pious expression had arrived in Egypt. Theories abound as to why Sadat drew on religion in such ill-conceived ways. The President, many thought, hoped to kill two birds with one stone. Religiosity would underline his legitimacy and, at the same time, crush the noisy self-described leftist and progressive voices of opposition. For a short while Sadat appeared to have succeeded, or so thought outside observers. Declaring Shari'a "the prime source" instead of "a main source" of legislation earned him general praise.[58] That this amendment to the constitution was merely symbolic still did not matter to many at home. Setting free the Ikhwan, whom Nasser had imprisoned, earned him the gratitude of many of them. And as soon as he took power Sadat also promoted influential *'ulama*, including al-Ghazali, whom he appointed minister of *awqaf*, in command of Egypt's directorate of religious instruction and preaching. However, the rift between him and many scholars of Islam grew wider over time.[59] As it turned out, measures with which Sadat hoped to bolster his Islamic credentials mostly failed, and the devout became the source of his gravest troubles.

A man or a cockroach?

In one swoop on a crisp autumn day in 1981, Sadat ordered the incarceration of almost every critical voice in his country, including that of the Coptic pope and of Muslim scholars. Many women representing all colours of Egyptian activism were consequently thrown together into police trucks. Later in the day, they found themselves huddled together in the same prison cell. The prisoners included Nawal al-Sa'dawi, a radical feminist; Widad Mitry, a Coptic Christian, Marxist, and campaigner for a secular state; Amina Rachid, a French-speaking professor who belonged to one of Egypt's old aristocratic families, and a self-confessed communist; Shahinda Muqalad, an avid Nasserist and a farmers' rights activist; and Safinaz Kazim, once an avant-garde journalist who had become a passionate Islamist and campaigner for a Shari'a-governed state. Notwithstanding their differences, Islamist, Copt, communist, Arab nationalist, and die-hard feminist all appeared to share strong bonds nurtured by their common struggle against a repressive state and by the humour they found in their collective misery cemented in age-old Egyptian ways. In a documentary that featured four of these women, prepared by one of their acquaintances, Safinaz Kazim recalled how in Sadat's jail they took turns to warn each other of sudden perils.[60] Prison hazards included crawling insects and unannounced men who might see their usually veiled fellow inmates without their headscarves. Lost in her thoughts, whenever she heard a comrade's warnings, the aristocratic professor of French literature frequently inquired: "What is it? A man or a cockroach?"[61] The women chuckled at the memory of the misery of their internment. They felt that they had to look after one another. In prison, just like outside it, their experiences indicated that no clear division of conservative against liberal—in the Western meaning of the word—set these modern Egyptian women apart. The vision of each appeared to have itinerant emphases, with their positions continually rearranged in the face of new threats. Like al-Ghazali, who at the time remained outside Egypt in fear of arrest, these women drew heavily on their shared communal memories; and all of them found inspirations in modern Western ideas, albeit in varying shapes and degrees. Whether they identified as liberal secular, communist, Christian, Muslim, or anything else, their various loyalties—including to notions of religion, womanhood, Egypt, and perceptions of Egypt's destiny—had as many similarities as differences. The tensions of these continually shifting visions generated energy and imposed limitations, both of which play a central role in al-Ghazali's and modern Egypt's story.

This particular Egyptian episode came to an end when attempts to harness Islam as a force to sustain Sadat's rule spectacularly backfired. Shouting "Death to the Pharaoh", an army officer who subscribed to Islamist thought turned his weapon on the President as he saluted the troops in October 1981. Sadat was killed on the spot; but instead of expressing the usual exaggerated expressions of grief, Egypt fell silent. "Why was Cairo calm?" was the question that an incisive American-British documentary posed to highlight a significant aspect of this incongruity: why, when world leaders rushed to President Sadat's funeral, did ordinary Egyptians largely gave it the cold shoulder?[62] Had not the masses intensely mourned the death of his predecessor, Gamal Abd al-Nasser, who had led Egypt into the 1967 defeat? Had not more than a million citizens of this predominantly Muslim country attended the funeral of Umm Kulthum, a woman singer a few years earlier?[63] Had not Sadat united Islam, modernity, and peace in his country, according to the Western narrative? Who then propelled reform in Egypt and who impeded attempts to shake off out-dated medieval practices? This important question remains without definite answers; but here too, labels such as liberal, conservative, secular, or moderate proved irrelevant: these all-too-familiar markers cannot explain the conflicts between Sadat and the varied forces in his country, including Muslim sentiments, any better than they can explain commotion in the region at any time. Rather, they blur them. For whatever Sadat's plans might have been, it is al-Ghazali whom many in Egypt credit with fighting for women and enlightening their society about women's freedoms. It may sound unfair, but decades after both men's deaths, Egyptians seldom remember Sadat's words, except to ridicule him, while al-Ghazali's quotes continue to permeate public discourse, despite his association with disturbing episodes. Here, the value of gauging the stresses and changes that result from actual crises can help situate some of the constantly moving solutions chosen by Egyptian society; and Muslim fanaticism is not one of them. Examined together, rather than in isolation, the commotion in the above accounts of seemingly disjointed disturbances, rather than some essentialist *fiqh* hypotheses, appear to be what shaped the Shari'a rules that al-Ghazali deduced, and to have determined how his Egyptian contemporaries received them. The chapters that follow take note of this.

Notes

1. Nationalist leaders in early modern Turkey and Iran felt ambivalent about Islam, some even blaming it for holding their societies back. Accordingly, in the hope of shoring up the energies of their countries, their governments also intervened in favour of Western dress codes. In Iran, Riza Shah's government officially banned the *chador* (Iranian veil) and, in some instances, removed women's veil by force. In July 1935, when Iranian worshippers at Imam Ali Reza Mosque refused to comply, the state sent forces into the mosque, killing over a hundred of its occupants and wounding over twice as many. See Dilip Hiro, *Iran Under the Ayatollahs* (London: Routledge and Kegan Paul, 1985), 28. For a further account on the story of modern Iran see Ervand Abrahamian, *A History of Modern Iran* (Cambridge: Cambridge University Press, 2008).

   In Turkey, Kemal Ataturk did not ban women's traditional dress outright. However, in its efforts to effect the wholesale adoption of Western dress, his government dealt especially harshly with men's traditional (thought of as Islamic) gear. In 1925 the Turkish state banned the Turkish fez and other traditional male modes of dress and made the wearing of Western hats obligatory. Public humiliation, not just the law, played a role in such dress transformations. During a public speech the leader made in the early 1920s, Gazi Mustafa Kemal singled out a man who sat "in the crowd in front of me; he has a fez on his head, a green turban on the fez [...] [W]ould a civilized man put on this preposterous garb and go out to hold himself up to universal ridicule?" And, by 1934, the state introduced another law to prohibit the wearing of all religious-related garments. See Bernard Lewis, *The Emergence of Modern Turkey* (Oxford: Oxford University Press, 2002), 100–102, 266–271,

409–411. For detailed insights into the making of modern Turkey, see Erik J. Zurcher, *The Young Turk Legacy and Nation Building: From the Ottoman Empire to Atatürk's Turkey* (London: I.B.Tauris, 2010); M. Sukru Hanioglu, *Ataturk: An Intellectual Biography* (Princeton, NJ: Princeton University Press, 2013).

2. Devout Egyptians' attitudes towards dress have changed more than once in the course of the twentieth century. To remind his countrymen of these attitudes when Hasan al-Banna led the Muslim Brotherhood, in the memoirs of their sister, Fawziya, the provocative Gamal al-Banna included pictures that show her in 1946, dressed in a western skirt, without her hair covered; on horseback clad in modern riding attire; then, as she moved to Sudan, in Sudanese dress, head barely half-covered. After the assassination of her brother Hasan, and the repression of the Ikhwan that followed, Fawziya subsequently moved to Saudi Arabia, where she adopted a different lifestyle and a stricter mode of dress. See Gamal al-Banna, *Dhikraiyat Fawziya al-Banna* (Cairo: Dar al-Fikr al-Islami, 2009), 30, 23, 68. With his close association with al-Banna, it is reasonable to conclude that, at one time or another, al-Ghazali accepted all such modes of dress modes as respectable or at least unobjectionable.
3. For illustration, see the memoirs of Hoda Sha'rawi, an important feminist figure in Egypt at the time, translated and introduced by Margot Badran under the title *Harem Years: Memoirs of an Egyptian Feminist 1879-1924* (New York: Feminist Press, 1987). Numerous illustrations can also be found in the arts, including popular art works, between 1910s–1950s, which provide excellent sources for modern Egypt's social history, but which remain largely untapped.
4. Mohammed al-Ghazali, "Qissat Haya", *Islamiyat al-Ma'rifa* 2/3 (2007): 210.
5. Ibid., 207–214.
6. Ibid., 205–210.
7. Salah Jahin, "Ta'amolat Karicatiryia fi al-Mas'ala al-Ghazaliya", reported in Mohammed Shalabi, *Al-Shaykh al-Ghazali wa Ma'rakat al-Mushaf fi al-'Alam al-Islami* (Cairo: Dar al-Sahwa, 1987), 90–99.
8. *Al-Ahram*, 30 May, 1962, 7. Reported in Mohammed Shalabi, *Al-Shaykh al-Ghazali*, 9 (author's translation).
9. Karima Hasan, "Ma'rakat al-Manbar wa al-Karikatir bayn al Shaykh wa al-Rassam", *Al-Masri al-Youm*, 28 December, 2009 (online: http://today.almasryalyoum.com/article2.aspx?ArticleID=87970).
10. Egyptian media, which was state-owned at the time, reported Sartre and de Beauvoir's visit of March 1967 as a momentous event in their country.
11. Shalabi, *Al-Shaykh al-Ghazali*, 90–99.
12. Al-Ghazali, "Qissat Haya", 209–210.
13. Ibid., 210, 214.
14. Shalabi, *Al-Shaykh al-Ghazali*, 66–80.
15. Ibid., 66–67.
16. Mohammed al-Ghazali, *Min Huna Na'lam* (Cairo: Dar al-Kutub al-Haditha, n.d.), 29, 30, 31, 63, 66, 128.
17. Ibid., 100.
18. Al-Ghazali, "Qissat Haya", 211.
19. Yahyia Haqi, *Al-Ahram* (Cairo), 11 June, 1987, 8.
20. Al-Ghazali, *Min Huna Na'lam*, 198. His view on face-covering conflicted with Shaykh Yusuf al-Qaradawi's, as discussed in "Portrait of a Seminar" in Chapter 8.
21. Mustafa abd al-'Al, "Fi Hiwar Khas Jidan ma' Saidati, al-Shaykh al-Ghazali yatahadath 'an al-Jinn wa al-'Afarit", *Saidati* 792 (11–17 May, 1996): 72–74.
22. Mohammed al-Ghazali, *Al-Sunna al-Nabawiya Bayna Ahl al-Fiqh wa ahl al-Hadith*, 5th edn (no location: Sahara, 1989), 86.

23. Ibid.
24. Ibid.; al-Ghazali also told an interviewer: "Islam says wear what you wish; do not tell me I have to wear this [or that type of garment], all Islam ordered is decency and dignity" (videotape interview #SYS-1). Also, he criticized the Muslim obsession with women's dress instead of paying attention to their dignity and well-being in comments he made following a public lecture by Abd al-Halim Abu Shuqaa. *Nadwat Tahrir al-Mar'a*. Lecture moderated by Ali Goma, 6 July, 1994 (Cairo: IIIT publications, n.d.), 19–21.
25. Mohammed al-Ghazali, *Al-Da'wa al-Islamiya Tastaqbilu Qarnaha al-Khamis 'Ashr* (no location: Dar al-Salasil, 1980), quoted by Yusuf al-Qaradawi, "Natharat fi Turath al-Shaykh Mohammed al-Ghazali", *Islamiyat al-Ma'rifa* 2/3 (2007): 41.
26. Al-Ghazali, "Qissat Haya", 227.
27. Abd Allah al-Masri, *Al-Da'yia al-Shaheed al-Shaykh Mohammed al-Ghazali* (Cairo: Al-Rawafid al-Thaqafyia, 1996), 43–48.
28. Ibid.
29. Ibid., 227–228.
30. Ibid., 228.
31. Taha Jabir al-Alwani, "Kalimat al-Tahrir", *Islamiyat al-Ma'rifa* 2/3 (2007): 12–13.
32. Mohammed al-Ghazali, *Nadwat Tadris al-'Ulum al-Shar'iya, Fadilat al-Shaykh Muhamad al-Ghazali: Taqdim wa Idarat Dr Gamal Eldin Attia* (Cairo: IIIT, n.d.), 13.
33. A Cairo newspaper reported that in 1994, during the *Eid al-fitr* holiday, over 100,000 worshippers attended al-Ghazali's sermon at 'Amr Ibn As Mosque (*Al-Wafd* [Cairo], 14 March, 1994).
34. Taha Jabir al-Alwani, "Kalimat al-Tahrir", *Islamiyat al-Ma'rifa*, 12. In a later interview al-Ghazali defended 'Amr Ibn al-'As, in particular, and the *sahaba*, in general, against abuse directed at those early figures ("Fiqh al Da'wa wa Mushkilat al-D'oa", *Al-Umma* [Doha], 15 Rajab / 13 March, 1408/1988 AH/CE, 143).
35. Ibrahim al-Deek, *Al-Sunna al-Nabawiya fi al-Qarn al-Sadis li al-Hijra* (PhD diss.; presumably in Egypt but no date or location given) publicized in al-Ghazali, *Turathuna al-Fikri*, 158–168; idem, videotape interview (#W-1).
36. Mohammed al-Ghazali, *Turathuna al-Fikri fi Mizan al-Shar'i wa al-'Aql*, 2nd edn (Cairo: Dar al-Shuruk, 1991), 108–114.
37. Mohammed Al-Ghazali, *Al-Da'wa al-Islamiyah Tastaqbilu Qarnaha al-Khamis 'Ashr* (no location: Dar al-Salasil, 1980), 159.
38. Ibid.
39. Al-Ghazali, "Qissat Haya", 159.
40. Al-Ghazali, videotape interview (#MUL-2).
41. Al-Ghazali, *Al-Da'wa al-Islamiyah*, 159. For a good summary of the history and historiography of this controversial incident, see Andreas Goerke, "Muhammad and Zaynab bint Jahsh: Between History and Exegesis", paper presented at Islamic Studies in Scotland: Retrospect and Prospect, University of Edinburgh, 24 October, 2015.
42. Quoted by Qaradawi in "Natharat fi Turath al-Shaykh Mohammed al-Ghazali", 41.
43. Al-Ghazali, *Turathuna al-Fikri*, 119.
44. Anwar al-Sadat, "Qisat al-Wihda al-Arabiya", translated under the title "East and West: Shall They Meet?", in Kemal Karpat, ed., *Political and Social Thought in the Contemporary Middle East* (New York: Praeger, 1982), 197–204.
45. Ibid., 201. Before and after the Free Officers assumed power in Egypt in 1952, Sadat served as their key link with the Ikhwan and other Islamist groups. Until he himself assumed the presidency in 1970, Sadat's official posts all appeared propagandistic, designed to prop up Nasser's presidency. They included serving as overseer-editor of *Al-Gomhouriya*, a national newspaper, acting as secretary general of the Islamic Conference and as secretary general of the Socialist Union, and appointed head of Egypt's National Assembly.

46. Ibid., 204.
47. Ibid., 202–203.
48. Once in power, Sadat courted populist religious sentiments in order to enhance his legitimacy as president, calling himself *al-ra'is al-mu'min* (the believer/devout president). For his own autobiographical account of this journey, see Anwar al-Sadat, *In Search of Identity* (New York: Harper and Row, 1978). For a reading of his relationship with the Brotherhood, see Saad Eddin Ibrahim, "An Islamic Alternative in Egypt: The Muslim Brotherhood and Sadat", *Arab Studies Quarterly* 4 (1982): 75–93. For a general observer's account of the rise of Islamist sentiments in Egypt, see the *Washington Post*'s former Cairo bureau chief, Caryle Murphy, *Passion for Islam: Shaping the Modern Middle East: The Egyptian Experience* (New York: Scribner, 2002), 59–65.
49. On 27 April 1974 a demonstration erupted against Sadat's order to ban al-Ghazali from giving sermons at Ibn al-'As Mosque. The protestors marched from the mosque to the Parliament building. More than a decade earlier, in June 1962, also in support of al-Ghazali, another march started from al-Azhar Mosque to the *Al-Ahram* building (already discussed in the first *Portrait* section above).
50. Al-Ghazali, videotape interview (#W-2).
51. Al-Ghazali, quoted in a Cairo seminar held to highlight the rights of women in Islam, "Fi Nadwa 'uqidat fi al-Qahira: Munaqashat Jaryi'a li Huquq al-Mar'a al-Muslima Tanawalat al-Isma wa al-Mirath", *Jaridat al-Khalij*, 15 January, 1993.
52. Text provided in Shalabi, *Al-Shaykh al-Ghazali*, 83–86:
فرد الشيخ الكبير برسالة لجريدة الأهرام المصرية يقول فيها: "إنني أتقاضى أكثر مما قلت، ورغم ذلك أنا على استعداد لترك الراتب الأعلى للعودة لمسجد عمرو إمامًا وخطيبًا، إن الفلوس لن تهمني وأنا أطالب بالعمل في مصر، لكنني لن أسكت علي باطل"
53. This included being active in the fascist Young Egypt, according to Jon B. Alterman, "Introduction", *Sadat and His Legacy: Egypt and the World, 1977–1997* (Washington, DC: Washington Institute for Near East Policy, 1988), ix, vii–xx (online: https://www.washingtoninstitute.org/uploads/Documents/pubs/SadatandHisLegacy.pdf.pdf).
54. Anwar al-Sadat, *Al-Bahth 'an al-Dhat* (Cairo: al-Maktab al-Masri al-Hadith, 1978), 47–73.
55. Al-Ghazali, "Qissat Haya", 181. Although his anti-British occupation sentiments led to 'Aqqad's incarceration, in the 1940s he warned his people against supporting "the blood-stained ideas" of Nazism, which was then fashionable among some patriots who hoped to rid Egypt of Britain's control. Abbas Mahmoud al-'Aqqad, *Hitler fi al-Mizan* (Cairo: Mo'assasat Hindawi, 2012).
56. Gamal al-Banna, *Kala thuma Kalala* (Cairo: Dar al-Fikr al-Islami, 1994), 14–16.
57. Ibid.
58. The 1980 amendment to Article 2 of the Egyptian Constitution proclaimed the principles of Shari'a "the prime" source, instead of "a main" source of legislation.
59. On the history of modern tension between al-Azhar and the state, see Tamir Moustafa, "Conflict and Cooperation between the State and Religious Institutions in Contemporary Egypt", *International Journal of Middle East Studies*, 32 (2000): 3–22.
60. Tahani Rashed (dir.), *Four Women of Egypt* (National Film Board of Canada, 1997).
61. Ibid.
62. Ofra Bikel (prod.), *Why Was Cairo Calm?* (BBC and WGBH, 1982) A summary with comments about this insightful documentary can be found in a blog by Adam Curtis, in which he traces distorted Western criteria for describing Egypt and its neighbours only to 1979. Adam Curtis, "Sadat's Dat", *The Medium and the Message* (21 February, 2011; online: http://www.bbc.co.uk/blogs/adamcurtis/entries/443ca7cd-6f8a-3c6b-8344-f91d0bddd80b).
63. Egyptians' farewell to this woman singer at her 1975 funeral can be seen on YouTube (e.g.: https://www.youtube.com/watch?v=JA2lZ8YRY8c).

FOUR

Untidy Texts: Al-Ghazali versus al-Ghazali

This chapter continues to highlight al-Ghazali's elusive, yet essential, Shari'a texts. Although the material is diffuse, these sources not only indicate how al-Ghazali as a *faqih* responded to a particular crisis, but also how society at the time responded to the Shari'a rules deduced by him. The chapter includes a portrait of al-Ghazali back in Egypt in 1992–1993, and at the centre of yet another public controversy unfolding shortly before his death. This is the period where many locate al-Ghazali's progressive credentials. But when distinguished experts describe al-Ghazali as a voice of moderate Islam they mostly pass over in silence the events discussed here—an incident in which al-Ghazali appears to have abandoned his own beliefs about the centrality of moderation and reason.[1] The importance of this episode goes beyond the vision of this one shaykh, raising central questions in the book of tension: Is Muslim government faith imposed by force, with *'ulama* such as al-Ghazali having the power of life or death over members of society? Or should Islam's system of rule mirror its people's choices, seeking reason and a sense of justice—as many, including al-Ghazali, have often argued? How and who decides these Shari'a rules, in the past and now?

Islamic state? Or what Islamic state?

When two highly respected Azhari scholars openly challenged the predominant accounts of the community's political history, they faced the wrath of believers and accusations of heresy even though they were not questioning a tenet of Islam. The first attempt was by Shaykh Ali abd al-Raziq in the 1920s, when he reconsidered accounts of the early Islamic leadership,[2] and this was followed in the late 1940s by Shaykh Khaled Mohammed Khaled, who raised criticisms about the Muslim experience, especially its government and its *fuqaha*.[3] Faced with indignation and objections, in the end both scholars retreated, albeit in different ways.[4]

Al-Ghazali was a voice of great credibility among the devout, and he had also been prominent in key religious institutions in Egypt and the Arabian Peninsula. It was no small matter, therefore, that by the 1980s this forceful, seemingly conservative leader of the Sunni majority unexpectedly entered the controversy over the Muslim political legacy and openly spoke of Muslim dynasties not as keepers but as corrupters of Shari'a over many centuries. Al-Ghazali's criticism of the Muslim past was received differently from the ideas of Raziq and Khaled, and his popularity as a spokesman of Sunni Islam in fact increased. But it was not only the devout who endorsed his defiance; some in the secular camp also found his critical approach useful. Recognizing al-Ghazali's authority must have been difficult for them; in a way, it placed al-Ghazali on the progressive side that championed reason but, just as troubling, it bolstered, rather than diminished, the role of religious discourse in society.

But difficult times required difficult choices: Egyptians had witnessed the futility of their governments, whether left- or right-leaning, in dealing with social and economic problems, and their rulers often lacked legitimacy. As modern, Western-inspired systems, which the Egyptian nation-state exemplified, consistently failed to address their sufferings, increasing numbers contemplated an Islamic alternative, even though the Islamists had no coherent programme for the Islamic state that they advocated, beyond popular catchphrases.[5] Feeling vulnerable and hopeless, many would no more oppose the concept of a strong Muslim polity than they would oppose Prophethood itself. According to *fiqh* mantras and the stories that they advanced, under Muslim dynasties their society had been strong, just, and prosperous.

Context, not fanaticism, decided Egyptian choices here, and whatever al-Ghazali's true colours may have been, some secularists recognized in his challenge to popular perceptions a most effective antidote against the deluge of claims about the perfection of Muslim governments. Farag Foda (d. 1992), a leading campaigner for secularism, was one such writer. He had trained as an agricultural expert, but had found fame as a talented writer and political commentator. His sharp and witty arguments posed a real obstacle to the advance of the discourse of religious groups in his country, and al-Ghazali must have been embarrassed to find Foda praising and using his critiques of Muslim history. Foda's endorsement appeared to validate the charges levelled against al-Ghazali at the time by his Islamist adversaries, who accused him of siding with the enemies of their faith when he disparaged the Muslim past. Foda and al-Ghazali both recognized the real strength of the other in the battle over Egypt's identity and its political future; but this awareness put al-Ghazali in particular under duress.

The Cairo Book Fair Debate

The ancient book markets that still exist in old Cairo testify to the long-established popularity of the written word in Egyptian culture, even if modern Egyptians are far from avid readers of books. Perhaps that is why Cairo's International Book Fair has become an annual cultural festival in which many Egyptians, including children, are eager to participate. When the 1992 Book Fair included a debate entitled "Islamic State [or] Civil State?", it was a must-watch event.[6] Its prominent discussants openly deliberated visions of government for Egypt, and the session is now commonly referred to as the Book Fair Debate. Three speakers advocated for an Islamic state: Ma'mun al-Hudaybi (d. 2004), a lawyer by training who later became head (general guide) or *murshid* of the Muslim Brotherhood and who was the son of their second leader Hasan al-Hudaybi (d. 1973); Dr Mohammed 'Imara, an academic who at various times had subscribed to Marxism, socialism, and Arab nationalism before embracing religion and establishing his reputation as a historian of Islam; and al-Ghazali. Equally prominent were the two representatives of the secular side: Dr Mohammed Khalafallah (d. 1998), a recipient of a numerous Egyptian State Awards for his contribution to Arabic literature;[7] and Foda.

Farag Foda shined above the rest, anchoring his adamant rejection of an Islamic state in historical precedent and contemporary reality, a twin structure in which the *fuqaha* have themselves long claimed to anchor their own arguments when discovering correct Shari'a rules.[8] In contrast, with arguments often marred by confusion and anachronism, the Islamic side at the debate appeared ill-at-ease and boorish. In making their case, its representatives often resorted to hurling accusations against their opponents instead of providing answers to the points which their rivals raised. At one point, 'Imara's response to Khalafallah was to ask God to guide him away from his erroneous ways; he also dismissed Foda's knowledge of history as based on the fictitious tales of *The Thousand and One Nights*,[9] although he never convincingly explained how he concluded this was the case. However, on the side that championed a secular state, Mohammed Khalafallah also painfully lacked clarity, and the structure of his arguments did not much differ from those of the Islamist panel. At times, his claims too appeared anachronistic and weak. In the confusion of terms and ideas which these Islamists and secular scholars infused into their debate, the two sides would have found parity at the end; Foda tipped the scale.

From the transcript of the proceedings, throughout the debate Foda appeared composed, well-informed, and to the point. He was also courteous to his opponents, before he systematically dismantled their arguments. But he singled out al-Ghazali for praise, to the apparent unease of the latter: "By God, I sincerely say it, for [the past] quarter century now I have listened to you and never have I stopped admiring your views or person", Foda told him. To warn against a government that speaks in the name of Islam, Foda invoked al-Ghazali's critique of Muslim history as a valued, authoritative, modern reference, before he took the shaykh's contradictions about sound governance. Whatever else he may have written or said on other occasions, if Foda disparaged Islam, as his opponents constantly claimed, nothing he said in this Book Fair Debate showed contempt or impertinence. What came across that evening was that, overall, his eloquence overpowered the defenders of a religious government, and that none of these eminent figures matched his intellectual prowess. The other side's many supporters did not see it like this, though. In Foda's cultivated discourse Islamists only saw an extension of the cultural hegemony of the West, to which large portions of Muslim intellectual space had already been lost in modern times. Consequently, instead of launching helpful discussions on how best to organize their chaotic communal lives, the Book Fair Debate inflamed fears of outside danger. The reaction to Foda's skill underlined a modern Muslim crisis: many semi-illiterate men and women felt cultural and political impotency, leading to widespread panic and rage. In the midst of this mob frenzy of perceived powerlessness, a few months later, in June 1992, two members of al-Jama'a al-Islamiya fatally shot Foda in the presence of his son as he prepared to launch a new political party.

The verdict: Rational or bigoted?

What followed was curious, and summed up the cultural and institutional chaos that engulfed Egypt in the late twentieth century. As the state prepared for the trial of Foda's assassins in June 1993, al-Ghazali volunteered his testimony as an expert witness on Shari'a rules. The assassins' lawyers welcomed this, and the public prosecutor did not raise any objections despite al-Ghazali's close connection to the case and his well-publicized loathing of the victim. Nor was his testimony challenged when he eventually took the stand. As an authority on Shari'a, al-Ghazali clarified its pertinent rules to the court and the country. He explained that the scholarly consensus (*ijma'*) among the *fuqaha* indicated that where an apostate refused to recant, and where the state neglected to punish this apostate, it was then acceptable for a member of the public to execute him.[10] In effect, al-Ghazali told his countrymen, two violations had taken place here: the first against the Shari'a (Foda's apostasy) and the second against the authority of a Shari'a-neglecting government (Foda's assassination). The implications were clear: Shari'a, which Muslims see as the foundation of justice and legitimacy, had to take precedence over rules set by an ineffectual government. To deduce this rule, al-Ghazali turned to the same *fiqh* constructs of which he had become openly critical. For almost a decade, and up to the eve of Foda's murder, al-Ghazali had been warning Muslims against corrupt rules that disguised themselves as part of Shari'a. He often cited violence and coercion in the name of religion as examples of *fiqh*'s distortion of their faith. He instructed his people that freedom of choice constituted a cornerstone of Islam, and that punishments for religious views employed suspect or little-understood Hadiths and Qur'anic phraseology heavily wrapped in invented *fiqh* constructs;[11] such constructs, as he saw it, included *naskh (abrogation)*, a device that effectively buried the Qur'an. For example, Qur'anic verses that gave Muslims in Medina permission to fight their enemies in specific contexts became permanent ferocious rule of aggression, by designating as revoked and thus no longer applicable the numerous verses that set out the actual Qur'anic message of peace and reconciliation.[12] For some time, al-Ghazali had been unequivocal about the troubled products of *fiqh*, including nonsensical rules that justified permanent war on all non-Muslims.

Yet in 1993, as it turned out, al-Ghazali in fact supported retribution against apostates, as the Foda murder trial showed. In his testimony he was careful to point out that he personally preferred imprisonment as punishment for apostasy, and did not favour this *ijma'*, the general consensus of the *fuqaha* on execution. His court appearance did not leave room for much doubt, however. Notwithstanding what he noted as his personal preference, or even Egyptian law (which presumably governs the court), from an Islamic legal perspective the gunning down of a writer for stating his views not only represented the lesser transgression but could even be regarded as lawful. In other words, there appeared to be two al-Ghazalis: one who declared that the tenets of Islam do not permit imposing faith by force, and another al-Ghazali who championed well-established *fiqh* rules that decreed a death punishment for apostasy. Here al-Ghazali, the Azhari villager, came face to face with al-Ghazali the well-travelled spokesman of Sunni Islam who eventually became an influential critic of his community. The tension that resulted from this confrontation was unbearable, and it immersed his country in a most unwelcome commotion. What impelled al-Ghazali to the centre of it provides insight into Muslim societies.

The storm

Al-Ghazali's testimony in the Foda murder trial prompted a major controversy between self-declared spokesmen of Islam and the self-declared secularists; yet in several ways they appeared to mirror one another. Only this time, al-Azhar's grandees fully entered this ill-tempered melee.[13] The battle left ordinary Muslims in Egypt with no rational compass. Rather than focusing on the intellectual or legal disarray in their society, which this incident (and the events that led to it) exposed, the two groups instead hurled clichéd insults at each other: Egypt's champions of secularism were condemned as apostates and a fifth column allied with neo-colonialism and the other enemies of their country and faith, while the Islamists were damned as terrorists, extremists, and backward.[14] Name-calling drowned out pertinent questions that their more alert fellow-citizens were trying to raise. These Muslims wanted to know whether or not the foundational sources of Shari'a (scripture or the Prophet's precedent in Medina) actually did contain a legal punishment for apostasy; and, if such a punishment indeed existed, who, according to Islamic tenets, had the authority to declare others apostates. Egyptians inquired about freedom of conscience in the scripture and how *ridda* (apostasy) should be defined. In other words, their flurry of queries about Shari'a rules usually revolved around methodological soundness and historical truth; the axis that al-Ghazali had fought to place at the top of the Muslim agenda. But this time neither he nor any other of the senior *'ulama* provided answers.

Some Egyptians insisted that despite their noise, the two screaming camps represented fringe minorities in their society. According to this view, one of the fringe camps believed that secularism meant consigning God to museums; consequently, many dismissed its spokespersons as former communists or cranks who deified Western trivialities. Similarly, they described the Islamist camp in terms of tiny mobs, albeit with dangerously illiterate members. The facts appear more complicated in the case of the Foda murder trial: for example, the supposedly tiny Islamist mob included many *'ulama* of al-Azhar, and so to dismiss this camp as peripheral is inaccurate. However, the records show it is equally inaccurate to conclude that this Islamist camp mirrored general Egyptian approval of the death penalty for apostasy, which the religious establishment supported.

In a chorus of testimonials, many senior *fuqaha* denounced Foda as an apostate, and they expressed their unequivocal support for al-Ghazali's court testimony. They also explained to Muslims the bases for Foda's punishment. In July 1993, Shaykh Yusuf al-Qaradawi, an Azhari expert with a global stature on *usul al-fiqh* and the State of Qatar's foremost Islamic authority at the time, declared: "There is not the slightest doubt about it, all the *'ulama* (scholars of Islam) would confirm al-Ghazali's testimony."[15] Alluding to Foda, al-Qaradawi added that, "a person who openly proclaimed his unbelief and mocked Shari'a can only be considered an apostate."[16] His declaration shows the rule as being far from a misunderstanding by fringe, ignorant mobs. In 1960 he had established Qatar University's first Faculty of Shari'a and, at the time of the Foda crisis, he had just founded the richly endowed Centre of Sira (the life of the Prophet) and Sunna at the same university. This great authority on how to make Shari'a laws explained that any *'alim* who truly feared God had to pronounce death as the punishment for an apostate, and that this rule had been long decided with the agreement of the community.[17] Even before the murder, some Azhari scholars who organized themselves under the name Jibhat al-Ulama (Muslim Scholars' Front) had denounced Farag Foda as an apostate,[18] although they avoided the pertinent questions that some of their countrymen increasingly now raised, such as whether the Qur'an or the Prophet's precedent in Medina did actually contain a legal punishment for apostasy.

The religious establishment appeared united on this specific Shari'a rule. Shaykh Mohammed Sayyid Tantawi (d. 2010), Egypt's grand mufti at the time, and supposedly also more liberal, declared in a letter published by Egypt's semi-official paper that al-Ghazali's opinion reflected the correct Shari'a rule.[19] Tantawi had a reputation as someone who did the bidding of the state, announcing religious edicts in the interests of the country's rulers. Did his firm support for al-Ghazali's testimony at Foda's murder trial mean that the state favoured an extreme punishment for citizens who criticized the common narrative of Shari'a, even if carried out on the streets of the capital? If not, why did Tanatawi take such a determined position on the subject of apostasy? His relationship with the government did not seem to suffer as a result: in 1996 the President put him in charge of al-Azhar Mosque-University, placing him at the head of the official religious establishment until he died, in 2010. How Tantawi and other eminent Azharis deduced the rule on apostasy to support al-Ghazali's testimony caused widespread concern in Egypt; this ought to have raised questions, but it did not. The mufti supported the apostasy rule by referring to a famous Hadith,[20] while Qaradawi cited the consensus of the *fuqaha* (*ijma'*);[21] but it was such Hadith reports, similar to those invoked by Tantawi, and *fiqh* construct-precedents, similar to those cited by al-Qaradawi, that al-Ghazali had challenged as valid sources of the Shari'a (as discussed later in this book). Why did he revert to making life-and-death rules based on what he concluded to be capricious and doubtful foundations? And, again, why was al-Ghazali at the centre of this apostasy debate in the first place?

The last question, regarding al-Ghazali's place in the midst of this controversy, is fundamental. He had not been the only Shari'a expert witness at the Foda murder trial. He had not even been the defence team's first choice. Initially, for an expert statement on correct Shari'a rules, the defence had turned to Dr Mohammed Mazroua, then head of *al-'aqida wa adyian* at al-Azhar's Department of *Usul al-Din*. Mazroua was unequivocal: this senior Azhari, who also taught creed (*'aqdīa*) and Islamic philosophy in Saudi Arabia, told the court that Shari'a dictated death for an apostate, such as in Foda's case. Unlike Mazroua, al-Ghazali volunteered his testimony, but in contrast to Mazroua's unequivocal statement, al-Ghazali's appeared less final. In court, he did not speak of a Shari'a-dictated execution rule, and even indicated that, personally, he did not prefer such a rule for apostasy, but would opt instead for imprisonment as punishment. Compared to the earnest declarations of other prominent Azhari scholars, who explained a death sentence for apostasy as a Shari'a decree, al-Ghazali's statement was ambivalent and trite. Yet, it was his opinion, not theirs, which occupied the centre stage in the case. Even a curious official Azhari attempt to counter al-Ghazali's testimony hardly mattered to anyone.[22] Why did the opinions of the grand mufti of Egypt at the time or that of famous *usul al-fiqh* experts matter less to their people than Mohammed al-Ghazali's view on the subject? What made his statement on apostasy the focus of this Shari'a debate in 1992–1993? These senior *'ulama* who declared death to be the Shari'a's punishment for apostasy held powerful official posts in the religious establishment at the time, whereas al-Ghazali could not secure such a post at al-Azhar or even a position in the Muslim Brotherhood.

Yet, to his supporters and opponents alike, al-Ghazali carried a far greater weight than other *'ulama*, including those of the official establishment. Perhaps having no state-sanctioned religious title helped him, evoking memories of the archetypical *faqih*, the genuine independent caretaker of Shari'a in society. Even Foda's killers are reported to have cheered in court upon hearing al-Ghazali's testimony, declaring that they could now die happy. Earlier, their groups had condemned all the *'ulama* as sell-outs, including al-Ghazali. Although previously enraged by his later campaigns, al-Ghazali's statement settled the matter for the assassins; they were now confident of the "lawfulness" of gunning down a writer.[23] Similarly, the country at large paid interest to al-Ghazali's sanctioning of killing apostates, even though, unlike other senior *'ulama*, he offered a qualified, and some would say convoluted, answer. Still, neither al-Ghazali nor any of the senior *'ulama* decided the matter.

Who finally decides Shari'a laws?

The *'ulama* are recognized as the trained experts in the methodology by which Shari'a rules are deduced, but, in practice, it is the community that ultimately decides on the validity of particular rules and determines their fate—or so it seems to keen observers of Muslim history in that part of the world.[24] The assassination of Farag Foda provides glimpses of this long-standing tradition; to note that most of the senior Azhari *'ulama* defended Foda's murder, not just a tiny radical minority of Islamists, and that al-Ghazali's views on the Foda's killing greatly mattered, is not the same as saying that it was either this key Sunni institution or al-Ghazali that decided the matter on rules relating to apostasy.

It is sadly alarming that, at the time, human rights groups portrayed the uproar that followed al-Ghazali's court testimony in terms of a confrontation between Shari'a and progressive forces that opposed it. This reflected the reductionist, self-indulgent imageries of the two noisy camps mentioned above, rather than the actual turmoil in Egypt at the time. In their well-intentioned calls for action against Shari'a law in the case of Foda, misguided human rights groups mirrored shoddy Western approaches to rights in Muslim societies because when it came to the murder of Foda, al-Ghazali's expert testimony did not sit well with many Shari'a-loyal Egyptians. Al-Ghazali suffered as a result, despite immense support from the religious establishment and loud Islamist groups. Devout Egyptians, rather than relentless daily attacks from secularists, made the summer of 1993 uncomfortably hot for al-Ghazali. Many of his admirers disagreed with his pronouncements on Foda and apostasy, and great numbers now agreed with critics on the Muslim scholarly fringes, such as Gamal al-Banna or Subhi Mansour, who taunted al-Ghazali about his inconsistency.[25] But the views of scholars such as these did not count for much in Egypt at this time: it was his supporters' widespread discomfort, especially among the educated public, that startled al-Ghazali. These Egyptians found al-Ghazali's approval of homicide curious for several reasons, such as his long-standing preference for working within the system, and not outside it. They did not hold back. If this was his position on Foda's murder, why did he instruct them that coercion and violent irrational practices were incompatible with Islam? Why had he campaigned against the Islamists and described them as dangerous? Did they not admire his courage that, unlike many of the *'ulama*, he did not mince his words? In a video interview, al-Ghazali described those who approached their faith in the angry terms of the late Sayyid Qutb as juveniles with "no mind, no *fiqh* (comprehension of Islam)" and "not worthy of serious consideration."[26] Up to the summer of 1993 al-Ghazali warned fellow Muslims not to corrupt the faith by tainting its doctrines with anger, no matter how justified. When it came to Foda's murder, however, far from being a champion of common sense and liberty (among the senior Azhari scholars of his time), al-Ghazali instead suddenly adopted the banner behind which marched furious mobs shouting for death to those with whom they differed. Scores of his countrymen noticed the discrepancy; many let him know of their concerns.

Ahmed Shawqi al-Fangari provides an illustration of such activist-professionals, whose collective voice has always held sway in shaping Shari'a rules.[27] As a medical doctor in Saudi Arabia, al-Fangari looked after members of the royal family and later worked in Kuwait, where he befriended some of the country's cabinet members. In the Arabic-speaking Gulf and in Egypt, Dr al-Fangari wrote frequently on Islam and became an outspoken critic of Israel's treatment of Arabs, publishing eyewitness accounts of his experiences in Gaza during the 1950s.[28] He too admired al-Ghazali, but in 1993, he declared that al-Ghazali had committed "a grave error" in his testimony at the Foda murder trial. Why could he not be like other prominent *'ulama* throughout the centuries, and "correct his mistake, even if it means he takes back his words [in the testimony]"? Who said that prominent *'ulama*, like al-Ghazali, could not make mistakes?, al-Fangari wondered.[29] "Mujarad Ra'i", Salah Muntasir's popular daily column at *Al-Ahram*, offers more glimpses of the general apprehension among Egypt's thinking public. For 19 days Muntasir pressed al-Ghazali on readers' concerns about his views on Foda's murder. Egypt's Mufti at the time wrote to the same columnist in response to al-Ghazali's beleaguered state as he faced these readers. Muntasir observed that it was al-Ghazali who frequently instructed Muslims that civil and informed dialogue with non-Muslims was a Shari'a-dictated duty, not a choice. If so, should not the same apply to debating with other Muslims?, the columnist asked.[30] He posed questions that preoccupied many readers about rules dealing with apostasy, most of which revolved around the foundations on which such rules were deduced. Al-Ghazali hurried to answer, but his weak responses to these structural questions entangled him further. He repeated general accusations against Foda: that he found him to hate Islam, or that it was Foda who had supported the death sentence "that imperialism has pronounced on our Shari'a and openly sided with our enemies."[31] Another journalist, Ibrahim Issa, wrote that it was love and reverence for al-Ghazali that meant Issa could not keep silent about what "our esteemed Shaykh maintained in his testimony to the State's Higher Court last week." In June 1993 Issa did not know how to explain how it was that, "suddenly we [hear] Shaykh al-Ghazali speaking in the language of Sayyid Qutb and, before him, Ibn Taymiya, [or of] Abu al-Ala al-Mawdudi."[32] Was not al-Ghazali the one who taught them about the venality "of hardnosed *fiqh* that [oppressors] had long used to tyrannize people"?[33] Such a line of questioning in effect challenged the entire religious establishment in Egypt. Other doctors, engineers, journalists, students at Islamic institutes, and representatives from various economic and professional backgrounds whom al-Ghazali had successfully won over through the years joined in, writing to remind him of his instructions, and noting that the Qur'an, the foundational source of life-and-death rules, contained no legal penalty for apostasy, and that the punishment of death was based only on *uhadi* Hadith reports, some of which al-Ghazali previously criticized as justifying practices that the Qur'anic message outlawed.[34] "You have abandoned the Qur'an [...] our Shaykh, and hurried to follow the [bulk of the] *fuqaha* instead [...] Whatever happened to moderation, to balance?", asked Mohammed Shibl, a retired army general. "Once upon a time you seemed to us the ray of light which guided those who walked in the sincere paths of the faith; and suddenly you have turned into the lightning bolt which strikes the enlightened", he wrote.[35]

These reactions give glimpses of the quiet, albeit intense, confrontation between many learned, influential Muslims and the main Sunni institution, al-Azhar. In 1993, Egypt's thinking public did not accept the rules on apostasy that those at the helm of the religious establishment declared as being Shari'a. These non-experts genuinely regarded themselves as representing the general sentiment in their country: in other words, many Egyptians held tightly to Islamic rules, but accused their experts on Shari'a of distortion. Many of these Sunni Muslims believed that al-Ghazali of all people should have known better.[36] The rising tide of Egypt's "thinking public" against him must have devastated al-Ghazali. Until recently, great numbers of the devout had looked up to him for inspiration. It was their support that helped to propel him into being an influential Islamic thinker, but now he watched open censure of his views pour in from every direction. Al-Ghazali knew that without this diverse segment of the population, he could easily be reduced to being just another Azhari graduate among throngs of villagers with feeble education and limited perspectives, such as those he often criticized.

This possibility reflects Egypt's two-tier system of education: one derived from the West, and the other—exemplified by al-Azhar, and perceived as appropriate for students with the lowest social and academic skills—focusing on Islam. Modern Egyptians value Azhari graduates for preserving Islam's legacy, but only to some extent, and they simultaneously write off Azharis as of inferior intellectual and social training. Social and cultural realities meant that without the support of Egypt's professional classes, al-Ghazali could soon be demoted to being another turban-wearing cleric from the obdurate Azhari mass. With mainstream Muslim criticism steadily escalating, a disciple of al-Ghazali, the newspaper columnist Fahmy Huwaidi, came to the rescue with an account calculated to limit the damage. In an article that was printed in both the Cairo *Al-Ahram* and the Kuwait City *Al-Watan*, Huwaidi distanced al-Ghazali from the *fiqh* death sentence in his testimony about apostasy.[37] As an expert witness, Huwaidi explained, al-Ghazali had only offered technical answers to specific *fiqh* questions that the defence team had posed. His answers therefore did not constitute al-Ghazali's personal *ijtihad* (deductions of correct Shari'a rules), nor were they meant as a fatwa on the matter, Huwaidi wrote, presumably with al-Ghazali's consent.[38]

It is not certain what percentage of Egypt's Muslims found al-Ghazali's testimony, or his attempts to justify it, acceptable, but it could be seen that popular support was uncharacteristically muted. In the 1960s demonstrators defied President Gamal abd al-Nasser and took to Cairo's streets to protest Salah Jahin's ridicule of al-Ghazali's call for Islamic dress; in the 1970s they filled the streets again when he objected to President Sadat's reforms to family law; but there was no similar mass expression of solidarity in 1993–1994, as scorching ridicule descended on the shaykh from every direction. An activist with al-Tanweer, a self-described "Enlightenment Association", likened al-Ghazali's testimony to extremists detonating bombs.[39] A former professor of history at al-Azhar, Dr Ahmed Mansour, called scholars such as al-Ghazali *fuqaha al-Gaz*, meaning someone on the payroll of oil-rich Gulf States who uses the issue of apostasy to persecute society.[40] Among them, al-Ghazali was a leader of the intellectual branch of terrorism, Mansour wrote.[41] It did not help al-Ghazali that he had been one of the rare senior Azharis who had actually admired Mansour's critiques of Muslim history. Al-Ghazali is even quoted at length in one of his books, which Mansour had been punished by al-Azhar for writing.[42] Similarly intense was the leftists' assault on al-Ghazali: Farida al-Naqqash scorned him for his consistently bad fatwas, as she put it.[43] A combination of arrogance and intellectual impotency led him to treat Islam as his private domain, to decide what was and what was not permissible, she wrote. Al-Naqqash described his role in Algeria as destructive and fascist. She censured the many in the Arab intelligentsia who showed him great respect, accusing them of empowering al-Ghazali's unjustified influence.[44] The firestorm continued: for months, typical *Al-Ahali* commentaries included titles such as "[...] There goes your Moderate Shaykh?", "Who is Not Afraid of al-Ghazali?", and "Ghazali: The Mask Falls".[45] Whatever happened to the remarkable expressions of support for al-Ghazali's positions on Shari'a against the country's modernist intelligentsia, or against the state, that Egypt had witnessed on earlier occasions? There were those who, in contrast, supported al-Ghazali's position on Foda's apostasy, but most of these persons appeared to belong to either the official religious establishment or the fringe belligerent Islamists who had acquired prominence during the Sadat era; but the mass of the Egyptian street did not join them. This time, in 1993, Egypt's *'ulama* huddled together in one camp, but the country's general thinking public and many of its ordinary men and women stood against them.

Why did the Egyptian street not rise in the early 1990s, to defend al-Ghazali against a ferocious onslaught, as it had done in the 1960s and again in the 1970s? Here an important but rarely noted element of Shari'a rulemaking comes to the surface: the role of the community in sustaining or rejecting rules that are designated as Shari'a. This highlights the question of what influence, if any, the Muslim public has had over rules deduced by the *fuqaha*. Over the centuries, communal reception, immediate needs, and powerful groups have ultimately decided which rules made in the name of Shari'a survived and which disappeared. Shari'a may have been the great cultural unifier of many societies across the continents, but it has also ensured their diversity. As discussed in Chapter 7, not only in practice but also theoretically, Shari'a methodology orbits around divine principles but also relies on choices. However, despite the evidence of this, the communal input in Shari'a rulemaking has long been buried in deep layers of *fiqh* constructs. Many of these concepts in fact originated in political confrontations over authority, hegemony, jurisdiction, and their aftermath;[46] Western images of a cast-iron Islamic law further conceal this communal input, an important feature of Muslim rulemaking. However, before further discussion of the influence of the communal voice on Shari'a rules, we must return to that old powerful tiebreaker in making Shari'a rules: communal memory.

The agency of memory

The murder of Foda and its aftermath underlines the importance of collective memory in Muslim societies in and around the Mediterranean. Despite appearances, the modern battles that rage between champions of reason and reform against the defenders of custom and inherited *fiqh* ideas have not produced two distinct camps in Muslim communities: at times when it has been felt that Muslim society is under attack, many of those who regarded themselves as advancing reason would retreat into tradition, seeking safety in the familiar arguments and practices of the *fuqaha*, even if they had previously criticized them. Chilling as his arguments may have been in the Farag Foda episode, it is inaccurate to designate al-Ghazali as an extremist or even a traditionalist, just as it is incorrect to regard him as a moderate or modernizer. Al-Ghazali can only be accurately considered in the context of a particular time, within the variables of his social world. In his area of the Mediterranean and its surrounding communities, past traumas had bred a deep sense of siege since the late thirteenth century CE, and whenever Muslims have felt overwhelmed by outside threats, they have turned inward,[47] whether or not the danger has been immediate and genuine or only an illusion. The West's colonialist ventures and, more recently, its interventionist wars, has further entrenched the impressions of encirclement. The lingering communal memories of outside threats often trigger responses that have made it harder for modern researchers to establish the line between the region's new camps: which of them adopt liberal ideas and attitudes that embrace change and which cling to tradition?

Al-Ghazali thus similarly rushed to take cover in the same shelter as his Islamist enemies. In his writings, we can sense his foreboding. In his view, of all the past *fuqaha*, his life most closely paralleled that of the thirteenth/fourteenth century CE scholar Ahmed Ibn Taymyia (d. 1328 CE), in whom many angry modern Muslim groups find inspiration. Ibn Taymiya had been born shortly after the destruction of the (Abbasid) Caliphate in Baghdad at the hands of the Mongols, "forcing [Ibn Taymiya] and his family to flee from one place to another, treading roads full of death, bewilderment, and incessant defeats."[48] Al-Ghazali noted that he had similarly been born a few years before another Caliphate (the Ottomans) had collapsed in 1923, making him a witness of similarly dark times in Muslim history.[49] Life in his Arab or Muslim neighbourhood had been full of danger and humiliation; he had long lived with a dread of outside enemies. Many of the charges that al-Ghazali and other Egyptians made against Foda carried strong intimation of danger to society, a fear of subjugation that appeared to them immediate and real. Mohammed Muru'a did not even understand why his fellow countrymen would denounce the killing of Foda; by the same logic they would have also denounced the execution of French traitors who collaborated with the

Nazi occupiers against the Resistance during the World War II, Muru'a remarked in his book *Secularists and Traitors*.[50] It is nothing short of a catastrophe that al-Ghazali also saw Foda as a member of a fifth column, instead of someone with a genuinely different point of view. Working for the enemy, encamped on their borders as it prepared to destroy his Muslim community, Foda's stance appeared intolerable. Al-Ghazali's overwhelming sense of siege may not provide much comfort to those whose lives may have been shattered by the consequences of such fears, but these perceptions are real nonetheless, and exist in the collective Muslim interpretation of the world around them. Like many of his people, when al-Ghazali lost his composure, he sought protection in the past, even though he may have rejected past ideas as flawed, both before and after the Foda episode.

A couple of years later, al-Ghazali sounded like his pre-Book Fair Debate self. In his regular column, "Al-Haq al-Murr" (The Bitter Truth), al-Ghazali wrote in 1995 to describe his fury at a young mosque preacher who claimed that the Qur'anic verse stating that there was no compulsion in faith was abrogated:

> I asked him: What about the verse on which [this supposedly abrogated verse] is based, was it also cancelled? [...] What about the verse before that, and besides them, around a hundred other verses explaining [Islam's] message and how to go about it. With what reason can one claim that all these verses had been abrogated?[51]

It is sad, the irate al-Ghazali concluded, that some poorly equipped people, "who could not be trusted with a simple business transaction, now see themselves fit to communicate the divine message to all people." Somehow the same al-Ghazali now appeared to fully understand the significance of advocating faith by force. "I weep", he added, "and I weep yet again for [every] intellectual defeat" in which the Muslims of his time exposed their "dearth of reason and dismal skills of dialogue".[52] As he watched another angry man translate his impotence into a lesson on Islam, al-Ghazali's impressions of outside danger seem to have abated.

We cannot be sure when precisely these perceptions of outside danger receded or to what degree did they recede. His readers are certain, however, that sometimes in his life's journey, al-Ghazali found many *fiqh* rules bizarre. It was his reconsideration of these rules and Shari'a methodology that made him the centre of a great commotion in Sunni religious circles. In his old and new approaches to Shari'a methodology, al-Ghazali provides an illustration of the enduring dialectic in Shari'a rule-/lawmaking: on the one hand, its age-old constant motion between layers of intellectual and material context, and on the other, the scriptural content. Chapters 5 to 7 provide examples of this dialectic in Shari'a rules on women.

Notes

1. Al-Ghazali, videotape interviews (#FTW-1, #TAYR-1, #TJD-1).
2. Ali abd al-Raziq, *Al-Islam wa Usul al-Hukm*, 2nd edn (Cairo: Matba't Misr, 1925).
3. Khaled Mohammed Khaled, *Min Huna Nabda'* (Cairo: al-Maktaba al-Anglo Misriya, 1969 [1950]), 41–84.
4. For a survey of Egyptian reactions to Abd al-Raziq's book and his academic fate, see Mohammed 'Imara, *Ma'rakat al-Islam wa Usul al-Hukm* (Cairo: Dar al-Shorouk, 1989). As previously noted, Shaykh Khaled later recanted his views on Muslim history in *Al-Dawla fi al-Islam* (Cairo: Dar al-Thabit, 1981) and *Rijal Hawla al-Rasul Sala Allah 'alayhi wa Sallem* (Cairo: Dar al-Fikr li al-Tba'a wa al-Nashir, 2006 [1999]).
5. The phrase "*al-Islam huwa al-hal*" (Islam is the answer), expressed a vision of governance that had swept across Egypt by the 1970s.
6. The transcript has been published as *Munadharat Misr Bayna al-Dawla al-Diniya wa al-Madaniya (Munathara fi Ma'radh al-Kitab), 1992* (Cairo: al-Dar al-Misriya li al-Nashr wa al-Tawzi', 1992). A video of the event can be seen on Youtube (https://www.youtube.com/watch?v=ubF2jHuHN1w).
7. The author of the current study is not related to Mohammed Khalafallah.
8. For more of Farag Foda's views on Islam, governance, and their history, see his *Al-Nazir* (Cairo: Dar Misr al-Gadida li al-Nashr wal-Tawzi', 1983); idem, *Al-Irhab* (Cairo: Dar Misr al-Gadida lil-Nashr wa al-Tawzi', 1988); idem, *Al-Haqiqa al-Gha'iba* (Beirut: Dar al-Ma'arif, 2003). In 1995 a collection of Foda's articles was published as *Shahid 'Ala al-'Asr* (Cairo: Dar wa Mat'abi al-Mustaqbal, 2005 [1995]).
9. *Munadharat Misr Bayna*, 32, 59.
10. Al-Ghazali testified on 22 June, 1993. The transcript of his court testimony can be found in *Al-Sha'ab* (Cairo), 25 June, 1993, and also in Gamal al-Banna, *Kala Thuma Kala* (Cairo: Dar al-Fikr al-Islami, 1994), 28–30.
11. Al-Ghazali wrote: "In my book *Jihad al-Da'wa bayna 'Ajz al-Dakhil wa Kayd al-Kharij* [Cairo: Dar al-Kutub al-Islamiyah, 1987] I enumerated more than a hundred Qur'anic verses that guarantee freedom of conscience and establish faith on personal convictions." (Mohammed al-Ghazali, *Al-Sunna al-Nabawiya Bayna Ahl al-Fiqh wa ahl al-Hadith*, 5th edn [no location: Sahara, 1989], 103–104).
12. Ibid.
13. Also of note is the self-described *'Ulama* Front (*Jibhat al-Ulama*), a group of Azharis who put Foda at the head of their 1992 list of Islam's enemies who were living in their midst. Its leader at the time, Dr Abd al-Ghaffar Aziz, headed the Da'wa Department at the College of Usul al-Din in al-Azhar University. Aziz later argued that Foda had been responsible for his own death (Abd al-Ghaffar Aziz, *Man Qatala Farag Foda?* [Madinat Nasr, Cairo: Dar al-'I'lam al-Duwali, 1992]). It was his assistant (and current leader of the same *'Ulama* Front) Shaykh Mahmoud Mazroua that the defence called as a Shari'a expert witness in the Foda murder case. Commonly referred to as "his eminence" (*fadilat*), al-Shaykh, Dr Mazroua worked as a professor of 'Aqida and philosophy at both Cairo's al-Azhar and Mecca's Umm al-Qura universities.
14. For examples of such slinging matches from the secularist side see Farida al-Naqqash and Rif'at al-Sa'id in *Al-Ahali*, and abd al-Sattar al-Taweela in *Rosa al-Youssef*; for the Islamist side, see the examples of Hasan Mohammed Katbi in *Al-Wafd*, Mohammed Sha'ban al-Mawgi in *Al-Haqiqa*, or in Abd al-Ghaffar Aziz, *Man Qatala Farag Foda?* (Madinat Nasr, Cairo: Dar al-'I'lam al-Duwali, 1992).
15. "Al-Qaradawi Yandhamu ila Qafilat al-Ulama al-Mu'aiydin li-Shihadat al-Shaykh al-Ghazali" (Qaradai joins the *'Ulama* who support Shaykh al-Ghazali's testimony), *Al-Nour*, 14 July 1993.

16. "Al-Qaradawi: Shihadat al-Ghazali Sahiha Miya fi al-Miya", *Al-Haqiqa*, 17 July, 1993.
17. Ibid.
18. For *Jibhat l-'Ulama*, see note 16 above.
19. "Risalat al-Mufti ila Salah Muntasir [...] Yu'aiyd fiha Mohammed al-Ghazali", *Al-Ahram*, 27 July, 1993. Tantawi's support of the testimony is also discussed in Hussam Salim, "Wa Hadha Maqal Nakhtalifu Ma'ahu", *'Aqidati*, 28 September, 1993.
20. Ibid.
21. "Al-Qaradawi: Shihadat al-Ghazali Sahiha Miya fi al-Miya", *Al-Haqiqa*, 17 July, 1993; "Al-Qaradawi Yandhamu ila Qafilat al-Ulama al-Mu'aiydin li-Shihadat al-Shaykh al-Ghazali", *Al-Haqiqa*, 17 July, 1993.
22. Curiously, an Azhar committee issued a fatwa against the punishment of death for apostasy at the very same time that al-Azhar's chiefs and senior professors declared their support for it. This "counter-fatwa" was published in Egypt's semi-official daily under the title "Lajnat Fatwa bi-al Azhar: La Yajuz an Yatahimu Ahad Insanan bi al-Rida aw Yu'aqibuhu", *Al-Ahram*, 9 July, 1993; also published in the Saudi international daily as "Al-Azhar Yarudu ala al-Ghazali wa al-Mazroua fi Qadiyat al-Rida", *Al-Sharq al-Awsat*, 10 July, 1993.
23. One of the men charged with Foda's murder, Safwat abd al-Ghani, told the Saudi paper *Al-Hayat* on 23 June, 1993 that al-Ghazali's court testimony sufficed as evidence of the righteousness of his act, whether or not he was sentenced to death. Ibrahim Issa, "Raghm shihadatuhi al-Khatira fi Qadhiyat Farag Foda, Takfir al-Shaykh al-Ghazali", *Rosa al-Youssef*, 28 June, 1993.
24. "Ya'tarif: Katamtu ba'dhu al-Fatawa Tajanuban li-Hiyaj al-'Ama wa Tashwish al-Jamidin", *Islamonline* (online in 2008, archived at http://web.archive.org/web/*/www.islamonline.net/Arabic/karadawy/part3/14.SHTML); also pubished in *Al-Dostor*, 23 April, 2009 and on *Shrouknews.com*, and *Al-naba.com*.
25. Al-Banna, *Kala Thuma Kala*; Ahmad Subhi Mansour, "Shi'ar Irhabi fi Yad Fuqaha al-Gaz; Hiwar al-Rida bayn al-Rafd wa al-Ta'iyyd", *Al-Ahali*, 17 November, 1993.
26. Al-Ghazali, videotape interview (#TAYR-1).
27. S.D. Goitein, "The Rise of the Near-Eastern Bourgeoisie in Early Islamic Times", in idem, *Studies in Islamic History and Institutions* (Leiden: Brill, 2010 [1957]), 215–241.
28. On al-Fangari, "Ahmed Shawqi al-Fangari, the Struggle of a Doctor in Gaza", Al-Jazeera TV report, 2 April, 2004 (online: http://www.aljazeera.net/NR/exeres/4DF7FA40-5847-446D-94AC-624027FB0697.htm).
29. Quoted in Gamal al-Banna, *Kala Thuma Kala*, 41.
30. Salah Muntasir, "Mujarad ra'i", *Al-Ahram*, 5 August, 1993.
31. Munatsir, "Mujarad ra'i", *Al-Ahram*, 21 July, 1993.
32. A typical expression of Egyptian discomfort at the time is Ibrahim Issa, "Raghm shahadatihh al-Khatira fi Qadhiyat Farag Foda", *Rosa al-Youssef*, 28 June, 1993:
لست مضطرا الى اعلان حبي واحترامي وتقديري للشيخ محمد الغزالي..لذلك لا نسكت عما قاله شيخنا الجليل في شهادته امام محكمة الدولة العليا في الاسبوع الماضي.....وفجأة نرى الشيخ الغزالي يتحدث بكلام سيد قطب وقبله ابن تيمية وابو الاعلى المودودى والفقه المتشدد الذي تم استخدامه مطية للتنكيل بالناس
33. Ibid.
34. For illustration, see al-Liwa Hossam Sowailim, "Hadha Maqal Nakhtalifu Ma'hu", *'Aqidati*, 28 September, 1993; idem, "La hukm fi al-Qur'an li qatl al-murtad", *Al-Gomhuriya*, 17 August, 1993; Al-Shaykh Mustafa 'Asim, "Na'am li-al-tanwir la li al-qatl wa al-takfir", *Al-Ahram*, 19 July, 1993; Dr Hamid Hasaan, "Had al-rida wa al-gholu fi al-din", *Al-Gomhuriya*, 24 September, 1993; 'Awni al-Hofi, "Lao Sahat al-Fatwa lakan Mustafa Mahmoud min 'Idad al-Dhahaya", *Akhbar al-Adab*, 8 August, 1993.
35. Mohammed Shibl, "Ya Shaykh al-Ghazali ... Haram 'Aliyk", *Al-Ahali*, 14 December, 1993.
36. As in his statement, "'Hasha an Ukafiru Musliman" (God forbid I ever proclaim a Muslim apostate) (Mohammed al-Ghazali, *Humum Da'iya* [Cairo: Nahdat Misr, 2004], 65, 66).

37. Fahmy Huwaidi, "Hashiya ala Shihadat al-Shaykh Mohammed al-Ghazali", *Al-Ahram* (Cairo), 6 July, 1993 (also published in the Kuwait City *Al-Watan*).
38. Ibid.
39. Mohammed Abu al-Is'ad, "Shi'ar Irhabi fi yad fuqaha al-gaz; hiwar al-Rida bayn al-Rafd wa al-Ta'iyyd", *Al-Ahali*, 17 November, 1993.
40. Ibid.
41. Ibid.
42. Mohammed al-Ghazali, *Turathuna al-Fikri fi Mizan al-Shar'i wa al-'Aql*, 2nd edn (Cairo: Dar al-Shuruk, 1991), 108–114.
43. Farida al-Naqqash, "Qadiya li al-munaqasha:al-Ghazali wa fatwah al-radi'a", *Al-Ahali*, 30 November, 1993.
44. Ibid.
45. Rifa'at al-Saíd, "Ya Do'at al-Islam al-siyasi Hakum Shaykhakum al-Mu'tadil", *Al-Ahali*, 30 June, 1993; Ghali Shukri, "Man la yakhaf al-Ghazali?", *Al-Qahira*, July 1993; Said Mahmoud al-Qumni, "Al-Ghazali wa soqot al-aqni'a", *Al-Ahali*, 22 September, 1993.
46. See Chapters 7 and 8 for illustrations.
47. By the thirteenth century CE the greatest Muslim urban centres had fallen one after the other under the twin invasions of the Crusaders (1091–1289 CE) and the Mongols (1219–ca. 1330 CE), leading to a fear of annihilation and a state of siege that swept the remaining Muslim landscape.
48. Mohammed al-Ghazali, "Qissat Haya", *Islamiyat al-Ma'rifa* 2/3 (2007): 156.
49. Ibid.
50. Mohammed Muru'a, *'Almani'yun wa Khawana* (Cairo: Dar Hira, 1996), 31.
51. Mohammed al-Ghazali, "Al-Haq al-Murr", *Al-Sharq al-Awsat*, 17 May, 1995.
52. Ibid.

FIVE

Textualizing Context: The Case of Women[1]

This chapter explores how contexts and various texts came together to determine how al-Ghazali deduced Shari'a rules, using rules about women as a case study. There are good reasons for selecting this topic, especially rules about women's eligibility for civic authority (*wilaya*), beyond the modern obsession with "women in Islam". The first reason is theoretical and foundational, while the second is practical and immediate. There is no doubt that fathers, husbands, or brothers did transfer their authority as leaders to female relatives, allowing some Muslim women to hold the reins of government, as celebrated examples from the past show. Such transfers might be accidental or deliberate, but in all instances the male as the original holder of power, rather than Shari'a, formed the basis for assigning civic authority to females. Famous *fiqh* rules make it clear: Islam dictates that power over men and the affairs of the community is restricted to men only. In modern times, those who have argued otherwise have often been regarded as Westernizers who flout or misrepresent Shari'a. The right to hold public authority has marked the line that women may not lawfully cross without causing harm to society.

The second, practical, reason for focusing on women is that of all the rules that al-Ghazali derived from Shari'a throughout his long career, there were two subjects that brought him—depending on perspective—either the most fame, or the most notoriety. These were the topics of women and of Islam's political principles. But these two areas played dissimilar roles in al-Ghazali's intellectual journey. The inequities of the occupation, corrupt government, the arrogance of Europeans in their midst, and abject poverty, all of which humiliated his people, cultivated in this Egyptian villager a deep sense of injustice very early in his life.[2] True, some of al-Ghazali's earlier views on Western political experiences changed significantly, but these changes did not denote structural shifts in his convictions about what constitute basic Islamic political principles. In contrast, al-Ghazali's approach to women and Shari'a led to genuine surprises, for himself and for the millions who listened to him. He accordingly deduced new rules, albeit if grudgingly. It may be hard to believe, but the notion of legitimate female civic leadership arrived in mainstream Muslim understanding of Shari'a only in the late twentieth century, and it did so thanks to al-Ghazali. This chapter explores what Shari'a rules he deduced and from what sources, but with equal attention to his arguments and the reality of women in al-Ghazali's day-to-day living. That many Western Muslims may find this chapter painful to read (and some of its details novel) is a testimony to the inroads that al-Ghazali made in his country's Muslim discourse from the late 1980s.

Orthodox texts?

Al-Ghazali stated Islam's position on women in the 1950s, most notably in his well-received *Min Huna Na'lam* (*From Here We Know*). He wrote that in contrast to a woman, "a man was characterized by strength in mind and ability to persevere."[3] As proof, al-Ghazali advanced what he then believed to be evidence from life:

> [I]t has been noted that the bodies of men are more beautiful and closer to perfection than the bodies of women. This is not only special to males and females of the human race but in all other animals.[4]

Still attentive to practical observation, he qualified this statement: "Of course not every woman is inferior to all men: there are some exceptions",[5] but to dispel any doubt about general female inferiority as a rule of nature, he explained that a female's advantage could only manifest itself across species, such as "the lioness being superior to male donkeys".[6] However, a woman could never, for example, exceed her father, brothers, or sons in intelligence or power.[7] Put another way, empirical observation over the centuries showed that women were of a lesser nature than men. Shari'a must regulate women's lives accordingly.

His book not only provided instructions on women; it also included the proofs he put forward to reach his conclusions. Any job a woman held outside her home was contrary to her nature and, consequently, contrary to Shari'a too. If, however, a woman found a pressing economic need to work, she could do so, but she could never hold any position of public authority. He explained that it was pure folly to import contemporary Western practices and to contemplate appointing Muslim women as judges or to government posts, for example. Society must exclude women from any civic positions, whether minister of state, head of a department, or even a mere clerk;[8] to place women in positions of influence would be "unfair to nature and [...] to public interests."[9] The general Shari'a rule that follows from this could not be clearer: women have no place in public life. They did not have any in the past, and should not in modern times. Nature's laws, long observed, were decisive: femininity is incompatible with *wilaya* (holding public responsibility).

When al-Ghazali declared war against Westernizers in Egypt, the cornerstone of his arguments had been to recall that Muslims do not make rules haphazardly; they must follow the parameters of the Islamic way—the Shari'a method of making rules/laws. At the time, he turned mainly to derive rules from a loose concept of valid precedent, which included Hadith, earlier *fiqh* rulings, and empirical evidence. Rulings concerning women especially relied on observations about the laws of nature; al-Ghazali's reasoning was based on what he understood to be wisdom distilled from centuries of "human experience", here meaning ancient quasi-scientific Greek knowledge that still forms a major part of the Islamic, including Azhari, educational curriculum. He also provided contemporary examples in support of the supposedly eternal verities about women. For example, he reported the case of an Egyptian woman lawyer who believed that neither she nor any of her gender should be allowed to become public prosecutors, there being crimes too delicate for women to hear about or deal with; she felt violated by her exposure to the details of such crimes.[10] Al-Ghazali quoted the lawyer's conviction (and, by extension his own), that "a simple villager with a baby in her lap was better for the nation [...] than a thousand women politicians or lawyers."[11] From these various tiers of precedents, al-Ghazali reached his conclusion of what constituted communal wellbeing.

Besides barring women from public posts, *Min Huna Na'lam* included rules that regulated their dress. The most suitable outfits for women were similar to "the garbs of Christian nuns [...] or peasant women from Monufyia and Sharqyia" or other Egyptian provinces in the area where both al-Ghazali and an ancient concept of piety associated with Christian monasticism originated.[12] In other words, al-Ghazali's eastern Mediterranean and Egyptian background provided the evidence he used to determine correct practice; the women of his childhood and a pre-Islamic, Christian view of women embedded in the rural Egyptian memory corresponded with "the closest to Islamic manners".[13] Further, in the early 1950s, the term "*hijab*" had not yet acquired its late twentieth-century meaning as only a head-covering; *hijab*, which meant "face-covering" in *Min Hina Na'lam*, offended al-Ghazali. He ruled it had no relation to Shari'a, being "neither Islamic nor did it protect (society) against seduction".[14] The context here is that peasant women have always made up an integral part of the workforce tilling the land; until other sources of income could be found, covering women's faces or secluding them would have brought economic ruin to Egyptian villagers. Al-Ghazali contrasted the face-cover, which reflected conditions of "collective impotence", with women covering their hair, which formed a definite Islamic rule.[15] "We observe decadence and chaos in [foreign] societies adopting the *hijab*", he wrote in reference to neighbours in the Arabian Peninsula, whom he contrasted with his "[Egyptian] villages, [where] peasant women without a blemish on their character roam without *hijab*."[16]

Al-Ghazali's association of face-covering with backward societies reveals another side of the limitations imposed by his immediate settings. Like modern Muslims, he located the origins of this practice in "the Bedouin habit of covering women's faces", resorting to colonialist perceptions of Arab societies: the less Westernized a community the more backward it is assumed to be. The shaykh indicated no knowledge that it had been urban women of the ancient civilized southeast Mediterranean societies (including Egypt) who had proudly embraced face-covering even before Islam.[17] In common with the secularists in his region, he also showed scant understanding of the diversity in his Arab neighbourhood, that not all "Bedouin" Arab societies practised covering woman's faces or suffered from collective impotence. For example, the conditions of women in what had been an exceptionally impoverished Kuwait decided the norms that separated them from their Muslim sisters in other corners of Arabia. While able-bodied men disappeared at sea for months during the pearl-diving season, leaving behind the old, the sick, and the very young, women looked after their community. Harsh circumstances gave these Kuwaiti women a higher stature than females elsewhere in Arabia or even in the Egyptian countryside. In other places in the Peninsula, until modern times women neither covered their faces nor were they ever really secluded. And old customs in what had become the states of Qatar and the UAE indicate that women could marry more than once without suffering from the stigma attached to widows and divorced women, which prevails in Egypt until today.

How are al-Ghazali's lamentations about the sorry state of women in his society to be understood? It pained him that during the then-recent 1948 Arab–Israeli War, that while "Jewish women heroically fought our men", passive ignorant Muslim women could not even find Palestine on a map.[18] Did not this expectation that Muslim women, like Jewish women, rise up in all fronts in the battle for Palestine plainly contradict Shari'a rules that barred women from public work, which he advocated in the same book? Inconsistencies pepper *Min Huna Na'lam*, and the work's approach to women is the most obvious example here.

Al-Ghazali's arguments faithfully followed the standard *fiqh* practices of his times. However, many of the supposedly universal principles about women that are found in the assortment of precedent often overwhelm the Qur'an, despite claims to the contrary. To illustrate, the *fuqaha* used this collective legacy to justify why they could not translate into a general rule the unrestricted divine right which the Muslim scripture accorded to women to have full legal personas, giving them, and not any of their male relatives, unqualified power over their own financial affairs.[19] Al-Ghazali followed suit: "True, a woman has the freedom to manage her own affairs just as a man", he conceded, in acknowledgement of the Qur'anic instruction, but "what relates to the welfare of nations and the interests of peoples is a different matter; women's abilities are below this", he wrote.[20] Again, his proof came from ancient Mediterranean assumptions which *fiqh* later codified. Muslims also accept an even higher (divine) category of precedent, according to which God spoke mainly through reports that claimed the Prophet as their author: Hadith (discussed further in Chapter 6). One Hadith in particular established the undisputed principle that barred women from government: "A people will not prosper if they let a woman be their leader."[21] Another instructed women to walk as close as possible to walls, if they had to use the roads.[22] Al-Ghazali used both of these Hadiths. In his mind, he believed that these rules were grounded in undisputed natural laws and, therefore, indicated divine intention and could not lead to anything but the good of society, including the good of woman. However, when the interpretation of natural laws alters over time, or novel challenges arise, influential *'ulama* have always reconsidered the rules, as well as the store of texts that generated them, including valid precedent.

New contexts, new texts

Observations from real life that indicated judicious practices, which matter a great deal in Shari'a rule-/lawmaking, had been fast changing in Egypt and its Arab neighbourhood. Egypt and its region underwent many makeovers during al-Ghazali's lifetime. These changes revealed contradictions in the fabric of Arab societies, and brought to attention inconsistencies in some authoritative precedents and in the rationale of *fiqh* arguments. With the social reality fast changing, the Islamic rules that al-Ghazali deduced also altered. By the time of his death in 1996, his position was that Shari'a did not bar women from holding any public posts, whether political or even religious. Muslims have usually met such liberal-sounding claims about Shari'a with distrust. In al-Ghazali's case, however, many of the devout applauded him, just as they had earlier when he explained to them that Shari'a barred women from any public authority. Others grudgingly conceded that al-Ghazali might be right here too. What did al-Ghazali convey to them that sounded different from modernists' arguments? Al-Ghazali urged Muslims never to make rules/laws haphazardly; they had to abide by Shari'a strictly, but he told them that their assumptions about reality, with which they approached Shari'a, had been thoroughly corrupted. The proof? Sound observation, again. New challenges have always triggered changes in Shari'a lawmaking, especially: (1) a review of assumptions about the laws of nature; (2) *fiqh* rules and arguments; and, if need be, (3) a closer investigation of the highest authoritative precedents, including approaches to divine universal principles.

Neo-orientalists brushed al-Ghazali aside with reductionist labels such as "fundamentalist", "traditionalist", or "modernist", but many Sunni Muslims understood him differently. These Muslims saw al-Ghazali in terms of how a *faqih* is celebrated in memory, as one who has to be always alert, recognizing not only threats but also identifying correct practices, regardless of their origins.[23] "[M]uch of their work meant coming to terms at least as much with their own society as with the Qur'anic challenge", to use Marshal Hodgson's words about the earliest scholar-activists, and this set the pattern.[24] The vocation of a *faqih* required that new information about women's realities had to be evaluated according to the Shari'a rule-making method and its sources. Therefore, developments need to be understood, and why they affected al-Ghazali in the way that they did.

Contexts: Women in reality

The portraits below show al-Ghazali in action, among women at work and at home at the time his views on women started to shift. The complex settings explored below show society's inconsistences, but also journeys of discovery and self-critique.

Portrait: In the Muslim Mediterranean (Algeria)[25]

Al-Ghazali sat waiting on a conference podium in a full public hall; his lecture would soon begin. The place: another city close to the Mediterranean Sea, like where he grew up, but in Algeria, a long way from home. The time: the 1980s, when Arabic-speakers hailed this Azhari scholar as a towering leader of Sunni orthodoxy.

At the outside entrance, two unveiled women arrived, hoping to challenge the "Islamic" vision that the lecture would promote. The men attending the doors spotted these women without head-covers, and barred them from entering what was a public event. A confrontation between the men and the two women quickly turned ugly. Algeria's Islamists are said to have spat in the women's faces in a fit of rage. Fahmy Huwaidi, a close associate of al-Ghazali and a famous columnist who happened to be passing by, found the ferocity of the scene distressing. He hurried to whisper it into al-Ghazali's ears, hoping that the prominent shaykh would include in his lecture words of wisdom on gentleness as an Islamic virtue, or something of the sort.

The shaykh stood up. With a bewildered Fahmy Huwaidi following behind, and without a word, al-Ghazali left the podium. Aided by his cane, he clumsily made his way towards the conference hall entrance, the scene of the quarrel. His appearance at the door stilled the scuffle. Everyone now stopped to look at al-Ghazali, the women in defiance, the men with pride. To the men's horror, a tearful al-Ghazali lashed at these self-styled defenders of Islam guarding the door: Is it in God's name that we now spit on people's faces?, he demanded. He is said to have then taken the hands of the two women, leading them into the conference hall, from which they had been barred earlier because of their "un-Islamic" dress, Fahmy Huwaidi recalls.[26]

Many Algerian Islamists would not forgive this incident or other similar episodes. Al-Ghazali had behaved scandalously, as they saw it; he had let them down. They discovered this famed fierce defender of Islam to have been a weakling at heart, "a stooge of the atheist West" who attempted to undermine their resolve, according to one such Islamist who sought asylum in Britain. At the time, "Ghazali could have been easily described as the most important man in Algeria, surpassing even the President of the Republic, Chadli Bendjedid", this Algerian said in an interview in London. He loathed al-Ghazali passionately, for not using his great popularity to enforce Islamic influence in his country.[27] At the same time, Algerian secularists equally hated al-Ghazali, but for opposing reasons (see Chapter 1).

For his part, al-Ghazali found much in the outlooks both of Algeria's self-styled defenders of Islam and of its self-styled secularists with which to disagree, not just their views on gender.[28] For example, a preoccupation with *jinn* and magical practices infuriated him. In the hope that the pious al-Ghazali could exorcise a spirit that was inhabiting his body, an Algerian man knocked at the shaykh's home one night. "You're a big guy, why do you not take possession of this *jinni* instead of it seizing you?", al-Ghazali scornfully advised him. He wanted those who were troubled by hearing voices to seek medical help, not exorcism. To some, this appeared flippant, the wrong "Islamic" answer to the possessed man's predicament, but al-Ghazali widely publicized the incident, challenging his people's perceptions. Why do the *jinn* seem to affect Muslims only? he asked; "I cannot understand it; why do they [*jinn*] avoid the Japanese or Germans?"[29]

At the centre of al-Ghazali's conflict in Algeria lay profound cultural disagreements with an angry younger generation seeking change. The clashes did not only originate in religious views, as al-Ghazali saw it; neither did they constitute proof of Algeria's sub-standard understanding of Islam. Instead, his North African troubles drew al-Ghazali's attention to how dangerous the boorish discourse of the twentieth-century Islamists had become, and how widespread. He recognized similar outlooks among these new spokespeople of Islam at home in Egypt, which he had previously overlooked.[30] According to an Algerian associate, one of the Shaykh's daughters, Afaf, finally led him away from the turmoil that surrounded him in North Africa. She travelled to Algeria to persuade her ailing father there was not much else he could do there. Mohammed al-Ghazali did not resist, and returned home to Egypt with her.[31]

The missing women

Before moving to Algeria, al-Ghazali had experienced another cultural conflict, which raised more questions than just about the place of women (as discussed in later chapters). From his own writings, it appears that these 1970s encounters in Islam's holiest places helped to spark his reconsideration of many popular *fiqh* rules. But why, following his clash with President Sadat—in which al-Ghazali had opposed new legislation that would guarantee women's rights—would have leaving Egypt to join Saudi Arabia's religious establishment have triggered a radical re-assessment of *fiqh* rules about women? As a celebrated guest of their elite circle of *'ulama*, every detail of al-Ghazali's world was catered for by his Saudi hosts, shielding him from the chores of daily life. That meant that in the absence of members of his family, he saw no women, talked to no women, and heard no women. Women vanished from al-Ghazali's world. At first glance such settings would seem consistent with the *fiqh* rules that restrict women's access to public space, which al-Ghazali advocated in his famous book *Min Huna Na'lam*, as the examples above show. While many twentieth-century Egyptian migrants ended up embracing the practices of their Saudi host society, insisting that these Saudi gender rules were the correct Islamic norms, al-Ghazali concluded the reverse. Why was that? Why did he see a significant clash between *fiqh*'s worldview and reality?

As a young boy in the green fields of his Nile Delta village, al-Ghazali constantly encountered, at weekly markets and town celebrations, not to mention as patrons visiting his father's tiny corner shop, "peasant women without a blemish on their character, roam[ing] without *hijab*", as he once described them.[32] Such women casually covered their hair with paper-thin black cloth in line with village custom, but not out of a particular religious zeal. As a renowned Azhari, his encounters with women increased rather than diminished. This *'alim* sat on committees in which he examined, applauded, or criticized women master's degree and doctoral candidates; his world included women colleagues of high stature, such as 'Aisha abd al-Rahaman (d. 1998), a celebrated Qur'anic scholar, or the younger Amna Nosseir, a former dean of the Azhar College for girls (in Alexandria) and one of his co-members in the Higher Council for Muslim (*fiqh*) Affairs (al-Majlis al-'Ala li al-Sho'un al-Islamyyia). In an interview, Nosseir provided a glimpse of the particular Cairo setting where senior *'ulama*, both men and women, mixed. She spoke at length of al-Ghazali's candid critiques of their learned community, remembering his good humour and some of the jokes with which he couched his criticisms of their scholarship.[33] The total absence of women from public life in his new Saudi Arabian settings, unpractical in Egypt, flooded al-Ghazali's mind with questions. A portrait from inside al-Ghazali's evolving life at home may help throw light on why his move to Arabia at that time, and for as long as it was, could have triggered reflections on the discrepancies between famous *fiqh* arguments which he advocated until the 1970s, and what he accepted as the right order of the world.

Portrait: From the family album: Hijab, marriage, and identity

Facing the Nile, the imposing old building had not lost its grandeur; neither revolution nor years of socialism had obscured its luxurious façade. Many floors up, inside the building, I stand facing the name inscribed elegantly on the door of the flat: Ihsan abd al-Quddous. A most unlikely place to search for al-Ghazali. It is here, in Ihsan's modern, plush Cairo home, where Mohammed al-Ghazali's legacy reigns supreme today, years after both al-Ghazali and Ihsan have gone. If it seems ironic, many in al-Ghazali's world, including his family and friends, find it ordinary.

No two figures better encapsulate the two opposing narratives that competed in twentieth-century Egypt than Mohammed al-Ghazali and Ihsan abd al-Quddous (d. 1990). If al-Ghazali embodies the Islamic vision in his time, abd al-Quddous became Egypt's most charming symbol of modernity. Their backgrounds also together sum up the emerging multi-layered modern Egyptian identity. Whereas al-Ghazali's story started with a villager father who decided his vocation, abd al-Quddous's started with an ultramodern mother who shaped her son's world in many ways. Born in Lebanon to a Christian family, Ihsan's mother, Rose al-Yusuf, came to Egypt as an orphaned child. At a time when Egyptian women were struggling merely to find their voices, the teenage Rose had begun a career in acting, which eventually earned her the nickname "the Sarah Bernhardt of the Arabic theatre", after the famous late nineteenth- to early twentieth-century French actress. As an adult, Rose converted to Islam and changed her name to Fatima. One successful career was never going to be enough for this energetic woman, who had acquired a taste of independence very early in life. Fatima therefore turned to journalism, setting up a magazine in 1925 which she named after herself: *Rosa al-Youssef*.[34] Long after this celebrated trendsetter died, the weekly *Rosa al-Youssef* continued to thrive as a forum for daring views. As a publisher, Fatima al-Yusuf also sought a voice in Egyptian political life, even organizing a campaign against the corruption of the Wafd party. More accomplished than her struggling actor husband, Ihsan's father, she divorced him and remarried twice, as she pressed forward with her sparkling career. She gave her adopted country a new model of womanhood, which Egypt embraced, entrenching this woman in the country's memory of its modern identity.

It is no small feat that abd al-Quddous's reputation eventually outshone that of his multi-talented mother; turning his back on a legal education, he worked for Fatima as a journalist at her magazine. Journalism appealed to abd al-Quddous's innovative nature and provided him with many public platforms that he effectively used to advocate civil freedoms and campaign for his country's independence. Reporting also allowed abd al-Quddous to gratify his talent for story-writing, and he eventually gained a reputation as a novelist. His artistic, dynamic character, not to mention his remarkably good looks, ensured Ihsan a distinctive place in his country's affluent circles, during a period that some called Egypt's *Belle Époque* before the Free Officers Movement takeover/ revolution in 1952. Even today, his career and dashing looks capture the imagination of his fellow Egyptians, inspiring storylines for many television soap operas.[35] Even after the Free Officers' Revolution altered the social and political life of the country, abd al-Quddous continued to shine as a journalist and novelist. Despite censorship and the nationalization of the media, he did not give up, even holding prominent positions at Egypt's two major newspapers, *Akhbar al-Youm* and *Al-Ahram*.

Al-Ghazali and abd al-Quddous both achieved fame during the 1950s, albeit for careers heading in strikingly different directions. Al-Ghazali called for restrictions on women's dress and their presence in public, while abd al-Quddous opened the doors to their most tantalizing worlds with titles such as *I Am Free*, *A Man in Our House*, and *A Nose and Three Eyes*. Some of his novels crossed the line set by Egyptian society as to the limits of decency in relation to gender issues; and many Arabic speakers who did not, or could not, read these stories instead saw the film versions or listened to radio adaptations, of which there have been many since the early 1960s. In the battle to shape the identity of modern Egyptians, al-Ghazali stood at one end and abd al-Quddous stood at the other: Islam and modernity appeared to be at loggerheads. Unchecked, the tension which resulted from this polarity has always had the potential to tear Egypt apart.

A VIEW OF THE NILE

A Nubian butler in uniform opens the door; he shows the way into the spacious sitting room that eventually widens into a splendid view of the Nile.[36] The youngest of al-Ghazali's daughters soon emerges, fully enfolded in a black dress and head-cover, and glowing with a welcoming smile. The child of the *faqih* who for many years disallowed women access to public agency (and spaces) is also the daughter-in-law of Egypt's symbol of modern secularism. The links between the two families tell a compelling story. If modernity and Islam stand at opposite poles, al-Ghazali's and abd al-Quddous's family ties reveal the complexity and nuances of this polarization in the second half of twentieth-century Egypt. They also symbolize the many turns that have enveloped Egyptian society since that time. Although Ihsan abd al-Quddous's name is still inscribed with pride on his home, the place has been transformed into another headquarters for the propagation of Islam as the solution for Egyptian problems. After I found my way there, Afaf recounted her memories and impressions in the course of three more visits, providing portraits from her family's album to help situate al-Ghazali in his multi-layered Cairrene milieu.

THE MARRIAGE

My first question was: How did the marriage take place between the children of two men who had been advocating conflicting visions for Egyptian modern identity? According to Afaf, the union took place when, in a chance visit to al-Ghazali's home, abd al-Quddous's son, Mohammed, ran into Afaf, fell in love with her, and asked her father for permission to marry her. In al-Ghazali's domestic setting, young men can see and talk to young women, albeit within appropriate decorum. When his daughter welcomed the young abd al-Quddous's proposal, neither Mohammed al-Ghazali nor Ihsan al-Ghazali objected to the union, according to Afaf. Al-Ghazali had one stipulation, however: first, he wanted to meet with her future father-in-law. The way she described it, this meeting between al-Ghazali abd al-Quddous revealed something of Egypt: they drank tea, ate sweets, and then exchanged jokes. Realizing that their children had put them in close proximity, these formidable men with opposing visions sought common ground, which they quickly found in their shared concern for social and political justice in their country. Subsequently, they turned this common concern into a new narrative: at the door of their homes, they let go of the Islamic-versus-modernist narratives of their respective camps; moving away from the "type" of discourse to its "goal", the Azhari Shaykh and the secular novelist saw in each other worthy champions of Egypt and the dignity of its vulnerable communities. The move served the two men well enough. Al-Ghazali, who openly attempted to censor other novelists, including the Nobel Prize winner Naguib Mahfouz, had only high praise for abd al-Quddous.[37] Al-Ghazali chose to highlight abd al-Quddous's patriotism, not his novels that exposed feminine passions. He explained to an interviewer that no "religious, civil, military, or artistic" leadership could ever prevail without the precious qualities that Ihsan abd al-Quddous possessed. When he stood up to Presidents Nasser and then Sadat, abd al-Quddous demonstrated his true calibre, al-Ghazali elaborated.[38] The way al-Ghazali adopted to converse with the novelist allowed him to view abd al-Quddous and himself in similar terms.

Seeing abd al-Quddous primarily as a man devoted to the service of their shared country, al-Ghazali did not object that, after her marriage, Afaf moved in with her husband's family in his Westernized, even secular, home; and Mohammed continued to be inspired by the Islamic vision of his father-in-law, not his father's modernist-secular perspective. There are many questions about how these two visions coexisted, and with what consequences. Their closeness does not match the common Western narrative on Muslim society, nor for that matter some Islamic rules on women which al-Ghazali explained in works such as in his celebrated book *Min Huna Na'lam*.

ISLAMIC DRESS

One such question relates to Islamic dress for women. Afaf duly provided more snapshots of their personal life, remembering how her father repeatedly counselled the family that a woman ought to cover her hair as well as dress in colours that emphasized self-respect. Al-Ghazali's five daughters responded differently to their father's advice. Some of her sisters listened to him, but as a teenager and university student, and even later, as a married woman, Afaf did not cover her head. And al-Ghazali did not force his wishes on his girls, she said. But, "thank God", she now embraced the *hijab*, which by the late twentieth century meant hair-covering only. She decided to cover her hair after years of living under the roof of Egypt's scion of modernity, Ihsan abd al-Quddous. In this thoroughly Westernized setting, the significance of the head-cover finally dawned on al-Ghazali's youngest daughter. Joining abd al-Quddous's world might have brought Afaf and her father into closer contact with modernity, leading to a nuanced appreciation of the West, but it also challenged the shaykh's daughter. The *hijab* may have served as the ultimate shield with which Afaf could peacefully defy the hegemony of a foreign culture that encircled her family life in Zamalek; her mode of dress became the persistent but silent expression of her independence. One can only guess. Afaf is not an exception among al-Ghazali's children: his devout sons married women who did not—and some still do not—cover their hair. In al-Ghazali's family, the head-cover was a matter of choice, and published photos show that this was also the case in the households of numerous Azhari shaykhs until the 1970s. Is it that power relations, rather than some doctrinal rule, decide the debates on women's dress, at least in the case of modern Egypt?

BOUNDARIES OF FAMILY LIFE

According to Afaf, her marriage to Mohammed abd al-Quddous brought her into a close family. She recounted a story of how compassionate her parents-in-law had been when she had been ill, although they fundamentally disagreed with her approach to treatment. She sought relief from her ailment in supplication at dawn prayers, while they insisted on, and indeed booked, a medical appointment in Switzerland. Although Afaf may have selectively retained only happy memories, her marriage to Mohammed abd al-Quddous and life at his parents' home has lasted for many years, revealing great accommodation and not only tensions in the lives of modern Egyptians with opposing visions. The region's age-old perceptions of family may have also facilitated this outcome. In Afaf's mind, her husband's loyalty to his parents, like her loyalty to her husband, was total and absolute. As proof of a wife's unquestioning obligations towards her husband (and his family), she recounts a Hadith in which the Prophet is reported to have said that, "If I were to command anyone to prostrate to a creature other than

God, I would have commanded woman to prostrate to her husband."[39] Hearing this, I fidget uncomfortably in my chair. Finally, I decide to remind al-Ghazali's daughter that her father had condemned that very Hadith as false, un-Islamic, and demeaning to women. "Oh, very well then; you know what I mean", she said, moving on calmly with her conversation. Despite its seemingly carefully defined exterior, as the rest of Egypt, the cultural plane on which Afaf and her family live allows considerable space for opposing visions.

In truth, Afaf and her husband Mohammed may have embraced much of Ihsan abd al-Quddous's legacy too. Or, maybe, observed from another angle, his and al-Ghazali's legacies were not all that different after all. That is how Mohammed sees it. This Islamist often writes about how he followed in the footsteps of his father, the inspiring Ihsan, in areas such as his championship of women, but from a Muslim point of view. Also, when the time came, the family did not send al-Ghazali's grandson to al-Azhar or a similarly Islamic institution; they instead sent him to a university in the United States. But, al-Ghazali's son-in-law noted, such liberal and Muslim views "do not conflict with one another".[40] Following in the footsteps of their famous forefathers, their children found the measure of their self-worth and faith in advocacy, the same vision that Ihsan abd al-Quddous and al-Ghazali shared. Afaf and her husband supported any voice of political or social opposition that raised an Islamic banner; for a decade after al-Ghazali's death, at every single demonstration that took place in Cairo during Mubarak's rule, without fail—whether demanding civil rights, or condemning American actions in Iraq and Afghanistan or Israeli bombings of Jenin—one was sure to find Mohammed abd al-Quddous at its head. At many of these desperate street protests, it was not unusual to find his wife Afaf marching by his side, albeit head-covered and in black clothing.[41] One of the earliest photos of the Tahrir Square Revolution shows five plainclothes policemen dragging into the street the man who was al-Ghazali's son-in-law and Ihsan abd al-Quddous's son: Mohammed was arrested on 26 January, 2011, the second day of the demonstrations that eventually toppled President Mubarak. Both al-Ghazali and Ihsan would have found in his protests a fulfilment of theirs.

About women or governance?

Al-Ghazali only drew on his surroundings. By the 1980s, in the world in which he lived the women of his village no longer played any central roles; normality now meant that his daughters went to universities, just like other aspiring middle-class young Cairenes of their age. He had learned from the Prophet about the obligation to educate girls as well as boys, was how al-Ghazali described his parenting philosophy.[42] And, learning did not translate into so-called Islamic education, such as the troubling diet which al-Azhar in its current state offered to students, and from which he had earlier suffered, he explained.[43] Instead, his children went to modern universities.[44]

A further catalyst to al-Ghazali's re-assessment of communal perceptions of women may have been the loss of his beloved wife: "Happiness deserted my world when she died", he lamented.[45] She also assisted him in preparing his books, he revealed, adding that "it is tough on a man to be with a stupid, ignorant woman."[46] However, nothing in al-Ghazali's personal life explains his reconsideration of Shari'a rules on whether a woman could legitimately lead men and rule over whole communities; yet he became the first leading *'alim* to tell the common Muslim that, when correctly applied, Shari'a did not bar women from holding senior public office. At last, Shari'a, and not accidents of fate, underpinned female civic authority in the Arabic-speaking world.

During a lecture in the UAE, al-Ghazali announced:

> By the One God, if in Egypt a woman came to me to say that she would follow Islam's ways, and [I find in her] a qualified leader, such as Thatcher is, I would tell her: "[Go ahead] rule [Egypt]; you are more eligible [to lead us] than those with moustaches and beards. Rule us."[47]

Al-Ghazali thus alerted his auidence to a hereto unknown Shari'a rule that had the potential to modify the political landscape: access to senior executive offices was open only to the competent, but this included qualified women. Political authority in accordance with Shari'a appeared suddenly to no longer require being a male. But why resort to the example of Margaret Thatcher so explicitly?

As expected, observers tie this radical new rule to al-Ghazali's changed perceptions of gender. However, his primary concern lay elsewhere. In fact, he was following his old pattern of the 1960s, when he raised the issue of Islamic dress. Although he continued to insist that hair-covering represented correct Islamic practice, he later clarified that he did not really wish to make it a priority; he condemned those who elevated outward appearances, including dress, into a central Muslim concern. As noted earlier, he actually wanted to oppose economic inequality and the disquieting loss of Egypt's cultural sovereignty.[48]

What proof could Margret Thatcher offer?

In the winter of 1990, during a lecture, a questioner complained: "At a time when crisis and [illicit] license abound", what was the wisdom of al-Ghazali's unprecedented "license" for women such as Thatcher to hold political office? Al-Ghazali could not resist the opportunity to discuss the ultimate taboo subject in the Arab region: governance. "What is it that disturbs you about Thatcher?", he challenged the questioner. "Was she leading Egypt or Saudi Arabia? [...] We have no woman who is [presently] seeking to be premier."[49] Not one to leave his position vague, al-Ghazali told the crowded hall: "Let me testify [here] that Thatcher is a far superior [head of state] than seventy [of our Muslim rulers] with beards and moustaches."[50]

A socialist at heart, al-Ghazali knew little about the image of "Thatcher, the Milk Snatcher", with which many Britons associated this Prime Minister. Writings such as *Qadhayia al-Ma'ra*, a book on women, indicate why she caught al-Ghazali's attention. A summary of one of her speeches, translated by the BBC, gave him the impression that Thatcher's sentiments accorded with Muslim principles, which encouraged faith and the quest for prosperity, and he praised how she made no apologies for being a Christian.[51] What interested him in Thatcher became immediately clear when, to conclude his discussion, al-Ghazali turned to a prominent journalist, Mustafa Amin, reiterating his plea for political accountability, which would allow the nation to know who governed it, instead of the Egyptian practice by which cabinet members appeared to spring "from the belly of the earth".[52] In other words, the example of Thatcher demonstrated what happens when people are able to choose who governs them, which al-Ghazali so longed for. Also, she gave him cover by which he could circumvent the ban on public discussions of political legitimacy; what Arab government would dare censor praise of Thatcher?

Seventeen years after her departure from office, the BBC's Andrew Marr described Margret Thatcher's years as "a one-woman revolution, a hurricane in human form" that transformed Britain from a state in terminal decline, where even the gravediggers went on strike late in the 1970s, into a richer and stronger country.[53] Al-Ghazali had seen that hurricane, and the contrast between Britain's returning vigour in the 1980s and the feebleness of Muslim political systems was a cause for pain. He was not alone: Thatcher's tenure raised in many Muslim minds questions that had little to do with her policies or even with Britain. Unceasing media reports about "the Iron Lady" challenged their understanding of Shari'a. Thatcher's leadership exposed conflict between plain evidence and Islamic rules. Thatcher also appeared at the right time—it was just as al-Ghazali began considering some *fiqh* rules on women that his travel experiences had brought to his attention, as the portraits above show. Until then, many Muslims genuinely believed that female leadership would necessarily weaken societies, as the famous Prophetic Hadith instructed. The seeming success—or at least fame—of the first woman British Prime Minister posed two fundamental questions: Could reality be at odds with revelation? How reliable are Shari'a rules? Both required urgent answers. It was *how* al-Ghazali derived and then applied the answers to these challenges that mattered most. Best of all, Thatcher's tenure offered a familiar illustration of a hereto unfamiliar reality. Thanks to the increasing oil revenues in the 1970s and new technologies, ordinary people in the Middle East had greater access to the outside world. In newspapers and on Arab television screens and radio bulletins, al-Ghazali and his fellow Arabic-speakers watched the news pouring in about this woman leader. They heard how other nations, including the two superpowers of the time, followed some of Thatcher's controversial initiatives.

Visiting Britain

A visit to the United Kingdom may have further advanced al-Ghazali's reconsideration of the age-old Muslim questions about the qualifications and parameters of public office. British Muslim leaders treated al-Ghazali like royalty when he visited their country. In their eyes, he signified a high religious authority, and they sought him out for answers to key challenges that faced them in the West. In his eyes, many of them appeared to be living in a precarious bubble. It struck this leader of mainstream Islam that a single, and what he regarded as irrelevant, question preoccupied the community's leaders: whether or not it was possible for Margaret Thatcher, a woman, to be what she already was, the British prime minister.[54] His hosts did not deliberate injustices in their communities or outside them; their only preoccupation concerned a woman leading their country. Everywhere he visited, the most influential of his British Muslim hosts urged al-Ghazali for a definitive "Islamic declaration" against the Thatcher aberration. However, he was instead preoccupied with comparing their Britain to the usual Arab system of government, including that of President Mubarak at home. Why had British Muslim leaders failed to grasp the obvious?, he wondered: that living in a woman-led Britain they had rights that Muslim rulers had extinguished for centuries. Their endless pious repetition of antiquated phrases irritated him no end. That his British Muslim hosts equated the soundbites that they had picked up from *fiqh* works or Hadith literature, without fully understanding their import, revealed "a dangerous vacuum of intellect", he said.[55] Al-Ghazali did not soften his criticism: he described these British Muslim leaders as no better than "a herd of sheep".[56] In France and the United States he also found much that disturbed him among Muslim communities.[57]

The following chapter discusses the process by which al-Ghazali deduced the new principle on women in public office from the Qur'an and the evidence of how to apply this Divine principle correctly. However, the novelty of an effective woman Prime Minster led to a painful self-search. Again, al-Ghazali turned to empirical observation, finding proofs in contemporary and historical records, which, he believed, Muslims had unwisely ignored. It had never been the United Kingdom's Conservative Party leader that really preoccupied al-Ghazali, but that the example of Thatcher offered an immediate and high-profile illustration. From thereon, al-Ghazali taunted his fellow Arabic-speakers: "Who defeated us, Muslims", over many centuries? He answered his own questions: states headed by females, such as Indira Gandhi, Queen Victoria, Queen Isabella, and Golda Meir.[58] As he saw it, historical and contemporary observation undermined Muslim assumptions rather than supported the Muslim perspective, as he had once believed.

It had not been modernism, feminism, or even women's rights that led to the radical change in Shari'a rules that he deduced concerning women's access to civic authority. It was a story of continuities, of an ancient, ever-altering rulemaking process and of resistance, taking up old unfinished battles in Muslim societies. Al-Ghazali's adjustment of these Shari'a rules can be summarized in two phrases: political resistance and historical narratives, and the result was Shari'a-prescribed female civic authority finally being accepted by the Arabic-speaking street.

Conclusion

Al-Ghazali began by reproducing familiar *fiqh* rules about gender. He connected the defence of these rules to the Muslim struggle against foreign powers over sovereignty.[59] In his mind, real sovereignty was cultural and intellectual, and did not derive from merely symbolic political gestures. However, day-to-day and intellectual experiences led him to conclude that some of these famous *fiqh* rules on gender were neither Islamic nor sound, and this led him to launch a full-scale war on how his old "orthodox" allies perceived women and, just as significantly, how they deduced Shari'a rules. Al-Ghazali spared no one. During the first Gulf War in 1990, by which time he was an icon of Sunni Islam, he openly ridiculed the Saudi religious establishment for banning female drivers at a time when their government had invited American women as part of the United States forces to defend the country against threats from Saddam Hussein.[60] The commotion that followed shows the shaykh and his Sunni enemies each turning their perspectives on the world into Islamic texts. However, nothing is novel or modern about these debates, or the changes in Shari'a rulemaking they produced. This raises important questions: if immediate contexts or political concerns lay behind many of the above-discussed rules, at least in the case of al-Ghazali, what then is specifically Islamic about them? Should researchers always examine *fiqh* arguments through the yardsticks of their particular contexts, rather than via often long-winded, and mostly irrelevant and vague, discussions on theology? What is it in the nature of Shari'a rule-/lawmaking that allows two opposite rules to be both referred to as Islamic? Chapters 6 and 7 address these questions, starting with how al-Ghazali employed divine instructions in deducing new Shari'a rules on women's eligibility to hold positions of public authority.

Notes

1. My gratitude to Professor Amira Sonbol, who very early on advised me to write an article based on sections of this chapter, which she later included among far more valuable contributions in her book Amira Sonbol, ed., *Beyond the Exotic: Women's Histories in Islamic Societies* (Syracuse: Syracuse University Press, 2005).
2. Mohammed al-Ghazali, "Qissat Haya", *Islamiyat al-Ma'rifa* 2/3 (2007): 155.
3. Mohammed al-Ghazali, *Min Huna Na'lam* (Cairo: Dar al-Kutub al-Haditha, n.d.), 180.
4. Ibid.
5. Ibid.
6. Ibid.
7. Ibid., 200.
8. Ibid., 206.
9. Ibid., 201.
10. Ibid., 202–205.
11. Ibid., 204.
12. Ibid., 198.
13. Ibid.
14. Ibid.
15. Ibid.
16. Ibid.
17. Leila Ahmed, *Women and Gender in Islam: Historical Roots of a Modern Debate* (New Haven, CT: Yale University Press, 1992), 11–39.
18. Ibid., 207.
19. Al-Ghazali, *Min Huna Na'lam*, 200. Similar arguments were advanced by his teacher, the famous Shaykh Mahmoud Shaltut, to restrict *ijtihad* of women in his *Al-Islam 'Aqida wa Shari'a*, 2nd edn (Cairo: Dar al-Qalam, n.d.), 567. Later, the shift in Ghazali's discussions on women becomes clearer when compared to his reformist teacher in Mahmoud Shaltut, *Al-Qur'an wa al-Mar'a* (Cairo: Jamiat al-Azhar, al-Markaz al-Dawli li al-Dirasat wa al-Bohouth al-Sukkanyia, 1975).
20. Al-Ghazali, *Min Hna Na'lam*, 200.
21. "*la yaflihu Qawmun walu amrihim imra'a*", al-Bukhari, *Sahih* (4425); and under "Ban on Women as Rulers", in Nisa'i, *Sunan* (8/227).
22. Al-Ghazali, *Min Huna Na'lam*, 197.
23. For a contemporary brief description of *ijtihad* requirements, in which a former head of al-Azhar's Fatwa Council discusses Shari'a lawmaking and realities, see Gamal Qotb, "Sources of Authority", *Al-Ahram Weekly* 864, 27 September–3 October, 2007 (Online: http://weekly.ahram.org.eg/2007/864/sc1.htm).
24. Marshal Hodgson, *The Venture of Islam*, vol. 1: *The Classical Age of Islam* (Chicago: Chicago University Press, 1977), 82.
25. Eyewitness account by Fahmy Huwaidi, given via telephone interview with author, 8 January, 2004. An account similar in tone, albeit with different details, appears in several reports, including one posted on *Islamonline* in response to a request for advice about how best to carry the message of Islam (*da'wa*) (online, archived at http://web.archive.org/web/20060724165111/http://www.islamonline.net/servlet/Satellite?pagename=IslamOnline-English-Ask_Scholar/FatwaE/FatwaE&cid=1119503545048).
26. Author interview with Huwaidi.
27. Author interview with Algerian asylum seeker in Britain who wished to remain anonymous, The Strand, London, 1997.
28. For al-Ghazali's Algerian experience, from an admirer's point of view, see Ammar al-Talibi, "Al-Shaykh al-Ghazali Kama 'Ariftahu fi al-Jaza'ir", *Islamiyat al-Ma'rifa* 2/3 (2007): 49–70; for

a general discussion of Algerian "Islamists", including al-Ghazali's influence on them, see Luc-Willy Deheuvels, *Islam et Pensee Contemporaire en Algerie* (Paris: CNRS, 1991).

29. Al-Ghazali, videotape interviews (#TAYR-1, #TAYR-2); Mustafa abd al-'Ala, "Fi Hiwar Khas Jidan ma' Saidati, al-Shaykh al-Ghazali yatahadath 'an al-Jinn wa al-'Afarit", *Saidati*, 11–17 May, 1996.
30. Al-Ghazali, videotape interviews (#TAYR-1, #TAYR-2).
31. Al-Talibi, "al-Shaykh al-Ghazali Kama", 55.
32. Al-Ghazali, *Min Huna Na'lam*, 194–195.
33. Author interview with Amna Nosseir, Madinat Nasir, Cairo, 29 March, 1999.
34. See www.rosaelyoussef.com/.
35. One example is the 1999 Egyptian soap opera *Hawanim Garden City* (*The Ladies of Garden City*).
36. Author interviews with Afaf al-Ghazali, Zamalek, Cairo, May 1998–September 2003.
37. On one hand, Shaykhs al-Ghazali, Mohammed Abu Zahra, and al-Sharabasi tried to persuade the Egyptian President Gamal abd al-Nasser to ban Nagib Mahfouz's novel *Awlad Haritna*. The reason, al-Ghazali later explained in the Kuwait City *Al-Watan* (24 January, 1992, 11), was its disrespect for the Deity and Prophets. On the other hand, he had nothing but praise for abd al-Quddous. See Midhat al-Bassyoni, *Al-Haqiqa al-Gha'iba bayna Khaled Mohammed Khaled wa Mohammed al-Ghazali* (Cairo: no publisher, 1979), 169–170.
38. "Al-Shaykh al-Ghazali Yatahdathu 'an Ihsan abd al-Qodous", *Al-Ahrar*, 17 November, 1994; Midhat al-Bassyoni, *Al-Haqiqa al-gha'iba bayna Khaled*.
39. Abu Hurayra reported the Prophet to have said, "If I were to command any creature to prostrate to another, I would have commanded women to prostrate to their husbands." This is a report found in a number of Hadith collections, e.g. *Sunan al-Tirmidhi*, 1159; *Sahih Sunan Ibn Majah*, 1853: "لو كنت آمرا احدا ان يسجد لغير الله لأمرت المرأة ان تسجد لزوجها".
40. Mohammed abd al-Quddous blogs under the name Ibn al-Tahrir wa Ibn al-Thawra (The Son of Tahrir and of the Revolution). There, he frequently celebrates what he describes as his exceptional father (Ihsan), grandmother (Rose al-Yusuf), and father-in-law (Mohammed al-Ghazali), insisting that their thought and aspirations for their country and peoples were not really antithetical, as some imagine (online: http://mohamedabdelkodos.blogspot.com).
41. The author first noted this couple at the head of a 1998 Cairo demonstration against Israeli bombing of Palestinians, then encountered Mohammed again several times in a much smaller gathering such as at Tal'at Harb Square, Cairo, in 2003. In this protest, a short distance from Tahrir Square, Mohammed abd al-Quddous held a loud-speaker calling his fellow countrymen to rally against Mubarak's undemocratic government.
42. Al-Ghazali, videotape interview (#S-1).
43. Ibid.
44. Al-Ghazali observed how al-Azhar refused to admit female students, and that when the Saudi state first introduced schools for girls, scores of that country's devout travelled to the capital Riyadh to object on the grounds that it violated Shari'a (Mohammed al-Ghazali, *Qadhayia al-Ma'ra bayna al-Taqaleed al-Rakida wa al-Wafida* [Cairo: Dar al-Shuruk, 1991], 36).
45. Al-Ghazali, videotape interview (#S-1).
46. Ibid. In the same interview al-Ghazali spoke admiringly of how he had read that the spouse of Thomas Arnold, the English historian who died in 1842, played an instrumental role in his work.
47. Quoted from a recorded lecture in Dubai, UAE, 1991. The private audio-recording was provided by Dr Mohammed Mushtahiri:

مداخلة لاحد المتشددين: "قلت له في..
والله لو جائتنى امرأة فى مصر وقالت انا سأقيم احكام الاسلام وكانت زى تاتشر كده فى القوة اقول لها احكمى،
انت احسن من ذوى الشوارب واللحى،

48. As noted earlier, al-Ghazali provided clues to why he wanted the state to impose Islamic dress in the 1960s. These included the cultural chaos in the Egyptian streets, and the stark economic disparities that dress further accentuated among his countrymen (Mohammed al-Ghazali, *Al-Sunna al-Nabawiya Bayna Ahl al-Fiqh wa ahl al-Hadith*, 5th edn [no location: Sahara, 1989], 86).
49. Mohammed al-Ghazali, *Al-Islam wa al-Mar'a* (Cairo: IIIT, 1990), 19.
50. Ibid.
51. Mohammed al-Ghazali, "al-Din 'Inda Thatcher wa 'Indina" (Comparing the Thatcher Government's Approach to Religion and Ours), in his *Qadhayia al-Ma'ra bayna al-Taqaleed al-Rakida wa al-Wafida*, 147.
52. Ibid., 148.
53. *Andrew Marr's History of Modern Britain* (TV documentary series, BBC, 2007).
54. Ibid.
55. Al-Ghazali, videotape interview (#W-2).
56. Ibid.
57. By the 1980s, al-Ghazali was voicing some strong views on Muslims living in the West. They included a warning that many who relocated from Muslim societies to Western ones imported old and corrupt ideas about Islam, instead of embracing its correct principles (interview by Nadir al-Quna in *Al-Watan* [Kuwait City], 14 February, 1997). A source who attended the Shaykh's meetings during his visit to the United States in the 1990s also claimed that al-Ghazali expressed concern about what he described as the psychologically troubled discourse of many converts to Islam in the West, "as if we do not have enough mentally troubled at home to be burdened with even more new ones", he is reported to have teased his American Muslim hosts.
58. "It was a woman, Golda Meir who defeated us in Suez; whatever happened to the bravado of the Arab macho men at the time? India's Indira Gandhi was the one who broke Pakistan's back, she too was a woman [...] Faced by her, Marshal Yahya Khan retreated [...] This is our problem. And who captured Andalusia? Isabella and her husband Ferdinand [...] So if you wish to think lowly of women, by all means do it, but never claim it is part of Islam. All I want is for the *umma* [our community] to understand its faith [... for many] people live in a fancy world thinking that the world will be bent according to their whims" (Quoted from a recorded lecture in Dubai, UAE, 1991; the private audio-recording was provided by Dr Mohammed Mushtahiri).
59. Al-Ghazali, "Qissat Haya", 194.
60. Al-Ghazali, *Al-Islam wa al-Mar'a*, 2.

SIX

The Contents: Scripture—The Almighty and Women's Leadership

It is a truism that Sha'ri'a rule-/lawmaking is regarded by adherents as being the interpretation of divine commands. However, although this is widely understood, there is less understanding of how instructions revealed by God actually determine *fiqh* rules. In the previous chapter, we saw how al-Ghazali's changing views on women and civic authority (*wilaya*) related to the contexts of his life; this chapter focuses on how he approached scripture to derive opposing rules on the same issue at different times.

The origins of many *fiqh* rules are to be found in how Muslims have dealt with the tension between the divine and the mundane over the centuries. This chapter starts with a discussion of Muslim approaches to what they believe to be the actual words of God, the Qur'an, using as an example how al-Ghazali employed its contents at different times to derive rules on women's leadership. It then discusses al-Ghazali's approaches to the Sunna, the second source of Shari'a rule-/lawmaking, which is derived from the reported sayings, deeds, or rulings of the Prophet. In time, these Hadiths themselves came to be considered scripture, albeit often implicitly, although layers of tension resulting from these developments were never resolved. The discussion below includes contemporary illustrations of this tension, which triggered al-Ghazali's concerns about the legacy of Hadith.

Approaching the Word of God

Until the early 1970s, al-Ghazali derived universal, sacred principles on women from famous *fiqh* arguments and Hadith reports. This has been the Muslim rulemaking norm for centuries, notwithstanding the prescription about the primacy of the Qur'an. By the late 1980s al-Ghazali had adjusted this approach. After reviewing Hadiths, he concluded that these common rulemaking practices that relied on Hadiths had effectively turned disorderly reports and human arguments into the main sources for Islam, thereby "burying" the Qur'an. He insisted that fellow Muslims must elevate the Word of God to the conclusive foundation of all universal principles in practice, not just in theory.

A *faqih*'s return to the Qur'an as the matchless source of Shari'a is not as straightforward as it may sound, however. Muslims have devoted great attention to their scripture from earliest times, treating it as the foundation of learning as well as the guide for living to which changing circumstances ought to be aligned. Communities in Asia, Europe, and Africa all used the Qur'an as the basis for research into any subject, including science and philosophy and other secular subjects, leading to the development of an enormous literary corpus of exegetical works (*tafaseer*, sing. *tafsir*). Many of these commentaries, and the narratives which sustained them, eventually acquired semi-sacred status, becoming indispensable lenses through which to read the Qur'an. Some modern Muslims recognized the burden and not just the value of this inherited library and successfully drew attention to the need to re-evaluate it; an example here is the school of Gamal al-Din al-Afghani and Mohammed Abduh at al-Azhar, discussed in Chapters 1 and 3. Al-Ghazali inherited both traditions: the *weltanschauung* that regarded old commentaries on the Qur'an as semi-sacred, and, from his famous Azhari teachers, the drive to appraise them critically.

Al-Ghazali eventually concluded that he too could no longer accept some of the preconceptions and methods with which celebrated works in the Muslim library approached the Word of God. Like other prominent modern Azharis, al-Ghazali rejected *naskh*, a key *fiqh* instrument whereby some Qur'anic texts are deemed to have been revoked and therefore do not apply in deducing rules.[1] *Naskh*, he believed, was a misguided human construct, particularly its "sick claim" that a Hadith report can abrogate verses of the Qur'an.[2] Al-Ghazali celebrated the wealth of information on Muslim cultural history that Qur'anic exegeses preserved, but, he insisted, they could not speak on behalf of the divine; *tafaseer* only reflected their authors' scholarly interests and the particular age in which they lived. He gave examples of how the branches of learning that preoccupied famous exegeses multiplied: into linguistic-grammatical exercises, as in *Tafsir al-Zamakhshari*; into philosophy and theology (*kalam*), as in *Tafsir al-Razi*; into collections of anecdotal and Hadith material, as in *Tafsir Ibn Kathir* and *Tafsir al-Tabari*;[3] and into the investigation of rulemaking, as in the *Tafsir* of *al-Qurtubi*, or *al-Khazen*.[4] Al-Ghazali liked this last *tafsir* "because it [was] easy and simple", but he went on to explain that a close inspection showed that "the man [al-Khazen] loved untruths, he opened a door of evil." Such an engaging, witty, and accessible *tafsir* "turned out to be a storehouse of superstitions", he said.[5] Centuries of comments on God's revelation did not just contain records of remarkable intellectual endeavour, al-Ghazali observed; they also contained a large assortment of entertaining, absurd, or even destructive material. Here too, he only restated a common Sunni concern, albeit less cautiously: it is one thing to draw on the Qur'an's substance, and to use its material as catalysts for intellectual projects, whether they be in philology, mathematics, physics, cosmology, philosophy, law, or other subjects; but it is quite another to equate its divine verses with human suppositions. With all the changes going on around them, al-Ghazali concluded, loyalty to the actual Word of God required constant reconsideration of the Qur'an's overall contents in line with new human discoveries.[6] He showed the way here, reviewing the rules that he previously discovered in the name of Shari'a and, following in the footsteps of his outstanding Azhari teachers and colleagues, he started his own thematic commentary on the Qur'an.[7] And in one of his later books, published in the form of a dialogue with Omar Ubaid Hassana, a well-regarded scholar, al-Ghazali appraised how Muslims might have used or abused the Qur'an over the centuries.[8]

What does the Qur'an say about women's leadership (*wilaya*)?

Later in his life al-Ghazali argued that he elevated the Word of God to the primary source for deducing or overturning legal principles in practice, not just in theory. He now observed in the Qur'an a recurring theme: a general equality between women and men.[9] Al-Ghazali also found long-neglected rules. When he applied Q27.23–44 (*Al-Naml*), he concluded that even the senior civic positions were open to both genders. From his comparison of the Qur'an's portrayal of the Queen of Sheba to that of the Pharaoh of Egypt, he derived a constitutional principle, not a feminist one: "It is not a question of femininity versus masculinity", he wrote. The matter concerned integrity and aptitude, al-Ghazali added.[10] The Queen appeared as a wise, cautious, and successful ruler who governed by consultation, eventually leading her people to "what pleased God".[11] In contrast, the same scripture depicted the macho Pharaoh as a self-aggrandizing despot who eventually led his people into ruin.[12] The stories of these two monarchs made clear that the criteria for public leadership (*al-wilaya al-'ama*) was not gender, but based on considerations such as personal talent and governance by consultation. Al-Ghazali thus deduced a new Shari'a rule.[13]

The tendency to read the Qur'an through medieval works, rather than treating Qur'anic interpretation as an essential ongoing project, means that important shifts in mainstream Muslim thought are overlooked. Compare al-Ghazali's reading of Q27.23–44 with that of *Tafsir al-Jalalyn*, a most revered Qura'nic commentary, authored by two fifteenth-century Shafi'i *faqihs*, Jalal al-Din al-Suyuti and his teacher, Jalal al-din al-Mahalli.[14] While al-Ghazali derived guidelines on sound civil authority, *Tafsir al-Jalalyn* primarily focused on the Queen's sexuality. The Qur'anic story explains how in their first meeting the Queen of Sheba raised her dress when she mistook the shining glass material that covered the brilliant floor of Solomon's palace for water. *Tafsir al-Jalalyn* adds the following details to clarify the import of this encounter between the two monarchs: seeing the Queen raise her dress stirred Solomon's desire, but the royal romance faced an obstacle because Solomon "disliked the hair on her legs". However, of all God's creatures, the devils came to the rescue, inventing a body wax that allowed the Queen to remove it. With the Queen's unsightly body hair removed, Solomon then "married her, he loved her, and permitted her to continue as queen", this exegesis informs Muslims. It barely touches on lessons on governance that could be drawn from the account of these two rulers. If there is a point with public-legal significance, it appears to be that the Queen's authority became a mere extension of the King's. *Tafsir al-Jalalyn* reports that Solomon allowed this female sovereign to continue to rule her people, while paying her conjugal visits "once a month, staying [each time] for three days", but that her rule came to an end upon his death.[15] Such an exegesis raises troubling questions in the minds of those who believe in the eternal pre-eminence of their scripture; did such influential *tafsir* re-interpret the Qur'anic account of Solomon's encounter with the Queen of Sheba? From where had such additions to the Revelation originated, and why had Muslims accepted them?[16] Later in his life, al-Ghazali's verdict was unequivocal and public: alongside brilliant achievements, the "Islamic culture and [...] literary sources [...] are [also] full of poisons and drugs; there is an urgent need to sift them."[17]

Scriptural evidence against women

Although al-Ghazali could now dismiss the supplemental claims that famous *tafaseer* imposed on the scriptures, such as the one above, this still left the explicit Qur'anic references that he previously invoked to prohibit women's civic authority. For example, in the 1950s, following eminent *fuqaha* from the past, al-Ghazali cited Q2.228: "and men are a degree above them [women]", which he followed with a question: "How could a woman ever have authority over all men, in general, when Islam gave [one] man authority over her at home?"[18] Another commonly used scriptural reference, which al-Ghazali also quoted when he opposed women's right to public positions, is a phrase in Q4.34: "men have authority over women, according to what God favoured some of them over the other."

Forty years—and many actual and intellectual journeys—later, al-Ghazali looked at these verses again. Naturally, he did not reject them, but he now saw that the word order did not correspond to their legal implications, as argued in the famous *fiqh* works which he had previously quoted. He described these Qur'anic quotes as phrases that had been extracted from verses or divorced from their larger contexts. Q2.228 began by stating the universal principle that "they [women] have equal [rights] as those [obligations] upon them", al-Ghazali now explained.[19] The verse then qualified this general equality of rights and obligations with an end-phrase, that "men have a degree above them", to indicate an administrative exception in the case of divorce procedures and family matters.[20] He also argued that the commonly used reference from Q4.34 indicated yet another exception to the universal rule of equality, but this time in regard to particular marital details. Mohammed al-Ghazali likened marriage to "a ship that must have an appointed captain"; the Qur'an "assigned the default option for this captaincy to man", but this was justified (also in the same verse) in mundane, circumstance-specific terms, such as the customary economic dominance of males, he pointed out.[21] None of these phrases, taken out of context, could establish a permanent principle, al-Ghazali now insisted; the general rule must lie in the frequent statements about the equality of believing men and believing women. The Qur'anic story of the Queen of Sheba corroborated this view. Muslims took truncated phrases and turned them into universal rules, he explained, finally settling the matter with this question: "Did a people who agreed to be ruled by a woman of such a precious type really lose?"[22] In discovering this neglected Shari'a imperative, common-sense observation replaced Hadith as the confirmation of the Qur'anic intention. The Queen led her people into what pleased God, while Pharaoh led them to disaster, according to al-Ghazali's reading of the scripture, as mentioned earlier.

Hadith: The other divine source

Al-Ghazali's reading of the Qur'an, whether or not more perceptive and accurate than that of other *fuqaha*, could not provide a decisive ruling on its own. The Sunna of the Prophet, being real-life applications that clarify Revelation's intentions, remained central to all Shari'a rulemaking. Therefore, he had to consider the Sunna's sources. Historically, divine instructions against women's leadership usually originated in the Prophet's recorded directives, not the Qur'an, and al-Ghazali had himself previously relied on a Hadith that predicted ruin to communities run by women. However, al-Ghazali now explained that, whether intentionally or not, Muslims had read this genuine Hadith report out of context. The Prophet used the term "woman" here to refer to Persia, which was led at the time by a woman. Mohammed had only been reiterating a Qur'anic statement that told believers that the Romans would eventually conquer the Persians; the Hadith did not provide a precedent on women's leadership. And to suggest that it was possible for observed reality to contradict God's order would deny a main tenet of Islam, he argued.

In historical records, which now preoccupied him, al-Ghazali found a connection between norms that repressed women and repugnant competition for power, especially tyranny;[23] practices he rejected as "political paganism".[24] The Qur'an provided a real-life application in this case. Its account concerning Solomon's encounter with the South Arabian queen did not revolve around women as such, and the relevant verses were actually about principles of sound governance, he argued. The Queen of Sheba as described in the Qur'an ruled through consultation, leading al-Ghazali to regard her as a constitutional monarch, of a sort.[25] Had the woman leader of Persia in the often-cited Hadith instead headed a polity in which the monarch similarly ruled by consultation, becoming as "effective and democratic as Golda Meir", the former Israeli Prime Minster, for example, the Prophet's remark would have been different, al-Ghazali wrote.[26] For him, social and political developments muffled the sources of Shari'a when Muslims wrapped their own choices in divine clothes. Thereafter, no *madhhab* (school of thought) fully escaped al-Ghazali's censure. When both the Qur'an and a well-known Hadith indicated otherwise, the Shafi'i and Hanbali schools appeared capricious when they allowed a father to marry his daughter against her will, for example. *Al-wali al-mujbir*, a rule that permits a male guardian to impose his choice of a husband on female relatives, illustrated how *fiqh* sometimes "toed the line of old customs that humiliated woman and degraded her personality."[27] Al-Ghazali arrived at two general conclusions: first, that some *fiqh* rules conflated human avarice and divine imperatives out of greed for power; and second, that corrupted claims about the Prophet's precedents had long served to validate vile practices at home, in the street, and in government. Al-Ghazali explained that forged or misunderstood Hadith turned the Sunna into a tool for suppressing the Qur'an and violating the vulnerable in society.[28] He had no doubt now that many *fiqh* blunders had originated in faulty approaches to the second source of Shari'a lawmaking—and not merely in the inaccuracy of Hadith reports. He noted the examples of a distinguished twelfth-century Maliki *faqih*, al-Qadi 'Ayyadh, who "resorted to twisting Qur'anic verses" in order to preserve a single suspect Hadith,[29] and of an influential fourteenth-century Shafi'i *faqih*, Ibn Kathir, who, according to al-Ghazali, preferred to "reinterpret [Qur'anic] verses in order to preserve bizarre Hadiths."[30] In his final campaign, al-Ghazali successfully persuaded many ordinary Muslims in his country to regard Hadith reports as "tentative" rather than "confirmed" evidence for the Prophet's instructions. That is, he had revived age-old deliberations about valid authority in Islam; a very delicate issue now as it was then.

The Sunna: An uneasy trajectory

Muslims often pride themselves on the accessibility of their scripture and what they see as its common-sense accounts of deity and prophethood. They equally praise the transparency of their rule-/lawmaking. However, the historical evolution of the Sunna into the foremost source of Shari'a does not always correspond with these sentiments.

Described in modern legal terms, the Sunna refers to valid precedents that clarify how to apply Islam's universal principles. The key challenge that has faced Muslims since Islam's early period has been how best to approach and interpret these sources.[31] In Muslim rule-/lawmaking, precedent does not refer just to the decisions of earlier court cases, but encompasses a variety of authoritative past legal applications. Unsurprisingly, the most cherished precedents have always been the rulings, opinions, and deeds of the Prophet. But those of his disciples (the *sahaba*), and the practices of his community in Medina were also incorporated as, or argued to be, Sunna. This also became so for practices initiated by key political leaders and, of course, the judgements and opinions of distinguished experts in Shari'a rulemaking, the prominent *fuqaha*. To complicate matters further, Hadith collections eventually acquired a sacred aura. The reports they contain were eventually also regarded as independent sources of universal principles. This multi-layered notion of precedent has never been effectively organized; Islam has had no central religious authority, whether in theory or in earlier practice, to have undertaken such an alignment. This has posed a great predicament. Adopting Hadith collections as divine instructions confronted Muslims with critical questions that remain without conclusive answers. Are these accounts of the past a part of scripture? According to Islam, it is a fundamental tenet of faith that the Qur'an, God's literal Word, is the only divine text. How can this be reconciled with the assertion that reports of the Prophet's sayings are also sacred? And can one ignore the chequered history of these collections?

Muslims disagreed over reports that claimed to originate from the Prophet from earliest times, and have continued to do so throughout their history. Further, some Hadith reports do not accord with Qur'anic tenets. Muslims have also differed over how to use these accounts in making rules/laws, and many of these disagreements have been recorded. Disputes over what the Prophet might have said or done gave rise to multiple schools of thought (*madhahib*), each adopting a distinct approach to the Sunna. Of the key schools that still exist today, the earliest Hanafi *madhhab* distrusted the accuracy of many Hadith accounts and sought sound precedent in how the Qur'anic message applied to particular contexts, while the early Maliki *madhhab* located the genuine Sunna in the actual practices of the people of Medina, the Prophet's capital. A latecomer, the Hanbali *madhhab* accepted Hadith as the backbone of the Sunna, while the Shafi'i *madhhab*, despite having sought to balance all the approaches, entrenched Hadith as the reservoir of the Prophet's Sunna and as an incontestable source of rulemaking. The reasons are to be found in the events of their time—and not in theology, as is often imagined. The clearest shift coincided with a crisis about valid authority that reached its climax in the ninth century CE, with Muslim society rebelling against its rulers' attempts to dictate religious beliefs and scholars allied to the palace. Consequently, any reports about instructions of the Prophet became the ultimate arbiter in disputes. By the twelfth century CE, all *madhahib* had finally surrendered to the Hanbali and Shafi'i arguments on the Sunna, fully subscribing to the ever-expanding corpus of Hadith as commanding precedents. Schools of thought which had once critiqued the doubtful characteristics of Hadith compilations retreated from a position of criticism. In the following centuries, Hanafi scholars even produced numerous anecdotes that depicted their early founders as having been devoted to Hadith, rather than critical.[32] The transformation of diverse historical accounts into divine texts redefined the Sunna beyond its linguistic and early meanings as authoritative precedents; from thereon, a Hadith report, or even a number of contradictory Hadith reports, that any one *faqih* or particular school of *fiqh* selected could serve as a source of universal rules and be regarded as divine, even if the content did not correspond to the Qur'anic message, and even though Muslims continued to believe in the primacy of the Qur'an as the source for their faith and its rulemaking.

Redefining the Sunna

As a feature of rulemaking, Sunna predated Hadith, as is evident in the eighth-century CE Malik Ibn Anas's above-mentioned view of it as *'amal*.[33] The subsequent elevation of Hadith to the principal source of Islam, not just the Sunna, had arisen following a confluence of circumstances, besides political and dynastic challenges. With Islam's geographical expansion, accepting anecdotal, sometimes contradictory reports about the Prophet helped diverse groups preserve their worldviews. Many Hadith accounts converted an assortment of social, cultural, and political preferences into Islamic wisdom and supported the position of a harassed community against its rivals. Thus the Prophet is quoted as both praising and vilifying the Arabs, the Persians, the Turks, the Blacks, the Indians, and the Rum—the same ethnic factions who were competing for benefits in a cosmopolitan Muslim expanse at the time that the Hadith collections were expanding.[34] Invoking the authority of the Prophet to improve the position of a group in society even goes beyond Muslims. For example, to this day the monks of St Catherine's Monastery in Sinai hold dearly to a letter supposedly from the Prophet in which he granted them a perpetual deed proclaiming their ownership of this monastery in the Egyptian desert. Besides other inconsistencies in this precious document, the 639–640 CE Muslim conquest of Egypt took place after Mohammed's death in 632 CE, and it was largely unplanned, especially by the rulers of Medina.[35] This "Testament of Mohammed" demonstrates the importance of Hadith and similar reports about the Prophet as the product of political and social development over many centuries, in contrast to the ahistorical tendency among modern Muslims to regard them as records of the Prophet's directives.

Some factors that entrench perceptions of Hadith as divine instructions endure to this day. The veneration of the relatives of the Prophet (*ahl al-Bait*) in Shia Islam broadened to include all other Muslims, but the Sunni, despite their formal disdain of human spiritual authority, have gone further, venerating anyone who met the Prophet and the Hadith accounts s/he reported.[36] The Muslim past is thus filled with sacred persons and, therefore, not to be questioned. Two main historical narratives—one Sunni and the other Shi'i—arose, both of which sustain views that bestow unquestioned spiritual authority on past figures. To maintain this perspective, an ever-expanding army of originally state-sponsored petty clergymen was created, whose training focused on entrenching particular narratives of the past. Today, at the first sign that the historicity or contents of a Hadith is under critical scrutiny, such *madrasa*-type clerics warn about the potential collapse of Islam. Without Hadith, they rush to caution, Muslims would not know how to pray or how many prayers to perform, for example.

Such statements are false, but they are not usually challenged, as neither these poorly-trained clerics nor the average modern Muslim know the facts about such mechanical mantras. After all, prominent *fuqaha* also turn to such reports, and the majority of God's instructions are accordingly derived from them. Not many who knew al-Ghazali expected him to spearhead a grassroots campaign to raise awareness about how Hadiths buried true precedents. In particular, he took on the army of clerics who defended Hadiths uncritically, believing it was they who ensured that a chaotic mass of anecdotes, rather than defined principles, remained the foundation of Islam and its rulemaking. However, al-Ghazali's concerns were not novel, as indicated in the following section, which briefly highlights Muslims' efforts to assess Hadiths and the precedents derived from them.

Testing historicity and substance (*isnad* and *matn*)

Reports about Mohammed that were supposed to clarify how to make rules in fact generated widescale confusion in early Muslim society. Instead of serving as authoritative precedents, they created disputes. The mayhem troubled learned Muslims; inconsistencies caused intellectual stress in a community that had put a premium on human reason. Very early, Muslim scholars recognized and openly confronted the problem of forged reports. They devised methods to address the irregularities that Hadith reports raised. By the third century AH (starting 913 CE), scholarly communities welcomed a two-part test designed to examine the historicity and substance of each report that claimed to originate in the Prophet's times. The first part of this test measured historical accuracy (*isnad*): the "how" and "who" of the human chain that reported the account under scrutiny. The second part then examined the content (*matn*), to determine whether the substance of the report accorded with the Qur'an. Every account was to be thus inspected before it was judged sound, establishing it as part of the Sunna.

Muslims also recognized that Hadith reports were subject to human error, not just forgery, and so more formulae were introduced to ensure that Hadith could not dictate or alter Islam's central doctrines. With admirable integrity, independent scholarly communities divided the memory of their Prophet's practices, the Sunna, into *mutawatir* (reported by a great number of sources since the very early years) and *uhadi* (reported by a limited number of sources, usually years after the Prophet's death). The *mutawatir* Sunna they judged to be an essential part of Islam's message. The precedents it set mostly included customs that detailed prayers, pilgrimage, and fasting; in short, all that the Prophet openly taught everybody in his community. Even if not recorded in any Hadith, these precedents were, therefore, certain, (*qati'*). In contrast, the same formulae designated the *uhadi* reports as *thani al-thubout* and *thani al-dilala* (tentative historically and in meaning).[37] With such classifications, Muslim scholars candidly acknowledged that both the origins and significance of *uhadi* reports were not fully certain. The bulk of Hadith reports belonged to this second, "only probable" category. None of this is secret: a former head of al-Azhar, the late Shaykh Mahmoud Shaltut (d. 1963), tactfully explained these limitations to the average person in a book about the tenets and the rituals of Islam.[38] The work became a staple of the Arabic library, to be found anywhere from stalls littering Cairo streets to Kuwait University syllabi.

A preoccupation with the integrity of Hadith in some specialized Muslim circles has therefore never truly died down,[39] and collective memory celebrates such efforts even today. Despite this vigilance, however, the assessment of Hadith has not always followed the procedures that attentive scholars set to guard against misuse of the Prophet's memory. Again, this was essentially a question of circumstances, not theology. The test of substance or content (*matn*) was often overlooked, even if a report flouted the tenets of the Qur'an or common-sense reasoning, as was the test to ensure historical accuracy. Although designated as only probable, *uhadi* reports have been frequently embraced as a definite source of law and even doctrine. With no central authority to systemize Hadith or rulemaking, chaos further engulfed the uses, terms, and classifications of these reports. As reformers who reviewed the legacy of Hadith observed, the seemingly admirable safeguards early Muslim communities designed to ensure the veracity of the Prophet's precedents eventually turned into notional tools. For all practical purposes Muslims replaced the Qur'an with Hadith as their ultimate source of rule-/lawmaking, as al-Ghazali later noted.[40] Officially, however, the Shari'a methodology remained unchanged.

Hadith in action

"As it stands now, I find in the Sunna what troubles me", al-Ghazali finally declared.[41] The accounts that follow discuss first-hand encounters from al-Ghazali's world, offering glimpses of the circumstances that nourished problematic approaches to the Sunna over time, and which led al-Ghazali to question the legacy of Hadith.

Snapshot: In the riqaws *of al-Azhar*

Sitting in on an advanced lesson at al-Azhar on how to examine Hadith, this author watched a celebrated professor of *usul al-fiqh* painstakingly explain the methodology of the thirteenth-century CE scholar Ibn al-Salah (d. 1245 CE).[42] In finishing his lecture, the Azhari professor asked his students this question: If we were to follow Ibn al-Salah's criteria for determining sound reports, would we not now consider *x*, a certain famous Hadith, unsound and an inappropriate source of Shari'a? Sitting by his side in the *riwaq* circle, his star student responded immediately: "No, I beg you, our Shaykh, Your Grace [*fadilatak*], God forbid you should suggest such a thing." Again, the shaykh challenged these would-be *fuqaha* and imams: Did it matter whether or not the assessment of a Hadith's reliability accorded with the criteria of Ibn al-Salah, a scholar who also defended Hadiths? "No, no, God grant you safety from every evil, my Shaykh, no, it is not possible", the outspoken younger man interrupted. The professor suddenly changed track. He allayed the anxiety of his puzzled students with a broad smile, reassuring them that he had no intention of challenging the Hadith in question, of course.

To understand the incident, this author caught up with the professor after the lesson. Did he really, as it appeared, give in when his students refused to apply the agreed criteria of sound Hadith, and if so, why? His response to my question showed the multiple and separate realities that a *faqih* often considers, how such an expert approaches the sources of Shari'a in practice and how the challenges of late twentieth-century Egypt dictate their use. "Step outside these walls [of al-Azhar], what do you see?" he asked. The senior shaykh did not wait for an answer: you will find:

> confusion, then more confusion and, thereafter, utter despair. Out there, favourite Hadith reports become the floating branches to which the vulnerable cling, maybe mistakenly, but they do so in the hope of saving themselves from drowning in the turmoil that engulfs everything around them.

He posed another question: "Is it right to snatch away a scrap of wood from a drowning man, no matter how paltry and ineffective it may be?"

Snapshot: In the corridors of power

In the 1950s al-Ghazali had chided his colleague Shaykh Khaled Mohammed Khaled for writing about an "obstructionist Muslim Church". No such thing had ever existed, al-Ghazali insisted at the time. Al-Ghazali's views changed, however. He concluded that frequently, and not exceptionally, many *'ulama* had first and foremost served dynasties and other power groups, not the cause of Shari'a or their communities;[43] and these *'ulama* used Hadiths as their main instrument, al-Ghazali concluded by the early 1980s. To illustrate, he recorded an incident. His friend, a senior state official, had sought out a famous Islamic scholar's advice about Hadith reports that discussed birth control. "Which did the government prefer, Hadiths to prohibit, or Hadiths to support birth control?", the famous *faqih* inquired upon receiving the state's request. Flabbergasted by this scholar's readiness to wrap in the Prophet's mantle whatever pleased the government, the Egyptian official pressed on. He placed an order for five Hadiths in support of and another five Hadiths against birth control. Apparently, the *faqih* duly complied. Al-Ghazali and his government friend chuckled at the incident. This *faqih*, they noted, made suitable material for religious officialdom, such as "the mufti of the [Egyptian] Republic, minister of *Awqaf*, or even shaykh of al-Azhar", al-Ghazali wrote.[44] That they could joke about it reveals aspects of the chequered relationship between the *fuqaha* and the state throughout Muslim history, and its shape in the modern nation-state.

Snapshot: Public versus private fiqh?

A high-flying Azhari who energetically helped this author to understand developments and discrepancies in the corpus of Hadith had one last request in 2000: "Never cite my name in Hadith discussions. I am but a man trying to support a family; I can ill afford such troubles." Soon, I would discover that such scholarly dread of the mob is common. As a result, researchers have often found it harder to document significant appraisals that take place in senior Azhari circles. The world had a glimpse of these trepidations and their impact when Shaykh Yusuf al-Qaradawi reported that a modern authority on *usul al-fiqh*, the late Shaykh Mohammed Abu Zahra, had kept his conclusions on the penalty for adultery secret for 20 years because he dreaded the responses of riotous crowds.[45] Shortly before he died in 1974, Abu Zahra disclosed these rules to a meeting of senior *'ulama* and why he had to keep them to himself. Shaykh al-Qaradawi revealed that, sometimes, he too did not impart all his views of correct Shari'a rules/laws, in fear of the furious reactions of poorly educated but noisy Muslim voices.[46] The eleventh-century CE *History of Baghdad* (*Tarikh Baghdad*) provides numerous examples of street beatings, mosque attacks, and even the murder of those who disagreed with the boorish hordes, al-Ghazali noted.[47] In these ancient accounts Mohammed al-Ghazali recognized a deep-seated quandary: the vulgar defined some Muslim norms and rules in the past and continued to do so in the present. Now, as then, prominent *'ulama* knew it too well, as further discussion in the next chapter shows.

Al-Ghazali wanted to rescue, not reject, precedent as the second source of Shari'a rule-/lawmaking, and especially that of the Prophet, as he saw it. Only sound historical inquiry, he proposed, could establish what the actual Sunna was and how the powerful and vulgar mobs had corrupted it. In other words, early Muslim conventions were better indicated by practices in Medina during Mohammed's lifetime, rather than eclectic and uncertain later Hadith selections. Al-Ghazali targeted the false Sunna that he believed unsound approaches to Hadith had allowed to flourish. One example was a report that instructed women preferably to pray at home, which al-Ghazali now dismissed as absurd. When they participated in general worship at all hours of the day and night, "no one ever heard the prophet saying to these women who joined him in the mosque [at Medina] that 'your homes are a preferable for you, go pray there'", al-Ghazali observed.[48] Lessons from Medina's early history further clarified how "human whims" struggled against the model that Mohammed established. When a son of Abd Allah Ibn Umar (a grandson of the second caliph, Umar Ibn al-Khattab) sought to prohibit women access to mosques, his father repeated the prophet's instruction not to question women's right of entry to God's mosques. "By God we shall prevent them", insisted the son. This lack of interest in the Prophet's instructions led Ibn Umar to refuse to have any further contact with his son. Al-Ghazali concluded with questions: How was it then, "that you [Muslims still] insist that Islam orders women to pray only at home not in mosques? From where did you derive this [rule]" when the early records show otherwise? As usual, he also provided the answer: by restricting women's access to mosques, later Muslims effectively buried the practices of the Prophet, replacing them with a rule invented by "a dimwit son".[49] Yet, such reports survived in Hadith collections. Al-Ghazali reminded his people of how, until not so long ago, many communities in Egypt and Arabia had subscribed to a supposed divine instruction not to teach girls to write. Although centuries earlier a Hadith scholar, al-Dhahabi, had designated this report fraudulent, Muslims chose to embrace this particular account and ignore all others, including its corrections, al-Ghazali observed.[50] So, in addition to open war against his society's choices that corrupted the Sunna, al-Ghazali turned his full attention on what actual models the Prophet had set and what principles to draw from them. The Sunna will always matter in deducing rules, as real-life applications of the intentions of scripture; still unsettled, however, is from where to derive this Sunna. Should Hadith be placed in the provisional or in the fixed ledgers of Shari'a rulemaking?

What did the Prophet instruct about women's leadership?

Only by introducing the pertinent Sunna reports could al-Ghazali confirm his reading of the universal (divine) rule on public authority. Thus, to verify his latest conclusions about women and civic leadership he had to satisfactorily answer the question: What practices of the Prophet could verify his reading of Qur'an? Could earlier *fiqh* discussions corroborate his conclusions? Would empirical observation validate them? He easily unearthed the views of prominent *fuqaha*, such as the tenth-century CE scholar al-Tabari (in Baghdad) and the eleventh century Ibn Hazm (in Andalusia), who both argued that women were qualified for some public posts.[51] Al-Ghazali then found real-life illustrations of past and contemporary competent women leaders, as discussed above and in the previous chapter. Most importantly, however, he had to find evidence in the actual practices that dated back to Mohammed and his community in Medina. He believed that sound historical inquiry could re-establish with some certainty the Prophet's instructions on how Muslims should organize themselves, and not just on gender matters. The search for genuine Sunna in records of the past had to always keep in mind the Qur'an's overall content, not just phrases taken out of context, he thought. Al-Ghazali started at the Prophet's home. He had prepared A'isha, his outspoken young wife, as a scholar, according to Sunni memory.[52] She set the model that Muslims had to follow, according to al-Ghazali. However, in practice Muslims did not accept this, even when it came to divine instructions on worship, as he saw it now.[53] The wilful neglect of the ninth-century CE Ibn Sa'ad of 'Aisha's critiques of Abu Hurayra provided an illustration: "He equated women with dogs and donkeys, God forgive him", 'Aisha is reported to have said when she heard what Abu Hurayra, a key transmitter of Hadith, had reported. Abu Hurayra claimed that he had heard Mohammed warn Muslims that these two animals, along with women, invalidated the prayers of whomever they passed before, presumably because they were all unclean.[54] 'Aisha did not hold back. She depicted Abu Hurayra as impetuous, and his understanding of the Prophet's instructions as slipshod. Her husband, she clarified, had actually been warning Muslims not to make such irrational claims; Abu Hurayra had arrived only at the end of their conversation, which he later publicized as divine instructions, 'A'isha explained.[55] These records, al-Ghazali now concluded, show that selecting Abu Hurayra's careless report over 'Aisha's careful corrections indicated a curious scholarship.[56] When, in later times, the *fuqaha* ignored her assessment of Hadith reports, they distorted both Shari'a rule-/lawmaking and their societies, he now argued. Inspired by an Azhari professor of Maliki *fiqh*, Shaykh Mohammed al-Madani, who encouraged his students to research treaties on the forgotten *fiqh* of 'Aisha, al-Ghazali sought the same remedy. He too invited doctoral researchers to study 'Aisha bint Abi Bakr's *fiqh*, proposing that this woman's critiques should constitute a basis for a review of all canonical Hadith collections, the *Sihah*.[57] 'Aisha exemplified the earliest Sunna that Muslim communities followed thereafter, al-Ghazali now thought. In an equally valuable Sunna, that of the Prophet's disciples (the *sahaba*), al-Ghazali also invoked the neglected account concerning al-Shifa, the woman that Umar, the second caliph, appointed as the first market supervisor (*muhtasiba*) of Medina, "with full authority over [...] men and women alike, legislating what is proper and forbidding what is improper, carrying out justice and seeing to it that no violations took place."[58] He concluded that the records show that this pattern had continued for some centuries, and that Muslim women having dynamic lives was a hallmark of Muslim societies during times of prosperity.[59] Now these records and the forgotten women they describe preoccupied him; he publicized their achievements and exceptional mobility. If such had been the Sunna, Shari'a rules that al-Ghazali deduced relating to women had to change accordingly. Herein lies the danger of historical narratives, as discussed in Chapter 7.

Shari'a-sanctioned premiership, at last

The Arabic-speaking world of the late twentieth century shunned the trend for accepting women as leaders that was evident in the rest of the world, including in non-Arab Muslim-majority states such as Pakistan or Turkey. Founded in 1947 as an Islamic polity, Pakistan nevertheless elected the young Benazir Bhutto as prime minister in 1988. Secular Turkey also elected a woman prime minister, Tansu Çiller, as the century drew to a close. However, these women seemed to be leading their countries in defiance of their Islamic heritage, not in accordance with it. In the 1990s, the first Islamist Turkish Prime Minister, the late Nacim al-Din Erbakan, infuriated many with his remarks on women.[60] Similarly, Pakistan continued to struggle with the question of Islamic regulations on women, even when it came to education.[61] Shari'a rules had little to do with these women politicians as leaders of their nations.

The notion of a woman head of government remained anathema in Arab countries at the time of al-Ghazali's death in 1996. However, and remarkably, in the 1980s the deputy of the all-important Kuwait Petroleum Corporation (KPC) and, more significantly, the dean of the College of Shari'a at Kuwait University were both women, despite Kuwait's conservatism:[62] at the time, the women of Kuwait could not vote, nor could they run for parliament.[63] More pronounced was the irrelevance of modernity to women in more liberal Arabic-speaking states, all of which nevertheless continued to exclude females from holding tangible authority over the public. Whatever posts that women held at that time had been largely cosmetic, whether in a pioneering Egypt, cosmopolitan and Westernized Lebanon, or the secular-socialist Ba'athist states of Saddam Hussein's Iraq or Hafiz al-Assad's Syria. Intended mainly to impress the West, women appointed to these country's cabinets oversaw social security or the environment, areas of little or no significance in these governments' priorities. If anything, the executive positions Arab women held in the late twentieth century reinforced images of their gender as capable of playing only secondary roles in their communities.

However, as mentioned in the previous chapter, women did head Muslim states. Modern research has brilliantly resurrected the memories of some examples, including the quick-witted Sitt al-Mulk (d. 1023 CE) and the brave Shajarat al-Durr (d. 1257 CE), both in Egypt; the skilled Queen 'Arwa (d. 1137 CE) in Yemen; and the astute Sultana Radhyia (d. 1239 CE) and Khadija bint Salah al-Din al-Bengali (d. 1368 CE) in India. But these women did not hold their position in accordance with Shari'a; their power devolved from male relatives, and only as extensions of male authority. In the predominant *fiqh* worldview, these women's rise to positions of authority marked the overturning of the correct order. No matter how exceptional these heads of states were, their tenure has been read as forced by circumstances, often in terms of chaotic and depraved times. More to the point, their leadership had no place in Shari'a: despite records of daughters, wives, or sisters of kings and sultans holding the helm of Muslim states, women continued to be ineligible to lead under the predominant view of Islam's proper rules. Modern improvements in education and the adoption of many Western practices had no impact on these rules, as al-Ghazali's contemporary spokesmen on Islam demonstrate. Among the *fuqaha*, for example, in 2004 a former Mufti of Egypt, Shaykh Nasir Farid, declared Islam's rejection of women running for his country's presidency.[64] The mufti based his evidence on the long-standing ban on women leading general prayers (*imamat al-Salat*) presenting his people with an irrefutable everyday, well-established fact.

Salat, usually translated as prayers, does not take place only on or at designated days and places; a Muslim must perform these recitals anywhere s/he might be. In so doing, believers renew their relations with the Qur'an and reset their priorities, by remembering the supremacy of the Almighty. They also re-enforce the link between individuals and their faith as they gather five times daily to face in the same direction: towards Mecca. Those who lead the *salat* are usually regarded as *bona fide* leaders of their people, regardless of what form their authority may take. Traditions surrounding this ritual have ensured the endurance of perceptions of communal authority, and not just in devotional matters; those commonly forbidden to lead prayers, such as the mentally unstable or women, are denied access to civic authority. Even in secular Turkey, until early in the twenty-first century worshippers from Fethullah Gülen's Nurcu group prohibited females from leading any prayers, including women-only prayers. In the absence of a male to lead them, in their gatherings each Turkish woman must pray on her own, a practice they believe that their Hanafi *madhhab* dictates. In Egypt, a boy of ten could lead in prayers a group of women that included his mother and his teachers, by virtue only of his gender. This form of Islamic worship as a divine marker of female inferiority is found not only in Egypt, but also elsewhere in its ancient Mediterranean neighbourhood and surrounding region. In London's Regent's Park Mosque, a commotion erupted in 2010 when a British Bangladeshi imam insisted that Islam did not and could not distinguish between how females and males prayed, as some in his community believed. Regardless of the resilience or success of any particular woman, therefore, prayers came to underpin the lesser status of her gender. Here al-Ghazali treaded carefully, but his intervention mattered a great deal to Muslims. To argue against age-old prayer practices as supposedly underlining the lesser status of females, he offered a contemporary Egyptian application. He told Safinaz Kazim, his Islamist interviewer, that it was unthinkable for Dr 'Aisha abd al-Rahaman (d. 1998), a renowned Qur'anic scholar, to pray behind men of lesser knowledge than hers.[65] The new question that challenged him was: Where is it in Islam that the well-informed had ever been instructed to follow the less-informed?

In the case of the *salat*, as in much else, the Prophet's precedent has always been central; and al-Ghazali had to search for it. Besides, the Qur'an contained few details of how to pray. Accordingly, al-Ghazali noted a long-neglected account from Medina, concerning when the Prophet instructed a female contemporary, Umm Waraqa, to lead her entire household, both men and women, in their daily prayers.[66] Usually later surrounded by various caveats, the rationale for this precedent, albeit implicit, appeared to him clearer: Islam entrusted the leadership of prayers to the person best versed in the Qur'an, which in this family was this woman.

Progressive al-Ghazali or just al-Ghazali?

Years after al-Ghazali's death, some Western Muslims held very public woman-led Friday prayer.[67] It had little in common with al-Ghazali, however. Whereas al-Ghazali deposited his absolute loyalty in the Qur'an, believing it to be the undisputed source of the Shari'a, the American professor who led men and women in this New York City Friday service challenged the Muslim scripture.[68] In contrast, by bringing the question of gender into rules on leadership, al-Ghazali hoped to catch two birds with one stone: Muslim confusion between the variable and permanent sources of Shari'a and, just as significantly, what he saw as their dismal political culture. Unlike members of the Progressive Muslim Union, al-Ghazali's key concern has never been women. As he reviewed Shari'a rulemaking, al-Ghazali suggested that Muslims' first loyalty had to be to Shari'a, which he believed disallowed haphazard rules. Al-Ghazali now felt that the *fuqaha* and society chose to neglect Qur'anic standards because these would enforce women's interests. In this, the *fuqaha* reduced the Qur'an into words for mere recitation only.[69]

Importantly, al-Ghazali candidly differentiated between systematic rulemaking, which he claimed to be at the heart of Shari'a, and the weight of social choices and customs. Al-Ghazali accepted that human preferences and the rules of Islam would never perfectly align. His community had to recognize that, whether considering their past, present, or future. If you want to humiliate your women, he told his audience at a lecture in the UAE, just do it—but never attach it to Islam.[70] Recognizing this tension even within himself, he spoke of his "natural" anxiety at the prospect of women taking control of anything, clarifying that he was neither a champion of women leaders nor of them heading states.[71] The clash between his upbringing and Shari'a meant that although he believed what he later deduced from Shari'a to be genuine rules of Islam, he still hoped to restrict the right of women to lead prayers, or lead communities in politics, to those who were qualified and outstanding; but as he saw it, "excellent women are few and far between."[72] Despite the immense inner strain that these new rules imposed on him, he may have significantly helped change the perceptions and practices of women and gender in Egypt.[73]

Summary: Scriptural trajectory of a Shari'a rule

For many years, precedent, and especially Hadith, was central to al-Ghazali's understanding of Shari'a. This was the common practice: a single Hadith report which warned against women's leadership provided an eternal principle on the disqualification of women to hold positions of public authority. More precedents corroborated the validity of this divinely inspired prohibition. For example, another Hadith instructed that if women had to use public roads, they must walk close to the walls, presumably to restrict their public exposure as much as possible.[74] Valid precedent included famous *fiqh* dictums, as well as long-observed human experience, including illustrations from modern times. Al-Ghazali invoked them all to deduce rules that banned women from public life; but later, he re-assessed these foundational sources and adjusted how he employed them.

In this, he started with the revelation, not with the usual pool of precedents. The Qur'an did not just serve as the first source, but as the only definitive source.[75] In championing the Qur'anic message, he only re-stated age-old beliefs. How al-Ghazali employed revelation changed, too. He now approached the Qur'an as a whole; its contents stood on their own, without props or *tafasir* scaffolds. Al-Ghazali wanted Muslims to discontinue plucking out phrases from their actual, and often very specific, contexts. Nor should they consider verses of the Qur'an in piecemeal manner, as fragments disconnected from the entirety of its message. This was a reversal of his earlier ways, when he had used what he now regarded as phrases taken out of context to give credence to rules that prohibit women from positions in the public realm.

It is false to claim that al-Ghazali rejected the Sunna. Instead, "we believe in the [complete authority of the] Book [Qur'an] and the Sunna", he wrote. However, the Sunna can only stand in the shade of God's word, for "we believe that the Sunna is a tributary [*far'i*], while the Book is the foundation [*asl*]."[76] Al-Ghazali defined this tributary as illustrative; that is, "the Sunna could only provide clarifications of the Qur'an, to confirm its particulars as well as broad indications." In short, "it is impossible for the Sunna to include a meaning or a rule that contradicted the Qur'an."[77] However, the sources from which to derive this binding precedent and how to read them had to improve, and al-Ghazali hoped to demonstrate this as regards women, among other subjects.

Al-Ghazali also condemned neglecting Muslim heritage. The abundance of extant sources from the past provided windows to understanding the Sunna, changing approaches to the Qur'an, and a rich variety of opinions and ideas.[78] It also demonstrated what he regarded as world-class intellectual efforts and methodologies with which early Muslims had enriched all humanity.[79] Changes and continuities now assumed the central role in the story of Shari'a rulemaking, as one of his last books, *How We Deal with the Qur'an*, makes clear. Other resources of rulemaking were human creations and had to be employed and studied as such. Besides the above-highlighted *tafaseer*, these included the now semi-sacred legacies of Hadith and *fiqh*, among others. Al-Ghazali noted how societies eventually "reduced [*fiqh*] to only mean rulemaking, to the exclusion of all other areas of knowledge", thus converting the Qur'an into a one-dimensional address to readers. This development did not accord with the full meaning of *fiqh*, nor did it fit how revelation employed *fiqh* to refer to a spectrum of knowledge which "entailed all dimensions of the word 'civilization'", he argued.[80] It became clear to him that Muslim culture and a great deal of its literary sources were both far removed from the Qur'an and the genuine Sunna.[81] The real threat to Muslim rulemaking, however, resided in the convenient silence over the confusion between the divine and man-made arguments in the Muslim heritage. It was petrifying, he wrote, that having acquired a sense of sacredness, past scholarship became "the wall that separated Muslims from the fundamental sources of their faith."[82]

What to do with a problem like uhadi *Hadith?*

In al-Ghazali's adjusted scheme of correct Shari'a rulemaking, the Sunna's standing remained high, but the place of Hadith shifted considerably. However, although he designated Hadiths to be non-scriptural, and thus no longer divine, his approaches to the Hadith legacy should not be oversimplified. In some instances, he showed caution and nuance; in others, his examples of what such reports did to the Muslim intellect exposed a particular Hadith as invalid.[83] Perhaps this quote best describes it: "I benefitted greatly from Muntheri's work, *Al-Targhib wa al-Tarhib*, when I taught worshippers in mosques." This was because this author "did not leave any issue without including something from this Hadith collection, albeit utterly fusing the genuine with the sick."[84]

Here too Mohammed Abduh had led the way: "The munificent Qur'an is the only reliable evidence for Islam. Anything else, such as material in Hadith reports, whether or not their *isnad* had been confirmed" according to later classifications such as *sahih*, *mashhur*, or *dha'if* "is unable to establish certainty".[85] Al-Ghazali placed this concern about the careless citation of *uhadi* Hadiths as among the concerns of key authorities at the centre of mainstream Islam. He quoted celebrated *fuqaha* from the four surviving Sunni schools—al-Bazdawi, Abu Hamid al-Ghazali, al-Asnawi, and al-Khatib al-Baghdadi—as well as Ibn al-Jawzi, Ibn al-Qayyim, and al-Shatibi, and he even quoted reports in *Al-Bukhari* and *Al-Muslim* Hadith collections.[86] He believed that he shared their conviction that "it is necessary to make sure that the Prophet has said [what it was claimed to be said], and that can only take place by measuring the *sanad* and the *matn* together."[87] But hindsight added new dimensions, as he argued it should. Long centuries demonstrated how *uhadi* Hadith had turned Muslim morality upside down; among other things, justifying spilling blood,[88] downright aggression,[89] and even imposing faith by force, thus overturning tenets of the Qur'an.[90] As al-Ghazali later saw it, *uhadi* reports became the choice tools of idiots and tyrants, and disfigured *fiqh*. Al-Ghazali did not want to discard Hadith altogether, but nor did he champion it. He wanted Muslims to adjust their approaches to *uhadi* reports as a matter of great urgency. As for the centuries-old argument that the community's consensus (*ijma*) transforms a Hadith report from probable to certain, al-Ghazali answered that the community did not even itself agree on such a premise.[91] When human inheritance took on a semi-sacred character, a long night disconnected Muslims from revelation, and had done so for long ages.[92]

Again, seeing rulemaking in terms of changes and continuities, al-Ghazali concluded that Muslims now "learn to read, not read to learn". They deserted the Qur'an in favour of the Sunna, then deserted the Sunna in favour of the opinions of key scholars, and then deserted even these human constructs in favour of senseless commentaries on older *fiqh* compositions.[93] It was time, he told them, to adjust their lawmaking in order to deduce better rules for better societies. Why and how al-Ghazali, or anyone else, could successfully adjust Muslim rules is the subject of the next chapter, which discusses the methodology at the heart of all acceptable Shari'a rule-/lawmaking.

Notes

1. For an English discussion of *naskh*, see John Burton, *The Sources of Islamic Law: Islamic Theories of Abrogation* (Edinburgh: Edinburgh University Press, 1990); for a brief contemporary Sunni *usul al-fiqh* exposition of *naskh*, see Ali Goma, *Al-Naskh 'inda al-Usuleen* (Cairo: Dar al-Nahar lil Tabi' wa al-Nashr, 1998).
2. Mohammed al-Ghazali, *Al-Sunna al-Nabawiya Bayna Ahl al-Fiqh wa ahl al-Hadith*, 5th edn (no location: Sahara, 1989), 103; idem, videotape interview (#FTW-1).
3. Mohammed Al-Ghazali, *Kaifa Nat'amal m'a al-Qur'an*, ed. Umar Ubaid Hassana (Herndon, VA: IIIT, 1992), 39–42.
4. Al-Ghazali, videotape interview (#TJD-1).
5. Ibid.
6. Mohammed al-Ghazali, *Turathuna al-Fikri fi Mizan al-Shar'i wa al-'Aql*, 2nd edn (Cairo: Dar al-Shuruk, 1991), 182.
7. Ibid. *Al-Naba' al-'Azim*, a Qur'anic commentary by Shaykh Abd Allah Diraz, approached the Qur'an's longest chapter (*sura*), *Al-Baqara*, as a single unit. This work especially inspired al-Ghazali. So did his teacher, Shaykh Mahmoud Shaltut, because, al-Ghazali said, Shaltut called for avoiding the all-too-common practice of examining Qur'anic verses as isolated phrases, without incorporating their larger Qur'anic contexts (videotape interview #U-1). It is worth noting here that nowhere did al-Ghazali acknowledge the then-popular *tafsir* of Shaykh Mohammed Mutawali Sha'rawi.
8. Mohammed al-Ghazali, *Kaifa Nat'amal ma' al-Qur'an*, ed. Umar Ubaid Hassana (Herndon, VA: IIIT, 1992). Syrian-born Hassana is presently a director of the Research Centre of Qatar's Ministry of Awqaf. and also a council member of the faculty of Shari'a, Law and Islamic Studies at Qatar University.
9. Al-Ghazali, *Al-Sunna al-Nabawiya*, 47.
10. Ibid., 51.
11. Ibid., 50; videotape interview (#SYS-1).
12. Al-Ghazali, videotape interview (#SYS-1).

13. Ibid.
14. Jalal al-Din al-Suyuti and Jalal al-din al-Mahalli, *Tafsir wa Bayan Kalimat al-Qur'an al-Kareem li al-Imamyin al-Jalilyin, al-Suyuti wa al-Mahalli* (Cairo: Dar al Fida al-Arabi, 1995), 380–381. Al-Mahalli died in 1459 CE, having only reached Chapter 12 (*Al-Tawba*). His student, the celebrated Jalal al-Din al-Suyuti (1445–1505 CE) completed the rest of the chapters.
15. Ibid.
16. Al-Ghazali believed that the *fuqaha* eventually turned their back on the Qur'an's accounts that attend to the history of civilizations and the natural laws (*sunat Allah ala al-ardh*) that govern societies and individual human conduct. As he saw it, instead of such lessons, many *fiqh* works show a proclivity to myths and superstitions (*Kaifa Nat'amal ma' al-Qur'an*, 67; *Al-Sunna al-Nabawiya*, 50–57).
17. Mohammed al-Ghazali, "Qissat Haya", *Islamiyat al-Ma'rifa* 2/3 (2007): 159.
18. Mohammed al-Ghazali, *Min Huna Na'lam* (Cairo: Dar al-Kutub al-Haditha, n.d.), 200.
19. Al-Ghazali, *Al-Sunna al-Nabawiya*, 32–33, 47.
20. Al-Ghazali, *Al-Sunna al-Nabawiya*, 48; idem, videotape interview (#W-1).
21. Al-Ghazali, videotape interview (#W-1).
22. Al-Ghazali, *Al-Sunna al-Nabawiya*, 50.
23. Although starting from opposite directions, closer scrutiny of their shared Muslim heritage appears to have led al-Ghazali and an outspoken Muslim feminist to similar conclusions about the connection between political tyranny and the oppression of women in Muslim societies; see Fatima Mernissi, *The Forgotten Queens of Islam* (Minneapolis: University of Minnesota Press, 1993), 179–189; idem, *The Veil and the Male Elite: A Feminist Interpretation of Women's Rights in Islam* (New York: Perseus Books, 1992), 15–62.
24. Al-Ghazali, *Al-Sunna al-Nabawiya*, 135.
25. Al-Ghazali, videotape interview (#SYS-1).
26. Al-Ghazali, *Al-Sunna al-Nabawiya*, 48–49.
27. Ibid., 32–33.
28. Ibid.
29. Ibid., 33, 127. Al-Qadi 'Ayyadh Ibn Musa (d. 1149 CE) was a prominent Maliki scholar of Yemeni origins who gained fame in his adopted lands of North Africa and Muslim Spain (Andalusia) (al-Ghazali, *Turathuna al-Fikri*, 181). Ibn Kathir (c.1300–1373 CE) was an influential Shafi'i scholar in Mamluk Syria and Egypt who wrote famous works on *tafsir*, history, and *fiqh*, among other things.
30. Al-Ghazali, *Kaifa Nat'amal ma al-Qur'an*, 181.
31. Increasing numbers of scholars found in the collected accounts about the Prophet a powerful "uncontested" authority with which to contain the influence on Shari'a rule-/lawmaking of their sovereigns and all others with executive, coercive powers. Thereby, they argued that such Hadith reports could create universal principles, a position that eventually found general acceptance among Muslims. This case for the supremacy of Hadith as evidence was most famously made by Mohammed Ibn Idris al-Shafi'i (767–820 CE), in his *Risala*. Still, many Muslims questioned the wholesale adoption of such a position and whether it challenged explicit Qur'anic verses, which led to unceasing interest in the authenticity of Hadith and debates about its place in deriving valid Shari'a rules. See Mohammed Ibn Idris al-Shafi'i, *Al-Risala*, ed. Ahmed Shakir (Cairo: Mustafa al-Babi al-Halabi, 1940).
32. Hence, this typical contemporary presentation of Abu Hanifa from Sunnipath.com:

    His coming was predicted by the Prophet (Allah Bless him and grant him peace). Abu Nuaym narrates in his Hiyat al Awliya, Bukhari and Muslim narrate from another Sanad from Abu Hurayra (Allah be pleased with him), Abu Bakr Shirazi narrates in his Kitab Alqab, Tabarani from Sa'd bin Ubaidah (Allah be pleased with him) and Ibn Masud (Allah be pleased with him) that the Prophet (Allah Bless him and grant him peace) said:—If Ilm was suspended from Pleiades and the Arabs are unable to reach it, then a man from the sons of Persia will be able to reach it. Imam al-Suyuti mentions that the *'ulama* have stated that that these Hadith are in favour of Imam Abu Hanifa and are authentic. (online: http://ahlussunnahwaljamah.blogspot.com/2008/05/hadith-about-imam-abu-hanifa-rh.html)

33. Malik Ibn 'Anas, eponym of the Maliki *fiqh* school, lived in Medina, and died there in 795 CE.
34. *Fadha'il* and *targhib wa tarhib* are illustrations of Hadith genres which also focus on the qualities of particular races or regions. So prevalent had been these compilations that, for example, in reporting the events of year 17 AH (638–639 CE), al-Tabari included a Hadith in which the Prophet informed that the trait of stinginess is composed of ten parts, nine of which belong to the Persians; that generosity is also of ten parts, nine of which belong to Blacks; that envy is made of ten parts, nine of which belong to the Arabs, etc. (Abu Ja'far M. Ibn Jarir al-Tabari, *Tarikh al-Tabari* [Riyadh: Bait al-Afkar al-Dawlyia, n.d.]), 655. For al-Ghazali's later assessment of such literature in praise of particular regions, see his *Al-Sunna al-Nabawiya*, 30–31.
35. Modern discussions of this document, known as the *Ashtiname* (a Persian term denoting a covenant), include John Morrow, *The Covenants of the Prophet Muhammad with the Christians of the World* (Hillsdale, NY: Sophia Perennis, 2013); for early-modern Western presentations of this document, see Richard Pococke, "The Patent of Mahomet, which he Granted to the Monks of Mount Sinai; and to Christians in General", in idem, *Description of the East*, vol. 1 (London: W. Bowyer, 1743), 268–270. In the absence of critical approaches to Islamic learning in modern times, contemporary Muslims usually attach this document to their Prophet's political legacy, as in Mohammed Hamidullah, *Majmu'ah al-Watha'iq al-Siyasiyyah li al-'Ahad al-Nabawi wa al-Khilafah al-Rashidah* (Beirut: Dar al-Nafa'ith, 1985).
36. By the ninth century CE, Ibn Hanbal's open-ended definition of who is a *sahabi* (a companion of the Prophet) gained currency: "a *sahabi* is any person who was in the company [of Mohammed] for a year, a month, or a day, or an hour [...] or even someone who just had a glimpse of him" (Shaykh Mohammed Abu Zahra, *Ibn Hanbal, Hayatuh, wa 'Asruhu, wa Ara'auhu* [Cairo: Dar al-Fikr al-'Arabi, n.d. (1947), 135]):
كل من صحبه سنة، او شهرا، او يوما، او ساعة، فهو من الصحابة، له من الصحبة علي قدر ما صحبه، وسمع منه، ونظر اليه ولو نظرة ...
37. For a contemporary restatement of this mainstream Sunni position on the place of *uhadi* and *mutawatir* Hadith reports in the Sunna, see al-Azhar's fatwa on this subject, Appendix 1.
38. Mahmoud Shaltut, *Al-Islam'Aqida wa Shari'a*, 2nd edn (Cairo: Dar al-Qalam, n.d.), 519–526.
39. For an academic discussion in English on the evolution and appraisals of the Hadith legacy, see G.H.A. Juynboll, *Muslim Tradition: Studies in Chronology, Provenance, and Authorship of Early Hadith* (Cambridge: Cambridge University Press, 1983); Jonathan Brown, *The Canonization of al-Bukhari and Muslim: The Formation and Function of the Sunni Ḥadith Canon* (Leiden: Brill, 2006).
40. Al-Ghazali, "Fiqh al-Kitab Awalan", in idem, *Al-Sunna al-Nabawiya*, 101–120.
41. Mohammed al-Ghazali, *Al-Islam wa al-Mar'a* (Cairo: IIIT, 1990), 4.
42. Abu 'Amr Uthman Ibn 'Abd al-Rahamn al-Kurdi, known as Ibn al-Salah, was a Shafi'i scholar who died in Damascus. His thirteenth-century CE *Introduction to the Study of Hadith* has served as the standard Sunni statement on this legacy; for a modern edition, see *Muqadimat Ibn Salah* (Beirut: Dar al-Kutub al-'Ilmiya, 1978).
43. Illustrations in Chapter 7, in "Portrait of a Seminar".
44. Al-Ghazali, "Qissat Haya", 198.
45. Works by Shaykh Mohammed Abu Zahra, one of the most distinguished modern experts on usul al-fiqh and its history, include *Al-Jarima wa al-'Uqoba fi al-Fiqh al-Islami: al-'Uqoba* (Cairo: Dar al-Fikr al-Arabi, n.d.); idem, *Tarikh al-Madhahib al-Islamiya fi al-Siyasa wa al-'Aqayid wa*

Tarikh al-Madhahib al-Fiqhiya (Cairo: Dar al-Fikr al-Arabi, n.d.); idem, *Usul al-Fiqh* (Cairo: Dar al-Fikr al-Arabi, n.d.).

46. "Al-Qaradawi Ya'tarif: Katamtu ba'dhu al-Fatawa Tajanuban li-Hiyaj al-'Ama wa Tashwish al-Jamidin." In eulogizing al-Ghazali, al-Qaradawi highlighted the departed Shaykh's exceptional mettle in terms of what he described as al-Ghazali's refusal to give in to the mob when it comes to discussing Shari'a rules (*Al-'Alam al-Islami*, 8 April, 1996).
47. Al-Ghazali, videotape interview (#TAYR-1). He was referring to the work of al-Khatib al-Baghdadi (d. 1071 CE), *Tarikh Baghdad* (Cairo: Maktabat al-Khanji, 1931).
48. For debates surrounding women's mosque attendance, see Marion Katz, *Women in the Mosque: A History of Legal Thought and Social Practice* (New York: Columbia University Press, 2014).
49. "Al-Shaykh al-Ghazali fi Hiwar ma Fannanat Ta'ibat", *Al-Gumhuryia*, Cairo, 23 February, 1995.
50. Al-Ghazali, videotape interview (#W-1).
51. Al-Ghazali, *Al-Sunna al-Nabawiya*, 47–48, 61; idem, videotape interview (#W2).
52. 'Aisha bint Abi Bakr, a wife of the Prophet and daughter of the first caliph (d. 678 CE).
53. Al-Ghazali, *Al-Sunna al-Nabawiya*, 16.
54. The Prophet's wife was referring to the account (below) which Muslim Ibn al-Hajjaj nevertheless included in his canonical collection on the authority of Abi Tharr, *Kitab al-Tahara, Sahih Muslim*, 9/339:
عن ابي هُرَيْرَةَ رضي الله عنه قَالَ : قَالَ رَسُولُ اللهِ صَلَّى اللهُ عَلَيْهِ وَسَلَّمَ : (يَقْطَعُ الصَّلَاةَ الْمَرْأَةُ وَالْحِمَارُ وَالْكَلْبُ ، وَيَقِي ذَلِكَ مِثْلُ مُؤْخِرَةِ الرَّحْلِ)
Also worth noting in the evolution of Hadith legacy is the defence of Abu Hurayra against 'Aisha's criticism, which many *fuqaha* advanced over the centuries, and up to the present day.
55. Bukhari 1/773; Muslim 4/229:
قالت عائشةُ رضي الله عنها-وذُكِرَ عندها ما يقطع الصلاة-: شبَّهْتُمُونَا بِالحُمُرِ وَالكِلَابِ؟! وَاللهِ! لَقَدْ رَأَيْتُ النَّبِيَّ صلى الله عليه وسلم يُصَلِّي، وَإِنِّي عَلى السَّرِيرِ بَيْنَهُ وَبَيْنَ القِبْلَةِ مُضْطَجِعَةٌ، فَتَبْدُو لي الحَاجَةُ، فَأكْرَهُ أنْ أجْلِسَ فَأوذِيَ النَّبِيَّ صلى الله عليه وسلم، فَأنْسَلُّ مِنْ عِنْدِ رِجْلَيْهِ. رواه البخاري [1/773]، ومسلم [4/229].
56. Al-Ghazali, *Al-Sunna al-Nabawiya*, 16, 22–24, 129.
57. Al-Ghazali, videotape interview (#1-U).
58. Al-Ghazali, *Al-Sunna al-Nabawiya*, 48; Those who objected to his arguments denied that al-Shifa' ever existed; see Abu Bakr al-Jaza'ri, *Al-Qawl al-Kareem al-Ghali* (Mecca: Maktabat Umm al-Qura, 1991), 43.
59. Al-Ghazali, *Turathuna al-Fikri*, 162–163; idem, comments following a lecture by Abd al-Halim Abu Shuqaa, *Nadwat Tahrir al-Mar'a*, 20.
60. Prime Minister Nacim al-Din Erbakan's views on gender infuriated many, including some of the devout in Tukey. He is reported to have defended "the idea that women could not take an active role in the decision-making mechanism" (Ruşen Çakır, *Direniş ve Itaat: Iki Iktidar Arasında Islamcı Kadın* [Istanbul: Metis Yayınları, 2000], 67). But with Turkey allowing public religious deliberations on Islam, the country's discourse on Shari'a and women moved on, showing a diversity of views and increased nuance. On the evolution of the Turkish Islamist discourse see idem, *The Changing Nature of Islamism in Turkey: A Comparison of Erbakan and Erdoğan* (MA diss., Bilkent University Ankara, 2002).
61. Because of foreign praise for her public advocacy of girls' education, a gunman in Pakistan shot a 15-year-old girl on 9 October, 2012. Malala Yousafzai survived. Although Malala and her family subsequently moved to Britain, their ordeal did not constitute an isolated act of lunacy, but rather mirrored an all-too-common view held by Muslims in regions extending across Pakistan and Afghanistan. Nor have such attacks on girls and women, in the name of Shari'a, stopped since that time, as is evident from news reports such as Simon Tomlinson, "Hundreds of Afghan Girls Poisoned by Toxic Gas at Two Schools in Suspected

Attacks by Taliban Militants Opposed to their Education", *Daily Mail* (London), 3 September, 2015 (online: http://www.dailymail.co.uk/news/article-3221073/Hundreds-Afghan-girls-poisoned-toxic-gas-two-schools-suspected-attacks-Taliban-militants-opposed-education.html).

62. Such important positions of authority should not be confused with later "modernizing" steps to raise the stature of women that governments of other Gulf States initiated decades later. The latter moves included Qatar's appointments of Shaykha al-Mahmoud as secretary of higher education, Shaykha al-Missned as president of Qatar University, and 'Aisha al-Manna'i as the dean of the Faculty of Shari'a at the same university where al-Ghazali once taught. However excellent such appointments may be, they have different trajectories from, and should not be confused with, the more organic women's advances that prevailed earlier in Kuwait, for example. The author interviewed three of these women in a variety of contexts: Drs 'Aisha al-Manna'i and Badriya al-'Awadhi as part of an Amnesty International project on the human costs of Guantanamo and, much earlier, Siham Razouqi, in the course of reporting on Kuwaiti oil production policies.
63. Kuwait, with a more chequered past than that of its neighbours, finally provided equal civil rights when four women won parliamentary seats in the 2009 general election.
64. Amani Majid, "Dr. Nasir Farid: La Yasihu an Tatawala al-Nisa mansibu al-Re'assa" (Women are not Eligible for the Presidential Position), *Al-Ahram* (Cairo) 20 March, 2005.
65. Al-Ghazali, videotape interview (#W-1); Dr 'Aisha abd al-Rahaman, who was a recognized Qur'anic scholar and a specialist in Arabic literature, died in 1998. She also explored the lives of women in early Muslim society in books and various newspaper articles. This modern woman scholar of Islam married her professor, the famous Shaykh Amin al-Kholi (d. 1966), and she wrote under the name of *bint al-Shati'*, the shore's daughter. Some of her popular titles in Egypt included *Al-Sayyida Zaynab, Batalat Karbala'* (Cairo: al-Hilal, 1965); idem, *Nisa' al-Nabi* (Cairo: al-Hay'a al-Misriya al-'Ama li al-Kita, 2000). Articles discussing her career in English include Issa Boullata, "Modern Qur'an Exegesis: A Study of Bint al-Shati's Method", *Muslim World* 64 (1974): 103–113; Sahiron Syamsuddin, *An Examination of Bint a-Shati's Method of Interpreting the Qur'an* (MA diss., McGill University, 1998); Mervat Hatem, "'A'isha Abdel Rahman: An Unlikely Heroine, a Post-Colonial Reading of Her Life and Some of Her Biographies of Women in the Prophetic Household", *Journal of Middle East Women's Studies* 7/2 (2011): 1–26.
66. Al-Ghazali, videotape interview (#W-1). On Umm Waraqa bint Abd Allah b. Al-Harith, see Ibn Sa'd, *Kitab al-Tabaqat al-Kubra*, vol. 10, ed. Ali M. Umar (Cairo: Maktabat al-Khanki, 2001), no. 5453: 424.
67. In March 2005, Amina Wadud, professor of Islamic Studies at Virginia Commonwealth University led public prayers in New York City. But Wadud's point of departure could not have been any further from al-Ghazali's: a month before she led the mixed-gender prayers, Professor Wadud gave a lecture in Canada, which was sponsored by York University (Canada) and the Noor Cultural Centre. In this talk, Dr Wadud explained that "in all honesty she could not continue with the hypocrisy of lying about how she felt about some verses of the Qur'an." According to her view, "it is the Qur'an that gives me the means to say no to the Qur'an" (Quoted in "Canada: Amina Wadud Lecture Disrupted in Canada" [online: http://www.wluml.org/node/1890]").
68. See the previous note.
69. Al-Ghazali, *Al-Sunna al-Nabawiya*, 46.
70. Quoted from a recorded lecture in Dubai, UAE, 1991. The private audio-recording was provided by Dr Mohammed Mushtahiri.
71. Al-Ghazali, *Al-Sunna al-Nabawiya*, 48.
72. Ibid., 50.

73. Egyptian women led the rest of their society in underlining the significance of al-Ghazali's changed views on gender. Among the first to critically survey this evolution in his thought was Heba Raouf Izzat, "*Al-Haqq al-Murr*: Qadhayia al-Mar'a fi Fikr al-Ghazali", *Islamiyat al-Ma'rifa* 2/3 (2007): 87–104. Also, as previously noted, Azhari Professor Amna Nosseir used him as a modern authority on Muslim rulemaking. Outside religious education circles, more women celebrated his memory too, as in the case of a renowned figure in Egypt's press corps, Sanaa el-Bissi, in her "Huwa wa Hiya, al-Ghazali ... Sayid al-Dowa'a", *Al-Ahram* (Cairo), 23 February 2008; on al-Bissi, see Amira Howeidy, "Sanaa El-Bissi, Reader, She Wrote It", *Al-Ahram Weekly*, 17–23 June 1999 (online: http://weekly.ahram.org.eg/1999/434/profile.htm).
74. Al-Ghazali, *Min Huna Na'lam*, 197.
75. Al-Ghazali, "Fiqh al-Kitab Awalan"; idem, *Al-Sunna al-Nabawiya*, 101–120.
76. Al-Ghazali, *Turathuna al-Fikri*, 181.
77. Ibid., 182.
78. Al-Ghazali, *Kaifa Nat'amal ma' al-Qur'an*, 164.
79. Al-Ghazali, videotape interview (#TJD-1).
80. Al-Ghazali, *Kaifa Nat'amal ma' al-Qur'an*, 68.
81. Ibid., 164.
82. Ibid.
83. For illustrations, see al-Ghazali, *Turathuna al-Fikri*, 179–182; idem, *Al-Sunna al-Nabawiya*, 68–79.
84. Al-Ghazali, *Turathuna al-Fikri*, 161.
85. Al-Ghazali, *Kaifa Nat'amal ma' al-Qur'an*, 164.
86. Al-Ghazali, *Turathuna al-Fikri*, 170–173.
87. Ibid., 181.
88. Al-Ghazali, *Al-Sunna al-Nabawiya*, 107.
89. Ibid., 104.
90. Ibid., 149.
91. Al-Ghazali, *Turathuna al-Fikri*, 173.
92. Al-Ghazali, *Kaifa Nat'amal ma' al-Qur'an*, 164.
93. Ibid. (al-Ghazali quoting his earlier work *Fiqh al-Sira*).

PART TWO

THE RULEMAKING TRAJECTORY OF SHARI’A

SEVEN

Shari'a: Dynamic Method or Fixed Law? Does it Matter?

Researchers will struggle to find an "Islamic law" associated with al-Ghazali, although they will be able to discern a definite mechanism, a method at the heart of Shari'a rulemaking to which he and his people subscribed. This chapter highlights the main technical and historical features of this Shari'a rule-/lawmaking process, noting the distinction between its variable and permanent sources, and exploring some of the significant influences on it over the centuries.

One thing stands out as a constant in al-Ghazali's life, which reinforced his influence among his fellow Muslims: his absolute loyalty to Shari'a. However, neither the sum of his texts, the various crises he triggered, the Shari'a rules he deduced, nor his own words, indicate that this loyalty was to an "Islamic law". Appendix 1 in this book includes a portrait of a seminar that al-Ghazali held in Cairo, which was attended by some of the most influential mainstream Islamic scholars in Egypt. Their deliberations provide a window on approaches to Shari'a and *fiqh* in the late twentieth century, underlining the question of whether it matters that Shari'a rulemaking is understood mainly in terms of a law or as a process. The disparity between the assumptions of the term "Islamic law" and how these Egyptian scholars, including al-Ghazali, viewed Shari'a reveals worrying gaps in understanding the experiences of Muslims, which in turn suggest that it is time to overhaul the academic discourse on Islam, especially when it comes to its rulemaking.

The Shari'a method of deducing rules

Muslims trace the method from which to deduce Shari'a rules back to the early days in Medina. Its outline remains fairly unchanged, in theory. As Muslims understand it, this way of deducing rules/laws draws on four fundamental sources (*usul*). Although not of equal weight, each of these sources forms a stage in an essentially four-step process. In modern legal phraseology, the Qur'an can be considered to be the "constitution", and Muslims designate it the divine and unchanging foundation of Shari'a. The three subsequent stages of Shari'a correspond to the modern notions of precedent, reason,[1] and communal input,[2] all of which are broad categories that appear under numerous Arabic terms. In theory, any learned, sound-minded Muslim can use this transparent process to discover or repeal a Shari'a rule/law. In practice, however, from an early period such work became the responsibility of *fuqaha*, experts with specialist knowledge of Shari'a, which they use to make—or challenge—rules/laws.

Although Muslims believe that the method employed was established at an early period, the first adjustments to key elements were made less than 40 years after Mohammed's death, and the method has continued to evolve since that time in response to events. Communal consultation (*shura*) provides an early example: when political authorities showed little appetite for consultation in the legislative process, the "thinking Muslim public" reworked *shura* to preserve the principle. *Shura* became *ijma'* (consensus), a more open-ended and politically acceptable expression that had not been used in Medina. Meanwhile, the Qur'an has been interpreted through particular cultural and political lenses, while precedent and what constituted valid legal reasoning have also been redefined (the former as discussed in earlier chapters). In order to preserve its outline, Muslims enshrined this basic methodology by means of a Hadith, whether genuine or not, in which Mohammed explained the process to his governor in Yemen.[3]

Who speaks authoritatively for this method has also changed. In response to a dynastic coup, early Muslim activists employed Shari'a rulemaking as a tool of political resistance, shifting the dynamic relationship of state, religion, and law in the nascent Muslim polity: after the capital moved to Damascus in (661 CE), the caliphs and their officials lost their poisition as the decisive authorities on this method. Resisting Muslims, who would become Islam's intelligentsia, the *fuqaha*, were able to lay down their own, and sometimes different, rules in diverse communities in Arabia, the Mediterranean, and beyond, and their labour marginalized the legislative authority of the state. As a result, a *de facto* separation of legislative power (managed by all who fall under the rubric of *fuqaha*) from executive power (held by a caliph and his palace officials) was a feature of Muslim society even in the first century of Islam.

However, from independent, learned activists, many of the *fuqaha* gradually organized themselves into church-like structures, despite the Qur'an's denunciation of clerics and the subsequent formal Sunni position that men do not speak with God's authority. Clerical groups eventually attached themselves to whatever dynasty the *fuqaha* lived under, at length becoming part of the state bureaucracy. By the fourteenth century CE, the relationship between such *fuqaha* and Muslim political authorities in many ways resembled the Byzantine church–state model. Historical practices thus sometimes clash painfully with the mainstream Muslim (Sunni) understanding of Shari'a.

With diverse communities discovering their own rules from this method, no central body, political or religious, could be identified as the ultimate authority on Shari'a rule-/lawmaking, and a variety of schools of thought, *madhahib al-fiqh*, flourished. Most of these are no longer extant, but among the Sunni majority four main schools survive. Their differences, as briefly summarized, consist of (1) how to weigh *usul*, the fundamental elements of Shari'a, against one another; (2) the supporting sources used to enhance the operational effectiveness of the basic method; (3) the particular schemes of deriving rules/laws from these *usul*;[4] and (4) their approaches to the general guidelines—*fiqh* maxims—that scholars deduced[5] from the tenor of Shari'a.[6] Thus a lively type of legal pluralism flourished in the Muslim landscape. Ibn Qudama's *Al-Mughni*, a key compendium of *fiqh*, illustrates the outcome of this decentralized approach to one method.[7] Shaykh Abu Zahra notes the example of the rule on counting gold and silver for the purposes of *zakat*; *Al-Mughni* records two different positions on the matter,[8] both of which originate with Ibn Hanbal (after whom the Hanbali school is named). In one account, he allowed counting the two precious metals together, but in the other he forbade it. Al-Khallal, a founder of the Hanbali school, chose the rule allowing it, while his student, another key Hanbali scholar, chose the position that forbade it.[9] How then is it possible to see in these divergent, often contradictory rules, that *madhahib al-fiqh* have preserved over many centuries a law, let alone a rigid one? How changes to this basic methodology over time were effected and by whom remains the largely unwritten story of Muslim lawmaking.

What continued, what changed

Despite significant changes over the centuries, Muslims continue to understand Shari'a rule-/lawmaking in terms of the four-step method described above. They believe this method to be divinely dictated, but not their efforts to deduce rules from it. Approached in this way, Shari'a is a process, not a code of law, meaning that Muslim rules/laws have been constantly changing. *Fiqh* schools, or (as in the above Hanbali example on counting gold) scholars within one school or even a single scholar, might deduce different rules from this method, all of which are labelled as "Shari'a". This enormous variety has not especially troubled Muslims, however. Even today, many continue to praise Shari'a as orderly, egalitarian, and dynamic, believing it can meet any of life's contingencies. That explains why in August 1995, seven months before his death, the International Islamic University (in Malaysia) celebrated al-Ghazali's achievements by hailing him as a defender of Islam's orderly approach. Presenting him with the award, Anwar Ibrahim, the University's president at the time, cited his book *From Here We Know* (*Min Huna Na'lam*) as evidence of the shaykh's emphasis on systematic thought.[10] Many, especially in the West, would find Ibrahim's choice of *Min Huna Na'lam* as an illustration of rationalism curious; but the Malaysian scholar and statesman was not concerned with rules that denied women public authority, which al-Ghazali had later reversed. Like many fellow Muslims, Ibrahim admired al-Ghazali for his unwavering loyalty to Shari'a as a methodological process, which *Min Huna Na'lam* loudly defended in the late 1940s. A further continuing demonstration of this loyalty, as they see it, was al-Ghazali's campaign in the 1980s to save the same method from becoming historical debris. Muslims could legitimately embrace, abandon, or reverse rules that al-Ghazali or other *fuqaha* deduced from the method of Shari'a; but what cannot change, at least formally, is the method's core and foundational sources. As these Muslims see it, they cannot subscribe to rule-/lawmaking that derives from whims or expediency; they cannot blindly copy traditions of the past or gullibly imitate prevalent trends. Scholars who defend this kernel of Shari'a rule-/lawmaking, as his Malaysian hosts believed al-Ghazali to have done, have often gained the gratitude of their fellow Muslims throughout the centuries.

Permanent and variable sources of Shari'a

It is true that Muslims believe that Shari'a rulemaking is divinely inspired and that the Qur'an, the first source of Shari'a, from which its permanent principles originate, cannot be challenged. Equally true, however, is that its other three fundamental sources/stages (*usul*) have been left for humans to determine. No matter how some dressed them up, the collective aspect of rulemaking in Islam (whether presented in terms of *shura* or *ijma'*) and the various kinds of legitimate reasoning involved (whether *rai'*, *qiyas*, *ijtihad*, or any other) are all human products. This is also true of precedent, the second source of Shari'a. Although it came to mean mostly, but not exclusively, the Sunna of the Prophet, the *fuqaha* recognized the tentative nature of Hadith when they allowed different schools to choose opposing reports about the Prophet depending on which they judged to be more accurate. This flexibility in Shari'a rulemaking became integral to Muslim legal and cultural memories; the method had allowed their forefathers to perfect, adapt, or update rules when they governed societies far more complex than those of Arabia.

The two predominant discourses with which Islam is currently described block out this historical and procedural dynamism. The first, a centuries-old Muslim narrative, does not reject the dynamism of Shari'a outright, but it blurs its history. Its warring sub-narratives all follow the same outline that uses the sacred to promote the right to rule of a particular party; Chapter 8 discusses the impact and limitations of this essentially political discourse. The alternative predominant discourse on Islam is more recent and Western, but its lens informs academic research and the media worldwide, not only in the West. Conceived in the context of colonialism, this orientalist narrative too is essentially political, although heavily wrapped in pretensions of scholarly impartiality,[11] and its neo-orientalist successors not only clinched to the posturing in old politically inspired Muslim accounts, but also entrenched many of their narratives as historical truths. Its experts constructed a concept of "Islamic law" that bordered on the exotic, and this can be seen in Western academic approaches to al-Ghazali's first famous book, *Min Huna Na'lam* (as discussed further below).[12]

Orientalists and neo-orientalists have often dismissed evidence of Shari'a's flexibility, or they argue that its dynamism is exaggerated. However, for the most part these experts' assumptions correspond neither to past historical developments nor to current mainstream Sunni Muslim legal constructs. The question of how to apply Islam's divine principles is a matter that has been largely, and openly, left to communities, or rather to their thinking public, to determine.[13] Even the grand design behind Shari'a rule-/lawmaking, commonly referred to as *maqasid* or the intentions of Shari'a, was left to humans to determine, with the *fuqaha* identifying several broad purposes. Imam Abu Hamid al-Ghazali famously listed them as the protection of faith, life, progeny, mind, and property, and the bulk of the *'ulama* concurred. Shaykh Ibn 'Ashur (d. 1973) added freedom as a sixth goal, and Mohammed al-Ghazali further added a seventh: justice, encompassing social, emotional, and political justice.[14] None of these *maqasid* concerns theology, however; they all centre on the wellbeing of the individual and the community. Nor do they sound peculiar to Islam. A fourteenth-century leader of the literalist—some would say rigid—Hanbali school of thought, Ibn Qayyim al-Jawzyia (d. 1350 CE), summarized this understanding of Shari'a rule-/lawmaking as the pursuit of human benefit. He explained that a rule or legal argument

> that departs from justice, to turn into injustice, from compassion, to become its opposite, from benefit [*maslaha*] to lead to [a state of] decay, and from wisdom, to wind up as folly, then [this rule/argument] would not be part of the Shari'a, even if [man had] attached it to it.[15]

Ibn Qayyim entitled this account, "A Section on Change to Fatwa (Discovering Shari'a rules/laws) and its Variety According to the Changes in Times, Place(s), Circumstances, Intentions, and Benefits". Ever since, whether they subscribed to his Hanbali thought or not, many Muslims have considered such statements as only restating Qur'anic teachings.[16] Like al-Ghazali, Ibn Qayyim previously contested what had become orthodox *fiqh* arguments and rules in his own times.

He too prevailed, and Muslim scholars from other *madhahib* have subsequently regarded Ibn Qayyim as one of Shari'a's foremost legal minds, even if they have not advocated his Hanbali school.[17]

That which benefits the good of individuals and communities has often been included as an additional source of Shari'a, or at least an indication of the correctness of rules deduced from it. Muslim scholars gave such "benefit" various designations, such as *al-maslaha*, *al-istislah*, or *al-isitihsan*.[18] The *fuqaha* also disagreed on how valid interests and benefits should be defined, or what their weight should be as a source of Shari'a rulemaking. Their perceptions of correct human practices were not always in accord, either. There are also many examples of how, by putting forward their interests as public benefit, the powerful (whether the political and economic elites, or the mob) have browbeaten whole communities into accepting unsavoury practices as of Shari'a. Why did Muslims not see such legislative permissiveness as a flaw? And how did they reconcile it with their belief in Shari'a's unchanging scriptural principles?

Empirical observation as divine source

The Muslim quest to continually update Shari'a rules/laws does not always stem from expediency; rather, it originates in two central tenets of their faith. The first is that the universe and divine revelation have the same consistent author: God. The Qur'an, therefore, can never contradict true scientific or natural laws. The second tenet is that God's intentions lead only to benefit; they cannot cause harm to either the individual or the community. To substantiate these beliefs, Muslims erected a bridge between revelation and reality in the form of practical observation. Evidence from life, regardless of its origin, thus became a key Muslim tool for discovering God's laws, as they relate both to interpreting physical phenomena and identifying social practices that either benefit or harm human society. Observation also clarified the meanings and intentions of Islam's scriptural principles: even the most simple-minded among the *fuqaha* have had to consider how to harmonize the Qur'an and practical information, and Muslims are agreed that contradictions here can originate only in human misunderstanding. In short, it is a principle that Muslim lawmaking cannot ignore the Qur'an or dismiss sound empirical information.

If deducing Shari'a rules correctly relies on information about reality, then the sources of this information deserve attention. When examining *fiqh* rules/laws, the crucial questions must always be: Where does a particular *faqih*, mufti, or *'alim* turn to for reliable observation?, and How does this *'alim* then interpret the information distilled from observation? The answer is that it comes from the prevailing communal worldview, a society's *weltanschauung*, and it is ahistorical to assume that all Muslim communities throughout the ages and everywhere embraced one, unchanging worldview. Whenever or wherever circumstances changed, communities sanctioned new practices by translating them into Shari'a rules. How Muslims have perceived learning, collective identity, orthodoxy, or even mundane matters such as commerce, for example, demonstrate the fascinating variety and transformations in the social and legal tapestry of Islam. But it is precisely because Muslims recognized empirical observation as a main tool of Shari'a rule-/lawmaking that their thinkers sought in times of crises to control what counts as valid real-life evidence, or at least to identify its parameters. Without such supervision, influential scholars argued, decisions would be made on whims and chaos would reign. Thus some of the *fuqaha* moved a step further, to restrict the instances where the interpretation of empirical evidence would apply. However, despite wave after wave of restrictions and fears, no school or community could definitively revoke the centrality to Shari'a of practical observation; instead, as powerful figures in Muslim societies discovered, it is easier to shape the sources and meanings of reality. *Madhahib* eventually became fortresses that preserved such reconstructions of the world by sanctifying particular interpretations of empirical evidence.

Changing discourses under familiar rubrics

Muslim enemies outside Egypt accused al-Ghazali of reiterating the old errors of Abu Hanifa.[19] They sought to dismiss, or at least contain, his critiques of their approach to Shari'a rule-/lawmaking by presenting them as the familiar mistake of a particular *madhhab*. Before Hadith had swept the Muslim landscape by the late ninth century CE, the early Hanafi method of discovering Shari'a rules did not favour wholesale reliance on reports that claimed the Prophet as their author; but, as later *fiqh* works indicate, the Hanafis eventually toed the line. The remaining four schools in the Sunni landscape eventually formulated an adjusted construction of rulemaking, which also entrenched a particularly standardized view of reality. In al-Ghazali's case, claims that his *madhhab*'s gaffes showed he was in error, along with references to a dispute between *madhahibs*, largely fell on deaf ears where it most mattered, in Egypt. In al-Ghazali's lifetime, while Egypt served as a great centre of Sunni *madhahib* learning, few outsiders appreciated the extent to which the country had adjusted its general views of these *fiqh* schools. As mentioned elsewhere, Abduh's reconsideration of *fiqh*'s legacy, which Hasan al-Banna then took to the country's streets, had altered how Egyptians approached the Muslim legal heritage. The common Egyptian no longer concerned her/himself with, or even subscribed to, a particular *madhhab*. By the late twentieth century new perceptions held sway; most of those who could read and write generally saw common disagreements over the details of Shari'a in the name of one school of *fiqh* or another as a flawed legacy from a troubled past that only the ignorant or covert enemies of their faith would advocate. The landscape created by Abduh/al-Banna was fertile ground for al-Ghazali's last campaign. His open critiques did not disturb many in senior Azhari circles, including *'ulama* who belonged to *madhahib* closely associated with Hadith. In 2006, even the Shafi'i *usul al-fiqh* scholar Shaykh Ali Goma described as "brainless" those Muslims who believed in the conclusive authority of *uhadi*, singular reports (the bulk of Hadith). Those who make such claims presented "inconsequential voices, not learned ones", an adamant Goma said in an interview.[20] A senior Maliki scholar, who wished to remain anonymous, sounded less diplomatic. After discussing his own thought-provoking research on Hadith, he griped about what he called "Hadith-inspired paganism" everywhere: in homes, streets, buses, and workplaces.

The nature and import of constant adjustments to Muslim "orthodoxy" and the self-critiques within Islam's scholarly ranks are not of great interest to many studying Islamic law, even when they note them, and even though the history of Shari'a today and in the past has revealed these elements as central to Shari'a rulemaking. Prominent *'ulama* have understood the constant uncertainty and discontent to which the nature of their rulemaking method could give rise, and there was concern over how the lack of any central authority meant that it could be threatened by either the mob and/or the powerful. These concerns, integral to Shari'a rulemaking, had little to do with details in *madhahib*, the static universe which many academic experts inhabit. As discussed in the previous chapter, al-Ghazali was aware of the violence recorded by al-Khatib al-Baghdadi in *Tarikh Baghdad*, the eleventh-century CE history of the Shafi'i faqih.[21] Abu al-Faraj Ibn al-Jawzi (d. 1201 CE), a pillar of the Hanbali School in the twelfth century CE, echoed his concerns;[22] although his school designated accounts about or from the Prophet as an ultimate source of valid precedent, Ibn al-Jawzi complained about the mob's fixation with Hadith.[23] Diversions from what he believed to be the correct way of Shari'a rulemaking also disturbed this Hanbali scholar. Such developments have little significance in the imaginary world of "Islamic law", however, which prefers to posit some essentialist Hanbali (or other) *madhhab*. For Ibn al-Jawzi, what modern experts suppose to be "classical Islamic law", instead described a tumult led by a mob wanting to sanctify the Hadith collected by the eponym of his school. Ibn al-Jawzi did not believe that this reflected the rule-deducing methodology of his school, or the intention of Ahmed Ibn Hanbal, even though some scholars had now started to follow the mob,[24] and he recorded his concerns:

> Some of those who have embraced Hadith asked me: "Could there be any [report] in *Musnad Ahmed* [Ibn Hanbal's collection of reports] that is not correct?" I said: "Yes". My reply shocked some [...] At first I did not pay much attention to them thinking they are unlearned.

When he found that such approaches were spreading to dominate rulemaking, Ibn al-Jawzi expressed his surprise and dismay:

> I said to myself: What a development! Even those who claim to be scholars have now also joined the throngs; they employ Hadith [reports] just because they heard of them, neglecting to research which [report] is true and which is shoddy. [...] They suppose that anyone who says what I said to them is attacking Ahmed's [Ibn Hanbal] work [...] That is not correct. For Imam Ahmed [merely] reported all accounts that circulated [in his time], which included the good and the flawed. [Consequently h]e [Ahmed Ibn Hanbal] rejected a lot of the same Hadiths that he reported and did not use [them in deducing Shari'a rules].[25]

Whether or not Ibn al-Jawzi's disapproval of the crowd's calls to sanctify suspect stories which his master had collected as Hadith reflected the real views of Ibn Hanbal, there is no escaping the disorder in this "classical" rulemaking. The record of his concerns also shows that unwelcome modifications to Shari'a's basic methodology, and not just Hanbali thought, occurred even when they contradicted earlier interpretations or the intention of the original authors. To support his view on Ibn Hanbal's uses of Hadith in rulemaking, Ibn al-Jawzi quoted early figures from his school: Abu Bakr al-Khallal (d. 923 CE)[26] and, from more than a century later, al-Qadi Abu Yala al-Farra (d. 1066 CE).[27] Discussing a particular rule, Abu Yala al-Farra explained that, "Ahmed collected in his *Musnad* all circulating reports; he did not mean [to divide these stories] into the genuine and the corrupt." Ibn Hanbal's son and student, Abd Allah, was reported to have said that his father described his *Musnad* as only "a record of *ad hoc*" accounts about early Islam that had spread in his times, adding that had he chosen only reports that he thought were genuine, his work would have included only very few accounts. "But, my son, you know such is my approach to [collecting] Hadith", Ahmed is reported to have said. From this, al-Qadi Abu Yala al-Farra concluded "that since Ahmed himself told us about his scheme of compiling [his] *Musnad*, [that must] mean that anyone who uses it as a definite [permanent] source [of making rules/laws] ignores Ahmed's purposes."[28] Hanbali leaders, al-Khallal in the tenth century CE, al-Farra in the eleventh century, and Ibn al-Jawzi in the twelfth century all fretted about the mob altering Shari'a rule-/lawmaking under the pretext of observing valid precedent.[29] So did many other *'ulama* after them, including a Hanafi shaykh in the twentieth century, Mohammed al-Ghazali.

Al-Ghazali may be far less known than the forefathers of the Hanbali School in previous centuries, but, like these *fuqaha*, his alarm mirrored long-held concerns about how ill-tempered crowds hijack aspects of Shari'a rulemaking. Geography, not only chronology, has dictated the outcome of such debates at any particular time. As mentioned above, in the case of late twentieth-century Egypt, thanks to the seeds that Mohammed Abduh had planted in al-Azhar, the Egyptian narrative on Shari'a had evolved in distinctive ways, and this helped al-Ghazali when the time came for him to advocate a modified approach to Shari'a. In other countries, he might have become a pariah, but in the context of Egypt he instead became a magnet for his country's dynamic Islamic thinkers, even if many of them did not share his *madhhab*, background, or even some of his views. A seminar which al-Ghazali gave to members of Egypt's religious establishment, and which is summarized in Appendix 1, shows how these senior scholars of Islam perceived Shari'a in the late twentieth century[30] and highlights a key, if not the key, conclusion of al-Ghazali's career: that as it now stands, *fiqh* entrenches a corrupt political culture that has poisoned Muslim societies and their civilization. In this, the path al-Ghazali charted differed structurally from that of many famous modern Muslim scholars, including his admirers.[31] Whereas contemporary Muslim thinkers read *fiqh* works as offering enlightened constitutional thinking and wise instruction on governance, al-Ghazali reasoned the opposite. *Fiqh* works dealing with principles of government in fact exposed an appalling dearth of constitutional thinking and revealed the main faultlines of Muslim history, not the profound ideas that some pretended to read in them.[32] Only Qur'anic principles, such as the stress on equality and freedom, and precedents of the early efforts to apply these ideals, saved Muslims from the total ruin that the political traditions of empires and their *fuqaha* would warrant, he thought.

In illustration, al-Ghazali compared *fiqh*'s criteria governing Muslim relations with non-Muslims to those that he believed Islam taught. For centuries "our relationships with others have mainly revolved around *jizyia* (poll taxes that non-Muslims paid) or war. That is what Azhari students learn up to this day", he observed.[33] However, *fiqh* misses that Islam primarily presents "an invitation to a comprehensive package that included monotheism, justice, and democracy."[34] A Muslim has no business beyond extending this invitation to those unfamiliar with it, he added. If Islam's call was rejected, he said, then all a Muslim had to insist on was the freedom to believe in and speak about this invitation, no more. The bulk of *fiqh* ideas that dealt with non-Muslims ignored this underlying principle, exposing how distant *fiqh* literature had become from the Qur'an, the Sunna, and sensible thinking, al-Ghazali said.[35] On the whole, its works on governance include no more than sketchy or primitive notions about running a community. Some of *fiqh*'s political constructs cultivated poor thinking, which disfigured much in Muslims' lives—all in the name of Shari'a. Worst of all, he thought, they turned their back on the gift that the principles of the Qur'an offered in organizing power relations—a gift which other communities struggled to acquire.[36] Ruthless tyranny, starting early in Islamic history, eventually silenced all legal or any other discussions of the ruler's rights and responsibilities.[37] "Something dangerous took place in Muslim history", he told an interviewer.[38] Despite so much lip service to Islamic principle, the muzzling of Shari'a in areas that touched power relations marked "the first broken ring in Islam's chain".[39] Al-Ghazali did not mince his words: he came generally to regard those who yearned for past Muslim governance as idiots or outside enemies. In commemorating the fifteenth century of hijra (1981 CE), al-Ghazali wrote about how talk of "returning to Islam" as a state filled him with "bad tidings". Those who advocated such a thing, he explained, added to the irrationality that afflicted his community, eager to revive traditions of governance that were of little use to Muslims or the world at large.[40]

Al-Ghazali was far from alone among late twentieth-century senior *'ulama* in worrying about how gullible approaches to the Muslim literary legacy misrepresented Shari'a. Curiously, on the night of the seminar, it appeared that the Azhar-reared scholars had less deference to old *fiqh* works than non-Azhari scholars of Islam. A former Azhar dean of Arabic and Islamic studies, Shaykh al-Sayyid Rizq al-Taweel, echoed al-Ghazali's warning that continuing to approach "*fiqh* compositions in the current ways [...] squandered [Muslim] time, their lives, and intellect."[41] Al-Taweel remembered how his fellow Azhari students regularly exchanged what they learned of the foolish premises of their various *madhahib*.[42] More comments by this Azhar doyen further dismantled impressions that there was any such thing as "Islamic law", even as regards family law. The so-called personal/family Shari'a code in Egypt, for example, merely included the preferences of those who drafted it, which they selected from among a variety of questionable *fiqh* ideas, al-Taweel lamented.[43] Throughout the seminar, the energetic and influential Muslim scholars who gathered around al-Ghazali appeared unified by anxiety about what could be described as the state of "cultural necrophilia" that gripped their communities, to borrow Simon Schama's expression.[44] Shaykhs al-Taweel and al-Ghazali wanted to cure the delusion that works from the past should be equated with Islam. Fellow Muslims had turned their rich heritage into sacred corpses, around which they constantly whirled; "the past-tensers", an English-speaking regular in al-Ghazali's crowd, Taha Jabir al Alwani, called them in an interview.[45]

Poor law, brilliant method

If it were a law, Shari'a would indeed be inadequate. Many of its rules are out of date and unable to support visions of structural change, as discussed in the next chapter. Its rules are also chaotic and hard to determine, as the examples in the early part of this chapter show. However, as a method, Shari'a injects order into even the most unruly settings. It provides its users with timeless principles, as well as standards for how to use them. It also requires users to make choices and not to fear legal and normative differences. In other words, this is a rulemaking process that expects its users to be always alert, both socially and intellectually.

It offers societies a transparent methodology, in which those who employ it must constantly re-assess their observations and, accordingly, their evidence. If they fail to do so, their deficiencies will be reflected in the laws they deduce and in their choices from among existing rules. The method of determining Shari'a does not offer a checklist or impose unattainable, purist regulations on the diverse communities that use it to organize their lives; rather, it provides a systematic outline for how to deduce rules, along with effective and stable points of reference. As individuals and communities, Muslims—not God—have had the responsibility of concluding from this process the practical details for regulating their lives. It has also been left to humans how to apply these rules/laws according to changing contexts. Conceiving the Shari'a-rulemaking process as "law" overturns this inbuilt energy, and it particularly blurs the element of choice. It also discards Shari'a's characteristic of enquiry: misunderstood as a fixed perfectionist code, it deprives Muslims of their most effective historical tool for making nonviolent adjustments to their societies. Worse, it converts bad practices, as long as they derive from the past, into God-given law. Below is a brief summary of the elements of Shari'a lawmaking as Muslims understand them.

Key features of the Shari'a method and the rules derived from it

Continuing loyalty to the method of Shari'a has produced a medley of precedents, proofs, scholarly opinions, and accepted customs across a wide geographical area. As a process of evaluation rather than a code, Shari'a requires constant intellectual re-assessment. The method brings both opportunities and challenges, and theory and practice have not always been aligned. The *fuqaha* who have benefitted (socially, economically, and politically) from blurring the essential distinction between Shari'a and *fiqh* would initially agree that their rulemaking should be stripped of divine pretensions, before immediately proceeding to qualify this caution—although none of these learned Muslims have dared make the absolutist claims that the Western construct of "Islamic law" entrenches. It is true that for centuries it suited many *fuqaha* to dispense *fiqh* preferences as being somehow sacred, resulting in confusing contradictions in scholarly explanations of Shari'a. Shaykh Yusuf al-Qaradawi offers an illustration here: his book on clarifying Shari'a places its rulemaking in two spheres.[46] In the first part of the book the *fuqaha* appear to speak in God's voice; *fiqh* is treated as precise and sacred, although it is apparent that most of the discussed rules originate in precedents from the Muslim past or in man-made *fiqh* constructs. However, the second part of the book clarifies that no one can ever speak in God's voice.

Lawmaking appears on another plane, rational and revolving around a process, not a law. To put it in Qaradawi's words:

> The Wise Legislator [God] did not wish to make His texts detailed, exact codes. He intended them to be made as lighthouses that guide those wishing to follow His way. With a few rare exceptions, His purpose is to set the principles and goals, not to reveal a comprehensive, definitive order [of rules/laws]. His [God's] intention is to encourage the human mind and to open the door for Muslim intellect so [Muslims] may choose whatever order suited to their state, times, and circumstances, without [having to suffer undue] limitation or burden.[47]

However, despite plebeian perceptions of *fiqh* as divine Shari'a—whether unintentional or encouraged to enhance *fuqaha* standing in society—key *'ulama* have rebelled against attempts to sanctify *fiqh*, or at least the rulings of their competitors. An essential attribute of the rules deduced from Shari'a's method is their tentative nature, and there are many accounts in the Sunni legacy that show how earlier masters of *fiqh* stressed this key feature. Here are some examples:

> Imam Abu Hanifa [the eponym of the Hanafi School] said: "It is not permissible for anyone to advocate what we advocated until he first check from where we derived it. It is not correct that someone who is unfamiliar with [the sources of] my evidence/proof to base it [a rule] on what I ruled."
>
> Imam Malik [the eponym of the Maliki School] was reported to have said: "I am but a man, I [sometimes perceive] wrongly and I [sometimes perceive] correctly. Examine my opinion. All that is in agreement with the book [the Qur'an] and the Sunna [Prophet's precedent] then follow it. All that which is not, discard it."
>
> Ibn Hanbal [the eponym of the Hanbali School] was reported to have said to Abu Dawud: "Do not copy me, nor copy Malik, nor copy Shafi'i, nor al-Awzai, nor al-Thawri, but derive [your rules] from where these [*fuqaha*] derived theirs [that is, the sources and method of Shari'a]."[48]

Other reminders that rulings derived from the method of Shari'a should not be given divine pretensions abound. There is the standard etiquette of concluding *fiqh* rules or arguments with the qualifying phrase "*wa Allah 'alam*" ("but God knows best"), and Sunni scholars have enshrined this principle as an instruction of the Prophet. In the first part of *'Ilam al-Muwaqi'in*, Ibn al-Qayyim included a chapter on the prohibition of claiming that a rule deduced from Shari'a was God's rule. He cited the Prophet instructing one of his officers, Barida, that if they ask him to rule in a case or make a law that of God's, "do not do it; for you must know that whatever you deduce are only your conclusions; you cannot know for certain God's judgement."[49] By embracing notions such as this as a central feature of their rulemaking, early Muslim communities acquired legislative autonomy. It allowed them to unreservedly integrate into their narrow world the intellectual and cultural treasures of civilizations far more complex than theirs, and to do it in an orderly way. Rules deduced from Shari'a that a majority in any one community favoured became the Shari'a of that community; rules that a community did not especially favour faded away. Shari'a may be the oldest surviving system of collective communal rulemaking, but only as a method. Memories of a vibrant and cosmopolitan past, not fanaticism, usually lie behind many modern Muslims' loyalty to Shari'a. In their minds, its transparent procedure ensures fairness and cultural richness. Its elements brought many societies together: records show when early Muslims conceived valid rulemaking in terms of flexibility and a benchmark, they promoted legal and cultural unity in and around the Mediterranean Sea that stretched into parts of Asia, Africa, and Europe.

Neither armies nor empires were previously able to bring such unity to this variety of civilizations; consequently, a wealth of legacies that extend from Greece, across Persia, and into India have been preserved and developed thanks to Shari'a, not in spite of it. This memory of cultural richness lives on. Regardless of how isolated, even narrow-minded, Muslim communities have become, they still concede that diversity thrived when *al-salaf al-salih*, or their upright predecessors, ruled large areas of the world. Together with reason, which also plays an important part in this process, the evidence from Islam's formative years has meant that Muslims must welcome fruitful human experiences and sound values regardless of their origins. The restricted universe of "Islamic law", the antithesis of all things Western, dictates otherwise, however.

Egypt's former mufti Ali Goma drew attention to this confusion. Among the senior *'ulama*, even this devoted subscriber to *fiqh*'s historical constructs also insisted that "*fiqh* (legislative legacy), or what I refer to as *al-tashri al-Islami*, does not equal an Islamic law." The reason appeared clear to senior *fuqaha*: "in practical terms *al-tashri al-Islami* can order me to perform a certain act and simultaneously prohibit me from performing the same act; there, it is possible to find a rule and its exact opposite", he explained.[50] Al-Ghazali also expressed alarm when an interviewer described Shari'a as fixed. Sunni *'ulama* differentiate between Islam's principles that have legal implications and *fiqh* rules and constructs derived from these principles. In the words of Goma, a feasible law must be precise in order to serve both the judges who apply it and those to whom it applies. This contrasts sharply with *al-tashri al-Islami*, which consists of what the mufti called an eclectic "bundle" that guides the deducing of valid rules. This "bundle", he elaborated, includes approved "sources of legislation, purposes of legislation [*maqasid*], maxims [*qawa'id al-fiqh*], and various proofs derived from the Sunna [*ijma, qiyas, istidlal*], as well as from other admissible sources." As Shaykh Goma saw it, references to the *tashri al-Islami*'s collection as Islamic law can only be an implicit criticism, a term that carried an inherent censure of Shari'a.[51]

Rewriting the story of Shari'a

Ali Goma has a point. The term "Islamic law" redefines Shari'a, and it rewrites its story. It also imprisons Shari'a in a mythical "classical Islamic" age, which erratically wanders from medieval times up to the nineteenth century, yet rarely goes back to Medina. Instead, this "Shari'a law" consists of snippets culled from *fiqh* works. Academia rarely places these *fiqh* extracts, whether rules or arguments, in their actual contexts, or considers how various *fiqh* rules approach Qur'anic instructions and their settings. The resulting Islamic law is insular, self-absorbed, and petrified of the outside world, according to this construct. Exotic compositions or tracts that ooze fear, usually penned at chaotic times, are given prominence and represented as Shari'a law. Consequently, early in the twentieth century, orientalists presumed that Shari'a would have to eventually fade away in favour of Western law. Thus, the increasing support for Shari'a that was evident as early as the 1970s took academia by surprise, as did the fact that the growing attraction of Shari'a rulemaking included many Western-educated Muslims.

Why do orientalists and neo-orientalists continue to fiercely guard the construct of "Islamic law", then? Why do their academic tools always fail? The modern academic narrative on Islam is hampered by an obsolete lens, lack of regard for actual context, and lack of understanding of the role of the contents of the Qur'an. Its narrative on Islam and its societies originated in Europe during the medieval period, for the purposes of rallying European lands to battle. Its academic outline was then primarily assembled in colonial times, as Europe ruled Muslim lands; the circumstances of the times, including political ends, dictated European scholarship and described the world as its white masters wanted it to be. Like contemporary Islamists, the predominant Western discourses aim to entrench, not examine, ancient unfavourable assumptions about the Other. Shari'a is perceived as a difficult-to-dislodge but passing irritation to the West's eternal hegemony. Further, despite a declared emphasis on historical enquiry, Muslim legal history is not related to either past or contemporary challenges, and there is no understanding of the complex interactions between Muslims and their sacred text, the Qur'an. Western-centred scholarship on Islam is thus at best short-sighted, and this has affected the interpretation of al-Ghazali, as discussed below.

Academic insights into al-Ghazali and his world

Orientalist masters

Modern academia noticed al-Ghazali early on, and his battle with Khaled Mohammed Khaled for the Egyptian mind. In 1954, the American Council of Learned Societies started its Near Eastern Translation Program with five titles, all of which were from Egypt. They included al-Ghazali's *Min Huna Na'lam* (translated as *Our Beginning in Wisdom*) and Khaled's *Min Huna Nabda'*. Two of the most prestigious Western scholars of Islam, Franz Rosenthal and Gustave E. von Grunebaum, reviewed these titles,[52] and despite their eloquence, the medieval origin of their narrative set the tone. They presented Islam and the societies in which it flourished as unfathomable, or in Professor Rosenthal's words:

> The books before us have English letters and words. However, the ideas they contain are Islamic and Arabic and conditioned by Near East history. [...] Learn the languages, study the sources of Muslim religion, literature and history, and you might still not be able to understand the modern Near East in its complexity, but at least you can say that you have seriously tried to understand it.[53]

However, neither historical nor literary complexity concerned these scholars, and contemporary realities did not matter either. Instead, their reviews orbited around one subject: Islam and the West, in the narrowest sense. Von Grunebaum focused mostly on political fears. He correctly noted that the Muslims who bitterly opposed communism, at that time the West's main adversary, were "at the same time potentially if not actually the most formidable strongholds of hostility to the West";[54] also troubling to him was the possibility that the world of Islam might become "strong enough to determine for itself what its primary concerns should be, and strong enough perhaps to be no longer compelled to westernise for the sake of survival."[55] Rosenthal, having warned of the inaccessibility of the alien world of Islam, devoted much of his review to details of the translation.

As with many other Western investigations of Islam, context hardly mattered. Consequently, none of the five Egyptian titles triggered fresh questions in these reviews about political upheaval or enduring connections in Egyptian or Arab societies that could help "the western world [keep] abreast of developments in the Near East in a deeper sense than newspapers can be expected and sporadic research works depended on to do", as Rosenthal hoped.[56] Nowhere is this limitation clearer than in their discussion of al-Ghazali's arguments to rebut Khaled's theses.

That both Rosenthal and Von Grunebaum read *Min Huna Nabda'* and *Min Huna Na'lam* side by side was important. But that too did not seem to produce worthwhile enquiries. Rosenthal had little to say about the battle of the two shaykhs over their fellow Egyptians' minds or, for that matter, the content of the books he reviewed, except that they indicated "the great interest of Egyptians in the rejuvenation of traditional Islam as the regulating force of life in all its aspects."[57] They did not explain why or what constituted "traditional Islam" in such settings. Still, Von Grunebaum devoted most of his review to a comparison of the two titles, from which he deduced that Shaykh Khaled's arguments were the most workable. His disregard for contemporary and historical realities led him to infer that "it could be said without malice that the lack of originality of Khalid's ideas—for he does little beyond elaborating familiar notions with unusual effectiveness—could be adduced as an argument for their practicality."[58] However, far from seeing Khaled's arguments as practical, most Muslims doubted them from the start; and eventually even Khaled came to agree with this early assessment and publicly recanted the ideas he had expressed in *Min Huna Nabda*.[59]

Rosenthal described al-Ghazali as "taking the position of the moderate traditionalist of our times, and his work is as good an exposition as can be found anywhere of the official attitude of Islam toward all the burning social and economic problems."[60] More bluntly, Von Grunebaum elaborated on a mainstream "official attitude of Islam" as exemplified by al-Ghazali, "whose every instinct is outraged by modernism."[61] What this expert meant by "outraged by modernism" raises troubling questions about this scholarship. For example, he did not approve that al-Ghazali described America's foreign policy and its treatment of African-Americans at the time as "a systematic violation of every moral virtue humanity has ever known".[62] Von Grunebaum thus declared that Islam would always oppose the spread of Western ways. What constituted "Western ways", however, is not explained.

In essence, both experts shared identical conclusions that emphasized Egyptians' intellectual weakness, by which was meant that all five authors they reviewed "reveal[ed] a considerable lack of true understanding of the West", in Rosenthal's words.[63] Their conclusion confirmed the superiority of Western truths—in the same way that Islamists use Western works, not to better study its societies, but as proof of the superiority of Islamic ways. Al-Ghazali gave Von Grunebaum "the impression [of] a man who knows the West from obsolescent books and adverse propaganda."[64] Perhaps this statement is the most revealing of Western modern discourse on Muslim societies. For, at the time, al-Ghazali's experience of Western societies may indeed have been limited, but his knowledge of the West did not come from obsolescent books, as Rosenthal and Von Grunebaum believed. Throughout his life al-Ghazali's first-hand encounters with the West included European soldiers and administrators. In his village, in prison, in the bombings of his country and the humiliation of his brothers in Algeria, in the Arab-Israeli wars, and elsewhere in the region, he saw the way that Western armies and governments treated his people. Could these encounters have had anything to do with his fears about the West? Neither orientalist scholar considered this possibility in evaluating al-Ghazali's ideas. In contrast, their reviews of al-Ghazali's book, like much else in their other works, suggest that it was these famous orientalists who approached contemporary Muslim societies, such as Egypt, "from obsolescent books and adverse [political] propaganda" (to use Von Grunebaum's words). Their book reviews show no appreciation of Muslim experiences of the past or contexts of the present, and their use of the "West" as a benchmark with which to examine the peoples and events in what they then called "the Near East" is also questionable. Such are the outlines, methodological structures, and tools used in formulating "Islamic law".

The neo-orientalist outline

Starting in the 1970s, attention has been given to a greater range of sources in the study of the Muslim past. But despite some excellent contributions, which have refined our knowledge of legal history in relation to subjects such as women, Hadith, or historiography, for example,[65] the underlying assumptions and research tools developed by orientalists in colonial times remain in place. The scholars of a neo-Islamic law narrative that arose to challenge the orientalists have been obsessed with the narrative which they sought to defy, leading them to see the world only through the orientalists' lens. More troubling, they have turned their back on reality, including how Muslims actually understand their faith—the supposed subject-matter of their research.

In the process, neo-orientalists in the West constructed their own "Islam", and modified orientalism only insofar as a few conventions deemed "politically incorrect" were abandoned. Like the old European masters, neo-orientalists resorted primarily to *fiqh* texts in order to explain Muslim rulemaking, neglecting almost all other evidence and particular contexts. They also showed no awareness of the tension in Muslims' continuous interaction with the content of the Qur'an and how this has generated varying legal products. Consequently, although sounding different in tone, neo-orientalist academic conclusions about Muslim rulemaking do not differ in substance from those of the early orientalists: Shari'a is a medieval law unfit for modern times; it had skilfully responded to new challenges but was rigid in reacting to changes in society, or it was excellent but unfeasible, all at once, as in the works of Wael al-Hallaq, a leading neo-orientalist scholar[66] who judges that "shari'a is no longer a tenable reality" and that "it has met its demise nearly a century ago", because it can only exist in past "classical times". It is not clear if he means Shari'a in general (which Muslims regard as a cornerstone of their faith), or *fiqh*, but his is the vision that colonialist scholarship has sought to impress on subject Muslims, although without great success.[67]

Whereas the limitations of early European orientalism lay partly in the sources available to its scholars and partly in their perspective as the overlords of most Muslim lands, neo-orientalism's limitations are due to its gullible, jumbled approaches to old *fiqh* sources. Despite academic pretentions, "Islamic law", as understood by neo-orientalists, betrays a poor understanding of history as a process. This has meant that the subject of Islamic law has not been able to interpret human experiences—at least Muslim ones—in terms of changes and continuities, even when some of its experts invoke these terms.

Decades ago, the great historian Albert Hourani recognized this limitation in modern academia's approaches to Muslim experiences, including in his own work. In the preface to an updated edition of his seminal 1962 book *Arabic Thought in the Liberal Age*, which remains a standard reference work for the ideas of al-Afghani, Abduh, and their students (the school to which al-Ghazali and his prominent Azhari teachers subscribed), Hourani indicated that the modern-sounding ideas of these *'ulama* may not have been epistemological and cultural ruptures, as often imagined, but instead showed processes that Muslims have long employed to calibrate their world. Ever attentive to historical changes as well as contemporary realities, Hourani cautioned the reader that

> to some extent I may have distorted the thought of the writers I studied [...] [T]he 'modern' element in their thought may have been smaller than I implied, and it would have been possible to write about them in a way which emphasised continuity rather than a break with the past.[68]

In contrast, neo-orientalists' "Islamic law" has an inbuilt disdain for contemporary Muslim experiences, and it deposits "real" Islam in unchanging medieval practices. New developments in Muslim societies almost always puzzle its experts; but instead of re-assessing their assumptions and methods, neo-orientalists place contemporary Muslim thought into categories of their own making—such as modernist, progressive, traditional, extremist, political Islam—all of which are substitutes for thorough analytical investigation. The lens of "Islamic law" consequently cannot differentiate between unfolding Muslim experiences, and so it regularly dismisses them all as either merely aping the Western masters or as politicized, and therefore a corruption of "real" Shari'a. Approaching the subject in this way misses the essence of Islam's methodology as it regulates all power relations: Shari'a rulemaking, as an ongoing process, is necessarily political.

And whereas orientalists sought to describe Islam mainly in terms of how they saw it then, neo-orientalists' work is to define "genuine" Islam, particularly to misguided Muslims. Even insofar as the neo-orientalist construct of "Islamic law" may approach the subject sympathetically, it contradicts key Muslim beliefs. Al-Hallaq's example serves as a brief but useful illustration of the subject's leading experts; they believe that Shari'a belongs to times long past, that its values and procedures are out of place in the modern age and are antithetical to all things Western.[69] The millions of Arabic-speaking Muslims who found in al-Ghazali the voice that elaborated their understanding of Shari'a did so mainly because he bonded Islam's ways to the belief that Qur'anic tenets required an unceasing search for sound universal values, whatever their origins.[70] Al-Ghazali told these Muslims that the pursuit of such learning (*fiqh*) had no restrictions of time or place and was far greater than that of Abu Hanifa, Shafi'i, or any other scholar.[71] Like other *fuqaha* across the centuries, al-Ghazali also increasingly worried that the confusion between *fiqh* and Shari'a by the unlearned invalidated Islam's central tenet, monotheism. Neo-orientalists ignore all that; they describe Shari'a and *fiqh* as one and the same "Islamic law". Consequently, and despite his impact on Arabic-speaking Muslims, al-Ghazali remained of little interest to experts of Islamic law, because of how he understood Shari'a, among other things. If he is noticed at all, his adjustments to some famous rulings are automatically located outside "classical Islam", and as such undeserving of being included in discussions on authentic *fiqh*. It is therefore impossible to examine al-Ghazali alongside neo-orientalist literature; they blur each other's story.

Despite its good intentions, neo-orientalism created a new religion, not an academic discipline. It neatly constructed an internally consistent picture of an "Islam" that neither al-Ghazali nor his people would recognize, nor reflected their historical experiences. However, it is a construct that some Muslims in the West have embraced, equating "neutral" references to Muslim rulemaking by non-Muslims as positive support and seeing them as a counterbalance to the onslaught on their faith which reproduces European medieval images of Islam. Such a strategy is born of desperation: ex-Muslims or ex-terrorists are often celebrated as scholarly and enlightened, and condemning Islam, offending Muslims, or making risible calls for Islam to be modified can be a pathway to residence at top universities and research centres. It can also guarantee access to key Western media outlets.[72]

Herein lies the main problem at the heart of "Islamic law": whether defined in an academic neo-orientalist and reconciliatory format, or in a way that is hostile to Islam, rarely does its "expertise" reach the parameters of the modern study of history, law, or the theories and multi-faceted practices of *usul al-fiqh*, which are the main areas it discusses; Islamic law operates outside the bounds of these disciplines.

The high price of living under the shadow of Islamic law

At first glance, this confusion in semantics seems academic. However, conceiving Shari'a as a fixed medieval law has had unwelcome consequences that have affected everyday life in our modern world and revealed worrying gaps in understanding Muslim experience. The broad reach of the narrative that leading scholars such as Professors Rosenthal and Von Grunebaum crafted eventually influenced many Muslims too, especially those directly touched by Western education. The media, educational institutions, and human rights groups often describe Muslim faith in terms of "Islamic law", responsible for daily reports of the humiliation and slaughter of women and minorities. Muslims reared on this regimen demonstrate the small-mindedness and confusion created by the open transformation of Shari'a from a method into a medieval system of law. Consequently, well-meaning efforts to address untenable *fiqh* suppositions or amend medieval practices almost always take place outside the parameters of Shari'a. Chapter 5 above, on women, offers illustrations of this; a more recent example is how a group of Muslim professionals in London held a lecture to clarify Shari'a in order to dissociate themselves from ISIS's (Da'esh) atrocities. The expert that the group invited announced that, "unlike the Qur'an, which Muslims consider the Word of God, the Shari'ah is a man-made construct developed after the death of the Prophet by early scholars of Islam."[73] Al-Ghazali and his Arabic-speaking followers would shudder at this statement. The Islamic law scholar did not understand that the Qur'an describes its divine message as the Shari'a sent to those who submit to his will. The lecturer also did not realize that it was Western academia, with which he was associated, that confused Shari'a with *fiqh*, by "using them interchangeably".[74] As a result, attempts to address Shari'a difficulties and protect against outside perils have had little impact or relevance for the majority of Muslims. "Islamic law"-reared Muslims have wandered from irrational irrelevance to irrational intransigence. A little-reported experience of an Azhari scholar who took political refuge in Britain in 1976 provides a glimpse of this. For decades, British Muslim leaders fought Shaykh Zaki Badawi (d. 2006) when he confronted this orientalist/neo-orientalist narrative that they had imbibed. Badawi called on British Muslims to raise outstanding British citizens engaged in intellectual and civic activism, while the British Muslim leaders feared contaminating their faith with the values of the alien culture of Britain.

But it was how Badawi discussed Shari'a that angered them the most. He criticized British Muslims' rigid views on rule-/lawmaking in Islam, and he openly dismissed *fiqh* schools, explaining that the *madahib* had all failed to mirror Shari'a adequately.[75] Badawi urged his community in Britain to take advantage of the freedoms that their new country offered them, so that they could formulate informed critiques of the Muslim literary legacy. However, as the British Muslim patriarchs saw it, such calls contradicted their "Islamic law", as did his challenges to many of its ideas and practices. Worse still, Badawi explained that Shari'a rulemaking and its culture necessitated such critical reviews: "Irreverence is part of [...] my training at al-Azhar", Badawi once told a London *Times* reporter in 2003. His education as a *faqih* taught him to "refuse to be deferential", he added.[76] Muslims who accepted the construct of "Islamic law" interpreted this as insolence. In defending the authority of *fiqh*, British Muslim leaders spent many years fighting Badawi. But they were not villains; they only knew of a definite "Islamic law "in which Shari'a was firmly deposited in "classical" and "traditional" rules and practices, that reflected an "authentic" Islam (usually the practices of the villages from which they originally hailed).

In the end, after years of bitter confrontation, many British Muslims conceded that Badawi possessed significant scholarship, and those who had previously fought him flocked to his Muslim College office in Ealing, west London, to seek advice on Shari'a rules. The details of his advice, however, continued to confound them. As head of the Shari'a Council, for example, Badawi insisted that Muslims had to abandon *al-wali al-mujbir*, a *fiqh* rule by which a parent or a relative could legally force his female ward into a marriage she did not want. Many, especially Muslims in Britain's Yemeni and Pakistani communities who subscribed to this practice, appeared dumbfounded, according to Badawi. Like al-Ghazali, Badawi declared such rules as offensive practices from the past that had no place in a healthy society that applied Shari'a. British Muslim leaders listened in wonder.

Other products of modern Islamic law also suggest that it is time to overhaul the discourse and study of Islam; converts and those who newly turn to religion in the search for answers to feelings of social and cultural disenfranchisement demonstrate the all-too-real dangers of "Islamic law". In 2013, two such persons, brandishing large knives, slaughtered Lee Rigby, a British soldier, in a London street in broad daylight.[77] Adopting the name Boko Haram, which means "Western education is forbidden", a Nigerian group has kidnapped schoolgirls and burnt churches on Christmas Day; ISIS, an angry gang of disfranchised and graduates of torture,[78] to which young Muslims from the West have subscribed, have happily recorded themselves slaughtering charity workers, destroying centuries-old regional communal fabric, and smashing historical treasures in Iraq and Syria. All such groups have sought to impose a new order that revolves around a code of law displayed on public walls. These modern Muslims have drawn inspiration from "Islamic law", conceived as insular and dissimilar to all modern values, as any truly Islamic state system supposedly had been and must be. Al Qa'ida sympathizers bomb commuters on their way to work in London in accordance with their "Islamic law", with another group of devout British Muslims could not think of any other way to protest publishing depictions of the Prophet which offended them but to harass worshippers at St Paul's Cathedral.

These seemingly fringe voices are far from being alone in the ways they conceive Shari'a lawmaking. Muslims who embrace the orientalist and neo-orientalist "Islamic law", in which whatever *fiqh* they come across becomes one and the same as Shari'a, present themselves, as well as the communities in which they live, with a conundrum. Their understanding of legitimacy and genuine rulemaking breeds chaos and obscurantism. Al-Ghazali and Badawi both grew up amid limiting economic and political circumstances, but they knew of a different Shari'a and took an altogether different path than the one that many Muslims raised on the narrative of "Islamic law" have taken. Al-Ghazali, however, differed from other reformers, including Badawi. Late in life he identified the key motivating factor for approaches to Shari'a that he, Badawi, and other Azhari scholars regarded as corrupt: unless addressed, common narratives of history designed to prop up political ideologies would always impede attempts to restore the sound method of Shari'a rule-/lawmaking, al-Ghazali believed. Chapter 8 examines his ideas on the role that history has played in influencing the Muslim legal legacy.

Conclusion: the life of a method

Technically and historically, there has never been an "Islamic law", let alone a "classical Islamic Law". What Muslims embraced, and still do, is an early outline of a rule-/lawmaking methodology. This benefitted them greatly. But, like any human experience, this outline has evolved over time, and Muslims have changed it, adjusted it, or tried to recapture its original form, with varying results. Time, geography, and circumstances mattered and still do. For example, how Muslims in al-Ghazali's twentieth-century Egypt saw *fiqh* rulemaking differed significantly from the perspectives of many Muslims in Turkey, Pakistan, or in the West at the time. Despite the wasted ink on "Islamic law", Shari'a's method of making rules/laws is likely to continue to produce changing or adjusted rules. It is unlikely to ever become an "Islamic law", if Shari'a is to survive. Efforts to turn it into a code or list of rules, from Ibn al-Muqafa to al-Majallah, to Boko Haram and ISIS (Da'esh), defeat the purpose and mechanism of Shari'a. Muslims have found in all such efforts little that they recognize as belonging to their faith or of benefit to their communities. So, far from being a modernist phenomenon, influential leaders of mainstream Islam over the centuries, like al-Ghazali, have known how agile their rulemaking can be and therefore have also worried about the mob's approaches to Hadith. All of these scholars, however, have been children of their times attempting to preserve the integrity of this rulemaking method, as they understood it. In this agility lie both the vulnerability of Shari'a rulemaking and its strength and durability. In al-Ghazali's case, circumstances led him to look again at the basic trajectory of Shari'a and to compare records. He judged that established ideas in the enormous bequest of *fiqh* texts showed disturbing irregularities in approaching the contents of the Qur'an and valid precedent. He also observed a clear legal lacuna in vital areas that *fiqh* left without detailed rules or penalties. These related to crimes including rape, misappropriation of orphans' money, and violations resulting from political corruption. All such breaches of clear Qur'anic directives rarely entered the realm of essential legal discussions or gave assigned specific mandatory remedies, even if they were routinely condemned as sinful, according to al-Ghazali.[79] In contrast, *fiqh* discussions regarding matters of far less urgency to both the individual and community swelled into what resembled a cancerous growth, al-Ghazali thought.[80] As Muslims have always done throughout the centuries, he taught his people that the time to change these *fiqh* practices had come. Through al-Ghazali's perspective and that of the Arabic-speaking millions who subscribed to his views of mainstream Islam, Shari'a cannot be "Islamic law" and will never be "Islamic law", unless it is first dismantled into what it has never been and reconstructed into what it is not.

Notes

1. *Ra'i* literally means "opinion", "what one sees". However, a literal translation in this context might be misleading. Taha Jabir al-Alwani, a member of the Islamic *Fiqh* Council in Jeddah, and at the time also President of the School of Islamic Sciences in Leesburg, Virginia, defined *ra'i* in this Hadith to be synonymous with *ijtihad*. For the purpose of this discussion about deducing rules, a better translation would be "analytical reasoning", in contrast to Greek formal reasoning, he added (author interview at IIIT, Herndon, Virginia, 1999).
2. The requirement of communal input in Shari'a rulemaking can take many shapes, including consultation or agreement.
3. "The Prophet questioned Ma'th before he sent him to govern Yemen thus: 'How will you find a rule [or judgement for a case]?' He [Ma'th] said: 'From God's Book.' [The Prophet] asked: 'But what if you could not find it [there]?' He [Ma'th] said: 'From the Sunna [precedent set in examples of] God's Prophet.' He [the Prophet] asked: 'But what if you could not find it [there]?' He [Ma'th] said: 'Through my personal reasoning.' Hearing this, the Prophet thanked God in approval" (author's translation of this Hadith from version found in Abu al-Hasan al-Mawardi [972–1058 CE], *Al-Ahkam al-Sultanyia* [Beirut: Dar al-Fikr al-Arabi, n.d.], 66–67). According to Shaykh Taha Jaber al-Alwani, after researching this Hadith he finally concluded that although it expressed a genuine early outline of Shari'a rulemaking, this particular report was not authentic. Instead, it showed how in later times, when Muslim scholars felt threatened by the arbitrary power of the state, they would have advanced such a "made-up" statement to give permanent authority to an already existing outline for deducing valid rules, he added (Author interview, ibid.).
4. كيفية استخراج الفروع من هذه الاصول
5. القواعد الضابطة للفروع
6. Mohammed Abu Zahra, *Ibn Hanbal, Hayatuh, wa 'Asruhu, wa Ara'auhu* (Cairo: Dar al-Fikr al-'Arabi, n.d. [1947]), 10–11.
7. Ibn Qudama (d. 1223 CE), *Al-Mughni wa yalih al-Sharih al-Kabir*, 17 vols (Cairo: Dar al-Hadith, 1996).
8. Abu Zahra, *Ibn Hanbal*, 173.
9. Ibid. Another famous illustration of this decentralization of lawmaking and its preference to deciding Shari'a rules away from the executive can be found in Abi Yusuf Yaqob Ibn Ibrahim al-Ansari, *Ikhtilaf Abi Hanifa wa Ibn Abi Laila* (Cairo: Matba't al-Wafa, 1357/1938 AH/CE).
10. Anwar Ibrahim, *The IIU President's Conferment Award for Sheikh Muhammad al-Ghazali, 22 August 1995* (online: http://ikdasar.tripod.com/anwar/95-19.htm). This was one of Ibrahim's most important speeches, according to Peter Riddell of Melbourne School of Theology (Peter Riddell, *Islam and the Malay-Indonesian World* [Honolulu: University of Hawai'i Press, 2001], 245).

11. Edward Said famously discussed the scholarly legacy of Islam and the Middle East that arose under the European colonialists' flags in *Orientalism* (New York: Pantheon Books, 1978).
12. This is discussed further below, using the examples of professors Gustave E. von Grunebaum and Franz Rosenthal.
13. To rephrase Christiaan Snouk Hurgoronje's useful description of "the thinking section of the [Muslim] people" in his "The 'Foundations' of Islamic Law" (1882), in idem, *Selected Works*, trans. Joseph Schact (Leiden: Brill, 1957), 274. Since the formative years of Islam, important agents of change have emerged out of such a thinking public, especially in relation to Shari'a rulemaking.
14. Mohammed al-Ghazali, *Nadwat Tadris al-'Ulum al-Shar'iya, Fadilat al-Shaykh Muhamad al-Ghazali: Taqdim wa Idarat Dr Gamal Eldin Attia* (Cairo: IIIT, n.d.), 17.
15. Ibn Qayyim al-Jawzia, *'Ilam al-Muwaqqi'in 'an Rab al-'Alamin*, vol. 3 (Beirut: Dar al-Jil, 1973), 333. Also cited by Yusuf al-Qaradawi, *Madkhal li Dirasat al-Shari'a al-Islamiya* (Cairo: Mu'assesset al-Risala, 1993), 180:

في تغير الفتوى واختلافها يحسب تغير الأزمنة والأمكنة والأحوال والنيات والعوائد

بناء الشريعة على مصالح العباد في المعاش والمعاد : هذا فصل عظيم النفع جدا وقع بسبب الجهل به غلط عظيم على الشريعة أوجب من الحرج والمشقة وتكليف ما لا سبيل إليه ما يعلم أن الشريعة الباهرة التي في أعلى رتب المصالح لا تأتي به فإن الشريعة مبناها وأساسها على الحكم ومصالح العباد في المعاش والمعاد وهي عدل كلها ورحمة كلها ومصالح كلها وحكمة كلها فكل مسألة خرجت عن العدل إلى الجور وعن الرحمة إلى ضدها وعن المصلحة إلى المفسدة وعن الحكمة إلى العبث فليست من الشريعة وإن أدخلت فيها بالتأويل فالشريعة عدل الله بين عباده ورحمته بين خلقه وظله في أرضه وحكمته الدالة عليه وعلى صدق رسوله ص أتم دلالة وأصدقها وهي نوره الذي به أبصر المبصرون وهداه الذي به اهتدى المهتدون وشفاؤه التام الذي به دواء كل عليل وطريقه المستقيم الذي من استقام عليه فقد استقام على سواء السبيل فهي قرة العيون وحياة القلوب ولذة الأرواح فهي بها الحياة والغذاء والدواء والنور والشفاء والعصمة وكل خير في الوجود فإنما هو مستفاد منها وحاصل بها وكل نقص في الوجود فسببه من إضاعتها ولولا رسوم قد بقيت لخربت الدنيا وطوي العالم وهي العصمة للناس وقوام العالم وبها يمسك الله السماوات والأرض أن تزولا فإذا أراد الله سبحانه وتعالى خراب الدنيا وطي العالم رفع إليه ما بقى من رسومها فالشريعة التي بعث الله بها رسوله هي عمود العالم وقطب الفلاح والسعادة في الدنيا والآخرة

16. Such as in Q7.29.
17. Al-Ghazali, videotape interview (#TJD-1).
18. These notions include public interest and the common good as sources of law, and have been adopted by Maliki, Shafi'i, and Hanbali *fiqh* rule-/lawmaking methodologies (albeit with varying weights and conditions). For a summary discussion of public interest and the common good in Muslim lawmaking, see Madjid Khadduri, "Maslaha", *Encyclopaedia of Islam*, 2nd edn (Leiden: Brill, 1999).
19. One example here relates to the compensation for the unlawful killing of a woman (*diy'yat al-ma'ra*). See Abu Bakr al-Jaza'iri, *Al-Qawl al-Karim al-Ghali fi al-Difa' 'an al-Da'iya al-Ghazali* (Mecca: Maktabat Umm al-Qura, 1991), 36–40. Al-Ghazali condemned (non-Hanafi) schools of *fiqh* which make compensation for a woman's life half of that for a man, judging that they deduced such a rule based on a forged Hadith.
20. Author interview, Dar al-Ifta', Cairo, March 2006.
21. Al-Ghazali, videotape interview (#TAYR-1). Al-Ghazali was referring to al-Khatib al-Baghdadi, *Tarikh Baghdad* (Cairo: Maktabat al-Khanji, 1931).
22. Ibn al-Jawzi was a renowned Hanbali *usul al-fiqh*, Qur'an, and Hadith scholar who also wrote on history. For examples of his work, see Ibn al-Jawzi, *Al-Mawdhu'at*, 3 vols (Medina: Mohammed abd al-Mohsen of al-Maktaba al-Salafiya, 1966); idem, *Gharib al-Hadith* (Beirut: Dar al-Kutub al-'Ilmyia, 1985); idem, *Al-Muntazam fi Tarikh al-Muluk wa al-Umam* (Beirut, Dar al-Kutub al-'Ilmyia, 1992).
23. Abu Zahra, *Ibn Hanbal*, 153–154.

24. Ibid.
25. Ibid.:

    "قد سألني بعض اصحاب الحديث:هل في مسند ابن حنبل ما ليس بصحيح؟ فقلت: نعم. فعظم ذلك علي جماعة ينسبون الي المذهب، فحملت امرهم علي انهم عوام. واهملت ذكر ذلك وإذا بهم كتبوا فتاوى، فكتب فيها جماعة من اهل خرسان، منهم أبو العلاء الهمزاني، يعظمون هذا القول ويرددون، ويقبحون قول من قاله، فبقيت دهشا متعجبا، وقلت في نفسي: واعجبا، صار المنتسبون الي العلم عامة أيضا، وما ذاك إلا لأنهم سمعوا الحديث، ولم يبحثوا عن صحيحه من سقيمه، وظنوا انه من قال ما قلته قد تعرض للطعن فيما أخرجه أحمد. وايس كذلك. فإن الإمام احمد روى المشهور والجيد والرديء، ثم هو قد رد كثيرا مما روى، ولم يقل به، ولم يجعله مذهبا، اليس هو القائل: في حديث النبيذ مجهول، ومن نظر في كتاب العلل الذي صنفه أبو بكر الخلال رأى أحاديث كثيرة كلها من المسند، وقد طعن فيها أحمد. ونقلت من خط القاضي أبي يعلى محمد بن الحسين الفراء في مسألة النبيذ، قال: إنما روى احمد في مسنده ما اشتهر ، ولم يقصد الصحيح، ولا السقيم، ويدل على ذلك أن عبد الله قال: قلت لأبي: ما تقول في حديث ربعي بن خراش عن حذيفة؟...... قال: قصدت في المسند المشهور، فلو أردت ان أقصد ما صح عندي لم أرو من هذا المسند إلا الشيء اليسير ولكنك يابني تعرف طريقتي في الحديث....قال القاضي: وقد أخبر عن نفسه كيف كان طريقه في المسند فمن جعله أصلا للصحة فقد ترك مقصده."

    "وختم ابن الجوزي مقاله بقوله: وقد غمني في هذا الزمان أن العلماء لتقصيرهم في العلم صاروا كالعامة، وإذا مر بهم حديث موضوع قالوا قد روي، والبكاء ينبغي ان يكون علي خساسة الهمم، ولا حول ولا قوة الا بالله."
26. Ahmad bin Mohammed bin Harun bin Yazid al-Baghdadi was one of Ahmed Ibn Hanbal's most energetic students, and records his teachers' views in 20 volumes.
27. Ibn al-Farra is another key Hanbali *usul al-fiqh* scholar (Henri Laoust, "Ibn al-Farrā'", *Encyclopaedia of Islam*, 2nd edn [Leiden: Brill, 1999]).
28. Quoted by Mohammed Abu Zahra, *Ibn Hanbal*, 154.
29. Throughout the centuries, prominent *fuqaha* from schools other than the Hanbali followed in Ibn al-Jawzi's footsteps. For illustration, see the late fifteenth-century CE Shafi'i scholar, Jalal al-Din al-Suyuti, *Al-La'ali al-Masnou'a fi al-Ahadith al-Mawdhoua'* (Cairo: Dar al-Ma'rifa, 1975).
30. Al-Ghazali, *Nadwat Tadris al-'Ulum al-Shar'iya*.
31. Taken at face value, some arguments about the compatibility of Shari'a and modernity, famously advanced by Muslim scholars in the West, sound like al-Ghazali's later ideas. These include Professor Khaled Abou El Fadl, *The Great Theft: Wrestling Islam from the Extremists* (New York: HarperCollins, 2007), and Professor Tariq Ramadan, *Radical Reform: Islamic Ethics and Liberation* (Oxford: Oxford University Press, 2008). For al-Ghazali's views on Islam and democracy see Chapter 8.
32. Al-Ghazali, *Nadwat Tadris al-'Ulum al-Shar'iya*; see also Appendix 1; idem, "Fiqh al Da'wa wa Mushkilat al-D'oa", *Al-Umma* (Qatar), 15 Rajab, 1408 AH [3 March, 1988], 139–140.
33. Al-Ghazali, *Nadwat Tadris al-'Ulum al-Shar'iya*.
34. Ibid.
35. Ibid.
36. Mohammed al-Ghazali, *Azmat al-Shura fi al-Mujtama'at al-Arabia wa al-Islamiyia* (Cairo: Dar al-Sharq al-Awsat, 1990), 36–37; idem, *Kaifa Nat'amal ma' al-Qur'an*, ed. Umar Ubaid Hassana (Herndon, VA: IIIT, 1992), 181–182.
37. *Kaifa Nat'amal ma' al-Qur'an*, 90.
38. Al-Ghazali, videotape interview (#TAYR-1).
39. Al-Ghazali, *Kaifa Nat'amal ma' al-Qur'an*, 66.
40. Mohammed Al-Ghazali, *Al-Da'wa al-Islamiyah Tastaqbilu Qarnaha al-Khamis 'Ashr* (no location: Dhat al-Salasit, 1980), 158; idem, *Azmat al-Shura*, 33.
41. Ibid., 4.
42. Ibid.
43. Ibid., 42–43.

44. Adam Sherwin, "Schama, Fellowes, and the 'Cultural Necrophilia' Row that would Make Lady Grantham Grimace", *Independent*, 18 January, 2012 (online: http://www.independent.co.uk/news/media/tv-radio/schama-fellowes-and-the-cultural-necrophilia-row-that-would-make-lady-grantham-grimace-6291113.html).
45. Author interview, Cairo, November 2010.
46. Yusuf al-Qaradawi, *Madkhal li Dirasat al-Shari'a al-Islamiya* (Cairo: Mu'assesset al-Risala, 1993), 146–147, 155–161, 182, 203; for his broad definition of Shari'a, see 218–219.
47. Al-Qaradawi, *Madkhal li Dirasat al-Shari'a al-Islamiya*, 160.
48. General Sunni discussions of their rulemaking include a variety of accounts such as the above, included in Jassim Muhalal al-Yassin, "Al-Safha al-Dinyia", *Al-Watan* (Kuwait City), 31 January, 1997, 13; see also Fahmy Huwaidi, *Al-Qur'an wa al-Sultan* (Cairo: Dar al-Shorouk, 2002), 43–44.
49. Ibn Qayyim al-Jawzia, "La Yanbaghi an Youqqal hatha hukum Allah", لا ينبغي ان يقال هذا حكم الله *'Ilam al-Muwaqqi'in 'an Rab al-'Alamin*, vol. 1 (Beirut: Dar al-Jil, 1973).
50. Author interview, Doki, Cairo, March 2007.
51. Shaykh Goma reasoned that it was obvious why one must "distinguish between *al-tashri al-Islami*, including *fiqh*, which is pluralistic and allows *ijtihad*, and God's Shari'a." Islamic law "could only refer to a specific legal code, limited by time and place", Goma said. Such an Islamic law may be "derived from one, or more, or even all of the Islamic legal schools and literature of *al-tashri al-Islami*", the mufti added. Author interview, Doki, Cairo, March 2007.
52. See reviews by Franz Rosenthal (in the *Journal of the American Oriental Society* 74/2 [1954]: 100–103) and Gustave E. von Grunebaum (in the *Journal of Near Eastern Studies* 14/3 [1955]: 200–202. Works by the latter that became classics in the Western library on Islam include *Medieval Islam: A Study in Cultural Orientation* (Chicago: University of Chicago Press, 1946); idem, *Classical Islam: A History, 600 A.D. to 1258 A.D.* (London: Allen and Unwin, 1970); idem, *Theology and Law in Islam* (Wiesbaden: Harrassowitz, 1971). Similarly, Franz Rosenthal helped shape the study of Islam in Western academia with works that include *A History of Muslim Historiography* (Leiden: Brill, 1952); idem, *The Classical Heritage in Islam* (Berkeley: University of California Press, 1975).
53. Rosenthal, review, 103.
54. Von Grunebaum, review, 202.
55. Ibid.
56. Rosenthal, review, 100.
57. Ibid., 103.
58. Von Grunebaum, review, 202.
59. Khalid Mohammed Khalid, *Al-Dawla fi al-Islam* (Cairo: Dar al-Thabit, 1981); idem, *Rijal Hawla al-Rasul Sala Allah 'alayhi wa Sallem* (Cairo: Dar al-Fikr li al-Tiba'a wa al-Nashir, 2006 [1999]). On the opposing views of Khaled and al-Ghazali, see Chapter 2.
60. Rosenthal, review, 103.
61. Von Grunebaum, review, 201.
62. Ibid., 202.
63. Rosenthal, review, 103.
64. Von Grunebaum, review, 202.
65. When Ronald Jennings turned his attention to the Ottoman Shari'a court records, he excavated from them new perspectives on the Muslim legal system of the sixteenth century. Ever since, looking beyond *fiqh* texts, interest in new sources has resulted in research efforts that have revised some assumptions on women and on what Shari'a meant in the practices of Islam's early central lands in and around the Mediterranean. See Ronald Jennings, "Women in the Early 17th Century Ottoman Judicial Records: The Sharia Court of Anatolian Kayseri", *Journal of the Economic and Social History of the Orient* 18 (1975): 53–114; idem; *Studies on Ottoman Social History in the Sixteenth and Seventeenth Centuries: Women, Zimmis and Sharia Courts in*

Kayseri, Cyprus and Trabzon (Istanbul: ISIS Press, 1999); also G.H.A. Juynboll, *Muslim Tradition: Studies in Chronology, Provenance, and Authorship of Early Hadith* (Cambridge: Cambridge University Press, 1983); Abraham Marcus, "Women and Property in 18th century Aleppo", *Journal of the Economic and Social History of the Orient* 26 (1983): 137–163; idem, *The Middle East on the Eve of Modernity: Aleppo in the Eighteenth Century* (New York: Columbia University Press, 1992); Judith Tucker, *Women in Nineteenth-Century Egypt* (Cambridge: Cambridge University Press, 1985); Margaret Meriwether and Judith Tucker, *A Social History of Women and the Family in the Middle East* (Boulder, CO: Westview Press, 1999); Jonathan Brown, *The Canonization of al-Bukhari and Muslim: The Formation and Function of the Sunni Ḥadith Canon* (Leiden: Brill, 2006); Amira Sonbol, ed., *Women, the Family and Divorce Laws in Islamic History* (Syracuse, NY: Syracuse University Press, 1996); idem, "Women in Shari'a Courts: A Historical and Methodological Discussion", *Kelam Araştimalari* 2/2 (2004): 25–56; idem, ed., *Beyond the Exotic: Women's Histories in Islamic Societies* (Syracuse, NY: Syracuse University Press, 2005); idem, "Negotiating and Disputing Marriage and Business in Early Modern Egypt and Palestine", *L'HOMME: Europäische Zeitschrift für Feministische Geschichtswissenschaft* (2006): 1–24; Marion Katz, *Women in the Mosque: A History of Legal Thought and Social Practice* (New York: Columbia University Press, 2014); continuing the theme of canonization, but as to rule/lawmaking approaches, in the case of al-Shafi'i, see Ahmed El Shamsy, *The Canonization of Islamic Law: A Social and Intellectual History* (Cambridge: Cambridge University Press, 2013); and research such as Hannah Hagemann, "Authors, Editors, Compilers? Al-Baladhuri, al-Dinawari and al-Tabari on Kharijite Origins", paper presented at Conference on the Authors, Editors and Audiences of Medieval Middle East Texts, Cambridge University, 1 September, 2014.

66. All the above premises can be found in Wael al-Hallaq, "The Use and Abuse of Evidence: The Question of Provincial and Roman Influences on Early Islamic Law", *Journal of the American Oriental Society* 110/1 (1990), 79–91; idem, "On the Origins of the Controversy about the Existence of Mujtahids and the Gate of Ijtihad", *Studia Islamica* 63 (1986), 129–141, idem, "The Logic of Legal Reasoning in religious and Non-Religious Cultures: The Case of Islamic Law and Common Law", *Law and Legal Theory in Classical and Medieval Islam* (Brookfield, VT: Variorum, 1994 [1986]), 79–96; idem, "Can The Shari'a Be Restored?", in Barbara Stowasser and Yvonne Haddad, eds, *Islamic Law and the Challenges of Modernity* (Walnut Creek, CA: Altamira Press: 2004), 1–52, 42; idem, *The Impossible State, Islam, Politics, and Modernity's Moral Predicament* (New York: Columbia University Press, 2014). See expert critics from relevant fields: Christopher Melchert, "Review of Wael B. Hallaq, *The Origins and Evolution of Islamic Law*", *Law and History Review* 24/3 (2006): 675–676; Shaykh Mohammed Akram Nadwi, "Review of *The Origins and Evolution of Islamic Law*, by Wael B. Hallaq", *Journal of Islamic Studies* 19/1 (2008): 109–115; and Georgetown University Law Centre's Lama Abu-Odeh, "Reviewing Wael B. Hallaq, *The Impossible State: Islam, Politics, and Modernity's Moral Predicament*", *International Journal of Middle East Studies* 46 (2014): 216–218.
67. "[T]raditional Sharia can surely be said to have gone without return", was al-Hallaq's unequivocal answer to the question of whether the Shari'a could be restored. He reasoned that there was a rupture, "one of epistemology and [that] goes deep into the inner structure of legal thinking" between modern *fuqaha* and the traditional ones. As al-Hallaq understands it, Islamic law can only survive in special conditions, not related to ever-changing Muslim circumstances or Qur'anic tenets. He was speaking at a symposium held at Georgetown University in 2001 under the title "Arab Legal Systems in Transition", later published as Wael Hallaq, "Can The Shari'a Be Restored?"
68. Albert Hourani, *Arabic Thought in the Liberal Age, 1798–1939* (Cambridge: Cambridge University Press, 1983), viii, ix.
69. Perhaps an obvious indication of the muddle of Islamic law as a scholarly discipline is how little it benefitted from the varieties and advances that the study of European history has made.

70. For illustrations see al-Ghazali, *Kaifa Nat'amal ma' al-Qur'an*, 47, 88, 94, 182, 223.
71. Al-Ghazali, videotape interview (#W-2). He told another interviewer that the thought of the greatest *fuqaha* presented no more than organizational, social, economic programmes, and that a Muslim can opt in or out of any of them; they did not constitute divine text, as illiterate impressions might see in them (videotape interview #SYS-1).
72. Muslims in the West face a deluge of curious expertise on Islam, much favoured by Western media and academic institutions, which include Irshad Manji, *The Trouble with Islam Today: A Muslim's Call for Reform in Her Faith* (New York: St Martin's Griffin, 2005); Sam Harris and Maajid Nawaz, *Islam and the Future of Tolerance—A Dialogue* (Cambridge, MA: Harvard University Press, 2015); Ayaan Hirsi Ali, *Heretic: Why Islam Needs a Reformation Now* (New York: HarperCollins, 2015). At the time, as an all-out war against Tahrir Square / Arab Spring Muslim discourse took off in every corner of the Middle East—in which, according to human rights groups, human rights lawyers, journalists, and activists were hounded, detained, or tortured—attention turned instead to these "Islam-must-be-reformed" calls, including in a chorus of articles also published in 2015. For a Muslim response which includes an overview of such articles, see Mehdi Hasan, "Why Islam Doesn't Need a Reformation", *Guardian*, 17 May, 2015 (online: http://www.theguardian.com/commentisfree/2015/may/17/islam-reformation-extremism-muslim-martin-luther-europe).
73. Ebrahim Moosa, "How Relevant is the Shari'ah Today?", lecture arranged by the City Circle Group, London, 29 January, 2016.
74. Ibid.
75. Shaykh Zaki Badawi, Islamic Legal Narrative Seminar, Sinai Centre for Islamic Mediterranean Studies, London, Muslim College, 16 July, 2005.
76. "I have always refused to be deferential, even to heads of state", Badawi is reported to have said in a 2003 interview. Quoted in his obituary: "Zaki Badawi: Leading Voice of Moderate Islam who Believed Passionately in Interfaith Dialogue and the Idea of the British Muslim", *The Times* (London), January 25, 2006 (online: http://www.timesonline.co.uk/tol/comment/obituaries/article719195.ece).
77. Fusilier Lee Rigby, 25, was a British soldier murdered in southeast London by two converts, Michael Adebolajo and Michael Adebowale, on 22 May 2013. See, e.g. BBC News, "Lee Rigby Murder: Map and Timeline" (2014; online: http://www.bbc.co.uk/news/uk-25298580).
78. As demonstrated in Martin Chulov, "Isis: The Inside Story", *Guardian*, 11 December, 2014 (online: http://www.theguardian.com/world/2014/dec/11/-sp-isis-the-inside-story); Liz Sly, "The Hidden Hand Behind the Islamic State Militants? Saddam Hussein's", *Washington Post*, 4 April, 2015 (online: https://www.washingtonpost.com/world/middle_east/the-hidden-hand-behind-the-islamic-state-militants-saddam-husseins/2015/04/04/aa97676c-cc32-11e4-8730-4f473416e759_story.html).
79. Mohammed Al-Ghazali, "Fiqh al Da'wa wa Mushkilat al-D'oa", *Al-Umma* (Doha), 15 Rajab, 1408 AH [3 March, 1988], 130.
80. Al-Ghazali, videotape interview (#FTW-1).

EIGHT

Shari'a and the Telling of the Muslim Story

When al-Ghazali's perceptions of the past changed, he adjusted, and sometimes even reversed, well-established Islamic rules, as described in earlier chapters. Towards the end of his life he saw a paramount connection between Shari'a and understanding Muslim history, which he then put at the centre of his final campaign. He believed that he had discovered troubling faultlines in the telling of the Muslim story, and his drive to impart to the common Muslim the urgency of having a sound understanding of their history may be his greatest—but so far his least noted—accomplishment. This chapter considers this last preoccupation of al-Ghazali, and its unexpected consequences. It explores why the connection between Shari'a and past precedents troubled al-Ghazali more than anything else at the time that it did: Why did he battle even loyal Sunni groups as he tried to highlight the paramount importance of historical perception to the making of rules that Muslims derive from the foundational Shari'a method? In a search for answers, the current chapter briefly discusses the evolution of the now commonly accepted Muslim historical narratives, and in what way their subtexts shape rulemaking in modern times. It then offers contemporary portraits from which the reader can glimpse how, in real life, impressions of the past determine relationships of power in Muslim communities even today. These portraits focus on women and governance, the areas where al-Ghazali triggered the loudest commotion.

As events transpired, the war to recover the proper subtext of Muslim experiences that al-Ghazali ignited on the Nile's banks exploded many years after his death. He managed to sow the seeds of a new mainstream Muslim discourse that rested on criticism of its own historical narrative: "When I hear some Muslims speak about 'return' to Islam, I feel depressed", he told Egyptians as late as the late 1970s. "Should Muslims listen to these calls [return to an Islamic state]", al-Ghazali explained, "they would only add to [Muslim] senselessness, [for] what they are likely to 'return' to is the worst days [...] of [governance], which contributed little to Muslim societies or to the world."[1] In time, the ordinary Muslim who learned the contours of this new discourse provided the grassroots support that powered Egypt's Arab Spring Revolution in 2011. Nowhere did the common descriptions of Islam's role in politics, whether in the modern media or academia, appear so inept as during and following this uprising, as the world watched in surprise. For the unforeseen Revolution and then the great conflict that followed was not a clash of secular and theocratic; and nor was it a class war or a gender war or even a war between different generations. It was a life-or-death war between two Muslim mainstream Sunni discourses of government that unsettled the world, as illustrations in the Epilogue show.

God and history

In Egypt, religion and history matter, and they always will. As soon as they toppled Mubarak in 2011, many Egyptians turned to the Muslim past as they competed to reshape the country's identity. Whether they saw themselves as religious, liberals, Arab nationalists, or any other identity, Egyptians filled newspapers, magazines, and social media with notes from ancient Muslim precedents and imageries to demonstrate the continuities of their visions with the past. Appealing thus to Islamic history did not necessarily indicate religious devotion; and activists did so each in his or her own way. Younger Egyptian activists, for example, brazenly asserted their convictions about the radical changes they wanted to see in their country's ways. Yet even a self-declared atheist such as Maikel Nabil, a Copt by birth, turned to Islamic precedents as an authority. On Twitter, he wrote in April 2012 that Ibn Taymiya described how God favours a just state, regardless of its faith, to an unjust, seemingly pious one, concluding that social and political justice must have the priority over religious beliefs. In support of his opposition to military conscription, Nabil re-Tweeted that the hated seventh-century army general, al-Hajjaj, had been the one to introduce forced military service into Muslim society.[2] Meanwhile, a Muslim Brotherhood supporter with religious and political views diametrically opposed to those of Nabil used the same image to mock a secular opponent's "Hajjaj-like interpretation of democracy".[3] Three years and great deal of troubles later, under the name Coptic Revolutionary, a Christian youth, albeit another self-declared atheist, proudly Tweeted: "Revolution is a delayed prostration in prayer that requires no imam."[4] Muslim imageries and precedents mattered to the revolutionary older generations too. The editor of the daily *Al-Dostor*, Ibrahim Issa, explained modern liberalism, to which he subscribed, as intellectually comparable to the Hanafi and 'Ashari schools; liberal economic ideas as akin to those of Othman bin 'Affan and abd al-Rahman Ibn

Aouf, two disciples of Mohammed; and liberal political systems in which an even-handed law reigned supreme, as similar to the real-life practices of the second caliph, Umar Ibn al-Khattab. Other gems of Muslim memory in which Issa found parallels to liberal values included favouring reason, as in the examples of Ibn Rushd (Averroes), Ibn Sina (Avicenna), and Mohammed Abduh. Issa's approach to the Islamic experience is not uncommon,[5] and in 2013 Issa embarked on a project to rewrite Muslim history to neatly accord with his views of current events. He then announced Islam's triumph when the army toppled the elected president, the Muslim Brotherhood's Mohammed Morsi, and he proceeded to write on Muslim history in order to explain it all.[6] A die-hard secularist and archenemy of Islamist political expressions, Wael abd el-Fattah re-Tweeted posts to invoke the excellent model of Umar Ibn abd al-Aziz, a Muslim caliph who ruled for only 30 months, as a way of expressing objection to the president.[7] Like many Egyptians, this opponent of political Islam also turned to the cherished precedents of early Medina. In reference to Morsi's attempt to claim descent from Medina's second caliph, another Umar, el-Fattah, Tweeted:

> Oh Umar: You ruled with justice and, therefore, you felt secure, able to sleep [casually under a tree], whereas the miserable, petty dictator that pretends to be related to Umar hides in a palace with barbed wires separating him from the people.[8]

Framing the quest for a democratic, egalitarian Egypt in precedent from Muslim history thus marks an obvious break with the European and American liberal discourse which has inspired many of these Egyptian revolutionaries. At least, seeing democracy through this lens distinguishes the Egyptians' vision from that of their Western friends. But it also marks a break with centuries-old Muslim traditions; this modern appeal to history is not about toeing the line, but rather about searching for a new narrative that includes whatever Egyptians cherish from their past. The angry younger generation of the 2011 Revolution liked to surprise and even outrage: they happily elevated obscenity as a preferred language of politics, freely hurling abuse against their opponents, including eminent members of the Muslim and Christian religious establishments and the military leaders of their country. The question is why, by 2011, did large sections of society stretching from deep Upper Egypt to its Mediterranean coast and along the shores of the Red Sea and Suez Canal participate in this seemingly unorthodox discourse, that doubted the common story of Islam and disregarded their religious leaders? The short answer is that it was because by this time al-Ghazali, 15 years after his death, had provided legitimacy to scrutinizing Muslim perceptions. Thanks to his tenacity, questioning the past became associated with righteousness. The potency with which he delivered his critiques from the 1980s eventually paved the way for street confrontations between two opposing Muslim readings of their story, and this is what lies at the heart of the Arab Spring.

In the early days of the Arab Spring, the above-mentioned editor of *Al-Dostor* quoted the "great *'alim*, Shaykh Mohamed al-Ghazali" in support of the Revolution and calls for change.[9] So did many other revolutionaries, peppering Twitter, Facebook, and newspaper pages with excerpts from al-Ghazali's works. Egyptian Muslims who sought change turned to al-Ghazali because, as seen in previous chapters, he accepted it was legitimate to ask the question that in modern times worries Muslims the most: Why should empirical observation or seemingly sound practices often contradict the norms of their faith? For answers, he delved into the Muslim past, including its vast *fiqh* legacy. Al-Ghazali found that many of those he engaged were not necessarily modern. In previous centuries other *fuqaha* had already raised many questions about women and authority, for example, reaching all sorts of conclusions. But to these Shari'a debates on gender, al-Ghazali added another dimension when he placed the consideration of changes and continuities at the top of the agenda.

It started when he located the core problem, or what he described as Islam's main enemy, in a particular worldview, a *weltanschauung* that Muslim societies have long embraced. By the 1990s al-Ghazali was telling Safinaz Kazim, a woman writer and Islamist activist, that before the late nineteenth century, when al-Afghani, Mohammed Abduh and his students confronted this worldview, for centuries Muslims "had no social or cultural foresight; whatever vision they had had, was merely sexual." Such a narrow perspective "extended to all other aspects of their lives"; it did not only manifest itself in laws that regulated women, al-Ghazali now declared.[10] The force that lurked behind all such cracks in the Muslim worldview, as he saw it now, was a misreading of the past. Blurring the Muslim story thus disfigured Shari'a too, he believed. Put another way, the past appeared to him as the primary tool that Muslim societies used to entrench unsavoury habits. As a result, his approach to history changed. Earlier, al-Ghazali dismissed undesirable episodes in Muslim history as isolated and unrepresentative,[11] but in his later years he spoke of centuries-old Muslim misconduct. Shari'a and the subtext of history were thus formally linked. From there on, al-Ghazali tracked faultlines in the predominant Muslim narrative. He also outlined a route map for change, starting with a sound assessment of Islamic records. Only by clearing away the debris that al-Ghazali saw as contaminating collective Muslim intellect can Muslims truly come nearer to their faith and revitalize their societies, he explained.

Faultlines: Predominant Muslim narratives

Two historical narratives have come to dominate the Muslim landscape: that of the Sunni majority, and that of the Shi'i minority. Although both originally served political purposes, both eventually gained religious sanctity. Their specific claims about early conflicts over government control became commonplace truths, transforming perspectives on seventh-century events into permanent, even sacred principles. In this way, the lines that separated human experience from divine instructions became blurred, or disappeared altogether. Even though their conclusions differ, the two accounts have identical frameworks, and careful scrutiny reveals the extent to which they drew on each other. Important here is the example of how the Sunni majority has derided the Shi'i minority for believing relatives of the Prophet to be inviolable. Such veneration, the Sunnis insist, contradicts monotheism, the central tenet of Islam. In theory, that indicates that historical figures and events have no sanctity and can always be candidly re-assessed, meaning that conclusions derived from past events belong to the variable sphere of Shari'a rulemaking. Theory and practice, however, were not in accord. As time went on, political interests, literary products, and pre-Islamic ideas of which Muslims had made use—whether Greek, Persian, or Indian—eventually came to be regarded as sacrosanct, or very close to it. In a radical shift in perceptions, such "Islamic sciences" and their authors were embraced as God-inspired authorities. However, the conflict between theory and practice did not go unnoticed.

This contradiction has prompted Muslim concerns over the centuries, as well as re-appraisals of the past. The approaches and consequences of such Muslim critiques of their history vary greatly, although al-Ghazali's impact stands apart: while the learned and senior *fuqaha* have often confined these critiques to scholarly or fringe circles, al-Ghazali succeeded in placing his critique into everyday Egyptian conversations. He similarly differed from popular Islamists. For example, unlike Sayyid Qutb or Abu 'Ala al-Mawdudi, al-Ghazali did not want the devout to isolate themselves from the outside world or from other Muslims, whereas Islamists believed engagement represented a departure from the ways of early Muslim society.[12] He urged Muslims to instead share in all good ideas, regardless of their origins (as illustrated below in the example of democracy), and to pray and work alongside the rest of society. Also, in contrast to contemporary Islamists, he especially condemned secrecy, preferring to work openly within the system that he confronted.[13] These dissimilarities may have helped al-Ghazali reach more deeply and widely among Arabic-speakers. Circumstances also helped al-Ghazali: thanks to the abundance brought about by oil wealth, as incomes grew in his region, so did literacy, mobility, and greater access to news from the outside world. With this relative prosperity, increasing numbers of

Egyptians found al-Ghazali's pursuit of historical knowledge engaging. Al-Ghazali made public everything that he distilled from records of the past, defiantly disturbing common images of the "orthodox" Muslim story in his country.

Drawing on the canvas of history

How a community perceives "when" and "in what way" it travelled from one point to another can be understood as a canvas on which members illustrate their collective identity. It is also a map of the world around them, and a guide to their future destiny: their worldview, or *weltanschauung*. In the case of Islam, precious records of the supposedly model past have not always supported the competing visions that arise in an expanding society. However, since Islam has been the cement that holds this community together, competing groups with political ambitions have raced to promote favourable "Islamic" accounts to advance their claims with legitimizing narratives, often distorting the most straightforward interpretations of early events or giving them a completely opposite meaning. The *weltanschauung* that the Abbasid Caliphate advanced in the eighth century CE is an example of one of the most successful propaganda machines in world history, in which the rulers succeeded in assembling new communal themes and moral codes. By following a shrewd course that combined extravagant rewards and ruthless punishments, the interests of the powerful were thus developed into universal truths with which to interpret reality, the main source of authority here being the rewriting of key events of Islam's formative years and what they signified. The rewritten past provided an interlinking store of precedents, meanings, and predefined frameworks with which to approach knowledge in general; even the *fuqaha* who had resisted this Abbasid scheme, including significant figures such as Abu Hanifa, Malik, and many others, had their stories reinterpreted to serve the ruling house. Thanks to the worldview that this propaganda machine created, from a dynasty with doubtful legitimacy, the Abbasid caliphate became an essential Islamic institution that was to last until the end of time.[14] No matter how vacuous their authority later became, the discourse that the Abbasids promoted guaranteed their long survival. Even when a Shi'ite army conquered their capital in the tenth century CE, its Buyid general-sultans elected to live under the entrenched Abbasid umbrella.[15] So did another formidable Shi'ite army that eventually acquired its own empire:[16] these Ismaili Fatimids copied, not dismantled, the masterfully crafted Abbasid institution of the caliphate, albeit with modifications. So, modifying Islam's precedents became a long-established means of acquiring legitimacy; each dynasty reconfigured the parameters of the Muslim story to create a sense of continuity.

The post-caliphate narrative

It was not always rulers or the powerful figures in their courts who sought to promote particular historical narratives. Well-meaning scholars also sought the power of the past to manage crises. In the thirteenth century CE, as enemies attacked Muslim lands from every direction, the supposedly everlasting Baghdad caliphate came to its end. Its rival caliphates, the Umayyad in Andalusia and the Fatimids in Egypt, had disintegrated even earlier. The devastation of all their illustrious intellectual-cultural centres in East and West further deepened the predicament that the fall of the ultimate and supposedly perfect political institution, the caliphate, had created for Muslims. To meet the challenge of the times, including what to make of the conviction that Islam and the caliphate were forever linked, required modifying the communal lens, and in this period energetic *fuqaha* attempted to reconnect society to its crumbled past. Ibn Taymyia (d. 1328 CE), Al-Dhahabi (d. 1348 CE), Taj al-Din al-Subki (d. ca. 1370 CE), Ibn Kathir (d. 1373 CE), Ibn Khaldun (d. 1406 CE), Ibn Hajar al-Asqalani (d. 1449 CE), Mohammed al-Sakhawi (d. 1497 CE), Jalal al-Din al-Suyuti (d. 1505 CE), and many more brilliant scholars of the following Mamluk era helped to standardize a modified, some would say new, Muslim historical narrative.[17] Building from the debris, these scholars gave sanctity to the order of things they had recently lost, as they worked to re-establish a sense of Muslim community in their unexpected new circumstances. Even the sequence of their seemingly "mechanical compilations" of history were designed to tell the community how to read the world. The modified worldview that they eventually assembled has had a profound impact on Shari'a rule-/lawmaking: the great influence of the post-thirteenth-century *fuqaha* does not arise from theology, but from the filter that they developed for interpreting old precedents to understand new realities. To this day, many Muslim perceptions of their past and the world around them originate in this late period rather than in the formative centuries of Islam and the precedents from that time that supposedly provide the legal principles to guide Shari'a rulemaking.[18]

The inherently subjective nature of interpreting the past does not make it an arbitrary pursuit; many Muslim historians made careful records and offered sober appraisals of events and figures of a past that they clearly loved. However, the injection of political ideology into the communal discourse brought with it erratic and irrational ways of approaching both the world and the divine message. Some of the self-evidently absurd assumptions about human experience and the common good that developed would not have greatly mattered, were it not for their impact on Shari'a rule-/lawmaking. After all, other communities around the world also embrace some outlandish views of their past. Such a historical lens becomes a matter of significance when views of the past promote or obstruct effective social transformation. How a community understands its origins can generate powerful emotions that become forces of change; no matter how far-fetched ideas may be, the world of perceptions creates new realities. Al-Ghazali and his Sunni enemies both demonstrate the magnitude of such impressions. He shared their loyalty to Shari'a, and like them he believed in its fundamental sources and its method of rule-/lawmaking. However, he differed with them on how to read the past. Looking at historical precedents through a different lens, al-Ghazali read evidence, especially empirical observation, in ways that clashed with his Sunni adversaries. As a result, and despite their identical beliefs about Shari'a's tenets, al-Ghazali and his Sunni opponents produced contrasting Shari'a rules.[19]

Twentieth-century Muslim views of history

Interest in the past is already evident in Mohammed al-Ghazali's earlier works, but once he acquired a sharper sense of history, he parted ways with significant aspects of the Sunni mainstream narrative of the past. He observed discontinuities, while his community often stressed only continuities. At the heart of the predominant twentieth-century Azhari view is the presumption that the world saw little change from the triumph of Mohammed's message in the seventh century CE until the West asserted its technological supremacy and military dominance in Muslim lands. This lens assumes that Muslims continued to live in accordance with what their Prophet had first taught them until the early nineteenth century. It was some Azhari *'ulama* also who most effectively challenged this narrative, such as Mohammed Abduh and those who followed in his footsteps. The challenges they posed about the past informed al-Ghazali, who took their ideas from specialist circles into the Egyptian street.[20] However, the Azhari *fuqaha* continued to see the West as the real agent of historical change in modern times. According to this narrative, actual transformation in Muslim societies only arrived with European conspiracies, which placed Muslims in political subjugation, and Western inventions, which reorganized the ways in which the world operated.[21] As for the rise and fall of Muslim institutions and states over the centuries, these are often explained in terms of predetermined, regressive stages which the Prophet (recorded in Hadith) had already charted for them anyway. Whether the *fuqaha*, the Sufis, or the Sufis' Salafi archenemies, all Sunni groups adhere to this, regarding the ideas to which they subscribe as uninterrupted ancient knowledge that dates from the time of the Prophet, even if these traditions cannot actually be traced back to early times or to scripture. Each Sunni group marks its traditions as sacred, therefore, perceiving their society as essentially unchanging, and thereby adopting the European colonizers' assumptions of a vigorous West in contrast to a static East (here meaning Islam).

The supposedly religious Muslim narrative therefore views Western scholarship on the past as simultaneously antagonistic but superior and objective. In theory, predominant Muslim accounts and European orientalist and neo-orientalist narratives ought to be in conflict. In reality, however, they confirm each other's authority and politically motivated perspectives.

Here, al-Ghazali took a new direction, although he never became an expert historian. Contradictions are not hard to spot in some of his ideas, but he now identified poor familiarity with sources, the failure to recognize constant changes, and what he regarded as detrimental faultlines in the predominant Muslim storyline (both Sunni and Shi'i) as the main intellectual challenge that faced Muslims. Of what he knew of Western academic accounts on Islam, al-Ghazali did not change his disparaging views—yet he acknowledged Western scholarly diligence, for example admiring the extent of Goldziher's sources, which included manuscripts that according to al-Ghazali most Muslim scholars rarely consulted.[22] In other words, although he turned his back on Western outlines of Islamic history, al-Ghazali also increasingly appeared to draw less on the premises of his society's common story of the past, as the portraits below show. Instead, towards the end of his life he acquired a new worldview that could not be described as either secular or religious, nor was it necessarily tied to a particular educational or social background. It was just different. For illustrations, one needs look no further than common Egyptian perceptions of womanhood or political authority.

Portrait: The modern intelligentsia discuss women

If a corrupted worldview is formed by a venerated historical narrative, as al-Ghazali saw it in his last years, then reforms around gender and politics may prove to be of limited use. The suppositions of this narrative have deep roots that thrive in Muslim communities alongside modern practices, as an example illustrates. In his *Kitab al-'Itibar*, the twelfth-century scholar Usama Ibn Munqidh (d. 1188 CE) described how his mother, in order to prevent her daughter being captured by the enemy, placed the girl at the edge of a cliff, ready to push her to her death should the encircling Ismailis (the Assassins) succeed in breaking the town's defences.[23] Faithful to the values of this worldview, a modern Egyptian novelist, Gamal al-Ghitani, heaped praise on this account which, to him, indicated Muslim gallantry. It also revealed Ibn Munqidh's high "respect for women", al-Ghitani wrote.[24] Al-Ghazali had also praised the same account, as demonstrating the exalted place of honour among Muslims. But unlike al-Ghitani, he found its tenor problematic, softly probing: why, instead of throwing the girl to her death, was she not trained to fight, following the example of Muslim women in Medina?[25] In the 1990s, al-Ghazali posed the same question again. This time his unequivocal answer showed the extent of his departure from the discourse with which his community commonly reads its records. Al-Ghazali found Ibn Munqidh's account simply unacceptable; for centuries Muslims "raised women to be helpless and mindless and then blamed [women] for being [helpless and mindless]."[26]

In scholarly settings al-Ghazali's new approach to the Muslim past is distinctive, such as in a 1990s Cairo event to discuss *The Liberation of Women* (*Tahrir al-mar'a*), a multi-volume work by Abd al-Halim Abu Shuqaa. Senior *fiqh* figures and members of the Egyptian intelligentsia attended the meeting. During the discussions, a female university professor identified the reason behind the decline of the status of women in one woman's interference in state affairs in the Ottoman Empire.[27] The professor was referring to Hürrem, or Roxelana (d. 1558 CE), who started life as a slave of East European origin and died as the wife and confidante of Suleiman the Magnificent (d. 1566 CE). When the Sultan ordered the killing of Mustafa, his eldest son from another slave girl, Hürrem was blamed as the instigator of this awful act, while the Sultan escaped responsibility. It did not help her case that after her death he killed one of her sons, too. Whatever Hürrem's culpability, in a political culture that embraced violence as a legitimizing convention, this woman was not seen as a victim, but rather served as the convenient scapegoat who as such has been blamed for many subsequent Ottoman failures. Even if she had wanted Mustafa dead, as a mother, Hürrem might have sought to save her sons from execution by their elder brother upon their father's death, as was the Ottoman custom at the time. Her real crime appears to have been that until Suleiman fell in love with her, Ottoman tradition held the sultan above the institution of marriage; the sovereign neither married nor even lived in the same quarters with his sexual partners. Yet Suleiman allowed Hürrem to move into the imperial palace with him, as his wife, and even corresponded with her about affairs of state when he was away from his capital.[28] Ottoman historians and *'ulama*, not Suleiman the Lawgiver (as his people knew him), were the ones to decide his wife's ultimate place in history. They charted a story of inevitable decline brought about by female interference in public life and disregard for conventions.[29] The elevation of Hürrem into partner and aide to the sultan served as the starting point for this interpretation of Ottoman history. Thus, instead of probing assumptions, the Egyptian female professor embraced them, only adding modern-sounding layers to Hürrem's crimes. This beloved of Suleiman had been behind the rise of the demeaning institution of the harem and the introduction of the *niqab* or women's face-covering, the professor told the seminar.[30] None of the attending distinguished scholars questioned her information. Instead, Shaykh Yususf al-Qaradawi sought to tactfully defend the face-cover as a symbol of Islamic devotion.[31]

That evening al-Ghazali looked elsewhere for the source of women's troubles: in terms of cultural-intellectual crises. Why, he asked the gathering, did their community waste so much effort arguing about trivial matters, such as face-covering and head-covering (*niqab* and *hijab*)? Why did they continue to ignore "the destruction that Muslim women have faced over the past one thousand years"?[32] And why "do the [contemporary] *'ulama* in a certain Arab state continue to deny woman the right to drive [...]?" Further, why did some Muslim (Arabic-speaking) villagers desert their towns early in the twentieth century with the introduction of modern education, because they believed that education for girls was evil?[33] As usual, al-Ghazali answered his own questions. He blamed his people for embracing a worldview originating in a misleading narration of the past. He quizzed an often-quoted report praising a woman for cutting her long hair during war so that Muslim soldiers could turn it into ropes for their horses (also told by Ibn Munquidh); now al-Ghazali thought the story portrayed "women as feeble", contrasting it with earlier times when society subscribed to a different approach. He found alternative images in the twelfth century CE, when Muslim women prospered, including as senior scholars, as he put it.[34] From the transcript of this seminar, no one else appeared to seize on this thread with which Mohammed al-Ghazali challenged the embedded messages of their collective memory. Instead, the usual search for scapegoats continued.

Portrait: Discourse of a political culture

The values embedded in a communal narrative extend beyond women and their rights, as a number of modern scholars have argued.[35] They permeate perceptions of power at every level, whether inside the home, in the street, or up to the highest echelons of government in society. "Political culture" is how this book refers to these conventions, by which a people regulate all power relationships. One modern trained historian, Hussein Mu'nis, provides an illustration. He often raised the all-too-important question of the problem of sources. In another 1990 Cairo lecture, this accomplished scholar intended to present a new approach to understanding the political history of the Prophet.[36] He included the tenure of the first two caliphs of Medina, Abu Bakr and Umar, because, according to Mu'nis, the Prophet as well as these two caliphs ruled benevolently, as fathers of their communities.[37] Conceptualizing the mandate of a ruler in terms of a boundless authority of a father over his offspring has long formed the cornerstone of Muslim political culture; in this, Mu'nis's presentation of Medina's legacy conformed to the outline of the common narrative, and it contained nothing new. Al-Ghazali distilled different lessons. True, he sometimes described these early caliphs in familial terms, as treating those older than themselves with the dignity they would have treated their fathers, those younger than themselves with the compassion they would have had for their sons, and the rest of the community as they would deal with their brothers and sisters;[38] but the Prophet's tenure at Medina, and that of his disciples as caliphs, al-Ghazali insisted, did not hinge on personal or familial ties, nor could it ever approve the monopoly of a family franchise on government, such as had been seen with the Umayyads, Abbasids, or the Ottomans.[39] Mohammed was indeed head of Medina's political community, albeit very rudimentarily, as well as being a Prophet, al-Ghazali maintained, but whereas no one in Medina but the Prophet could speak in the name of divine authority, when it came to civil matters, even Mohammed "had a duty to consult". The Prophet also had to abide by the results of this consultation, al-Ghazali persisted.[40] In line with this reading, he challenged his contemporaries: "If [consultation] is an obligation on the Prophet, by means of a Qur'anic directive, how is it then possible that any [other] ruler could dismiss it [as not required or not binding]?" Al-Ghazali further noted that this divine command to consult followed an incident in which Muslims actually disagreed with the Prophet's views at the Battle of Uhud; but tyrants and their *fuqaha* had every reason to confuse or distort Mohammed's civil legacy, al-Ghazali explained.[41] For despite its rudimentary political structures, he told fellow Muslims, when Medina was their capital, it was organized as a community of equals where men and women participated in making decisions about their worldly affairs. As al-Ghazali described it, the first Muslims always held their leaders accountable while in office. In contrast, notions such as political contract, accountability, or collective decision-making, which al-Ghazali placed at the heart of Medina's political life, were hardly discernible in Mu'nis's modernist discussion, in which Mohammed had been solely a Prophet and never a ruler.[42]

To describe Mu'nis's or al-Ghazali's views of their political history as religious or secular is a misnomer.[43] The devout and the not-so-devout in their part of the world have equally subscribed to a discourse that understands political authority in coercive paternal terms. In March 2011, as the events known as the Arab Spring escalated, Al-Jazeera Television broadcast a collection of clips showing Arab despots repeating identical arguments: Hosni Mubarak (in Egypt), Zein al-'Abidin Ali (in Tunisia), and Ali Abd Allah Salih (in Yemen); these heads of state all resisted calls to give up decades of autocratic control, because they had sacrificed years of their lives as patriarchs of their nations, as they described it. Fatherly rule presumably justified their exclusive grip on the public weal, lawmaking, and all else, managing it as they pleased. Key spokesmen of the religious establishment supported this perspective, counselling citizens to show these leaders the same obedience due to male heads of families.[44] Expediency was not always behind this advice; many of these Muslim figures genuinely conceived authority in absolutist patriarchal terms. Even the most peaceful acts of public opposition ushered in *fitna* (chaos), they feared. Some scholars went further, declaring all street demonstrations as forbidden by God (*haram*).[45] Their counsel makes abdication of political, civic responsibilities a Shari'a rule. Constructed over many centuries, such logic lies at the heart of the now predominant Sunni vision. However, despite being cloaked with Shari'a credentials, the political culture that these *'ulama* upheld was not necessarily anti-secular. In Muslim societies secular and religious jurisdiction had long been separated and entrenched by *fiqh* arguments constructed in order to justify the powers of army ringleaders (sultans) while simultaneously preserving what had become a ramshackle caliphate. The masses' call in 2011 for a society ruled by its citizens presented the grand shaykhs and Egypt's leading Christian clerics with a conundrum. Grandees of Muslim *fiqh* did not support the victims of state brutality in their streets, in their darkest days; and only after the cause of freedom appeared to have won did they hurry to pay lip-service to the sacrifices of the protestors. Christian patriarchs were just the same: seeing danger in Tahrir's political discourse, they told their congregations to stay away from democracy protests. By 2012, a British journalist described an awkward "line of reporting [...] Ahmed Shafik, the Mubarak loyalist, has the support of the Christian Copts, and Assad has the support of the Syrian Christians." In the Middle East, "Christians appeared to support the dictators", Robert Fisk observed.[46]

In the late twentieth century, al-Ghazali explained all such *fiqh* political thought as historical products, not religious instructions. Muslims had to shed them in favour of an older, more precious reservoir of precedents, he reminded the ordinary Muslim. During his lifetime, astute commentators recognized the magnitude of al-Ghazali's new battles, noting how he distilled from a formative (exemplary) Muslim community seemingly liberal-sounding, egalitarian principles, such as accountability of public officials and women's right to full participation in political life. Ironically, these commentators included Egypt's most articulate secularist, Farag Foda.[47]

Fiqh? Hadith? No: It's history, stupid!

An increasing number of Muslim academics have advocated the compatibility of Islamic rulemaking and modern values. In the West, Professors Khaled Abou El Fadl (an admirer of al-Ghazali) and Tariq Ramadan are the two most distinguished examples.[48] However, all such scholars fundamentally differ from Mohammed al-Ghazali, both in the core of their arguments and in their impact. Certainly, Abou El Fadl and Ramadan seek to address a real dilemma in Western Muslim narratives, but Arabic-speaking societies hardly notice them, despite their prominence in Western institutions. Their ideas mainly circulate among Muslims in Western academic circles and, in the case of Ramadan, French-speaking North Africans. Consequently, some specialists judge that their arguments are essentially directed to this Western audience and that they merely mirror outsiders' approaches to Islam.[49] However, a more fundamental difference between al-Ghazali and all such Muslim scholars, whether in the West or elsewhere, is how they approach Shari'a rulemaking. The latter have faithfully rested on *fiqh*, or what these Western-based scholars commonly describe as juristic literature. They legitimized liberal ideas (as being of Shari'a) by employing constructs culled from the same *fiqh* legacy which orientalists and neo-orientalists label "Islamic law". These reform-seeking Muslims thus leave themselves open to a question: Why handpick particular *fiqh* works as decisive authorities on civil tolerance or women's rights, for example, and not other *fiqh* works (sometimes by the same authors) that promote intolerance and misogyny? If old juristic literature is the divine law of Islam, why not accept it all? True, al-Ghazali admired, and openly defended, the legacy of *fiqh*; he defended the Hadith legacy too. However, he moved both legacies into a space that was preoccupied with history as the essential context of the extant literary heritage, whether *fiqh* or Hadith reports. He designated both as precious inheritance, to be cherished and studied, but not to be employed as universal precedents and ultimate authorities in rulemaking. Al-Ghazali declared this heritage chequered at best. He went further here than his great teachers and colleagues, other Mohammed Abduh-inspired Azharis who also openly highlighted serious flaws in the works of even the most eminent *fuqaha*.[50] Al-Ghazali added an essential step to deducing Shari'a rules from the reservoir of precedent, requiring these precedents or their interpretations to be examined in terms of political and cultural pressures and other historical developments. Through this prism, al-Ghazali had little use for *fiqh* works on governance; as discussed in Chapter 7, he considered most of them not to reflect Islam's values. His point of departure for Muslim lawmaking started with critical investigation of discontinuities and continuities in their records, including those that relate to valid Shari'a rules. This meant that, despite drawing liberal-sounding conclusions about Shari'a rules, he did not speak the same language as contemporary modernizing Muslims, especially those in the West. He relinquished his society's narrative on *fiqh* scholarship just as he equally rejected many Western ideas about Islam along with his audience's naïve views of the West.

Al-Ghazali did not introduce anything novel when he invited Muslims to use Medina as the measuring stick by which to deduce Shari'a rules. But as a leader of mainstream Islam, he surprised Muslims by campaigning for the re-examination of this formative history and especially its sources through a common-sense lens, rather than permeating this memory with invented meanings. Inside Arabic-speaking *fiqh* circles, the precedents of Medina, as al-Ghazali now taught them, sparked fierce opposition. He distilled from these early events principles of government that flew in the face of what the establishment had extracted from the same sources. When a senior *'alim* condemned democratic election as a novelty (*bida'*), of which Islam does not approve, al-Ghazali replied that, if so, then surely the ways of Islam were the "spilling of blood and violating" all that humanity cherished.[51] Al-Ghazali now saw danger embedded in the way the Muslim formative story was told. It offered his people two choices only, both of which Islam openly rejected: brutality or abandonment of civil responsibility. Al-Ghazali in this way raised queries that startled the region, the historical central lands of Islam. What if the quarrel between Ali and Mu'awyia had been settled through a referendum to decide the question of leadership?, al-Ghazali pondered, referring to the seventh-century conflict that has plagued Muslim societies ever since. Had these contestants opted for fair elections, allowing the people to choose between their political visions, Muslims might have avoided long centuries of (Sunni–Shi'i) violence, this "orthodox" *'alim* thus challenged the predominant Sunni and Shi'i narratives.[52]

Al-Ghazali recorded some of his confrontations against this common narrative. He especially targeted *fiqh*, believing that chaos and backwardness in Muslim communities originated in his peoples' wholesale abdication of civil responsibilities, which many *fiqh* ideas validated. In another reported encounter, al-Ghazali interrupted two men arguing about restrictions on physical contact with women. Why not spend their time promoting civil rights instead?, he asked them. Such matters "deal with politics; what [we are] discussing concerns *fiqh*", protested one of the men angrily. Al-Ghazali countered: no, that is the "[genuine] *fiqh* I am talking about." He explained to them that their exchange promoted "despicable policies to busy the masses with petty quarrels" over pointless details. Originally devised by "cowards or the intellectually feeble", such trivia as the two men discussed aimed at "diverting [...] attention away from [actual] *fiqh* that looks into [sound] governing practices and finance", al-Ghazali rebuked them.[53] Unaware of what *fiqh* really meant, "gangs of riffraff" preachers, as he described them, have kept such squabbles alive throughout many centuries. By regurgitating "sick phrases" from the Muslim past they helped dictators tighten their grip on Muslim societies, al-Ghazali wrote.[54]

The past therefore had to be confronted. Whereas he had previously reproached Shaykh Khaled Mohammed Khaled for comparing the *fuqaha* to medieval clerics who impeded progress, as discussed earlier, al-Ghazali now pointed the finger at them as behind the misinformation that continually destroyed political life in Muslim societies. He further concluded that the depravity of Muslim state systems had been pervasive, not isolated incidents. *Fiqh* either ignored or justified their tyranny, weaving the logic that sustained an ailing and violent culture and provided it with "scholarly" covering. *Fiqh*, the magnificent legacy of learning to which Islam gave rise, had such an all-encompassing meaning that the state and its scholars eventually presided over its demise.[55] Had Muslim states paid al-Farabi, al-Kindi, Hasan Ibn al-Haytham, al-Khawarizmi, Jabir Ibn Hayan, or other such scholars, some of the attention it paid its sycophants, the Muslim worldview would have evolved in a different direction.[56] Manifestations of these *fiqh*-validated political traditions in modern times included the conspiratorial and repressive outlook of the Muslim Brotherhood (after Hasan al-Banna's death),[57] and the focus on worship details at the expense of civil responsibilities by al-Jami'yia al-Shar'iyya and the Indian based Jam'at al-Tabligh; no one told the members of these groups that "prayers were only a small part of Islam". Islam, al-Ghazali explained, first and foremost sought to establish rights and stand against wrongs, especially in defence of the vulnerable. According to al-Ghazali, Hizb al-Tahrir al-Islami also contradicted the tenets of Islam by advocating that any means were justified in the pursuit of power, while the self-described Salafis of Egypt and Algeria of the late twentieth century had ideas of governance that showed them to be "insane, [indicating] the great disaster they are likely to precipitate" should their groups achieve power.[58] The same old repressive practices plagued the whole political landscape, including self-declared secular groups, whether they raised the banners of the Ba'ath party, Nasser's Arab nationalism, or other flags; al-Ghazali regarded them all as mercenaries.[59]

Al-Ghazali's public deliberations of the harmful role of *fiqh* and Hadith scholarship on society triggered loud condemnations against him. Many religious circles considered his statements defamatory of Islam. Notoriety, it turned out, was good for him. His consideration of the Muslim past also had an unpredictable impact, both on al-Ghazali and his people: he concluded that Muslim societies had long subscribed to a theology of power, not to principles of government derived from their faith. This assembled theology and its stories of the past, and not Islam's tenets, had shaped their worldview for centuries, he argued. No wonder that many of the religious had trouble even understanding the meaning of the Qur'anic-Medina term *al-shura* (consultation);[60] his country's Islamists only wanted to "restore the rule of al-Ghuri in Cairo", referring to a Mamluk sultan whose reign Egyptians regard as violent and arbitrary.[61] Al-Ghazali warned that the Islamists' loyalty to Mamluk political traditions proved their unfitness to hold public office or even to provide Islamic education. It was nonsensical to describe political convictions that draw on this theology of power, as opposed to what he believed to have been Medina's Sunna, as just being different interpretations of their faith. Al-Ghazali increasingly saw the vision of power, to which many in his community subscribed, as a product of a damaged collective psyche and as indicating a continuing mental turmoil. In contrast, he argued, the Sunna of Medina clarified Islam's tenets faithfully, establishing the principles with which to organize a sound political community.

The tenacity of a historical lens

It is misleading to imagine the evolution in al-Ghazali's ideas on the political Sunna in terms of neat, linear lines. For example, he found the thought of a strong polity that defended vulnerable Muslims everywhere impossible to resist, even as he increasingly criticized old empires, dynasties, and their caliphs.[62] Yet, by the 1980s al-Ghazali was furiously campaigning to establish historical context as a key yardstick with which to assess *fiqh* works; he judged their legal and religious legacy to have fallen into the service of tyrants, or at best as having sought to mitigate their evil in society. Al-Ghazali's bid to introduce historical inquiry to assess all *fiqh* products, of any age, may prove to be of immense import. Like other Muslim societies, that of Egypt has long equated governance with their experiences of coercion, and has defined effective leadership in terms of fierce soldiers, grim *walis*, and sultans, or else as mighty pharaohs and, in its most primitive form, as harsh tribal chiefs. Under such systems of rule, Egyptians have submitted to violence as the usual political language, but the *fuqaha* played a decisive role in this surrender to oppression. True, many *fuqaha* have kept alive the memory of early egalitarian traditions of government in Medina, and some have even questioned whether Shari'a prescribed the office of caliph at all.[63] However, ideas that sanctioned tyranny have been determined by immediate circumstances and the idealization of the past, not profound constitutional reflections: their authors preferred the brute force of a single governing group to the uncertainties and, indeed, the brutalities, of several groups competing for power. In time, *fiqh* became the tool that tied oppressive political customs to Shari'a, legitimizing "government-imamate by compulsion".[64] Many such scholars theorized that, without caliphs, sultans, or emirs, Shari'a could not be applied, and therefore would be lost. So it would be, they thought, with justice. Yet the same *'ulama* who had advocated this did not require caliphs and sultans to face *qadis* in common courts, when these rulers summarily killed their subjects, or their relatives and friends. What doubt did the great Harun al-Rashid's (r. 786–809 CE) sudden execution of Jafaar al-Barmaki, his friend and minister of state, and the imprisonment of al-Barmaki's family, cast on this grand monarch as a defender of Shari'a? Or Suleiman the Magnificent's (r. 1520–1566 CE) similar treatment of his friend and great minster of state, Ibrahim Pasha? None. By providing an abundance of Shari'a arguments that rationalized tyranny, Muslim memory in al-Ghazali's region has held two opposing perceptions of legitimate Islamic authority: one that celebrates an accountable and egalitarian Medina-type of administration, and another that embraces traditions of despotism, violence, and permanent inequality. For example, the vision of a splendid royalty residing above a society ordered into ranks, as suggested by the minister Nizam al-Mulk (d. 1092 CE; his name means "Order of Government") is celebrated as the ideal standard of Islamic governance. It was this Seljuk vizier who laid the foundation of the "formal" schooling of the Sunni *fuqaha*, as we know it now (the madrasa). Yet, equally celebrated as the backbone of Islam's principles of government are "Sunan al-Shaykhin", or the model of the first two caliphs as leaders answerable to a classless community of equals. Thanks to these conflicting perceptions of lawful power, Muslim political discourse sometimes sounds surreal.

In time, binding imperial grandeur to religious integrity struck deep roots. Religious-based magnificence also bound itself to communal honour; even today, images of a God-favoured, all-powerful ruler as the ultimate articulation of Islam and community permeate Muslim perceptions, and not just in Egypt and its Arabic-speaking neighbourhood.[65] When in 1996 a Syrian TV soap opera depicted Ottoman officials as oppressive, the then very secular Turkish government reacted angrily, leaving many Arabs bewildered as to why criticism of Ottoman rule outraged the state that had put an end to this dynasty.[66] It was because, in the Turkish case, the same predominant narrative has bound almost every aspect of communal selfhood to Ottoman imperial majesty. Some years later, in 2011, another historical soap opera, this time Turkish, caused a similar uproar. Instead of imageries of dominance, *Muhtesem Yuzyil* (*The Magnificent Century*) featured the harem intrigues and lavish lifestyles inside Suleiman's palace. The show provoked 70,000 complaints, many of them calling for its withdrawal. This time an Islamic government sat in Ankara, but like its secular predecessor in 1996, it rushed to safeguard communal honour, refusing to even consider arguments about historical accuracy. Angry Turkish officials included the then-deputy Prime Minister, Bülent Arınç. He is reported to have warned that "those who try to humiliate the important people of our history [...] should face retribution. What is necessary will be done."[67] Many of Turkey's intelligentsia, whether secular or devout, have also objected to such probes into their illustrious heritage. This reluctance to re-consider past ruling figures appears widespread among the intelligentsia in other Muslim societies. What or who can ever delegitimatize discourses that tie the integrity of community and religion to dynastic dignity? The weight of the Muslim street, not academic finesse or grand fatwas, is the short answer. Here lies the impact of al-Ghazali's final campaign: he taught ordinary Egyptian men and women that circumstances, not Islam, lay behind their inherited political traditions. He gave them examples of how conventions that they supposed were Islamic in origin were generally corrupt. Despite great opposition, al-Ghazali eventually convinced increasing numbers that inquiry into the past threatens neither society nor faith. His adjusted historical lens established a new signpost—an act some would say amounted to a menace—in the predominant Muslim story about themselves. He did not abandon all the accepted premises of this story, but he would have welcomed further probing into history, not just the practices that *Muhtesem Yuzyil* portrayed, despite the fact that these probes greatly anger the modern *'ulama*. These included not just "the destruction that Muslim women faced over the past one thousand years", as he put it, but also dynastic principles, Ottoman enslavement of Christian children (the *devişerme*), or the way the sultans killed their brothers, nephews, and even their sons.[68] For, as he explained, sound evaluation of the past meant a sound understanding of Muslims' political cultures. This, al-Ghazali thought, would help Muslims better understand their faith, and to grasp the contemporary problems they face.[69] Most of all, he insisted, it would help them understand the changes that have taken place in the name of Shari'a rulemaking. Somehow al-Ghazali got this message across to many ordinary people in his country and, perhaps, to some of its neighbours.

In his book *Islam without Fear*, the American political scientist Raymond Baker optimistically sees figures associated with al-Ghazali's scholarly circle as bringing about long-awaited changes to modern Muslim societies.[70] Baker is not alone; among Muslims, al-Ghazali's circle has enjoyed a reputation of intellectual courage in Egypt, propelling some of its members to political prominence as soon as the 2011 Revolution appeared triumphant. Many hoped that these scholars could fill the painful void in sound political thought from which their country suffered. But a reputation for reform is all they seem to have acquired, and after al-Ghazali's death there were rarely attempts among these scholars to widen al-Ghazali's inquiry into historical discontinuities and continuities. This was even though most appeared to have acceded to his key conclusions, albeit sometimes reluctantly, as could be gleaned from a seminar held by this elite gathering.[71] The continuing loyalty of these Islamic thinkers to the predominant historical narrative tipped many of their scholarly and real-life political choices. Although many in this so called *wasyattyia* (moderate) crowd greatly benefitted from the 2011 Revolution, within months they bewildered their countrymen, as they appeared to support preserving military control of the state (through the Supreme Council of the Armed Forces) or advancing the religious establishment as an alternative. Egyptians watched closely as the sympathies of Tariq al-Bishri, Salim al-'Awa, Mohammed 'Imara, or Kamal Abu al-Magd, for example, alternated confusingly between old familiar autocratic traditions and modern political visions of change. Consequently, between January 2011 and December 2012, the popularity of the men whose thought Baker had generously praised plummeted. No longer do their Muslim countrymen see in them what they saw in al-Ghazali: leaders in the image of the scholar-activists of early Islam. Instead of seeking them for inspiration, as many did in the past, Egyptians regularly scorn these scholars as symptoms of the cultural-political vacuum that now troubles Egypt.[72]

More ominously, perhaps, some in al-Ghazali's learned circle of reformers continue to object to a critical examination of the past. Shaykh Yusuf al-Qaradawi provides an example here. He has described al-Ghazali as his teacher and praised his "love for freedom and revulsion of tyranny".[73] Notwithstanding, in 2005 this key expert of *usul al-fiqh* found it necessary to warn that Muslim scholars such as al-Ghazali, Sayyid Qutb, Abu al'Ala al-Mawdudi, and others like them only aided the enemies of Islam with their criticism of the past.[74] Not even the eminent tenth-century CE al-Tabari has escaped al-Qaradawi's censure. He found in al-Tabari's reports, and other works of probing scholars like him, "unintentional unkindness" to Muslim history.[75] In contrast, Shaykh al-Qaradawi praised the twelfth-century Abu Bakr Ibn al-Arabi (d. 1148 CE) as a model historian, and his dreamy accounts in *Al-'Awasim fi al-Qawasim* as a "scientific consideration" of early Muslim history.[76] Al-Qaradawi's arguments demonstrate the contours and the tenacity of the narrative that Muslim societies have long embraced. It often pays lip service to reason, or "scientific consideration", to use al-Qaradawi's words, but it resists attempts to probe its stories, regardless of why. Thus when questioning the Sunni account common in the Arabic-speaking street at the beginning of the twenty-first century, al-Qaradawi hastened to defend its sanctity, even if he had to denounce early and contemporary Muslim historians, including al-Ghazali.

There is also a dimension to al-Qaradawi's apprehension which is specific to Egypt and which important Azhari *'ulama* share. Such Azharis warn listeners to look at the bigotry and the return to the superstitious practices of the nineteenth century which this uncertainty around the common story of Islam's history has bred in Egypt. These Azharis point to the rapid rise of extremist groups and the resurgence of Sufi *tariqas* in their country. More worryingly, they believe that populist suspicions of this common story have aided projects of religious fragmentation inside Egypt, especially Shi'i schemes hatched by the Iranian state theocracy or Indian-based Ismaili groups, and by every other group that scares them. By 2013 an official at al-Azhar, Shaykh Hussein al-Shafi'i, discarded diplomatic niceties during a joint press conference held at the conclusion of Iran's president's visit to this ancient Cairo institution. With Mahmoud Ahmadinejad and Iran's religious officials standing by his side, a visibly angry Shaykh al-Shafi'i complained of intense activity to convert Egyptians into their Shi'i sect.[77] However, Egyptian concerns were not confined to the possibility of clandestine, foreign-sponsored activity. Many of the country's *'ulama* genuinely believe that, when Egypt is compared to other societies, theirs reflects the most reasonable expressions of Islam. Overwhelmingly Sunni, modern Egypt has not experienced the all-too-familiar Sunni–Shi'i vehemence that plagues many other states. Also unlike other Muslim communities, Egypt's public no longer identify with a specific *madhhab*; many have accepted that only experts busy themselves with these methodological differences. In other words, for a time Egypt has spared itself the often ill-tempered religious rivalries that occur among competing Sunni schools, as well as Shi'i–Sunni tensions. Azhari scholars want to keep it this way; but they also recognize the intellectual and cultural paucity in their ranks. As perceptions change, a large number fear a deterioration in how Egyptians approach Islam, arguing that with its mediocre educational system and shoddy media, their country can ill-afford a deconstruction of its religious discourse.

These learned Egyptians were right in detecting a growing shift of perceptions in their streets, but its direction was headed elsewhere: in Egyptians' growing acceptance that freedoms, not great Muslim dynasties or even the *fuqaha*, have furnished the real settings for Shari'a. A book first published twenty years before the Tahrir Square protests erupted in 2011, by one of al-Ghazali's closest associates, provides an illustration.[78] Fahmy Huwaidi's *Al-Qur'an wa al-Sultan* started with the premise that what really mattered to all societies could be "summarized in two words: liberty and democracy."[79] This point of departure allowed Huwaidi to scrutinize Abu al-Hasan al-Karkhi (d. 951 CE), the master of the Baghdad Hanafi School, without offending the devout. As a product of historical failures, al-Karkhi's opinions repressed, not upheld Shari'a; Huwaidi reported that this Hanafi master had instructed that "any Qur'anic verse that contradicted our school is to be considered allegorical or abrogated."[80] In other words, ordinary Egyptian readers, sometimes starting in the 1980s, encountered another mainstream Muslim discourse, one that described political rights as perquisites of Shari'a and *fiqh* works as products of a chequered historical legacy—the same ideas that al-Ghazali fought hard to publicize towards the end of his life.[81] The religious establishment in Egypt faced a most serious challenge in the streets; but what do such changes in Egyptian perceptions of Muslim history mean in practical terms? What happens if the assumptions of the predominant story of the past are undermined, but without denting the tenets of Muslim faith? An indication is given in the way that large numbers of ordinary Arabic-speaking Muslims in and around the Mediterranean rewrote their conversations on democracy.

Scrambling all the clichés

The Arab street champions Western democracy?

> [T]he old nineteenth century [European] dream of a springtime of a people, where a nation can be reborn as a citizenry, [...] a community of citizens, seemed to be an impossible fantasy and one of the most inspiring and stirring things, actually, that in the Middle East of all places, one should not be saying that, I know, but that is the surprise for everyone is to see that happen [in the Middle East ...] It scrambles all the clichés.[82]

That was how in 2011 the British historian Simon Schama saw the events unfolding in Tahrir Square. But the real "scrambling of clichés" would take place later, without much fanfare, in the epic confrontations between Sunni discourses that are continuing even now, in 2016. Far more difficult, for many modern experts, is to consider how al-Ghazali of all people could have played an important role in his region's embrace of democratic values, eventually leading its "reborn citizenry" into breaking ancient barriers during the Arab Spring. This book has charted the course by which a confluence of events, texts of earlier times, and scriptural contents led al-Ghazali to his final views, including those on the nature of legitimate political authority in Islam. When he blamed a lack of well-developed political thought and a profusion of poor governance for many of society's troubles, al-Ghazali chose not to focus on long drawn-out technical arguments as responses. Instead, he took his concerns to the streets. Al-Ghazali instructed the common man and woman in the central lands of early Islam that historical circumstances, not any requirement of Shari'a, shaped most of their political ideas. This advice appeared to fly in the face of his earlier views. In the 1950s al-Ghazali had defended Muslim political memories over many centuries as models to follow. At the time, he condemned Western claims to democracy as a sham—merely an exercise of hypocrisy.[83] He noted how the West, while speaking of human dignity and freedom, savagely treated the rest of humanity and then portrayed its victims as savages.[84] Recalling the time when British soldiers had occupied his country and other Europeans were subjugating the rest of his region, often brutally, al-Ghazali found nothing in the colonizers' political practices from which Muslims could learn.

By the 1960s and 1970s realities had changed. Arabs had won their long struggle for independence and acquired immense oil wealth, but they appeared to have lost their battle for dignity. They neither reflected healthy self-governing communities nor even the riches of their heritage. Whether revolutionary new republics, which he initially supported, or tribal-like monarchies, which he previously criticized, they all failed the societies over which they ruled, al-Ghazali complained. He also started to visit Europe and America, in the cities of which he observed their world first hand. This led al-Ghazali to reconsider Western democratic experiences in a new light. As he saw it, his Western enemies, despite a history of ruthlessness, had the courage to confront their own demons, which meant that they often now succeeded in the test of civilization, whereas his own people often failed. No longer did he approach the West in monolithic terms. He abhorred its appetite for aggression against outsiders, which manifested in Western foreign policies, as much as he appreciated its peoples' efforts to rein in the same forces in their societies. In the end, the shaykh delivered his verdict openly: "I say it and will continue to say it over and over again: [...] there is no sense in arrogantly snubbing the benefits" of sound Western political ideas, he explained.[85] He urged Muslims to drop their pretence of superiority and to learn from other societies, especially the practices of good governance in the West. This took his people by surprise. Al-Ghazali clarified how he arrived at this new conclusion: "My [first-hand] experiences and my study of history", he said, showed how Western peoples' quest for political rights eventually created mankind's healthier political traditions.[86] He conceded the imperfections of democracy, yet he wholeheartedly championed the egalitarian spirit and the perseverance that cemented the rule of law and conventions of representative governments. As he saw it, the institutions that resulted from these struggles for communal justice generally encouraged cooperation among Western states, entrenched belief in civil freedoms, and established a church–state relationship that guaranteed religion a role in society.[87] As usual, al-Ghazali did not do things by half measure, and he described as the greatest Muslim failing the absence of a system of elected government in which all members of the community participated. He gave a chapter of a book on *al-shura* the title "Why Not Draw [Our Political Scheme] from Western Democracies?"[88] Until then, contemporary Sunni *fuqaha* had insisted that only the caliphate provided a perfect political system; their senior members either rejected democracy outright, or if not, they did not dare to come to its defence as superior to Muslim governance throughout much of their history. Many taught that criticizing the grand empires of the past hurt Muslims; a position expressed in the above example of Shaykh al-Qaradawi. Praising their European colonizers for nurturing societies more just than those of their victims hurt millions reared on this common narrative even more. Still, many of his people found al-Ghazali's core argument hard to ignore, because he told them that Shari'a was at stake. If Muslims wished to breathe life into their faith, they had to truly appreciate these foreign political experiences. For, according to al-Ghazali, Shari'a and authoritarian rule could never coexist. Within a decade of his death in 1996 increasing numbers of devout Arabic-speaking Muslims embraced the same beliefs.[89]

The importance of the timing and reasoning of al-Ghazali's assault on the predominant Muslim worldview and its historical roots cannot be emphasized enough. Neither can his suggestion that democracy is a key ingredient to any Muslim reforms. Following the events of 11 September, 2001, Muslim critiques of fanaticism and statements about their faith's compatibility with democracy became common, even fashionable. And no longer did "Islamic" outward appearances attract special privileges in the name of religiosity or religious freedom, as they had done during the time al-Ghazali criticized associating Islam with beards or certain garments. Al-Ghazali, who died five years before the events of 2001 and the ensuing War on Terror, had had to confront Muslim mindsets and their preoccupation with appearances at the height of the Islamists' political and financial power, even in the West, during the 1980s and 1990s. Britain at that time provides a glimpse of the situation: scores of its Islamists blatantly carrying placards around the centres of British cities, boasting of the caliphate's imminent rule over the United Kingdom and posting their threatening messages everywhere, including on public litter bins. Their leaders established an exclusively British Muslim Parliament to keep at bay the aberrations of Western democracy, which had produced a female prime minister. True, al-Ghazali persisted in damning

American and European meddling in his people's affairs and the Muslim and Arab governments that facilitated this continued subjugation; but alongside battling Muslim subservience to neo-colonialist powers and mindsets, he now observed that thanks to their historical struggles for rights, peoples of the West had succeeded where Muslims had abjectly failed. They had created better societies than most past and present Muslim state systems. Such views, made so publicly, took everyone by surprise. Not only did al-Ghazali rock the seemingly triumphant Islamist boat of his time; he also threatened his reputation as a key spokesman of mainstream Islam. But he did not sink. Why? *From Here We Know*, the title he chose for his first famous book, provides a clue. As discussed previously in Chapters 2 and 5–7, from then until he died, al-Ghazali did not see Shari'a as fixed articles of law. He approached Shari'a as a reliable *modus operandi* that revolved around a set of recognizable sources and depended on accurate information. Al-Ghazali did not change his mind about Shari'a, nor did he change his mind about its central place in society: he merely believed that he had discovered how his people's worldview had suppressed this dynamic and self-correcting rulemaking mechanism. He therefore prescribed two surprising remedies to rescue Shari'a rulemaking, both of which revolved around history. The first required a sound approach to investigating Muslim records candidly; the second, a genuine appreciation of past developments that had seen the West creating democratic structures to hold their governments accountable. As noted in Chapter 3, al-Ghazali recognized the challenges: sound historical knowledge required scrupulousness, aptitude, and the courage to re-examine many of his society's assumptions;[90] but scrutinizing records of the past, concerning both the modern period and before, would uncover the most reliable evidence with which to deduce better-informed rules from Shari'a, he now thought. In the end, al-Ghazali used the critical examination of historical sources as the means to bridge Shari'a, self-governance, the rule of law, and successful Western democratic traditions. When he linked the core Muslim lawmaking process to another people's historical struggle for their rights he furnished many Egyptians with a new roadmap for non-violent political change, which, he told them, sustained rather than demolished Islam. He did not know it then, but in so doing al-Ghazali provided many of his people with a rationale for their 2011 uprising, regardless of its outcome.

With the benefit of hindsight, establishing a convincing link between Shari'a, its history, and Western democracy, one that the average Muslim could accept, appears to have been indispensable to sowing the seeds of a grass-roots civil rights vision in the region.[91] The alternatives have failed: decades of Ba'ath secular ideology in Syria and Iraq did not embed modern political ideals in these countries. Albeit less doctrinaire, other secular states such as Tunisia or Egypt fared no better. Repression also thrived under governments that ruled in the name of Islam. As a principal tool of communal organization, coercion dominated the political landscapes in Iran, Afghanistan, and Sudan, to name just a few states that embraced various versions of the well-entrenched politically inspired narrative on Islam. Western efforts to bring democracy to Muslim societies further highlight how little they affected the grassroots. Decades of Western-sponsored programmes and cultural council activities had done hardly anything to support Muslim freedoms. Their politically inspired events and publications often irritated, and even raised suspicions about their intentions, rather than building any lasting awareness of civil rights in the host countries. Early in the twenty-first century, Western governments went a step further. They sent armies to impose democracy by force in Afghanistan, Iraq, and then Libya. There, too, the results do not look promising despite the immense loss of lives and resources. But especially within Western societies, where citizens enjoy many freedoms and economic and social benefits, its Muslim communities do not appear to have become genuinely inspired by democratic values.[92] The authoritarian memory often lives on. The bulk of Western Muslim activists have divided into two strands: those who measure Islam and its civilization in terms of "imperial might", with many aspiring to resurrect the caliphate's grandeur, as in the Abbasid or Ottoman cases, even through coercion; and those who see themselves as modern and fully integrated members of their new societies, yet who regularly urge their governments to curtail the freedoms of fellow Muslims who subscribe to views they oppose. Hizb ut-Tahrir, its offshoot al-Muhajiroun, and numerous instructors of so-called traditional Islamic institutions are examples of the former strand;[93] the Quilliam Foundation, the Sufi Council of Britain, and the Islamic Supreme Council of America exemplify the latter.[94] Although with seemingly opposing viewpoints, spokespersons of both strands hold identical images of authority, finding in autocracy the standard of political life. The majority perceives executive offices in terms of men dictating God's will over a people, but their Muslim opponents give the same authority to the British, American, or any other Western government.[95] This does not mean that the activists are "bad", just that they link their faith to the same communal memory of legitimate political culture. Adopting the vocabulary of modern ideas of government has not helped them. When the Revolution at Tahrir took off, the head of the Quilliam Foundation, Majid Nawaz, made the rounds of UK media outlets, rushing to support Mubarak's appointment of Omar Suleiman as his deputy at the end of January 2011.[96] Suleiman, dubbed Egypt's torturer-in-chief, was the best qualified to lead his country into democracy, according to Nawaz, a Briton of Pakistani background who served time in Egypt on terror charges.[97]

It was supposed to happen the other way around. While in 2011 scores of Muslims in Tunisia and Egypt spoke a new political language, a majority of Europe's devout Muslims aspired to see a caliphate that would enforce God's law by the sword, while an opposing minority, championing repressive measures, urged their governments to curtail the rights of the former group and to prevent any other Muslim dissent. At the time, the call for freedom at Tahrir Square, coming from men and women who included Salafi and Muslim Brotherhood members (whose patriarchs had either condemned the protests outright or stayed away from them), did not quite excite European Muslim minds. Their visions of the best way for Islam to organize governance could not comprehend the sentiments and activities at Tahrir, despite constant international media reports. As a community, the majority of Western Muslims did not claim the struggle for civil rights in the Arab Spring as theirs; many regarded it with suspicion, while others either attacked or dismissed it as insignificant. The freedoms and opportunities that Western Muslims have enjoyed have not nurtured nuanced and mature political thought which could be labelled Islamic. The lofty barriers of two predominant narratives on Islam in the West ensnared them. In stark contrast to these Muslims, a majority of the non-Muslim intelligentsia in their countries celebrated the Arab Spring as an extraordinary event; some continued to mourn every setback to these calls for freedom, which this thinking Western public saw as belonging to a universal vision. When Syria's turn came, a majority of Western Muslims either supported the old tyranny of President al-Assad, under secular pretexts, or supported ISIS, the group largely made up of Saddam Hussein's former secular army, the damaged products of US-led torture camps such as Abu Gharib, and those enraged by the clampdown on the Arab Spring uprising.[98]

Perhaps al-Ghazali might have anticipated such reactions. He had warned that simply replicating Western political, legal, or any other structures would not lead to genuine transformations. Despite fully championing democratic change and inviting his people to learn from Western experiences, al-Ghazali wanted Muslims to reform their worldview first. Even if democratic institutions offered the most workable mechanisms of self-rule and proved far better than any Muslim system of government except that of Medina elections alone are no remedies, however. The rejuvenation of society resided elsewhere: in polishing their collective lens, al-Ghazali contended. Because "our *umma* [the Muslim collective] suffers from intellectual and moral disorders", as he put it, Muslims had to "first effect structural changes in the way we live."[99] As the now-aging shaykh saw it, besides self-rule, real progress required letting go of narratives that sustained a corrupt worldview. Many years after he died, al-Ghazali's willingness to criticise Muslims at home and in neighbouring Arabic-speaking countries prompted an unexpected turn of events. As Egypt's former mufti expected (and feared), Mohammed al-Ghazali had a significant impact on their society, as illustrations in the epilogue that follows show.[100]

Notes

1. Mohammed al-Ghazali, *Al-Da'wa al-Islamiya Tastaqbilu Qarnaha al-Khamis 'Ashr* (no location: Dar al-Salasil, 1980), 158.
2. @maikelnabil (February 2012):
   عفوا لكن أول من أوجد التجنيد الإجباري في الإسلام هو الطاغية الحجاج بن يوسف الثقفي
3. @almogheer (1 December, 2012):
   حمزاوي بيقول الاستفتاء انقلاب على الديمقراطية والسؤال هنا هوا انت يا حمزاوي كنت بتقرأ لمين في شرح الديمقراطية؟ للحجاج بن يوسف؟؟؟
4. @C_Revolutionist (21 September, 2014), الثورة ركعة قضا، مفيهاش إمام بينم!
5. Ibrahim Issa, "Bi al'aks ... Fazat al-Libraliya!" (On the Contrary ... Liberalism Won!), *Al-Dostor al-Asli* (Cairo), 3 January, 2012 (online: http://www.almogaz.com/opinion/news/2012/01/3/138065).
6. Ibrahim Issa, "Al-Youma Intasara al-Islam", *Al-Dostor al-Asli* (Cairo), 3 July, 2013. Articles by him legitimizing the army takeover in terms of Islamic history included "'Abd Allah Ibn Sarh" (series of two articles), *Al-Dostor al-Asli*, 9–10 August, 2013; "Khaled Bin al-Waleed, sayfu Allah al-Maslul" (series of three articles), *Al-Dostor al-Asli*, 12–13 and 17 August, 2013; and "Al-Dohat al-Arba'a" (series of seven articles), *Al-Dostor al-Asli*, 12–18 October, 2013.
7. Re-Tweet by Wael abd al-Fattah (@abu_fajr, 9 December, 2012):
   اللى بيقولك مينفعش الحاكم يصلح فى فترة قصيرة .. عمر بن عبد العزيز حكم 30 شهر وجاء بعد طواغيت ومع ذلك لقب بخامس الخلفاء الراشدين لعدله
8. Re-Tweet by Wael abd al-Fattah (@abu_fajr, 1 December, 2012):
   حكمت فعدلت فامنت فنمت يا عمر. والديكتاتور البائس والهزيل الذي يدعي وصلا بعمر يختبأ في قصره تفصل الاسلاك الشائكة بينه وبين الشعب
9. Ibrahim Issa, "Al-Bah'th 'an al-Hurriya wa al-'Adala", *Al-Dostor al-Asli*, 1 August, 2012 (online: http://www.masress.com/dostor/66505).
10. Al-Ghazali, videotape interview (#W-2).
11. Mohammed al-Ghazali, *Min Huna Na'lam* (Cairo: Dar al-Kutub al-Haditha, n.d.), 37.
12. For a brief but insightful summary on al-Mawdudi, see Fazlur Rahman, *Islam and Modernity: Transformations of an Intellectual Tradition* (Chicago: University of Chicago Press, 1982), 116–118; on Qutb, John Calvert, *Sayyid Qutb and the Origins of Radical Islamism* (New York: Columbia University Press, 2010).
13. Al-Ghazali, videotape interview (#IKH-2); idem, "Qissat Haya", *Islamiyat al-Ma'rifa* 2/3 (2007): 203–204, 208.
14. A brief illustration of such old discussions on Muslim leadership can be found in Fakhr al-Din al-Razi, "Al-Bab al-'Ashir: Fi al-Imama wa fihi Massa'il", *Kitab M'alim Usul al-Din* (Beirut: Dar al-Fikr al-Lubnani, 1992), 101–109; for a succinct outline in English on the institution of caliphate, see Wadad al-Kadi and Aram Shahin, "Caliph, Caliphate", in Patricia Crone, Wadad Kadi, Devin J. Stewart, Muhammad Qasim Zaman and Mahan Mirza, eds, *The Princeton Encyclopedia of Islamic Political Thought* (Princeton, NJ: Princeton University Press, 2012), 81–86.
15. The Buyids (934–1062 CE) were a Shi'ite dynasty that eventually extended its rule to modern-day Persia, Afghanistan, Syria, Iraq, and, most significantly, Baghdad, the capital of the Abbasids.
16. The Fatimid Caliphate (909–1171 CE) was an Ismaili Shi'i dynasty that extended its control into North Africa, Egypt, Syria, Hijaz, Yemen, and, notably, Islam's holy places in Mecca and Medina.
17. For some key and varied works of these Mamluk-era scholars that shaped Muslim perceptions of history and Shari'a in later times, see Selected Bibliography.

18. For observations on twenty-first-century Egyptian perceptions of the caliphate, see John Casey, "Isis are Barbarians—But the Caliphate is an Ancient Muslim Ideal", *Independent* (London), 4 July, 2015 (online: http://www.independent.co.uk/voices/comment/isis-are-barbarians—but-the-caliphate-is-an-ancient-muslim-ideal-10365201.html).
19. An investigative Egyptian journalist and Sinai specialist, Ismail Alexandrani, observed how Egyptians inspired by ISIS employed ancient terms such as *gazwa* in reference to the attacks they conducted against Sisi's state, or *wali* (an Islamic governor) to refer to their leaders. Ismail Alexandrani, "Athar Da'sh 'ala Misr", lecture organized by Misr al-Qawiya Party, Cairo, 21 June 2014 (online: https://www.youtube.com/watch?v=ubvb8T1Z4Tc).
20. It must be noted that modern Azhari *'ulama* had also been the most effective in challenging this old narrative, as in the famous case of Mohammed Abduh, his students, and those inspired by them. Al-Ghazali transformed the questions that these scholars of Islam had posed to the common narrative of their past from the discourse of learned circles into the Egyptian street.
21. This is an account of Shaykh Ali Goma's description of his country's modern history during two author interviews in April 1999 and February 2007; also, between 2002–2007, the author had discussions with other Azhari shaykhs, including Usama al-Sayyid al-Azhari, Goma's protégé and recently appointed as President Sisi's advisor. They showed unsettling views of the past; see also Yusuf al-Qaradawi, *Tarikhuna al-Muftara 'Alayh* (Cairo: Dar al-Shorouk, 2005), 25–26. This common reading of history revolves around three assumptions: first, that nothing has changed in Muslim societies since the coming of Mohammed (seventh century CE) up to the eve of European colonial rule in modern times; second, that before such Western incursions, Muslims had a far superior system of governance and justice, and enjoyed greater general prosperity than the modern West; and third, that ever since, the West has become the only cause of change in Muslim societies. It is worth noting, however, that by 2014 Shaykh Goma had adjusted some of his views on the history of *usul al-fiqh* in *Tarikh ilm Usul al-Fiqh* (Cairo: Dar al-Moqatam li al-Nashr wa al-Tawzi', 2014).
22. Al-Ghazali, videotape interviews (#TAYR-2, #Mul-2).
23. An English translation of *Kitab al-'Itibar*, titled *An Arab-Syrian Gentleman and Warrior in the Period of the Crusades*, trans. Philip Hitti (New York: Columbia University Press, 2000).
24. Gamal al-Ghitani, *Muntaha al-Talab ila Turath al-'Arab, Dirasat fi al-Turath* (Cairo: Dar al-Shorouk, 1997), 64.
25. Mohammed al-Ghazali, *Humum Da'iya* (Cairo: Nahdat Misr, 2004), 61–62.
26. Mohammed al-Ghazali, comments reported in the transcript of a lecture by Abd al-Halim Abu Shuqaa, *Nadwat Tahrir al-Mar'a* (Cairo: IIIT, n.d.), 19–21; idem, *Al-Islam wa al-Mar'a* (Cairo: IIIT, 1990), 5–6.
27. Leila al-'Anani, comments reported in Abu Shuqaa, *Nadwat Tahrir al-Mar'a*, 10–11.
28. Leslie Peirce, *The Imperial Harem* (Oxford: Oxford University Press, 1993), 61–64, 86–90, 94, 121.
29. Ibid., 86–90, 109, 143, 154, 242, 277, 281 ff.
30. Al-Ghazali, comments reported in Abu Shuqaa, *Nadwat Tahrir al-Mar'a*, 10.
31. Ibid., 18.
32. Compare al-Ghazali's above remarks to the views of the North America-based Muslim scholar Gamal Badawi in his *The Status of Woman in Islam* (Riyadh: World Assembly of Muslim Youth, 1997).
33. Al-Ghazali, comments recorded in Abu Shuqaa, *Nadwat Tahrir al-Mar'a*, 19–21.
34. Ibid., 20.
35. Famous examples include Leila Ahmed, *Women and Gender in Islam* (New Haven, CT: Yale University Press, 1992); Fatima Mernissi, *The Forgotten Queens of Islam* (Minneapolis: University of Minnesota Press, 1993); for recent discussions examining the link between the

status of women and the formation of the nation state, see Amira Sonbol, "Shari'ah and State Formation: Historical Perspective", *Chicago Journal of International Law*, 8/1 (2007): 59–83.

36. Hussein Mu'nis, *Usus al-Hadhara al-Islamiya fi al-'Asr al-Nabawi* (Cairo: Markaz al-Dirasat al-Ma'rifiyya, n.d.).
37. Ibid.
38. Mohammed Al-Ghazali, *Azmat al-Shura fi al-Mujtama'at al-Arabia wa al-Islamiyia* (Cairo: Dar al-Sharq al-Awsat, 1990), 35.
39. Ibid., 31, 74–75.
40. Al-Ghazali, videotape interview (#SYS-1).
41. Al-Ghazali, *Azmat al-Shura*, 41 ff.
42. Ibid., 12, 36–37.
43. Mu'nis was known for his critical discussions on Muslim sources of history as in his *Tanqiyat Usul al-Tarikh al-Islami* (Cairo: Dar al-Rashad, 1997). Other Western-trained figures also known for their modernist approaches to Muslim history did not really part ways with older narratives, including Taha Hussein, as illustrated in his *Al-Fitna al-Kubra* (Cairo: al-Hay'a al-Misryia, Maktabat al-Usra, 2013). On modern historiography of Islam, see Ahmad Dalal, "Appropriating the Past: Twentieth-Century Reconstruction of Pre-Modern Islamic Thought". *Islamic Law and Society* 7/1 (2000): 325–358.
44. For illustration, see the passionate arguments in defence of President Mubarak by the famous preacher Shaykh Khaled al-Gendi (online: https://www.youtube.com/watch?v=nIx5Aedtj0w).
45. An example here is the Azhari professor and leader of the group called Salafi Movement, Usama abd al-Azim. He declared that Shari'a banned all public demonstrations, especially those like the Tahrir Square protests that called on Mubarak to step down as president. Abd al-Azim further explained that protests contained acts of debauchery which involved drugs and illicit sex. The response came from within al-Azhar, too. Azhari students who supported Tahrir Square accused this Salafi leader of being a traitor in the service of tyrants ("Al-tulab yuhajimoun al-doctor Usama abd al-Azim", *Al-Dostor*, 18 May, 2011 [online: http://www.dostor.org/politics/egypt/11/may/18/4257]).
46. Robert Fisk, "Hosni Mubarak has Fallen. Assad Clings On. Yet the Fate of their Nations is Anyone's Guess", *Independent* (London), 4 June, 2012 (online: http://www.independent.co.uk/opinion/commentators/fisk/robert-fisk-hosni-mubarak-has-fallen-assad-clings-on-yet-the-fate-of-their-nations-is-anyones-guess-7814810.html).
47. See Chapter 4, section "Ghazali versus al-Ghazali".
48. Khaled Abou El Fadl, *Islam and the Challenge of Democracy* (Princeton, NJ: Princeton University Press, 2004); idem, "Conceptualizing Shari'a in the Modern State", *Villanova Law Review* 4 (2012):56 ; also Tariq Ramadan, *Islam, the West, and the Challenges of Modernity* (Leicester, UK: Islamic Foundation, 2003); idem, "Tariq Ramadan: My Absence Would Certainly Be The Most Powerful Speech I Have Ever Given At ISNA", 14 August, 2014 (online: http://theislamicmonthly.com/tariq-ramadan-my-absence-would-certainly-be-the-most-powerful-speech-i-have-ever-given-at-isna/).
49. Richard W. Bulliet, "Islamic Reformation or Big Crunch? A Review Essay", *Harvard Middle Eastern and Islamic Review*, 8 (2009): 7–18.
50. A modern nuanced illustration can be found in former head of al-Azhar Shaykh Mahmoud Shaltut's *Al-Islam 'Aqida wa Shari'a*, 2nd edn (Cairo: Dar al-Qalam, n.d.), 72–80, 300–306, 568–571.
51. Al-Ghazali, *Azmat al-Shura*, 42, 49.
52. Al-Ghazali, videotape interview (#SYS-1).
53. Al-Ghazali, *Azmat al-Shura*, 83.
54. Ibid., 43; al-Ghazali, videotape interview (#SYS-1).

55. Al-Ghazali, *Kaifa Nat'amal ma' al-Qur'an*, ed. Umar Ubaid Hassana (Herndon, VA: IIIT, 1992), 68–70, 94–95.
56. Ibid., 47, 65–66, 89, 145–147.
57. Ma'alim al-Haqq Al-Ghazali, *Min Ma'alim al-Haqq fi Kifahina al-Islami al-Hadith*, 2nd edn (Cairo: Dar al-Kutub al-Haditha, 1963), 235–249.
58. Al-Ghazali, videotape interview (#TAYR-2); idem, *Al-Islam wa al-Mar'a*.
59. Al-Ghazali, *Nadwat Tadris al-'Ulum al-Shar'iya* (Cairo: IIIT, n.d.), 31.
60. Al-Ghazali, *Azmat al-Shura*, 33.
61. Ibid.; al-Ghazali, *Al-Da'wa al-Islamiya Tastaqbilu Qarnaha al-Khamis 'Ashr* (no location: Dar al-Salasil, 1980), 158.
62. Al-Ghazali, *Azmat al-Shura*, 38, 73, 76–77; idem, "Fiqh al Da'wa".
63. See footnote 16; Fakhr al-Din al-Razi, "Al-Bab al-'Ashir: Fi al-Imama wa fihi Massa'il", *Kitab M'alim Usul al-Din* (Beirut: Dar al-Fikr al-Lubnani, 1992); al-Kadi and Shahin, "Caliph, Caliphate".
64. Theorizing a Shari'a-accepted "government-imamate by compulsion" has been openly argued as in the example of the Shafi'i *faqih*, Badr al-Din Mohammed Ibn Jama'a (d. 1333 CE), *Kitab Tahrir al-Ahkam fi Tadbir ahl al-Islam*, ed. Fouad abd al-Monem Ahmed (Doha: Ri'asat al-Mahakim al-Shariya, 1985).
65. Immediately after the Egyptian 2011 Revolution, Islamist parties turned to the army's generals, who they saw as Islam's governors. Many in Egypt continue to remember how on 30 July, 2011 various Islamist groups, including Ikhwan supporters, organized demonstrations at Tahrir Square in which they dubbed the SCAF's (army) chief as "al-Wali" and urged him to follow in the footsteps of the Mamluk sultan Qutz and of the Ayubid Sultan, Salah al-Din al-Ayyubi (Saladin):

    وجه التيار الاسلامى بالتحرير رسالة إلى «الوالى طنطاوى» فى إشارة إلى المشير حسين طنطاوى رئيس المجلس الأعلى للقوات المسلحة تطالبه بـ«اتباع الشريعة كما اتبعها صلاح الدين الأيوبى، وسيف الدين قطز، لينصره الله على أعدائه، كما نصر سابقيه الذين حكموا بشرع الله» بحسب اللافتة التى رفعها البعض.

    (online: https://www.facebook.com/shorouknews/posts/249168981773394).

    Following the army's July 2013 coup against the Ikhwan's elected government, this and all other YouTube video clips showing Islamists' open demonstrations urging the military to step in as guardians of their vision have been removed (presumably by Islamists) and the following message appears instead: "The YouTube account associated with this video has been terminated due to multiple third-party notifications of copyright infringement." There are good reasons why Islamist political parties had to thoroughly erase these memories, which showed the reasons behind the rift between them and the rest of the Egyptians, who continued to support Tahrir Square calls for freedoms. The latter regularly posted these videos to taunt the Ikhwan and other Islamists about their blurred vision of democracy and their role in saving the repressive old political system, as illustrated by the following Tweets: @MSRY1112 (2 January, 2013):

    فيديو يجب ان يحتفظ به كل واحد ويوريه لعياله .. موقف الاخوان من الثورة

    http://www.youtube.com/watch?NR=1&v=bAUfGXTEpnc&feature=endscreen ...

    @AymanYousuf (1 August, 2013):

    حتي لا ننسى .. هتافات السلفيين والإخوان للمشير فى ميدان التحرير.

    https://www.youtube.com/watch?v=Z2RohV1C9LQ&feature=youtube_gdata_player
66. Najdat Anzour (dir.), *Ikhwat al-Turab* (TV drama, 1996). This serial tells the story of the country's revolt against the Ottoman governor in Syria, Ahmet Cemal Pasha (d. 1922), who later ruled the empire throughout World War I with two colleagues, Ismail Enver and Mehmed Talaat.
67. Suzanne Fowler, "Magnificent Century Divides Turkish Viewers over the Life Of Suleiman", *Guardian*, 20 March, 2011 (online: http://www.guardian.co.uk/world/2011/mar/20/turkish-drama-magnificent-century-divides); Esra Doğramacı, *A Revisionist Turkish Identity:*

Power, Religion and Ethnicity as Ottoman Identity in the Turkish Series Muhteşem Yüzyıl (MSc diss., London School of Economics and Political Science, 2013).

68. Al-Ghazali, comments reported in Abu Shuqaa, *Nadwat Tahrir al-Mar'a*, 19.
69. Al-Ghazali, *Azmat al-Shura*, 90.
70. Baker's informative book generally focuses on figures in al-Ghazali's circle such as Salim al-Awa, Tariq al-Bishri, Fahmy Huwaidi, and Kamal Abu al-Magd. Raymond Baker, *Islam without Fear: Egypt and the New Islamists* (Cambridge, MA: Harvard University Press, 2003).
71. See Chapter 7.
72. On 15 February, 2012, Egyptian activists disturbed a lecture that al-Awa was to give in London. They chanted "No to military rule, no to Ikhwan, Awa out". They also shouted that he scandalized religion and patriotism by supporting the military council (SCAF) that killed their fellow revolutionaries or imprisoned them (online: https://www.youtube.com/watch?v=9t2dIvL4jgA).
73. Yusuf al-Qaradawi, *Tarikhuna al-Muftara 'Alayh* (Cairo: Dar al-Shorouk, 2005), 61.
74. Ibid., 46–50, 56–57, 61–64, 83–85, 230–240.
75. Ibid., 230–231, 234.
76. Ibid., 235.
77. "*Al-Azhar Yu'wajih Saf'at Mu'lima li al-Ra'is al-Irani*" (al-Azhar deals a painful blow to the Iranian president) (online video: https://www.youtube.com/watch?v=cGieHJlfl9E#t=172); Fahmy Hwiedi, "'Itab Ghadhib", *Al-Shorouk*, 17 February, 2013 (online: http://shorouknews.com/columns/view.aspx?cdate=17022013&id=0c0e4371-ceb0-4c97-a877-117f19e7fde9).
78. Fahmy Huwaidi, *Al-Qur'an wa al-Sultan* (Cairo:Dar al-Shorouk, 2002). For more of Huwaidi's arguments in favour of democracy see his *Al-Islam wa al-Dimoqratyia* (Cairo: Markaz al-Ahram li al-Tarjama wa al-Nashr, 1993).
79. Huwaidi, *Al-Qur'an wa al-Sultan*, 20–21.
80. Ibid. 21.
81. Ibid., 21–58. Early in this century, alert observers in the West questioned the common academic assumptions about Islam's inherent hostility to democracy. See Michael Hirsh, "Bernard Lewis Revisited: What if Islam Isn't an Obstacle to Democracy in the Middle East but the Secret to Achieving It?", *Washington Monthly*, November 2004: 13–19 (online: http://www.washingtonmonthly.com/features/2004/0411.hirsh.html).
82. Simon Schama, speaking on BBC *Newsnight*, presented by Gavin Esler, 24 February, 2011 (online: http://news.bbc.co.uk/1/hi/programmes/newsnight/9407995.stm).
83. Al-Ghazali, *Min Huna Na'lam*, 69, 94, 100, 103, 198.
84. Ibid.
85. Al-Ghazali, *Azmat al-Shura*, 61–78, 81.
86. Ibid., 36–37, 81, 89, 90.
87. Ibid., 53.
88. Ibid., 69–78, 93.
89. See Epilogue for illustrations.
90. Mohammed al-Ghazali, *Turathuna al-Fikri fi Mizan al-Shar'i wa al-'Aql* 2nd edn (Cairo: Dar al-Shorouk, 1991), 119.
91. Al-Ghazali's debt to Mohammed Abduh's legacy cannot be overestimated. Whether regarding the tenets of Muslim faith, the relative weight of the fundamental sources of Shari'a rulemaking, and approaches to history and democracy in terms that Muslims found acceptable, all followed in the footsteps of Abduh's earlier arguments. That Abduh's presentations were familiar to many in Egypt also helped al-Ghazali. Where next and how al-Ghazali advanced these arguments meant that they took new turns, with important consequences, as the Epilogue shows.

92. Among examples, see David Kirkpatrick, "Online American Helps Fuel Attacks in Egypt", *New York Times*, 27 February, 2015 (online: http://www.nytimes.com/2015/02/28/world/american-agitator-helps-fuel-attacks-in-egypt.html).
93. On such institutions see Appendix 1, a summary of al-Ghazali and senior Muslim scholars' deliberations on contemporary Islamic institutions of learning.
94. Dominic Casciani, "Minister Backs New Muslim Group", *BBC News*, 19 July, 2006 (online: http://news.bbc.co.uk/1/hi/uk/5193402.stm); Mark Sedwick, "Sufis as 'Good Muslims': Sufism in the Battle against Jihadi Salafism", in Lloyd Ridgeon, ed., *Sufi and Salafi in the Contemporary Age* (London: Bloomsbury, 2015), 105–117; Richard H. Curtiss, "Dispute Between U.S. Muslim Groups Goes Public", *Washington Report on Middle East Affairs*, April/May 1999 (online: http://www.wrmea.org/1999-april-may/dispute-between-u.s.-muslim-groups-goes-public.html).
95. In 2010 the Quilliam Foundation presented the British authorities with a list of names of "dangerous" Muslims to watch, which alarmed some in Britain as being "McCarthyite"; see Vikram Dodd, "List Sent to Terror Chief Aligns Peaceful Muslim Groups with Terrorist Ideology", *Guardian*, 4 August, 2010 (online: http://www.theguardian.com/uk/2010/aug/04/quilliam-foundation-list-alleged-extremism); Jonathan Gthens-Mazer and Robert Lambert, "Quilliam on Prevent: The Wrong Diagnosis", *Guardian*, 19 October, 2009 (online: http://www.theguardian.com/commentisfree/belief/2009/oct/19/prevent-quilliam-foundation-extremism).
96. During the protests at Tahrir Square in January and February 2011, Maajid Nawaz presented himself as an expert on Egypt. In this capacity, he told Channel 4 News and the BBC that an army general in charge of intelligence, Omar Suleiman, would make the best candidate to lead that country into democracy after the fall of Mubarak. Video clips of these interviews are no longer available; but, in a news summary of its reporting on Tahrir events, BBC curiously designates Nawaz's organization as "the Arabic thinktank, the Quilliam Foundation" (online: http://news.bbc.co.uk/1/hi/9381309.stm).
97. Lisa Hajjar, "Omar Suleiman, the CIA's Man in Cairo and Egypt's Torturer-in-Chief", *Jadaliyya* (Washington DC), 30 January, 2011 (online: http://www.jadaliyya.com/pages/index/503/omar-suleiman-the-cias-man-in-cairo-and-egypts-tor).
98. Liz Sly, "The Hidden Hand Behind the Islamic State Militants? Saddam Hussein's", *Washington Post*, 4 April, 2015 (online: https://www.washingtonpost.com/world/middle_east/the-hidden-hand-behind-the-islamic-state-militants-saddam-husseins/2015/04/04/aa97676c-cc32-11e4-8730-4f473416e759_story.html); Martin Chulov, "Isis: The Inside Story", *Guardian*, 11 December, 2014 (online: http://www.theguardian.com/world/2014/dec/11/-sp-isis-the-inside-story). Chulov's documentation of the origins and make-up of ISIS gained recognition in 2015: see "Guardian Journalist Martin Chulov wins Orwell Prize for Middle East Coverage", *Guardian*, 22 May, 2015 (online: http://www.theguardian.com/books/2015/may/22/martin-chulov-wins-orwell-prize-guardian-middle-east-coverage) and "Guardian Middle East Reporter Martin Chulov Wins Journalist of Year", *Guardian*, 25 November, 2015 (online: http://www.theguardian.com/media/2015/nov/25/guardian-middle-east-reporter-martin-chulov-wins-journalist-of-year).
99. Al-Ghazali, *Nadwat Tadris al-'Ulum al-Shar'iya*, 50–51.
100. Author interview with Shaykh Ali Goma, al-Azhar Mosque, Cairo, May 1998.

EPILOGUE

What is in a Historical Narrative?

Uprisings

When Mohammed al-Ghazali targeted the popular Muslim understanding of Islam's history in the 1980s, his campaign triggered storms of controversy that were continuing at the time of his death in 1996. However, his arguments gave authority to a budding new mainstream Muslim discourse that by 2011 had found its way to prominence across the Arabic-speaking lands of early Islam. Although unmistakably Sunni, this discourse puts its own political (Sunni) narrative on trial. Yet, it is equally far from Shi'i political imageries or aspirations. Other scholars helped in various ways with the birth of this new narrative, but it was al-Ghazali who turned into a populist demand the idea that, to save Shari'a, his people must revisit the conclusions they had drawn from their past. He determined the outlines of the resulting new discourse and gave it its distinct voice: Muslim records and realities revealed that, when it came to power relations, lawmaking according to their faith had been stymied or neglected. In Saudi Arabia, the country whose religious establishment had led the campaign against al-Ghazali's views on Shari'a and history, many eventually turned to his arguments as appropriate Islamic reference points for reforms. Increasing numbers of popular Saudi Salafi figures, who had disparaged him in the 1980s and 1990s, at the beginning of the twenty-first century now sounded like al-Ghazali. An example here is Shaykh Salman al-Odah. In the late 1990s, he published a famous response to demonstrate al-Ghazali's errors in articulating Shari'a.[1] However, in 2005 he expressed regret over this response to al-Ghazali's *Al-Sunna al-Nabawiya*,[2] and by 2013 his website included a book that described al-Ghazali as a member of the fifth generation of remarkable modern Muslim reformers.[3] A year earlier, this Saudi champion of the Hadith legacy judged a Hadith stating that "the Sultan is God's shadow on earth" as forged, even though their great Shaykh Ibn Taymyia had accepted it as genuine. The report was intended to falsely wrap rulers in divine authority, al-Odah concluded.[4] He unhesitatingly celebrated as Islamic the Egyptian

Revolution's call for a civil and democratic state.[5] In May 2012 al-Odah tweeted to the devout that Shari'a did not recognize religious government, and that it opposes theocracy. His is not a lone Saudi Sunni voice,[6] and such views contradict their fellow Saudi Salafis, especially those of the state-appointed mufti. In a Mount 'Arafat sermon the mufti warned the Muslims gathered for Hajj against the notion of civil government and democracy. In this 2012 *khutba*, at Nimra Mosque (Mecca), Shaykh Abd al-Aziz bin abd Allah Al Shaykh declared that all such notions contradicted Shari'a and the fundamentals of their faith;[7] but signs that the Salafi Saudi discourse is changing are now too close to that society's core, and too many to ignore. For example, although previously known for his strict Salafi views on Shari'a, the younger Abd Allah al-Maliki, while still devout, wrote that political *fiqh* formulated under the shadow of an authoritarian state has no place in today's society. The growing embrace of the notion of "a contractual state" indicates that a new political *fiqh* is now being formed, al-Maliki added.[8] In November 2011, Abd-Wahab al-Triri, another strict Salafist from Saudi Arabia, re-Tweeted approvingly this statement of the younger al-Maliki: "I came to fully believe that democracy is the best space/setting for applying the Shari'a."[9] All such statements by an ever-vocal segment of Saudi Salafi leaders appear to echo Mohammed al-Ghazali's conclusions on democracy, which had shocked the Saudi devout decades earlier. Obviously, they contradicted other Salafi leaders in their country. Another al-Odah Tweet expressed the thought that it is incorrect to organize a government in terms of divine dictates;[10] instead, people "must put together [these details] according to each country's circumstances." The idea of change became a paramount duty; Muslims must constantly seek such modification, not blindly copy ideas of the past, al-Odah urged his followers. The Saudi Mohanna al-Hubail shared with the like-minded a Tweet that called for revising Islamic education to focus on areas such as the priorities and purposes of Shari'a.[11] A professor of Shari'a in Saudi Arabia, Dr Saleh Sultan, traced the bulk of Muslim problems to their neglect of what he described as Islam's guarantees of freedoms, equality, and justice for all members of society.[12]

Gauging the real import of any such statements is far from easy: they cannot be understood in terms of a linear progression.[13] Some authors lack coherence regarding the principles they now champion, and at times these Salafi statements sound like echoes of unfamiliar languages or a simple wish-list rather than the genuine products of long journeys of reflection. Notwithstanding, the surging popularity of these ideas among popular outspoken Salafis indicates considerable tension as well as new energy inside Saudi religious circles. Their conversations posed the ultimate threat to existing ways of governance, albeit very quietly, and they indicate that a newer mainstream discourse on Islam has spread inside Saudi Arabia, raising the following question: To what extend did the rise of this particular discourse in this influential country coincide with al-Ghazali's battles with his hosts in the religious circles of Mecca and Medina? The genuine revolution in such novel-sounding deliberations is in their adjusted approaches to history, not in theology. Al-Odah describes the formation of the caliphate in Medina as merely a "human experience", albeit one that successfully put together a government which distanced itself from coercion.[14] In contrast, al-Odah notes that the Abbasids (the dynasty most associated with championing the Sunni-Hadith legacy) failed to keep their promises even to those who helped maintain their state.[15] Seeing early Muslim governments in terms of a positive experience in Medina versus bad practices under the Abbasids and in other cases has an impact on these Salafis' assumptions about Shari'a. One is that the enormous number of rules under the rubric of Shari'a appears in a different light; for example, according to al-Odah, only an oppressive community has detailed rules to control its members' lives.[16] He concluded that only with persistent efforts can Muslims overcome centuries of tyrannical legal traditions that sought to subjugate them.[17] The late Dr Mohammed al-Rasheed, a former Saudi secretary of education, and dean of the Department of Education at Ibn Saud University, similarly challenged sensitive Shari'a rules in light of historical precedent. He too sounded like al-Ghazali when, in January 2013, he asked those who objected to women joining the workplace whether or not they knew that the first person to be appointed as market supervisor (*muhtasiba*) was a woman, al-Shifa bint 'Abd-Allah.[18] The former Saudi official found that no permanent Shari'a source of law prohibited appointing women to top public jobs, as long as they had the necessary qualifications. In some Saudi Salafi circles, wholesale reconsideration of history, in al-Ghazali-like ways, now matters in the making of Shari'a rules. All useful works on political thought, even if not Muslim, are embraced. Hence Salafi shaykh al-Odah's re-Tweet that included a link to "an admirable book to read": Montesquieu's *L'esprit des lois*.[19]

In Egypt, transformations in the Sunni discourse were far more noticeable than in Saudi Arabia. Without them, the mass participation in the Revolution of January–February 2011 across the country would not have been possible. The role that Facebook, Twitter, and other social media have played in the Arab Spring has attracted great attention. Yet, the agency of Islamic ideas that decided the character of this Egyptian Revolution, provided its grassroot support, and may still decide the country's long-term prospects, has not been thoroughly examined. Egypt's Tahrir activists quickly highlighted the limitations of their communication tools in effecting change. Modern social media helped them arrange the events that toppled their president, but the actual Revolution—that is, the shift in many of their countrymen's perceptions of governance and society—has had an altogether different trajectory. In a visit to London, a recognizable young face of the Tahrir 2011 protest maintained that describing it as a rebellion of a younger internet generation misrepresented and undermined the Egyptian Revolution.

Their uprising had been in the making for many years, said Gigi Ibrahim, an outspoken leftist.[20] Many of her countrymen agree.[21] This raises the question: If modern social media and a younger generation did not decide the battle for the Egyptian mind, which has led to some of the most radical confrontations since World War II (as Henry Kissinger once described the Arab Spring), what did?[22] A significant factor that paved the way for this political tremor is an emerging discourse that has been in the making for many years. It is Islamic and Sunni, for the most part, which makes it extremely unfashionable to the now predominant Western discourse on Islam. It is also very incomplete. Worse, perhaps, is that this vision provoked an upsurge of its opposing Sunni and Shi'a discourses. Whether as arguments for "Islamic" government and communal stability, or as protests or counter-protests, all such old visions recognize that if left unchecked, this new discourse will undermine their entrenched perspectives.

Mohammed al-Ghazali played a critical role in validating this adjusted Sunni political worldview. In linking Shari'a to communal self-governance in the way he did, the urgency of communal decision-making and accountability spread across his country. Even those who did not like this new discourse hurried in the first days of the Revolution to appropriate some of its imagery and arguments, including many Islamist opponents of al-Ghazali inside Egypt. His previously controversial Shari'a rules on governance, on women, and, more significantly, how he deduced them from Shari'a, became celebrated positions in Egypt following the 2011 mass uprisings. Five months after the fall of Mubarak, one of the former president's faithful associates, Shaykh Ahmed al-Tayyib, while still at the helm of the world's key Sunni institution announced an Islamic outline for Egypt's Shari'a-compliant governance: *The Azhar Document*.[23] It described a democratic, constitutional, and sociably equitable system of state. Other features included the separation of executive, legislative, and judicial powers; civil freedoms; and a call for sound, critical learning. This much-publicized *Document* also spelled out the origins of its eleven articles as universal principles derived from the fundamental sources of Shari'a. The texts and meaning of these Shari'a sources, according to the *Document*, must be definitive, *qatyyiat al-thubout wa al-dilala*. Here, the influence of al-Ghazali's final battles is not hard to see. In his last, fiercely fought, campaign he reminded his people that Muslim scholarship had long assessed the origins and meanings of Hadith reports as tentative. Therefore, he insisted, the bulk of Hadith literature could not serve as the sources for universal rules, as has been common practice. Nor can *fiqh* works. Only *qatyyiat al-thubout wa al-dilala* Shari'a sources can do this. Naturally, not all Egyptians accepted this view.[24] Some Islamists persisted in rejecting such wording about "definitive" sources of Shari'a rulemaking, even in the draft of the 2012 Muslim Brotherhood Constitution and then again in the army-engineered constitution of 2013. Notwithstanding, an important change had taken place in the street, in public, marking a shift in how

Egyptians discuss Muslim rulemaking. The religious establishment tried to follow suit.

Whether or not they genuinely subscribed to the new perspective, al-Azhar's grandees were not alone in openly adopting the outlines of the then-popular new Shari'a political discourse. Most leaders of Islamist groups in Egypt eventually gave homage to the same civic vision that many of their fellow Egyptians now embraced; most significantly, this was the principle of the sovereignty of the people, which they now accepted as Islamic. As the then-leader of the Muslim Brotherhood (Ikhwan) Party (FJP) Mohammed Morsi announced, his group wanted a civil state that represented all its peoples; such a position did not contradict Shari'a. Further, as Egypt's first freely elected President, Morsi told Egypt at Tahrir Square on 29 June, 2012 that "there is no person, party, institution, or authority over and above the will of the people."[25] Salafi leaders also paid homage to democracy and freedoms on the same terms as the Ikhwan and al-Azhar's establishment. More telling—indeed, more significant—were shifts and variations in Egyptian Salafi views of Islamic governance, which are discussed below.

Faith or political memories?

Of all the terms modern experts use to describe a "rigid and violent Islam", *Salafi* is the most common. Realities in Egypt, however, show its irrelevance. Some key Salafis continued to embrace a violent political vision, while others embraced an old "give-in-to-whoever-rules" attitude. Egypt's 2011 Revolution revealed yet another strand. In its early days, these Salafis spoke—and still speak—the language of Tahrir Square. They called for peaceful change, representative civil government, and due process. Prominent among the now-recognized names associated with Tahrir discourse is a former spokesman of Al Nour, the largest Salafi (strict Islamist) political party in Egypt. A scholar of early Muslim sources and a trained dentist, the late Mohamed Yousri Salama quit his Al Nour post when he judged its leadership still wedded to a corrupt, old narrative of government. He believed that only a civil party could deliver his country from its traditions of coercion and realize Salafi ideals. Days before he unexpectedly died in 2013, Salama Tweeted: "Not giving up hope despite all [...] Our Revolution continues, it will triumph despite all its enemies." To this day both Muslim and Christian subscribers to the new Tahrir narrative circulate the old Tweets of this prominent voice of Salafism in their country, and some even use his picture as a social media avatar. No sooner had an Egyptian court banned the pro-democracy 6 April Movement on 27 April, 2014, than his fellow citizens—modern women, Christians, and Muslims of all shades—turned to remembrance of this Salafi.[26]

They tweeted an image of an old blog that Salama had written shortly before his death: "Hold your head up high, you who belong to the 6 April Movement [...] You spoke up when the rest were silent."[27] Salama posted it at the time that Islamists of all backgrounds, who still subscribed to the old familiar narrative, were nicknaming the group the 6 Iblis (devil) Movement, regarding it as the spearhead of a civil state in Egypt. Many of Egypt's self-described secularists, liberals, and devout Christians stood on the same side as the Salafi Salama and against the old political culture. Bassem Youssef, a secular and liberal comedian, hosted him on his famous TV programme, *Al-Bernameg* and, when Salama died, Youssef wrote in celebration of his life.[28] The Egyptian-British novelist Ahdaf Soueif did the same: "I shudder thinking of what we lost by losing him", she wrote in 2013.[29]

In subscribing to the Tahrir discourse, Salama was not alone among the Salafis. On 30 January, 2014 another Salafi, also from Alexandria, Tweeted: "Our position is unchanged: against any repressive authority."[30] He approvingly re-Tweeted a Cairene woman's snipe at how the Salafi Hizb al-Nour supported whoever was in power. This party, she wrote, faithfully followed the principle that "whoever married my mother I call him uncle." He too, like the new breed of Tahrir-Square Salafis, opposed *other* Salafis' authoritarian views of governance, as much as he opposed the Ikhwan's practices and the similarly repressive ways of many of their country's liberals, secularists, and the army-led state that toppled the Muslim Brotherhood government. His outspoken pro-democracy views finally landed him in an army jail, for drawing Mickey Mouse ears on a picture of President Sisi.[31] A third Salafi wrote about his disgust of the loud and loutish Islamist voices which populated the media's landscape at the time of the Ikhwan government.[32] When the state jailed the social revolutionary activist Mahienour El-Massry, on charges of disturbing public order in Spring 2014, the Tahrir-discourse Salafis rallied behind her, seeing her as an Egyptian heroine. Some of them, fellow Alexandrians, attended her trial that year. From the courtroom, they Tweeted to celebrate the bravery of this woman who, without hijab, had in the past often led demonstrations in which these unwavering Salafi men participated.[33] Meanwhile, the Salafis who remained committed to the older model of power relations continued to blur female TV presenters' faces in clips they posted to YouTube of these women's interviews of their spokesman Nader Bakkar; female faces were not fit for any exposure, let alone to be seen with the communal leadership. Such Salafis allied themselves first to the Muslim Brothers when they were in government, then switched to the army when it toppled the Ikhwan president. The range of "Salafi" thought provides evidence of how this term has been misused.

The very young showed the extent of such structural shifts inside Egypt. Some Salafi teenagers who supported the Tahrir protests circulated a video, made by one of them, that criticized their familiar religious discourse, to which the devout worldwide subscribed. "Something seems to be wrong", said the boy in the video. Mimicking parents and teachers, he reflected on customary religious phraseology, especially at home. What they expressed now appeared to him a disturbing mix of faith and trivia that discouraged questioning and that were merely tools by which adults manipulate and coerce. "Can that really be what faith is all about? Often repeated mantras and symbolism?", he asked. "There must be another meaning, another lens" with which to see Islam, the young man added.[34] Within one month of posting it on YouTube, close to half million viewers had seen the clip. These young men and women had learnt the same Shari'a language of Tahrir Square in which others in their society now conversed.

But it was not only Salafis; many of Egypt's non-Salafi Muslims have also joined this new camp. Among them, Egyptians now recognize names such as Ahmed Samir, Abd al-Rahman Yusuf, and Ahmed Douma. Although having identical religious beliefs as the Muslim Brothers, these activists also spearheaded the protests against the Brotherhood's government as much as they later opposed the seemingly secular army coup. In doing so, Ahmed Douma stood against his father, a committed Brotherhood member. Morsi's government incarcerated Douma for poking fun at the President. Taking no chances, Sisi's state sentenced him to 25 years in prison for demonstrating.[35]

Similarly, Abd al-Rahaman Yusuf also stood against his pro-Ikhwan father, Shaykh Yusuf al-Qaradawi. As the world-famous al-Qaradawi urged Muslims to join the jihad against those who opposed the Muslim Brotherhood government, his son campaigned for it to go. The Ikhwan could not deliver peaceful reforms that would entrench the rule of law, as the younger al-Qaradawi saw it. Early in the summer of 2013, Abd al-Rahaman published an open letter to record his eyewitness account of the inept, undemocratic, and outdated practices of the Muslim Brotherhood.[36] After the army massacre of the Ikhwan protestors at Raba'a Mosque and its crackdown on activists and civil liberties, Abd al-Rahaman equally opposed the junta's repressive state.

The Shari'a-compliant society, 2011 model

This emerging home-grown Sunni narrative appears to have informed a majority of the revolutionaries. Many of them opposed religious political parties; as they described it, neither the military nor the clergy should ever have a role in running the state they were struggling to bring about. Yet these activists' posts on Facebook, Twitter, and other social media showed that neither Islam nor even Shari'a scared them; whereas the lingering, inherited power relations at home, in their schools, in the street, or in government did so. As Islamists appeared to hijack the process of writing Egypt's new constitution in November 2012, even the previously mentioned member of the socialist revolutionaries group, Gigi Ibrahim, Tweeted: "Then we will have shari'a mandates as part of our constitution, which is not a huge problem to me as much as the lack of freedoms & soc[ial] equ[ality]." Islamists' political traditions, not Shari'a, scared her.[37]

More significantly, as they fought for a civil, secular state, many young leaders of the Revolution appeared to be holding tightly to Islam, or their perceptions of it. Outspoken activists such as Wael Ghonim, Engy Hamdy (6 April Movement), Ahmed Doma (spokesperson for Youth of Revolution Coalition), or Taqqadum al-Khatib (National Association for Change) are but examples. At the time regarded as spearheading secularism in their country, the activists in the 6 April Movement issued a statement in 2012 that strongly advocated the adoption of Shari'a rulemaking. But Islam has no place for a religious state, their statement added: "The Shari'a that we espouse ensures justice and equality among all citizens." To clarify what the group meant, the 6 April statement included three illustrations, all from seventh-century Medina. Two concerned the second caliph, Umar, and the third the Prophet. Least noted of all is how the most diverse segment of the spirited Tahrir Square supporters coalesced around the same party in the first free presidential elections: a party headed by an uncharismatic figure who championed Shari'a, which he explained in terms identical to those of al-Ghazali.[38] Many in Egypt did not understand why their country's civil rights campaigners, liberals, and brilliant academics would gather around Abd al-Mon'em Abolfotoh. Hard to describe in the terms of the usual political criteria, his supporters included Wael Ghonim, a one-time Google executive whose Facebook page had promoted the 2011 protests at Tahrir Square and who had then become a world symbol of the young and modern face of the Egyptian Revolution;[39] Khaled Fahmy, a secular professor at the American University of Cairo; Issam Sultan, a leader of al-Wasat, an Islamic Party; Fahmy Huwaidi, a prominent Islamist columnist and one of al-Ghazali's closest associates; Wael Khalil, a self-described secular-leftist software engineer who turned into one of the most effective bloggers of the Revolution but later refused a post as advisor to president Morsi; and the irrepressible Safinaz Kazim, once an avant-garde writer who later became a strident Islamist. The same camp also included a secular, MIT-educated engineer from a grand family of former pashas; a devout Cairo taxi driver who travelled daily from his village to work in the capital; the owner of a small Cairo convenience store; and even a 14-year-old girl who, despite her parents' military background, started with her friends "Underage", a Facebook page to express their generation's opposition to all that military rule bred in society. Eventually, some who did not join this unusual camp noticed its originality and diversity, after their not-so-inspiring party leader lost the election. "I never supported Abolfotoh before", wrote the respected editor of the English *Al-Ahram Online*, Hani Shukrallah. The former presidential candidate and Shari'a supporter acquired some relevance to Shukrallah in September 2012. A month later, this writer, who happened to be a leftist and a Christian, sounded more certain. Having watched the team that ran Abolfotoh's campaign on TV the night before, Shukrallah thought them "amazing. Democratic islamism is coming", he tweeted.[40] "Democratic Islamism" did not arrive, however; the Muslim Brotherhood leadership came to power instead.

Muslim Brotherhood rule

With support from an organization that had been in existence for 80 years, the Muslim Brotherhood's candidate won the first free presidential elections to widespread celebrations. A break with the old ways of running their communal life finally appeared possible, and many joined in the celebrations.[41] The Ikhwan succeeded because they had long attended to the most vulnerable of their people, the needy and the sick that the state had long neglected. And, in a country with no legacy of permissible activism, theirs appeared the only name with a political programme that millions of Egyptians could understand: Islam's calls for social and political fairness, as a villager once put it when questioned by a British journalist.[42]

Once in government, however, al-Ghazali's old Brotherhood sided with police brutality against protestors and agreed that the army would remain unaccountable. Worst of all, in November 2012 the government announced President Morsi's sole control of all state powers; his decisions were not to be questioned and could not be repealed. With hindsight, the Ikhwan's fears of conspiring neighbouring powers against their government were realistic; but how they dealt with the threat laid bare their vision: arbitrary, tribal, and unaccepting of any dissent. In these critical days, nothing summarized public concerns about the Ikhwan's President in 2012–2013 better than the decades-old analysis of al-Ghazali. The Muslim Brotherhood leadership had an in-built tendency to quarrel with the majority of Egyptians, he had cautioned. They also "prefer unconstitutional practices and show troubling neutrality towards falsifying elections."[43] Indeed, many among the new discourse's activists had been former Muslim Brothers who judged the movement intellectually dull and politically dangerous.[44] The Islamists' Ikhwan-led botched attempt at a democracy allowed Egypt's customary system of coercive rule by men-in-arms to make a comeback within a year. Many in the country welcomed this return to "normal" ways.

Age-old martial rule

By June 2013 the warriors of the old regime had jumped on the Revolution's bandwagon too, when they joined the mass revolt against the Islamist interlude. The army chiefs, who found front-row seats in this now overcrowded bus, staged a coup—all in the name of the glorious call for change in Tahrir Square. In so doing, they only brought back to Egypt one of the most entrenched political traditions in Muslim societies: coercive rule. It had to happen. No sooner had the army and police generals taken over than an all-out war for survival broke out between two competing discourses: the familiar old view of power and the new one, a Tahrir-Square, Shari'a-friendly vision. The former gathered under various banners and came from all backgrounds. They included the devout—Muslims and Copts alike—as well as self-described liberals and secularists: women, businessmen, scientists, historians, musicians, actors, journalists, scientists, the poor and the wealthy, the old and the young. However, against them also stood the devout—again, Muslims and Copts alike, and with the same diversity. Each camp even had its own human-rights and women-rights organizations. What set these warring camps apart was how each side approached legitimate power: the old political culture saw violence as the realistic means of governing society, while the emerging culture emphasized government through negotiation and compromise to save society.[45]

Meanwhile, the usual frames of reference (many Western) with which we now approach the "Middle East" continue to blur these realities and the fast-moving events that they triggered, instead of explaining them. Unable to make sense of the dizzying commotion in Egypt, many outsiders found it confusing, and so they looked the other way. Others dismissed it in the belief that places like Egypt and peoples like the Arabs were not fit for peaceful self-rule.[46] The usual secular versus religious and other sectarian narratives—Muslim against Christian, orthodox against unorthodox Islam, Sunni versus Shi'i—were summoned in this key case too. Some even explained the war that broke out inside Egypt in 2013 in terms of those living in Zamalek, being the old moneyed, against the newly moneyed living in Madinat Nasr.[47] Regardless of how misleading, even comical, such analyses turn out to be, the usual narrative on the Middle East is thus preserved and even defended. Its neo-colonialist outline is not only simpler; its ready-made binaries are useful in justifying policies that go against non-violence. For Western governments competing to secure markets for national businesses, dictators are far easier to reach deals with than the multiple and often meddlesome forces of democratic settings. Still, had the experts looked at the real Egypt instead of the lethargic clichés on Egypt and Islam, they would have often encountered the likes of the above-mentioned Salafi Mohamed Yousri Salama, who often reminded fellow supporters of the discourse of Tahrir Square that the *folool* (supporters of the old guard and its traditions) were their aunts, their cousins, friends, and families, who now fought against the Tahrir dream. The pundits did not even note views written in English by the likes of Shukrallah, also mentioned above. While the Muslim Brotherhood government lazily watched Christian homes and churches burn across Egypt late in 2012, Hani Shukrallah wrote about the fuzzy and dangerous common presentations of the Revolution as a battle between civil and Islamic forces in Egypt. Describing the current events in his country thus "plays into the hands of those who want to introduce roots of sectarianism and portray democratic forces as pampered upper classes [*beys*]."[48] In another Tweet, this Christian writer, whom the Ikhwan once forced out of his job as editor of *Al-Ahram Online*, warned: "I repeat: Stop references to civil forces and Islamic forces. Our battle [in Egypt] is between democracy versus tyranny, between the Revolution versus the Counter-revolution—[so] why use the terms [with which] our enemies [cast this battle]?"[49]

Collapse of common perceptions: War of discourses

By the summer of 2013, all of the clichés, all the sacred assumptions about the Middle East, had been "scrambled" in Egypt; and they are yet to be reassembled to something more intellectually realistic. Neighbouring governments now openly and fully joined in the crucial Egyptian war of discourses, which also now threatened them. At the time, some Salafi states sided with Egyptian secularists, liberals, and nationalist generals against other Salafi states, while these other Salafi states sided with Sufi Islam.[50] Sufi states sided with Muslim groups that reject Sufi ways; Christians who subscribed to the old discourse hailed strict Islamic states under which non-Muslims have limited or no rights as excellent regional models and examples of fraternal bonds. And so on.

How to contest mass peaceful opposition that called for civil rights posed an extraordinary danger, not just a public-relations obstacle. This spreading Shari'a vision of governance posed an existential threat to the familiar ways in the region. The old guard, including in the media, intelligentsia, and businesses, put their full weight behind shoring up their world against the enemy within, regardless of its religious and secular-sounding aspects. It is hard to exaggerate the revenge that this entrenched political culture exacted on those who supported the Tahrir Square discourse.[51] Even the brutal crackdown against members of the Muslim Brotherhood in Egypt and in the greater part of the Arabian Peninsula was far from a confrontation between the religious and the secular, or between different sects. Astounding sights across Egypt told the story: women in hijabs beating other women in hijabs for supporting the Revolution or supporting the Muslim Brotherhood; men with beards praising Sisi, while their neighbours, other men with beards (and women in hijabs) demonstrating every Friday against him. Most telling, perhaps, were the descriptions in divine, religious terms of Egypt's army chief, later President Sisi, by the patriarchs of the Muslim and Christian religious establishments.[52] Meanwhile, famous Azhari scholars urged the authorities to execute the Muslim Brothers—who held not-so-different theological views from their own and who hailed from identical socio-economic backgrounds to theirs.[53] On the other side, devout Muslims ridiculed their grand religious scholars who until the eve of the Revolution had been revered as world authorities on Islam. Their new heroes included jailed secular friends whose pictures filled their social media posts.

The crackdown

The ferocious crackdown on the Muslim Brotherhood membership provided the cover to extinguish the greatest danger, the Tahrir discourse on peaceful civil rights. On the flimsiest of charges, the key movers of the Tahrir uprisings found themselves in prison. They included the 6 April Movement's leaders, Ahmed Maher and Mohamad Adel; two women lawyers, Yara Salam and Mahienour El-Masry; activists documenting the theft and destruction of Egypt's heritage, Mohamad Hussein and the poet Omar Haziq; and leaders of Tahrir activism such as Ahmed Doma, Alaa' abd al-Fattah, his 20-year-old sister Sana Saif, a disabled freelance photographer named Isra'a al-Taweel, and even a boy detained without trial for two years for the crime of wearing a shirt opposing torture.[54] The crackdown also led to the solitary confinement of a most outspoken human rights lawyer, Malek Adly, and torture to death for another lawyer, Karim Hamdy, when he turned up to see a client who had been detained without charge at a police station. Silencing all traces of the spreading new mainstream narrative became an unspoken priority. Hence, voices such as the famous comedy talkshow host, Bassem Youssef, the writer-dramatist Bilal Fadl, and the poet Abd al-Rahman Yusouf were also hounded, and prevented from working and travelling, or from returning to their country. Football players did not fare any better: those who joined calls for civil rights were accused of terrorism and sacked by their clubs—in a famous TV interview which underlined the old ways, a friend of Sisi and legal figure, Murthadha Mansour, dismissed Ahmed al-Mirghani, a player who dared to criticize repression, as nothing but a "black" man, fit only for working as a domestic servant.[55] No one representative of the state, which Murtadha Mansour defended against claims of repression, objected to his comments, and the club suspended the player. Others were not so lucky. Many shared the fate of the poet and activist Shaimaa al-Sabagh, who was shot and killed by the police as she laid flowers to commemorate the fallen at Tahrir.[56] But the vision of Tahrir had spread and struck some roots, so by 2015 many activists started to disappear, only for their dumped bodies bearing the marks of torture to appear days later. Some others could not simply take the despair; they committed suicide, like the young Tahrir activist Zaynab Mahdi and a flute player, Nada Salama. A Facebook post of 6 January, 2015 captured the extent of the efforts to quell the vision. The post's author noted the whereabouts of some of the Tahrir Square figures in a photo: the first from the left had immigrated to France; the second and third had each been sentenced to 15 years in prison for demonstrating against the trial of civilians in military courts; the fourth had fled to Turkey; the fifth and sixth had been drafted into the army; and the last had also ended in prison, serving a two-year sentence for demonstrating near Morsi's presidential palace when the Ikhwan ruled. This list "does not include the dead" friends, the post concluded. Perhaps the worst casualties of the crackdown were the youngest, those aged between 14 and 16 years old at the time of the Revolution, who had acquired a taste for civil activism, thus representing the ultimate long-term loss to the region. Millions of them had lost their voices altogether under strict instructions from their families and schools. Many found refuge in Hadith reports, unconcerned with their authenticity. And, outraged by what they regarded as the cruel crushing of their dream of justice, some who were brought up in trendy Egyptian neighbourhoods saw the only alternative in ISIS-like visions.[57] The solutions that self-described jihadi groups provided had been long embedded in narratives of resistance in the region.

Reactionary resistance

Al-Ghazali had sought to expose the bankruptcy of these old visions of opposition, even if every so often he sought them out for a bizarre but ancient sense of comfort.[58] Following the 2013 army takeover, however, all the ideas of violent resistance made a comeback. As the army chiefs fortified their grip on every aspect of the country's life, including the media and judiciary, many in Egypt hurried back to immerse themselves in convenient anecdotes that they regarded as divine Hadith reports; in this, they were no different than "a drowning man hold[ing] to a scrap of wood [...] no matter how paltry and ineffective it may be", as an Azhari scholar once described such uses of Hadith.[59] Others embraced the tradition of abdicating civil responsibilities, a course which had long been advanced as an Islamic principle. Political apathy is thus equated with devotion, and dissent with chaos and disorder (*fitna*). And, as way of venting their rage too, there were those who returned to the old and cruel Sunni–Shi'i battles in order to feel they were resisting evil. Superstitions and delusions became the shelter of millions, not only in matters of faith but also science. When the army announced that one of its generals had invented a system that not only cures both Aids and Hepatitis C, but also turns their viruses into kebabs-kofta, scores of the country's intelligentsia applauded the claim.[60] Centuries-old models of government were given a modern rationale; communal self-governance was thus enveloped in sham parliaments or simply declared un-Islamic. By the autumn of 2014, an English Tweet from Libya (on 14 October) read: "Voting like the one in #Egypt no thanks u can stick #Democracy lie in ur face we want #ShariaLaw Haq! Not man made lies." In this government-led slaughter, some who once saw hope in the Sunni Tahrir discourse but did not fully understand its vocabulary also retreated into ancient ideas of security and dreams of imperial grandeur.

Thus violence as an alternative form of protest re-emerged, not only among many of the religious but also those who subscribe to leftist and nationalist ideologies. As Muslims make up a majority of the population in that region, a return of the narrative that finds Shari'a incompatible with democracy also re-emerged in response to the suppression of peaceful activism. Many who wanted to change Egypt wondered about the effectiveness of the Tahrir vision to which they had once subscribed; enraged, some of them turned to new groupings born in dire settings such as Saddam Hussein's and al-Assad's Ba'ath ideology, or in Zain al-Abidin's Tunisia or post-Qaddafi Libya, where American torture sites and similar outrages provoked organized reactions.[61] The developments indicated that throttling the new Tahrir discourse in Egypt, which al-Ghazali had previously helped to spread across the length and breadth of his country, could pose a grave danger to the region. As a British observer of the region warned, if continued state brutalities made violence the only option for resistance, the consequences "will be of a magnitude far greater than the fall of Mosul to the Islamic State", and ISIS establishing itself in areas of Iraq and Syria.[62]

However, despite the all-out war against it, the greatest danger that threatens this new Sunni political discourse lurks within, in failing to attend to fresh reconsiderations of records of the past, which al-Ghazali had employed in his last campaign to great effect. His approach allowed him to "tidy up" or, to use his own image, to sift the extensive store of old precedents through a sieve of sound critical investigation. Herein lies the ultimate difficulty of the Arab Spring. Unlike old images of effective governance, this emerging mainstream Muslim worldview of "a community of citizens" speaking for themselves, which al-Ghazali promoted late in his life, had neither the advantage of imperial, regal dynastic memories, nor a legacy of *fiqh* arguments to support its vision of power. For Tahrir Square to survive against the odds, it needs to assert what is to its advantage: sound, critical attention to Islam's common story, including entrenching "other" precedents that underpin its vision. An impossible task, observers might argue. Tyranny in Muslim societies derives from a rich storehouse of customs and religious arguments, as al-Ghazali discovered; every repressive tradition is sustained by a sacred past. In contrast, the still-in-the-making Tahrir Square discourse finds itself at a disadvantage. For despite the principles of the Qur'an and the primacy of the model of Medina, which al-Ghazali now framed in terms of choices based on negotiated contracts and rigorous accountability, the common images of Islamic government revolve around bravado, dynastic majesty, and unquestioned patriarchy—not Shari'a-based self-rule. Without reinforcing the rationale by convincingly documenting this alternative vision of power relations, it may end up where it has resided for centuries in Islam: in hollow pensive longings for the best kind of governance.

At present, hopes for continuing what al-Ghazali started appear uncertain. Egyptians may have applauded this shaykh when he invited Muslims to push open the doors of their history and carefully examine its records if they wanted genuine reform; but, regardless of their leanings, most continued to show little appetite for systematic investigation of, or even familiarity with, primary historical sources. Nadder Bakkar, the spokesman of the largest Salafi party in his country, Hizb al-Nour, provides an illustration. In 2012, in support of seemingly democratic ideas, he wrote a series of articles on the precedents of governance that Muslims set in early Medina. He was much applauded. These political lessons, which Bakkar now drew from the administration of the second caliph, Umar Ibn al-Khattab, appeared identical to those that al-Ghazali sought to publicize towards the end of his life and for which Bakkar's Salafis disparaged him in the 1980s and 1990s. Consequently, the author of the current study requested Bakkar to cite the records from which he derived his conclusions. He could not offer any. Instead, Bakkar later explained that his assessment of Medina's government "was a literary analysis that did not require historical sources."[63] Bakkar's presentations of seventh-century CE events might have highlighted al-Ghazali's influence, but it did not originate in exploring primary sources, let alone critiquing them.

Bakkar is not alone in this, and nor are other Islamists. Egypt's secularists and liberals have also shown little interest in investigating primary records, despite the fact that many of the country's thinking public now welcomes criticism of the past. The bulk of learned Egyptians prefer to leave their enormous historical wealth to Western projects, which they then often condemn for bias and misusing their heritage. The persistence of this idle and arrogant approach to history could undo the nascent Muslim worldview that helped bring about the Arab Spring. It may be difficult to acknowledge or even to see it, but the connection between Islam and history is central to the 2011 mass awakening that the world once celebrated. In January 2016, Alaa al-Aswany, a novelist and bitter enemy of Islamic expression in civil space, admitted at an event in London that without the mass support for the new Tahrir vision in 2011, anti-Mubarak demonstrations by people like him would have remained irrelevant, merely a minor irritation in the country's political landscape. Another secular medical consultant who played an active part in supporting the Tahrir Revolution, Hossam Abdallah, saw it more clearly that evening: "Unless we transform Islamic forces into democracy's forces there is no realistic hope for Egypt's 2011 Revolution to survive." Many in the audience did not take much note, however. Some thought that such remarks exaggerated the role of religion in Egypt.[64]

Towards the end of his life, al-Ghazali believed that without rigorous inquiry into Egypt's rich storehouse of historical memories the past would remain a mainspring of repression and superstition. He also discovered that a thorough assessment of Muslim sources tied Shari'a to political freedoms. However, the prospect for a culture that cultivates historical tools appears weak. Many subscribers to the Tahrir discourse approached criticism of the past in the same way as those they now criticized as being the cause of their society's troubles. They too seek in historical records virtuous texts, ideas for the future; they do not see in them diverse testimonies from which to trace change and continuity in their society. In a 2015 illustration of "liberal" and supposedly critical new attitudes, a lawyer Tweeted a Facebook link which he described as an "important" post written by another famous activist and writer. In it, she warns her countrymen never to read Ibn Kathir's *Al-Bidaya wa-al al-Nihaya* (The Beginning and the End);[65] this fourteenth-century CE work contained nothing of value, she judged. Like the Islamists that they opposed, both the lawyer and his writer friend sought divine instructions in such old works, which they did not find in this particular one.[66] Such a superficial investigation of Islam's heritage is common, and may prove the undoing of this new Shari'a discourse.

Besides the approach to sources, there is also the question of precedent, which is central to Shari'a rulemaking. Just as al-Ghazali's critiques of Egypt's historical narrative had once nurtured calls for democratic rights across the country, the scarcity of further precedents of negotiated and egalitarian power relations, other than those he provided from early Medina, means this new popular Sunni vision may lack a homegrown rationale. Of equal importance are models of resistance that differ from the two customary options of violence, or abdication of civil responsibilities and even withdrawal from the world altogether. Without new "valid" forms of struggle, the kind of grassroots appeal that fuelled the events of 2011 will eventually shrivel.

Could new memories, born during the Revolution, help here? Could they provide valid precedents? In those heady days of the Revolution, loyalty to Shari'a included an image of a man, peacefully but defiantly standing in front of a tank; good-natured protestors chanting "*silmiya, silmiya*"; and a prostrating sea of people, encircled by the joined protective arms of Christians, as together they turned Egypt's central square into its largest mosque. This store of Muslim memories also acquired a new image, no less poignant: the image of a Tahrir woman protester, on her back, being dragged into the street by soldiers in riot gear, her black cloak pulled away, exposing her body. Scandalized by such nakedness, Islamists took the soldiers' side, pouring scorn on her. They asked what has become a notorious expression ever since: "*ih ili wadaha hunak?*"

(Whatever took her there?) Such Egyptians wondered what on earth was a woman doing at a public protest. But Salafis, the Ikhwan, and other devout Muslims, who all subscribed to the new Tahrir narrative, now saw gender differently. They nicknamed her "*Sit al-Banat*", the best of their girls. No longer did her dragged and exposed body or bright blue bra invoke shame. Covering *per se* did not designate morality; rather, morality was in a woman's rise to defend communal rights. For these Muslims, honour no longer resided in throwing women off cliffs to protect them against soldiers' brutality, as was previously commended.[67] Could guarding these newly made memories sustain the alternative mainstream Muslim discourse, the same way that the precedents of the 1919 Revolution had helped to redefine Egyptian identity?

The changes in Egyptian perceptions which the 2011 uprising revealed make it risky to predict the direction of the region's Sunni Arabic-speakers' future choices. For key among the Tahrir memories is how great numbers of the devout publicly defied religious establishments, including the Christian churches.[68] Later, a few even broke with al-Azhar altogether. Whether he wanted it or not, al-Ghazali had facilitated this novel shift. In the two decades before the uprisings that swept their country, many of Egypt's Muslims had been openly taught what no other Sunni instructions had identified as a foremost Islamic concern: that tyranny and prayers could, and did, sleep in the same bed.[69] By 2011 such Egyptians accepted that throughout the centuries many of the *fuqaha* had supported the suppression of freedoms, and, therefore, had censored Shari'a too, especially when it came to women and other vulnerable groups. The many centuries-old assertions in the dynastic narratives, which depicted a Shari'a-abiding, *fuqaha*-purified society, began to unravel on the banks of the Nile. This evolving Muslim understanding of traditions frustrated orientalist and neo-orientalist assumptions in the West: al-Ghazali's lessons about Muslims' political culture, which enraged every powerful group in his country and the region, nevertheless spread rapidly across Egypt, largely because he convinced his people of the connection between these new lessons and Shari'a.

Structural change in the Sunni discourse on Shari'a could not have been clearer on a bright spring day in 2013, when Egyptians organized a demonstration against the sexual violence that had become the punishment of choice used against women who supported the Revolution. On the afternoon of 6 February, 2013 the crowds first gathered in front of a mosque built in memory of Zaynab, a great granddaughter of the Prophet who had emigrated to Egypt in Islam's formative centuries. However, these subscribers to a new political discourse that accorded with Shari'a also carried banners that celebrated their early modern Egyptian grandmothers. Flags fluttered in the afternoon breeze; imprinted on them were images that included the likes of an early women's rights activist, Hoda Sha'rawi (d. 1947), and the singer most associated with modern Egypt's essence, Umm

Kulthum (d. 1975). It is worth considering who took part in this demonstration, what their demands were, and the reactions of the residents of Cairo's lower-class neighbourhoods through which the march passed. A middle-aged woman, fully clad in a purple hijab and armed with a loudspeaker, led the way through the streets of al-Sayyida Zaynab, heading towards Tahrir Square. The worn-down countenance of this leader underlined her urban working-class circumstances. Behind her, there were just as many women with hijabs as those without one.[70] These women included journalists, influential writers, 6 April Movement activists, medical doctors, engineers, a head of a college at Cairo University, and students, all following what would have been the most unlikely leader in their old culture. Men of all ages also trekked behind her. From the loudspeaker she chanted, and the crowd repeated: "They told us a woman's voice is an *'awra* [part of genitalia to be concealed];[71] a woman's voice is the Revolution"; "Raise your voice higher; women of Egypt defied death". But women had not been the sole concern of these women and men; they championed a novel political culture in their country, which at the time was being governed by the Muslim Brotherhood. It turned out this march opposed in equal measure both military rule and government in the name of religion, whether by an Islamic institution or a Church. On both sides of the protestors' route, people waved from their windows in support, or stood on their balconies chanting slogans that by then many of their countrymen knew by heart: "*Yasqut hukm al-murshid; yasqut hukm al-'askar; la kanisa wa la murshid*" (Down with a government run by the leader of the Muslim Brothers; Down with a government run by the army; Neither a state run by Christian churches nor a Muslim Brotherhood guide). Only a decade or so earlier, such visions of women and governance would have been alien to grassroots Egyptian sensibilities.

Whether or not the 2011 mass uprising in favour of democracy and civil freedoms will shrivel into a short-lived flicker in Egypt's long history, one thing will not change: once upon a time, a short distance from al-Azhar, the world's main Sunni centre of learning, Muslim men and women, from all backgrounds, walked the streets of Cairo to reprove the prospect of an "Islamic state", or one influenced by the Christian Coptic Church, and the usual premises about power, whether in relation to gender or citizenship, with which these traditions burdened them. It might have confounded outsiders; Muslims had found out for themselves that what they had learned about the perfect glory of their past governments did not match the actual records of their history. Most important, however, they now learned that many political traditions, which their religious scholars had entrenched, in fact violated the principles of Shari'a and its basic process of discovering rules to which many of them remained loyal. The great mass of the devout in this Egyptian crowd knew that rules for organizing their communal lives had to be amended. That is how Muslims who supported the Tahrir Square protests understood Shari'a and sought to protect its integrity.

Notes

1. Salman al-Odah, *Hiwar Hadi' ma' al-Shaykh al-Ghazali* (Riyadh: al-Ri'asa al-'Ama li'Idarat al-Bohouth al-'Ilmiyya wa al-Ifta wa al-Da'wa wa al-Irshad, 1989). Far less candid than al-Odah, some salafi Shaykhs are accused of copying from others, especially al-Ghazali, without giving acknowledgement. See this famous example, Hisham Man'na', "'Aidh al-Qur'ani ... Waqa'a fi al-Fakh!" *Vito*, 28 March, 2015 (online: http://www.vetogate.com/1555310; https://www.facebook.com/permalink.php?story_fbid=792832537479393&id=786246198138027; http://www.alarabiya.net/articles/2013/02/02/264018.html). A Saudi journalist who wished to remain anonymous noted that many of those who rose to dismantle al-Ghazali's latter ideas now mirrored his arguments, presenting them in terms of the essence of the genuine Shari'a: "Ghazali has silently become Islam's superstar among many in Saudi Arabia; most popular religious figures resort to his ideas", the Saudi journalist added (author interview, London, 29 May, 2013). Perhaps this observation is verified by a rather glowing biographical article in English in the Saudi *Arab News*: Adil Salahi, "Scholar of renown: Muhammad al-Ghazali—III", *Arab News*, 12 August, 2002 (online: http://www.arabnews.com/node/223295). Illustrations of Saudi social media exchanges (discussed below) show that some popular Salafi figures have indeed adopted a discourse on women and democracy similar to that with which al-Ghazali surprised and angered them in the last ten years of his life.
2. Al-Odah first signalled the shift in a somewhat oblique television interview with Turki al-Dukhail, in 2005 (online: http://www.turkid.net/?p=16). Ever since, the shift has become far more pronounced. Many Salafis continued to use his earlier arguments against al-Ghazali, however. In 2012, Al-Odah is reported to have made his position clearer in another TV appearance, insisting now that in Shari'a women had important public roles, just as men, including in politics, a main point of Saudi Salafi contention to al-Ghazali's later arguments ("Dr al-Odah: Dor al-Mara' la yaqilu an al-Rajul hata fi janib al-siyasa", *Al-Basheer*, 14 Ramadan, 1433 / 2 August, 2012 [online: http://islamtoday.net/albasheer/artshow-12-171381.htm]).
3. Mohammed Yunis, *Tajribat al-Shaykh Mohamed al-Ghazali fi Tajdid al-Fikr al-Islami* (Cairo: Maktabat al-Thaqafa al-Diniyya, 2013), posted on Salman al-Odah's page: (online: http://www.islamtoday.net/salman/artshow-99-194064.htm).
4. @salman_alodah (1 July, 2012):

   حديث "انما السلطان ظل الله في الارض" وهو يمنح السلطان القداسة ويجعل حكمه الهيا ومع استشهاد ابن تيمية بالحديث وتأويله إلا انه حديث موضوع

   Here Salman al-Odah is not alone among the Salafis of Saudi Arabia. A year later he explained that "al-Sultan", the Arabic term commonly used to refer to absolute rulers, is used by the Qur'an to mean something altogether different: providing convincing proof. Idem (24 November, 2013):

   غالب لفظ السلطان) في القرآن يعني الحجة وليس السلطة، مما يدل على أن الإقناع أهم من الفرض

   His Saudi followers sought to provide further proofs as in this re-Tweet of @Binshamer: @salman_alodah

   كثير يظنون أن العدل والحرية وحقوق الانسان التي جاءت في مقالك اليوم أنها نظرة غربية وما تدبروا قول الحق ليقوم الناس بالقسط

5. Following the Tunisian and Egyptian Revolutions al-Odah published *As'ilat al-Thawra* (Riyadh: Markaz Nama' li al-Bahth wa al-Dirasat, 2012).
6. Other Salafi figures in Saudi Arabia, including Shaykh Abd al-Wahab al-Triri, similarly challenged Hadith reports calling for political obedience, which had been especially popular among Salafis as the following tweets indicate: @altriri (March 2012):

   .إن من حق الناس أن يتكلموا فيما يمسهم من قرارات وإجراءات، وأن يستمع إإليهم ويبين لهم

@altriri:
قسم المصطفى مالاً فأعطى أناساً وترك آخرين فبلغه أن من لم يعطهم عتبوا عليه فخطب وقال: إني لأعطي رجالاً لما جعل الله في قلوبهم... الحديث

@altriri:
إذاً هناك من الصحابة من تحدث في قسمة المال العام ثم بلغت مقالتهم المصطفى، فما عاتبهم ولا وبخهم، ولكن (فبلغه) خطب وجلى الموقف وبين السبب

@altriri:
.قسم المصطفى غنائم حنين فأعطى المؤلفة قلوبهم ولم يعط الأنصار فقال بعضهم: يغفر الله لرسوله يعطيهم ويدعنا

@altriri:
بلغت المقالة رسول الله فما غضب ولا عتب ولكن جمعهم وبين أنه أعطى أناساً يتألفهم، وأعطاهم نفسه الشريفة، فطابت نفوسهم وحق لها أن تطيب

@altriri:
هذه المشاهد النبوية تبين أن الحديث العام في الشأن العام ليس من باب النصيحة الخاصة التي يطلب فيها السر أو مواجهة .الوالي

@altriri:
وقد جرى عمل الصحابة على ذلك في وقائع كثيرة منها مراجعة أبي بن كعب لعمر في المسجد: حتى قال:يا عمر أتريد أن تكون عذاباً على أصحاب رسول الله

@altriri:
ومراجعة علي لعثمان في متعة الحج ، ومراجعة بلال ومن معه لعمر بن الخطاب في وقف أراضي الفتوح، وغيرها من الوقائع

@altriri:
واكثر ما يعترض على ذلك بحديث : من أراد أن ينصح لذي سلطان بأمر فلا يبده له علانية ولكن ليأخذ بيده فيخلو به فإن قبل فذاك....الحديث

@altriri:
وهذا الحديث وإن صححه بعض أهل العلم لكنه ضعيف الإسناد منكر المتن : أما ضعفه فللانقطاع في إسناده، وضعف بعض رواته

@altriri:
واما نكارة متنه فلمخالفته لوقائع كثيرة منها هذه وغيرها في حياة الرسول صلى الله عليه وسلم والخلفاء الراشدين وهي .أصح

7. "Al-Hujjaj yaqifoun 'ala Say'id 'Arafat", *Al-Jazeera*, 25 October, 2012 (online: http://www.aljazeera.net/news/arabic/2012/10/25/الحجاج-يقفون-على-صعيد-عرفات).
8. @iAbuhesham (19 December, 2012):
الفقه السياسي الذي تشكل في ظل دولة التغلب استنفد غرضه وحاجته مع زوال تلك دولة . ومع مجيء الدولة التعاقدية سيتشكل فقه سياسي جديد
9. @iAbuhesham (19 December, 2012), Retweeted by @altriri:
مؤمن ايمانا عميقا بأن الديموقراطية هي الفضاء الامثل لتطبيق الشريعة
10. @salman_alodah (25 July 2012): المجتمع يسحق أفراده بالتحكم في تفاصيل حياتهم وعيشهم
11. @MohannaAlhubail, @aloshari:
نحن بحاجة الي دورات في فقه الخلاف وفقه اولويات الشريعة ومقاصدها الاخلاقية والاجتماعية عبر مؤسسات متخصصة لرفع الوعي
12. @_salehalsultan (15 July 2012):
غياب كثير من المعاني التي جاء بها الاسلام من العدل والمساواة وضمان الحقوق والحريات وعدم التمييز بين الناس هو سبب كثير من كشاكلنا وأزماتنا
13. All such statements were made between 2011–2014 before the rise of ISIS. For recent scholarship investigating some of the differences in Saudi Salafi political views, see Stéphane Lacroix, *Awakening Islam: The Politics of Religious Dissent in Contemporary Saudi Arabia*, trans. George Holoch (Cambridge, MA: Harvard University Press, 2011); focusing on Shaykh Salman al-Odah, see Madawi al-Rasheed, *Muted Modernists: The Struggle Over Divine Politics in Saudi Arabia* (London: Hurst, 2015); Roula Khalaf, "Saudi Cleric's Rebellious Spirit Returns", *Financial Times* (London), 23 March, 2012 (online: http://www.ft.com/cms/s/0/bdfc8940-74d8-11e1-ab8b-00144feab49a.html#axzz3u1seHqg8); Max Fisher, "Motorcycle Sheikh

Sparks Saudi Controversy: Does the Koran Approve?", *Washington Post*, 31 October, 2012 (online: http://www.washingtonpost.com/blogs/worldviews/wp/2012/10/31/motorcycle-sheikh-sparks-saudi-controversy-does-the-koran-approve/).

14. @salman_alodah (24 July, 2012):

- أبو بكر شاور الناس في مرضه، ثم اختار عمر وأوصى به وصية غير ملزمة

idem:

السقيفة تداول رشيد إنساني، أبو بكر لم يتولها بالسيف ولا عمر

@salman_alodah (September 2012):

لا أفضل ولا أصح تدينا ولا أتم فقهاً من الصحابة الذين نهاهم النبي أن ينزلوا الناس علي حكم الله، لانهم لا يدرون هل يصيبون فيهم حكم الله أم لا

15. @salman_alodah (24 July, 2012):

كان العباسيون ينكّلون بمن ساعدهم في الحكم ولذا يقال : الملك عقيم

@alaglan_i (19 March, 2012):

أئمة السلف أنكروا على أخطاء الأمويين والعباسيين ولم يقل عنهم أنهم خرجو باللسان ومن يجهل مواقفهم في هذا الباب فليته يسكت عن التحدث باسم السلف

A younger such Salafi, wrote: @iAbuhesham (18 February, 2014)

الدولة اختراع بشري، ومنتج اجتماعي وتاريخي، والدين حقيقة غيبية إلهية منزلة.. الله تعالى لم ينزل من السماء دولة.. إنما الناس يصنعون دولتهم

@iAbuhesham (29 May, 2013):

المشكلة هي الخلط بين الاسلام من ناحية ودولة تاريخية سمت نفسها الخلافة وبين غطاء الرأس وبين غطاء الوجه من ناحية أخرى ...والمحزن والمؤلم هنا أن كل الانظمة تم وضعها تحت شعار (تطبيق الشريعة)

16. @salman_alodah (25 July, 2012):

المجتمع يسحق أفراده بالتحكم في تفاصيل حياتهم وعيشهم

Following the events of the Arab Spring, al-Odah wrote on the subject of Revolution, especially in the West and Arab experiences, in *As'ilat al-Thawra* (Riyadh: Markaz Nama' li al-Bahth wa al-Dirasat, 2012). This title is reported to have been banned from the Riyadh Book Fair in its year of publication.

17. @salman_alodah (24 July, 2012):

تحول العربي إلى الديمقراطية السياسية والاجتماعية يتطلب جهداً ووقتاً لأنهم تطبعوا على الاستبداد لأجيال حتى أصبح مكوناً ثقافي

18. @MAMRasheed (1 January, 2013):

ألا يعلم المعترضون على عمل المرأة أن الشفاء بنت عبدالله هي أول من تولى جهاز الرقابة العامة على الأسواق بتكليف من أمير المؤمنين رضي الله عنه

Also, see the younger Saudi Salafi view regarding supposed Shari'a restrictions of women: @iAbuhesha:

لأجل عيون الرجل ولأجل خاطره ومزاجه وحتى لا يفتن مولانا يتم التضييق على المرأة ومنعها من حقوقها وتحريم ما أباحه الله لها .. أي فقهِ هذا ؟!

19. @Issam_ElAttar, re-Tweeted by @salman_alodah (29 November 2012):

من الكتُبِ التي أُعجبتُ بها كتاب: "L'ESPRIT DES LOIS" MONTESQUIEU "روح القوانين" للفيلسوف الفرنسي مونْتسكيوُ ...

http://fb.me/1mmA0hA5U (the online citation is part of his Tweet).

20. Gigi Ibrahim, video recording at a Socialist Workers Party (UK) event entitled "Arab Revolutions" (online: https://www.youtube.com/watch?v=At53dCTw9p4); see also her assessment of the events a year later, at an SWP event entitled "How can the Egyptian Revolution Win?" (online: https://www.youtube.com/watch?v=8U9LLB1N_4k).
21. Evronia Azer, "The Facebook Revolution", *Swedish Pen*, 10 September, 2014 (online: https://www.dissidentblog.org/en/articles/facebook-revolution).
22. Henry Kissinger speaking to Krishnan Guru-Murthy, *Channel 4 News*, 1 February, 2011 (online: http://www.channel4.com/news/egypt-the-biggest-change-since-world-war-2).
23. "Shahed al-Tayyib, "Shaykh al-Azhar Yasdiru Wathiqat al-Dawla al-Madaniya wa Yarfudhu al-Dawla al-Dinyya", *Masry al-Youm*, 21 June, 2011 (online http://www.masralyoumnews.com/2011/06/video-sheikh-al-azhar-declares-support.html); see also "Dr Ahmed

al-Tayyib Yu'linu Wathiqata al-Azhar al-lati Tuda'imu Tas'sis al-Dawla al-Madaniyya al-Dimokratiya", *Masry al-Youm*, 20 June, 2011 (online: http://www.masralyoumnews.com/2011/06/dr-ahmed-al-tayeb-al-azhar-declares.html). At the time many of Egypt's Muslims celebrated this document ("Muslim Brotherhood Endorses al-Azhar Document on the Future of Egypt", *Ikhwanweb*, 18 August, 2011 [online: http://www.ikhwanweb.com/article.php?id=28948]). For a pdf English rendition of the Azhar Document, see *Al-Azhar Document for Basic Freedoms* (online: https://danutm.files.wordpress.com/2012/04/al-azhar-document-for-basic-freedoms.pdf).

24. For illustration, see "Waqafat ma wathiqat al-Azhar", 27 June, 2011 (online: http://islamstory.com/fr/node/14985); "Al-Thanni wa al-qaty'i wa al-tanasul min al-Shari'a al-Islamiya" (online: http://afkarblog.com/2011/07/02/الظنيّ-والقطعيّ-والتنصل-من-الشريعة-ال/).
25. "President Mohamed Morsi's Speech in Tahrir Square, Friday June 29, 2012", *IkwanWeb*, 30 June, 2012 (online: http://www.ikhwanweb.com/article.php?id=30153), also quoted a year later in Umar Farooq, "Seeking New Leadership, Millions of Egyptians Take to the Streets. The Arab Spring, Take Two", *The Atlantic*, 30 June, 2013 (online: http://www.theatlantic.com/international/archive/2013/06/seeking-new-leadership-millions-of-egyptians-take-to-the-streets/277419/).
26. For illustrations of such social media exchanges, see Haifaa Khalafallah, "Modern Egypt's Unheeded Revolution, and Why It Matters Today", paper presented at the Centre for Citizenship, Civil Society and Rule of Law, University of Aberdeen, 22 October, 2015.
27. Ibid.
28. On 24 March, 2013, the day after Salama died, the talkshow host Bassem Youssef Tweeted: "Why is it in this country only the beautiful people die?" Dubbed "Egypt's Jon Stewart", Youssef is a secular liberal voice who subscribes to Tahrir discourse. Bassem Youssef hosted the 2015 International Emmy Awards in New York City (online: http://www.cc.com/episodes/pjkw01/the-daily-show-with-jon-stewart-august-6—2015—-jon-stewart-s-final-episode-season-20-ep-20142). Despite his fame, after the coup in 2013, Youssef had to leave his country after incurring the wrath of army generals.
29. Ahdaf Soueif, "'An al-Khanat wa 'Abirr'iyha", *Al-Shorouk*, 27 March, 2013 (online: http://www.shorouknews.com/columns/view.aspx?cdate=27032013&id=5cc68ed3-0284-4117-9e2f-88e7ffd5968b). For further illustrations, see also: "Political Figures from Across the Political Spectrum Offer Condolences on Death of Mohamed Yousri Salama who Died on Sunday Aged 39", *Ahram Online*, 24 March, 2013 (online: http://english.ahram.org.eg/News/67611.aspx); Belal Fadl, "Mohammed Yousri Salama Youmathiluni" (Salam represents me). *Al-Shorouk*, 30 March, 2013 (this last article has been removed from the newspaper's website after the crackdown on freedom of the press).
30. Amr Nohan @ANohan (30 January, 2014), "موقفنا ثابت: ضد اي سلطة فيها قمع"
31. Mona Daoud, "Jailed for Putting Mickey Mouse Ears on Sisi?", *Cairo Scene*, 20 October, 2015 (online: http://www.cairoscene.com/BusinessAndPolitics/Jailed-for-Putting-Mickey-Mouse-Ears-on-Sisi).
32. Ahmad Almougy @drahmedelmogy (8 January, 2013):
لكم مني كل الأحتقار ... من أول رئيس القناة للعاملين للمذيع للي بيصورا للي بيتفرجوا من الرموز ومش بيتداخلوا بمكالمة....(الاخوانى محمد العمده و نبيه الوحش للشعب المصريى: يا ولاد الكلب هنعلمكوا الادب بالمركوب)
https://www.youtube.com/watch?v=-Hz6rRcE4g
33. For illustrations, see Khalafallah, "Modern Egypt's Unheeded Revolution".
34. Video uploaded by @AxeerStudio on 6 February, 2013, at https://www.youtube.com/watch?v=ju4o15g941Q&sns=tw.
35. "Egypt Court: Activist Ahmed Douma among 230 Sentenced to Life in Prison", *BBC News*, 4 February, 2015 (online: http://www.bbc.co.uk/news/world-middle-east-3113422).
36. "Abd al-Rahman Yusuf al-Qaradawi Yaktub: Afwan Abi al-Habib, Morsi la Shar'yyia lahu", *Al-Youm al-Sabi'*, 7 July, 2013:

عبد الرحمن يوسف القرضاوى يكتب: عفوا أبى الحبيب ... مرسى لا شرعية له
http://www1.youm7.com/News.asp?NewsID=1152641&SecID=12 ،،الأحد202013% يوليو 20%207%
(page removed following army's crackdown)
An English-language report regarding this letter can still be found: Ramadan al Sherbini, "Abdul Rahman Accuses Former Islamist President of Not Fulfilling Promises", *Gulf News*, 8 July, 2013 (online: http://gulfnews.com/news/region/egypt/egypt-activist-criticises-father-al-qaradawi-over-pro-mursi-fatwa-1.1206648).

37. Gigi Ibrahim, @Gsquare86 (28 November, 2012).
38. "Ara'a Abd al-Mon'em Abolfotoh hawla Tatbiq al-Shari'a" (online: http://www.youtube.com/watch?v=2zN3J2UyNnE) آراء د عبد المنعم أبو الفتوح حول تطبيق الشريعة الإسلامية. Abolfotoh's TV interview, *Al-'Ashria Masa'* on 15 May, 2011 has been removed (https://www.youtube.com/watch?v=P5N5a6gPD9A). Impressed by what he heard, a staunchly secular US educated Egyptian wrote in an email on 17 May, 2011: "Personally, I have no sympathy for the Moslem Brothers, but I found this man to be head & shoulders above any other presidential candidate. Keep an eye on him."
39. Perhaps Wael Ghonim best captured the new vision that attracted diverse and dynamic figures at the time in a post he wrote on 14 April, 2012: "I back a president who believes that Egypt is far greater than any political trend [...] A leader who does not think of his role as Salah al-Din, but that of a mere executive manager (of our collective affairs)":
وائل غنيم: انا مع الرئيس الي مؤمن ان مصر اكبر من اي تيار واي حزب ... الي عارف انه مش هو مش صلاح الدين .. عارف انه مجرد مدير تنفيذي.. مع عبد المنعم ابو الفتوح.
Two years later, when the Revolution appeared in retreat, Ghonim restated that their vision did not orbit on great figures; it only revolved around the sovereign will of a people who found their voice: @Wael Ghonim (14 January, 2014):
أفضل ما في ثورتنا (والحكم للتاريخ) أنها بلا قائد ولا منقذ ولا رمز ولا مخلّص. وأنها لم تسع للسيطرة على السلطة بل أعادت حق الاختيار للشعب
40. @HaniShukrallah (25 October, 2012), "despite unfortunate choice of party name, abdel-monem abul-fotouh and team on *ontv* yesterday were amazing—democratic islamism is coming".
41. For example, although he did not vote for Morsi, the then-head of history at the American University in Cairo, Khaled Fahmy, appeared jubilant in international media interviews the day Morsi won the presidential elections, because it was the first time in Egypt's long history that his fellow Egyptians had got to vote for who ran their government. Others in the Tahrir crowd, who dubbed themselves "The Lemon Squeezers", also celebrated the victory of the majority's choice, although they found it difficult to digest much about Mirsi and his party.
42. Jonathan Rugman, interview with a farmer in Fayoum (a town 100 km south of Cairo) as part of Rugman's coverage of Egypt's first post revolution election campaign, *Channel 4 News*, June 2012.
43. Al-Ghazali, videotape interview (#IKH-2).
44. For illustration, see Ismail Alexandrani's haunting 28 November, 2013 Facebook post entitled "Kulukum Usama", about his old friend and fellow Ikhwan member, Usama al-Sayyid. The friends parted when Alexandrani, a journalist and former fellow at the Woodrow Wilson Center, found the Ikwan also wanting, and he turned into one of their vocal Muslim critics inside Egypt. Usama al-Sayyid continued to support the group until he was killed in Muslim Brotherhood protests that followed the army's massacre of their brethren at Rabaa Mosque in 2013.
45. "*Kulukum Usama al-Sayyid*", 26 November, 2014 (online: https://www.facebook.com/ismail.alexandrani/posts/10207842508717675). Alexandrani's Facebook and other social media accounts were later closed, however, when the army arrested him on 29 November, 2015 upon his return from Germany. He is accused of disseminating harmful information about the Egyptian state (see online: http://ecesr.org/en/2015/12/01/

release-ismail-alexandrani-andall-prisoners-of-conscience-societies-are-built-with-freedom-joint-statment/). For a brief discussion of this battle of the discourses, see Haifaa Khalafallah, "Taking Sides in Egypt's Troubled Revolution: But Which?", *Open Democracy*, 8 May, 2014 (online: http://www.opendemocracy.net/arab-awakening/haifaa-g-khalafallah/taking-sides-in-egypt%E2%80%99s-troubled-revolution-but-which).

46. Examples here include a former British ambassador to Syria and to Saudi Arabia, Andrew Green, "Why Western Democracy Can Never Work in the Middle East", *Telegraph* (London), 16 August, 2014 (online: http://www.telegraph.co.uk/news/worldnews/middleeast/11037173/Why-Western-democracy-can-never-work-in-the-Middle-East.html; and a "former Chief Executive Officer of a major Saudi bank", Elie Elhadj, "Arab Democracy is Fantasy. Democratic Ideology cannot Defeat Islamic Theology", *Joshua Landis*, 23 February, 2010 (online: http://www.joshualandis.com/blog/arab-democracy-is-fantasy-by-elie-elhadj/); for an opposite equally hands-on point of view, see Nicholas Kristof, "Unfit for Democracy?", *New York Times*, 26 February, 2011 (online: http://www.nytimes.com/2011/02/27/opinion/27kristof.html).
47. A Quilliam Foundation founder and senior advisor to Tony Blair's Faith Foundation, Ed Husain, advised that the events of July 2013 originated in class-related conflicts. The explanation shows unfamiliarity with the Tahrir Revolution's main figures and lack of awareness that great numbers of Sisi's supporters come from places like Nasr City, just as many who opposed the general lived in the most exclusive parts of Cairo, including Zamalek. At the time a Senior Fellow for Middle Eastern Studies at the American Council on Foreign Relations, Husain wrote: "The fact that many Brotherhood leaders live in Nasr City in eastern Cairo, away from the exclusive neighborhoods favored by the elite—Zamalek Island or the compounds in Sixth of October—is symbolic" (31 October, 2013; online: http://www.cfr.org/egypt/reforming-muslim-brotherhood/p31765).
48. @HaniShukrallah (19 December, 2012):
المنظور الشائه لقوي مدنية في مواجهة قوي اسلامية يلعب في أيدي من يريدون تكريس الطائفية ويساعدهم علي تصوير القوي الديمقراطية كبهوات مترفين
49. @HaniShukrallah (19 December, 2012):
أكرر: فلنكف عن القول بقوي مدنية وقوي اسلامية. معركتنا هي بين الديمقراطية والاستبداد، الثورة والثورة المضادة- لماذا نستخدم مفردات الخصوم؟

    Hani Shukrallah, "Qadhiyatuna hiya al-Dimokratiya fir Mowajahat al-Istibdad", *Al-Shorouk*, 29 November, 2012 (online: http://www.shorouknews.com/columns/view.aspx?cdate=29112012&id=0bf14903-f3e1-4b03-8897-4f8963bd41ff).
50. Once the battle of discourses took off outside Egypt's borders, the Muslim states in the region appeared to be fighting a life-or-death battle in which they let go of the usual labels. The supposedly "Salafi-Hanbali" Qatar sided with the predominantly "Sufi" Turkey in order to shore up the "anti-Salafi and anti-Sufi" Muslim Brotherhood group. Meanwhile, Sunni Arabic-speaking sister Gulf States, such as Saudi Arabia, Kuwait, Qatar, and the UAE, entered into an open war of words against one another.
51. After the army took over in July 2013, many who opposed the state were imprisoned, harshly silenced, sometimes even kidnapped, tortured, or massacred in daylight. Human Rights Watch, Amnesty International, and various other human rights groups documented a great number of these violations,which can be found in their reports.
52. Most telling were Muslim and Christian religious establishments' patriarchs' divine-like descriptions of Egypt's army chief, later president, Sisi. For brief illustrations in English see Khalafallah, "Taking sides".
53. The chair of the Department of Comparative Fiqh at al-Azhar University reiterated the difference between Shari'a and *fiqh*, but indicated a preference for the latter. He invoked *fiqh* rules to support his call for the immediate execution of 329 Muslim Brotherhood members without the possibility of appeal or the usual process which

required the mufti to sign off any execution sentence. According to *fiqh* tradition, Sa'ad al-Din al-Hilali said, as soon as a judge declares a death sentence, an executioner next to him carries it out. See "Dr Saad al-Din al-Hilali: Tah'iya li al-Qadha al-Shamikh fi Misr", *Al-Balad* TV, 24 March 24, 2014 (online: http://www.youtube.com/watch?v=TeEoY6nIbys); "Dr. Sa'ad al-Din al-Hilali: 'Idam 329 yajib tanfidhu bidon ra'y al-mufti aw al-isti'naf", *Al-Shorouk*, 25 March, 2014 (online: http://www.shorouknews.com/news/view.aspx?cdate=25032014&id=08c73402-3e84-4ae3-8cf4-537bf0760424). The arguments of this violent political narrative include a statement by another Azhari professor, also made in a TV interview. Shaykh Ahmed Karima declared that anyone who objected to being ruled by the military or who sounded a call to overthrow their government contradicted the Prophet and did not believe in his divine message ("Ahmed Karima: Man Yaqul Yasqut hukm al-'askr yukathibu wa yu'anidu al-Rasul", *Al-Youm al-Sabi'*, 15 February, 2015 [online: http://www.youm7.com/story/2015/2/15/أحمد-كريمة--من-يقول-يسقط-حكم-العسكر-يكذب-ويعاند-الرسول/2067635). A third, a professor of *fiqh* at the Department of Sharia in al-Azhar, Dr Ahmed Attia, told *Al-Tahrir* TV that as the ruler of the country, Sisi had the right to gouge the eyes of citizens in the process of implementing God's Shari'a (video was previously embedded at http://www.masrawy.com/News/News-Videos/details/2015/2/14/460325; the YouTube video was removed but the news item about its contents can still be found at "Shaykh Azhari: Yajuz li al-Sisi faq'i 'ayun al-muwatinin" [online: http://almesryoon.com/دفتر-أحوال-الوطن/669025-شاهد-شيخ-أزهري-يجوز-للسيسي-فقع-أعين-المواطنين]).

Divine support for rule through force and violence is a position commonly held among many contemporary *'ulama* who embrace the standard *fiqh* narrative of the past, as in the example of the dean of *dawa* at al-Azhar University, who declared that "anyone who opposed Sisi will be expelled from God's mercy" ("Ameed Kuliyat al-Dawa bi Jami'at al-Azhar 'ala Khuta al-Hilali: Mul man Yu'aridh al-Sisi Sayutrad min Rahmat Allah", *El-Sha'ab*, 14 May, 2015 [online: http://www.elshaab.org/news/178476/عميد-كلية-الدعوة-بجامعة-الأزهر-على-خطى-الهلالي-كل-من-يعارض-السيسي-سيطرد-من-رحمة-الله]). Identical visions that accepted coercion as a political ideology were held by Sufi and Shi'i groups in Egypt, who saw government in terms of association with the divine. But so did Islamist groups who fought pro-Sisi *'ulama*, many of whom continued to subscribe to the old political culture. Although anti-Sufi, many of these groups in Egypt saw the Turkish president Recep Tayyip Erdoğan as the caliph.

54. Concerning the t-shirt case, see *Amnesty International*, "Egypt Release Student Held for Anti-torture T-shirt" (online: https://www.amnesty.org/en/get-involved/take-action/egypt-release-student-held-for-anti-torture-t-shirt/).
55. Murtadha Mansour's comments were made during a TV interview with a talk show host, Wael al-Abrashi, on *Al 'Ashira Misa'*, 3 July, 2015 (online: https://www.youtube.com/watch?v=YSFwBa4ssfw). A self-declared enemy of the Tahrir Revolution, Mansour is also a famous lawyer and became a member of parliament in 2016.
56. Robert Mackey, "Egyptian Police Attack Marchers Carrying Flowers to Tahrir Square, Killing Protester", *New York Times*, 24 January, 2015 (online: http://www.nytimes.com/2015/01/25/world/middleeast/egypt-woman-is-killed-in-peaceful-cairo-protest.html); "Egypt Condemns Western Outrage at Fatal Shooting of Protester", *New York Times*, 27 January, 2015 (online: http://www.nytimes.com/2015/01/28/world/middleeast/egypt-condemns-western-outrage-at-fatal-shooting-of-protester.html).
57. As in the examples documented reported in "Islam Yakn or Amr Abu Wadhah al-Muhajir", *Egyptian Chronicles*, 3 August, 2014 (online: http://egyptianchronicles.blogspot.co.uk/2014/08/the-story-of-islam-yaken-story-of-good.html).
58. See Chapter 4.
59. See section "In the *riwaqs* of al-Azhar", in Chapter 6.

60. "Egypt's Military Leaders Unveil Devices They Claim can Detect and Cure Aids", *Guardian*, 28 February, 2014 (online: http://www.theguardian.com/world/2014/feb/28/egypt-unveil-device-detects-cures-aids).
61. As documented, for example, by Nadim Shehadi, "What is Hiding Behind Islamic State?", *The World Today*, December 2014 and January 2015; Martin Chulov, "Isis: The Inside Story", *Guardian*, 11 December, 2014 (online: http://www.theguardian.com/world/2014/dec/11/-sp-isis-the-inside-story); Liz Sly, "The Hidden Hand Behind the Islamic State Militants? Saddam Hussein's", *Washington Post*, 4 April, 2015 (online: https://www.washingtonpost.com/world/middle_east/the-hidden-hand-behind-the-islamic-state-militants-saddam-husseins/2015/04/04/aa97676c-cc32-11e4-8730-4f473416e759_story.html).
62. David Hearst, "Sisi is Pushing Egypt to the Brink", *Huffington Post*, 30 June, 2015 (online: http://www.huffingtonpost.com/david-hearst/sisi-is-pushing-egypt-to_b_7700560.html).
63. Nadder Bakkar, 12 August, 2012.
64. "Five Years on from Tahrir Square, is Egypt's Revolution Still Alive?", speakers Alaa al-Aswany and Jack Shenker, Ralph Miliband Lectures Programme, London School of Economics, 20 January, 2016.
65. Abu al-Fida Ismail Ibn Kathir, *Al-Bidaya wa al-Nihaya*, 21 vols (Cairo: Dar al-Hadith, 2012).
66. At the opposite end of Bakkar's religious spectrum, an activist lawyer, Malek Adly, shared Nawara Negm's Facebook post of 28 April, 2015, in which she said she wrote to save Egyptians from reading 13,000 pages of "human vomit".
67. See discussion in "*Portrait*: The modern intelligentsia discuss women", in Chapter 8.
68. For a brief list of al-Azhar's stance during the 25 January Revolution, see the Arab Studies Institute report, "Al-Azhar wa Thawrat 25 yanar", *Ma'had al-Dirasat al-Arabiya*, 15 October, 2012 (online: http://www.alarabiya.net/articles/2012/10/15/243828.html).
69. For examples, see Chapters 7 and 8, and the discussion of the seminar in Appendix 1.
70. The author walked in a section of the march led by this leader.
71. The impermissibly of women's voices being heard in public places is often presented as a Shari'a rule. The discomfort of women's names or voices in public became a common taboo across various classes in Egypt.

APPENDIX 1

Portrait of a Seminar: How Senior *Fuqaha* Saw Shari'a in the Late Twentieth Century[1]

This book has highlighted how instead of attending to both context and texts as responses to scriptural content, academia still deposits Shari'a rulemaking and other contemporary Muslim experiences into boxes of its own making: classical, traditional, extremist, modernist or progressive, and so on. The prevalent neo-orientalist narrative finds itself at a loss whenever these containers it designed for present-day Muslims spill into one another, or when their labels do not match reality.

Looking through this lens, anything that Western experts define as not classical or traditional is thought not to be Islam, or at least not "original" Islam but rather a modernists' replication of contemporary Western values. Muslim self-critiques are usually seen as being of this type, falling outside Islam proper. Significant contemporary assessments of and debates regarding *fiqh* are consequently ignored or dismissed. Neo-orientalist lethargy has a context too. Some of it has roots in old politically inspired Muslim narratives, while some originates in the little-discussed fear of Muslim scholars of incurring the wrath of the mob or other powerful groups, which gives inattentive outsiders the impression of certainty when in fact turmoil and change reign. True, cultural colonialism has led some Muslims to flimsily project Islam onto modern Western experiences. But, far from being a modern phenomenon, re-assessment and adjustments in Muslim rulemaking have been a characteristic of scholarship in senior *fiqh* circles. Orthodoxies come and go. Hence, Muslims express gratitude for the stability that the Qur'an provides as the ultimate source of their rulemaking. A modern-day illustration of this—describing the process of re-assessing *fiqh*, the tension this creates, and the changes in mainstream Muslim thought which this eventually produces—can be found in the following summary of a late twentieth-century seminar led by al-Ghazali. Here, senior Muslim scholars discussed Islamic learning, or what is commonly referred to as "Islamic sciences". Their debates show how some of these most established mainstream scholars saw Shari'a. They may also highlight why these readily available high-ranking *fiqh* discussions are often ignored or dismissed: they unravel academic Western classifications of Islam. The transcript of "Teaching Islamic Disciplines" describes it as a seminar/symposium, possibly to draw attention to the comments of its high-ranking participants, which followed his talk. This event, which took place in Cairo in the 1990s, was attended by many of the intelligentsia that gathered around al-Ghazali.[2] What follows is a brief introduction to these scholars and a summary of their deliberations.

The attendees

The attendees reflect the extent to which the intelligentsia rallied around al-Ghazali in the last two decades of his life. They constituted what could be described the high-ranking circle that promoted Muslim reform in the 1980s and 1990s, and many of them had a wide reach both inside and outside Egypt. In other words, they were the leaders of mainstream Islam, and not some fringe. The story of Islam in contemporary Egypt can only be fully understood when the evolution—and limitations—of each member of such a circle has been investigated. What brought these scholars together, what drove them apart, and what made many of them start to raise questions about Muslim practices is outside the scope of "theology". This group of men and women is also notable for the diverse backgrounds of its members, and those who attended the seminar are briefly profiled here.

Dr Gamal Attia: The event moderator, Attia originally studied modern law in Cairo and Switzerland. Besides practising as a lawyer, he served as an expert on Islamic banking and then as a member of the Jeddah-based Fiqh Council.

Dr Tariq al-Bishri: Al-Bishri trained in modern law and eventually held senior judicial positions in his country. Earlier in his career, al-Bishri championed secularism along modern Western lines, but he changed his mind after the Israelis defeated Egypt in 1967, shaken by his country's disintegrating conditions. Al-Bishri told a Mecca website that his initial preoccupation with Islam was in 1951, when he accidentally came across one of Shaykh Mohammed al-Ghazali's books. It completely captivated him; he could not put it down until he had finished it from cover to cover.[3] Eventually, al-Bishri became one of Egypt's most popular legal-Islamic leaning scholars. This reputation soared immediately following the January 2011 Revolution, only to greatly diminish within a year.[4]

Shaykh Ali Goma: Having first acquired a degree in commerce, Shaykh Goma turned to Islamic scholarship, in which he earned a doctorate from the Faculty of Shari'a and Law at al-Azhar University. At the time of this lecture-seminar, Shaykh Goma was fast becoming a world authority on *usul al-fiqh*, the discipline that studies Shari'a rule-/making. In 2005 he was appointed grand mufti of Egypt amid great public support. However, his political views on Egypt's 2011 Revolution reversed his great standing among many of the devout who previously regarded him as an exalted authority on Islam.[5]

Shaykh al-Sayyid Rizq al-Taweel (d. 1998): Al-Taweel was a member of Egypt's Higher Council for Muslim (*fiqh*) Affairs, and he served as Dean of Arabic and Islamic Studies at al-Azhar University, the main centre of Sunni learning worldwide.[6]

Dr Mohammed 'Imara: Al-Ghazali initially disparaged 'Imara's writings on Islam. Prior to joining al-Ghazali's circle, 'Imara had been a strident Marxist who considered a variety of other ideas, according to reports.[7] He became a student of Islamic philosophy, and he later found a niche as an author and prolific editor of Islam's literary heritage. These efforts eventually led to membership of al-Azhar's Council of Islamic Research, and to great renown. Following the 2011 Revolution, the ruling Supreme Council of the Armed Forces (SCAF) appointed 'Imara a member of al-Azhar's Assembly of Supreme *'Ulama*.[8] However, accepting the generals' patronage as an approved authority on Islam lessened his stature in Egypt.

Dr Mohammed Kamal Imam: Imam now heads the Faculty of Law and Shari'a at the University of Alexandria. In common with many who attended the seminar, Dr Imam's reach extends far beyond Egypt. He was a member of the International Union of Muslim *'Ulama*, and he also lectured at Riyadh's King Saud University and served as advisor to key Islamic institutions that included al-Azhar.

Dr Saif Abdal-Fattah: A political scientist with Islamic leanings, Abdal-Fattah has a professorship at Cairo University, and he has often lectured in Arab capitals. Following the Revolution, he joined the team of Abolfotoh, the presidential candidate whose views on Shari'a echoed al-Ghazali's the most.[9] When Abolfotoh lost the election, Egypt's new president, Mohammed Morsi, appointed Abdal-Fattah as one of his key advisors in 2012.

Dr Nasr 'Arif: Another energetic Cairo University professor of political science, 'Arif worked for the Virginia-based International Institute of Islamic Thought (IIIT) in its heyday (in the 1990s) before he moved half way across the world to teach in the UAE.

Dr Fawqyyia Hasan: A woman professor.

An unnamed Dean of the Faculty of Usul-al-Din at al-Azhar is also mentioned.

How did these leaders of Muslim thought approach Shari'a, nearly a decade before the 2001 destruction of the World Trade Centre, the ensuing War on Terror, and more than 20 years before the Egyptian Revolution of 2011?

What is wrong with Islamic learning, and how should it be revised?

Al-Ghazali set the tone for the discussions with a story: his friend and a Muslim Brotherhood activist, Shaykh abd al-Mu'zz abd al-Sattar, had hoped to spread Islamic education in Faqus, his birthplace in the Nile Delta. He started his lessons with instructions on ablution (*wudu*). For this purpose, Shaykh abd al-Sattar used *Al-'Idah*, a book on Hanafi *fiqh*. It instructs the believers that seawater, river-water, dew-water, snow-water, rainwater, lake-water, and well-water are suitable for this. "What are you on about? Why not use tap water?" a villager interrupted the shaykh. Taken aback, Abd al-Sattar put his notes away; the plan for Islamic lessons in the village folded. *Al-'Idah*, a text which al-Ghazali and abd al-Sattar had studied as Azhari students of Hanafi *fiqh*, "had been written centuries earlier for people who struggled daily to find clean water." Why, al-Ghazali wondered, did Muslims continue to use works composed to address ancient conditions of life as instructions on Islam today?[10]

Conflating yesterday's conditions with the tenets of Islam was both tragic and comical; so was imposing them on altogether different realities, according to al-Ghazali.[11] The reasons for this common confusion and how to address them turned out to be the subject of his talk that evening. He remembered how many years earlier, as an imam at a central Cairo mosque, he had jotted down in a few short lines all that a worshipper ever needed to know about correctly performing *wudu*. Why, then, the shaykh asked this audience of Cairene experts, had fellow Muslims continued to harp at great length on the subject of *wudu* and fight over its details? Why did an eminent scholar such as Ibn Hazm (d. 1063 CE), write two hefty volumes on the rules of ritual washing? Al-Ghazali answered his own questions: at some point in their history, Muslim societies substituted *employing* Islam with *conversing* about it. In contrast, he wanted to underline the role of collective choices. For far from disliking Ibn Hazm, al-Ghazali found his *fiqh* otherwise sound.[12] According to al-Ghazali, communal preferences eventually turned *fiqh* from "a brilliant intellectual project" into "a dead discipline of learning", a situation that continued until the present.[13] Consequently, for the most part, discussions of *fiqh*, like its study in modern times, were misspent efforts, he concluded.[14] Later in the lecture, al-Ghazali took on another *faqih* that he otherwise admired: Ibn Taymiya.[15] This celebrated early fourteenth-century Hanbali scholar tended to delve into areas in which he had no real expertise, leading him to derive curious assumptions about the nature of God based on verbose linguistic analysis.

Al-Ghazali's message to senior members of the religious establishment in Egypt that evening was clear: as Islam's scholarship had evolved over the centuries, it had taken directions which did not always reflect the faith or benefit the common good; as it stands today, this legacy appears counterproductive and damaging to Muslims. Often used uncritically, renowned *fiqh* works froze time and terms, he added. As a result, what masqueraded as Islamic education in contemporary times generated disorder in the communities that relied on old works for instructions. What he saw as the all-too-common gullible approaches to earlier *fiqh* scholarship served only to disconnect Islam's extensive literary corpus from common sense and the contemporary world in which Muslims lived. It threatened to bury their faith altogether.

Feeding a corrupt political culture

Nowhere did al-Ghazali see the shortcomings of Muslims' scholarship more clearly than in how *fiqh* polluted Muslim societies' political culture. Whereas a majority of modern Muslim thinkers, especially in the West, read in *fiqh* works excellent constitutional rules and Islamic political principles, al-Ghazali concluded that, for the most part, *fiqh* works dealing with governance exposed an appalling dearth of constitutional thought, and not the weighty theories that some pretend to read in them.[16] In this, he differed from modernist Muslim scholars, including those among his admirers.[17] On the whole, *fiqh* works on governance included no more than sketchy or primitive notions about running a community, according to al-Ghazali. As he now saw it, with the exception of some discussions on administration, which reflected how a few early imams had addressed the circumstances of their times, there is nothing of value in the *fiqh* works on political management. For illustration, al-Ghazali compared what Azharis learned about the criteria governing Muslim relations with non-Muslims and what he believed Islam to teach. In *fiqh*, "our relationships with others [non-Muslims] have mainly revolved around *jizyia* [poll taxes that non-Muslims paid] or around war. That is what the Azhari students learn up to this day", he observed.[18] But such an outline contradicted the essence of their faith, as al-Ghazali saw it. In reality, Islam presented only "an invitation to a comprehensive package that included monotheism, justice, and democracy."[19] A Muslim had no business beyond extending this invitation to those unfamiliar with it, and then only by giving a reasonable account of Islam's holistic features, he added. If Islam's call was rejected, he said, then all a Muslim had to insist on was the freedom to believe in and speak about this invitation, no more. There cannot be any resort to confrontation and hostility unless non-Muslims aggressively deny them this right, al-Ghazali said. He found such clear principles of international relations, as he labelled them, that were hard to distil from *fiqh* works. When organizing a community that included non-Muslims, for example, *fiqh* works exposed how distant from the Qur'an, the Sunna, and sensible thinking they had become, al-Ghazali thought.[20]

Worse, many *fiqh* works used phraseology or presented inconsistencies that corrupted Muslim political culture—all in the name of Shari'a. He gave contemporary examples. When "an Indian court recently saved a mosque that Hindus wished to demolish", he observed, "Arab media outlets ignored this [Indian] democratic, orderly decision."[21] Their society could not recognize a verdict which demonstrated the rule of law, al-Ghazali thought. Such blindness to fair practices afflicted every corner of Muslim lands. He found all Arab political parties, including those that invoked secularism, or nationalism as merely mercenary, incapable of creating the conditions for reform.[22] Parties with Islamic leanings did not fare better: by now al-Ghazali had acquired a reputation for criticizing the mean-spirited political culture of the Muslim Brotherhood and the dangerous notions of governance held by all contemporary Islamist groups. *Fiqh* lurked behind it all: its experts helped to entrench a bankrupt version of power relations in the communal fabric, which eventually scarred Muslim intellect and morality, he told this senior *fiqh* circle.[23]

Convinced that *fiqh* cemented despotism in their midst, al-Ghazali tied all genuine correctives to the reform of Muslim political culture. However, instead of doing away with *fiqh* learning, al-Ghazali thought that only Islamic scholars could provide the answers to the mammoth tasks that society needed to urgently address.[24] The *fuqaha* ought to lead critiques of their literary heritage; not only did they have the needed expertise, but, after all, it was the eventual alliance between the *fuqaha* and tyrants that had muddled approaches to the Qur'an, to Hadith, and to almost every other aspect of Islamic knowledge.[25] As noted elsewhere in this book, al-Ghazali found in sound historical inquiry the tools for sifting the ideas in Islam's vast library: "There must be a reconsideration of all Islamic *fiqh*, its topics, and its study", to remedy the distorted views of their faith, al-Ghazali announced.[26] Without such wholesale re-assessment, Muslims faced an insurmountable obstacle. Continuing to learn and teach *fiqh* works in their current form, he concluded, "waste[d] time, life, and intellect".[27]

Hadith

What al-Ghazali now identified as the slipshod use of reports about the Prophet at many levels was presented as proof of the disorganization of the community's collective intellect. In his quest to establish the genuine Sunna, al-Ghazali spared neither preachers nor specialists. He observed how a revered figure of Islamic resistance against Nasser, Zaynab al-Ghazali (d. 2005), had carelessly misused reports about the Prophet, thereby confusing the very message of Islam.[28] But far from originating in the imprudence of unlearned self-appointed preachers such as Zaynab, this sloppiness plagued experts too. He gave past and contemporary examples, starting at home. Al-Azhar taught Hadith poorly, al-Ghazali explained.[29] Why did al-Azhar not invite Nasr al-Din al-Albani or someone else of his calibre to join its faculty?, he wondered. This acknowledgement of al-Albani's substantial knowledge of *isnad* did not amount to an endorsement of al-Albani's thought, however; Al-Albani exemplified the structural cracks that damaged Muslim scholarship, and that were especially manifested in approaches to the Prophet's Sunna. Certainly, al-Albani excelled in the study of Hadith transmission chains, but he showed little understanding of the precedents these Hadith reports contained. Elsewhere in his lecture and in the discussion that followed, al-Ghazali and other senior *'ulama* provided illustrations of al-Albani's blunders relating to the Sunna.[30] Yet, at this stage of his life al-Ghazali wanted to shift the blame from individual scholars to a general Muslim outlook that had bred such ailing epistemological approaches. Al-Ghazali told these *'ulama* that, in common with many other such scholars of Islam, al-Albani pontificated on every discipline of learning under the sun, imagining himself qualified to deduce universal principles on them all. In other words, the *isnad* expert had mirrored a common outlook among his contemporaries who spoke in the name of Islam. Every last one of them, al-Ghazali thought, believed himself a final authority on every branch of knowledge.[31]

Causes

Al-Ghazali offered reasons for the general decline in Muslim intellectual energy, all originating in historical circumstances. One was the rise of trends that bred slavish veneration of certain ancient Greek notions; al-Ghazali did not object to his people opening up to the ideas of the world, but, he noted, even whenever some of Aristotle's statements indicated "a drugged state of mind", the *fuqaha* indiscriminately "gobbled them up" too.[32] By regurgitating the accepted Greek ideas of their times, these Muslim scholars disregarded central tenets of their faith. Discussions about the nature of the Deity provided an illustration of this. Al-Ghazali thought it peculiar for, in contrast to Greek thought, Islam put an end to speculation about God, rather than promoting it.[33]

Another crucial development was changes to the *fuqah*'s vocation. As many *fuqaha* elected to serve whoever ruled, instead of fighting for social and political justice, their new employment distracted their attention. Their interests changed; daily challenges faced by the ordinary people of their societies gave way to futile disputes, al-Ghazali contended. He gave as illustrations philosophical subjects, such as latter-day Mutazilite discussions that eventually gave rise to *ilm usul al-din*, a discipline in which al-Ghazali specialized at al-Azhar.[34] As he saw it, the time had come for Muslim society to recognize that these Muslim scholars had eventually transformed the dynamic intellectual project of knowledge (*fiqh*) into a burdensome inheritance.[35]

The remedies

When al-Ghazali found an Islamic cause, he did not do anything in half-measures. How Muslims approached the Sunna provided his most frequent illustrations that evening. He explained that close investigation of the most revered Hadith collection, *Al-Bukhari*, showed that it contained several false reports. Other canonical compilations (collectively, *Al-Sihah*) included "idiotic" accounts that that defied common sense and the tenets of Islam; these did not constitute instructions of the Prophet, al-Ghazali added.[36] To deal with the crisis in the legacy of Hadith he proposed a complete revision of Islam's approach to its heritage, which included Hadith terminology, history and—what he saw as the most neglected feature of all—the substance of Hadith reports.[37] However, proposals to sharpen the academic lens regularly enraged those who subscribed to the historical-religious narrative that al-Ghazali now challenged.[38] When he taught at the Cairo branch of the International Institute of Islamic Thought (IIIT), al-Ghazali suggested improvements to the study of Hadith, but the IIIT instructors had "totally discarded my proposal", he revealed. Religious convictions had not been behind their opposition, he thought; rather, it originated in entrenched intellectual "laziness". As al-Ghazali saw it, these instructors followed centuries-old habits that suspended critical thinking about tentative and often chaotic reports about the Prophet. Such attitudes to knowledge meant that contemporary Muslim education for the most part only churned out unskilled graduates who mirrored the ethical and scholarly lethargy of their institutions, as he now regarded all such "traditional" establishments.[39] Later that evening he offered illustrations (see below).

Towards the end of his life al-Ghazali called for two seemingly contradictory plans of action: to protect intellectual treasures of the most precious kind that were contained with the Muslim library, and to dismantle 15 centuries of fabrications, as he referred to many of their popular traditions in a private telephone conversation.[40] That is, he simultaneously campaigned to spread Islamic ways and also to clear away what he believed to be the obscurantism that approaches to *fiqh* had planted in their midst. Islam's massive literary legacy cried out for critical investigation; its wealth had been thoroughly mixed with dirt and toxins, the Shaykh said to these Muslim experts. It required "thorough excavation and filtering similar to the processes of refining crude oil", he urged. And such a review was overdue, he added, because poisons within *fiqh*'s legacy impinged on Islam's tenets.[41] That meant that disorder in the study of Islam did not only lie in approaches to Hadith reports; other disciplines also worried al-Ghazali.

Qur'anic exegeses

Tafaseer (sing., *tafsir*) came next. Al-Ghazali described the current study of *tafsir* as useless and mind-numbing. Fortunately, however, a few modern Azharis had made important advances in that area, he thought. Works that inspired new approaches to understanding the Qur'an included the "Salafi *tafsir* of [...] Shaykh Rashid Ridha", and *Al-Naba' al-Azim*, by Shaykh abd Allah Diraz. Al-Ghazali hoped that every student of Islam would read this latter *tafsir*, as a way of encouraging thematic commentaries on Islam's Scripture.[42]

Arabic

From the days of al-Shafi'i up until modern times, no *fiqh* deliberation could be complete without encouraging proficiency in the Arabic language. Yet, some modern Western observers see such advocacy in terms of Arab nationalism. This perception originates in the nineteenth century, when Arab nationalists strove to energize their language from what they saw as centuries of neglect under non-Arab rule. Prominent Christians in the Levant brilliantly led the way; but so did the late Shaykh Mohammed Abduh. This most famous mufti of Egypt shared with his Christian contemporaries their determination to revive the dynamism of Arabic. However, Abduh was not concerned with Arab nationalism, and rarely has it been a concern of the *fuqaha* raised in Abduh's tradition. Al-Ghazali himself provides an illustration here: he often condemned Arab nationalism as a parochial, spiteful vision and a defective import from the West.[43] Arabic, however, was another matter.

Al-Ghazali wanted Arabic moved to the top of the curriculum, superseding "worthless so-called Islamic disciplines". "Arabs had betrayed Islam" when they paid scant attention to teaching Arabic to those who embraced their faith, he contended. He believed that every Muslim had to learn the tongue in which God had addressed them, in order to participate effectively in discussions about their faith. In this way, they could remedy the historical shortcomings which now meant that "six out of seven Muslims understood no Arabic" and, therefore, had no direct access to Islam; this was a bitter harvest of the past that his community now reaped, according to al-Ghazali. It worried him that the majority of his people approached their faith only through hearsay or secondary sources, many of which often contradicted the tenets of Islam.[44] His prominent audience appeared to share these convictions; some provided further examples of the consequences of this low priority given to mastering the language of the Qur'an.

Usul al-Fiqh

That evening Mohammed al-Ghazali concluded his presentation with comments on *'ilm usul al-fiqh*, the study of the method and sources of deducing Shari'a rules/laws. He believed that the fundamental purposes of Muslim rule-/lawmaking, *maqasid al-Shari'a*, should form the actual cornerstone of the discipline. Further, besides the five or six purposes which earlier *fuqaha* had identified, al-Ghazali added a seventh: a comprehensive notion of "social, emotional, and political justice".[45] The *'ulama* had smothered these purposes of Shari'a, he thought; why else, he asked, did al-Azhar *usul al-fiqh* curricula censor works that focused on the purposes, *maqasid*, of Shari'a? For centuries, this key Sunni institution intentionally neglected the teaching of al-Shatibi's *Al-Muwafaqat* in favour of Ibn al-Hajib's "dead text", from which it taught *usul al-fiqh* to its students, he said.[46] The result, according to al-Ghazali, was that Azhari graduates only learned "methodological gymnastics" that had little relation to the world around them or even to the sound understanding of *fiqh*. He urged his colleagues to overhaul this discipline too; they ought to transform *usul al-fiqh* courses from irrelevant archival expeditions into dynamic lessons on pertinent Shari'a rulemaking.[47]

Shari'a experts respond

The comments that followed al-Ghazali's lecture provide a valuable window into modern *fiqh* debates. A great part of the tension within the ranks of these living authorities on Shari'a revolved around loyalty to a particular historical narrative, as opposed to those inclined to question it. Their discussions also show that al-Ghazali was far from being a lone critic of the common approaches to *fiqh*; he was only the voice behind which many such critics gathered. These Shari'a experts' deliberations on how to overhaul their scholarly legacy opens a world that Western discourse on Islam ignores, despite its mantra about the need for a Muslim reformation.[48] As it turned out, these Egyptian leaders of Muslim "orthodoxy" did not particularly subscribe to popular ideas about Muslim "orthodoxy". Their views on Hadith provide a good start.

Who dares doubt Hadith?

When in the late 1980s al-Ghazali published his book in which he claimed that Muslims repressed Shari'a and the true Sunna with their approaches to Hadith, he generated a great commotion in the Sunni establishment. However, this senior gathering is evidence of how his assessment of Sunna presentations chimed with the concerns of powerful sections of mainstream Muslim scholarship. Tariq al-Bishri also praised efforts to re-evaluate the contents of Hadith, judging Mohammed al-Ghazali's assessments "a signpost of *fiqh* and Islamic thought in our times";[49] Mohammed 'Imara supported calls to appraise the contents of Hadith in the light of the Qur'an and the *maqasid*, or the general purposes of Shari'a;[50] and Abd al-Aziz al-'Alami applauded al-Ghazali's assessment of the Hadith legacy as "a loud cry to awaken the careless and to stir the lazy among sound-minded Muslims." In al-Ghazali he saw the highest contemporary authority on Islam, calling him "the Shaykh of our Age".[51] Al-Sayyid Rizq al-Taweel also praised the quest to purify the memory of the Prophet from the falsehoods that currently envelop it.[52] To stress how the distortion of Sunna corrupted Muslim minds, he added his own example. Al-Taweel recounted his conversation with the Hadith scholar Shaykh Nasr al-Din al-Albani, who opposed the explicit meaning of a Qur'anic verse because it contradicted a Hadith report. When al-Taweel probed further he discovered that al-Albani did not remember the Qur'anic verse in question. When he confronted al-Albani, al-Taweel learned that, "the man who studied by heart thousands of Hadith reports did not bother to study the Qur'an in the same way, learning only some of its chapters."[53] This one-time Azhari dean found al-Ghazali's criticisms to have hit a chord that echoed his own "heart beats".[54]

Reforms and contradictions

Notwithstanding the frequent applause that evening, comments by some of these specialists exposed their discomfort with al-Ghazali's disparagement of their fields. Mohammed 'Imara pleaded the case of Islamic philosophy, in which he had earned a doctorate, and the Mutazilate doctrine, to which he had once subscribed. 'Imara restated the usual argument: such scholars turned to ancient Greek philosophy in order to argue Islam's cause with non-Muslims.[55] Ali Goma defended the texts that the Azhari professors, including himself, selected to teach *usul al-fiqh*. The trouble with the current study of *usul al-fiqh* stemmed from "the scarcity of competent professors of al-Ghazali's calibre", rather than the old texts themselves, Goma argued.[56] The unease underlined some of the faultlines inside circles of reform in the last decades of the twentieth century. Perhaps not all experts who called for the overhaul of Islamic learning fully accepted all its consequences, but despite hints of disagreement, all the attending scholars sounded warning bells about Muslim education and lawmaking, of which they painted a dismal picture. Herein lies their support for al-Ghazali, which in many cases was expressed generously.

What Islam did al-Ghazali represent?

Some of the Islamic scholars sounded a call for al-Ghazali to lead efforts to solve the crises in *fiqh*, Hadith, and Muslim history and scholarship. This was a curiously tall order for one person: a modern Egyptian law and Shari'a expert, Mohammed Kamal Imam, hoped that al-Ghazali's "crucial and resolute" views would mark the start of a process for implementing the Shaykh's suggestions for reforms.[57] Tariq al-Bishri, a senior public legal figure, wanted such reforms to bridge the gap between the modern Egyptian legal system and Shari'a in all areas, instead of restricting Shari'a to family matters.[58] Mohammed 'Imara believed that modern times marked the lowest point in Islamic scholarship, and that thousands were graduating as Islamic experts "while in reality they are utterly ignorant."[59] Ali Goma, as previously mentioned, noted the dearth of educators of Shaykh Mohammed al-Ghazali's calibre; addressing the dean of al-Azhar's Faculty of *Usul-al-Din* in their midst, he suggested that he immediately start a programme for academically accomplished students who would work under the tutorship of Shaykh al-Ghazali, entrusting him with preparing a roadmap to reform.[60] Goma reasoned that the *fuqaha* had to begin building the new edifice before demolishing the old;[61] speaking at some length, he reminded them of how learning in their country had split into religious, meaning dated and lethargic, and secular, meaning contemporary and dynamic. The line that separated this new dual system of education was rarely crossed, he observed. Trapping Muslims in "religious education' was hazardous, this future mufti of Egypt cautioned. In the nineteenth century, Shaykh Mohammed Abduh had warned them that such educational dualism produced ignorant *'ulama* and incompetent Shari'a judges, Goma reminded the gathering. So did other Azharis of Abduh's time, he also noted.[62] The trepidations of their predecessors proved well justified; Azhari education was now academically poor and suffered from a dearth of documentary sources, Shaykh Goma thought.[63]

Islamic institutions of learning

Al-Ghazali interjected after Goma's discourse. True, in modern times Islamic learning in Egypt had become associated with the weak, both socially and intellectually, but his criticism was not solely directed at al-Azhar (or Egypt's education), he clarified; it included all Muslim "traditional" educational institutions, such as al-Zaytouna (in Tunis).[64] The Islamic curricula manifested decay; contemporary Muslim religious institutions had no appetite for rational thinking, and this was the reason for their weakness, as al-Ghazali saw it.[65] He gave an example of this regression. As a student of *usul-al-din* himself at al-Azhar (in the late 1930s), he had to comprehend some principles of algebra, maths, geometry, biology, physics, and chemistry. At the time, no one could have graduated as an *'alim* had he held views similar to those of "Shaykh Bin Baz [the Saudi Mufti in the 1990s], which deny that the earth is round."[66] Far from providing the remedy, founding more such Islamic institutions of learning only produced "counterfeit medicine". These establishments could not help it, al-Ghazali insisted; their culture and the nature of their instruction only produced "badly informed *'ulama*", he further explained. To illustrate, al-Ghazali once again put forward the foremost Saudi religious authority, Shaykh Bin Baz. Considering that many seminar participants were serving in scholarly bodies in Jeddah, Mecca, Medina, or Riyadh, or had other close contacts with the Saudi religious establishment, it is hard to underestimate the import of this example. But, as al-Ghazali saw it, society should not celebrate limited aptitude and poor education because they were wrapped in godliness; piety did not necessarily translate into intellect or knowledge, and Bin Baz was an example of this, al-Ghazali warned. Although a devout, kind man who feared the Day of Judgement, the fact that many Muslims celebrated Shaykh Bin Baz's ideas underlined a communal, not an individual's problem.[67] God's sunna on earth was clear: the Almighty only raised the stature of peoples with intellectual prowess. Many of those who currently spoke for Islam "were mostly the half-learned, the illiterate, and the intellectually feeble." Consequently, he urged these senior Muslim scholars to "purify the studies [of Islam] from falsehoods, additions, and perceptions held by barbarian minds."[68] His verdict was unequivocal: contemporary centres of Muslim learning constituted travesties that inflicted offensive ideas on the rest of humanity. Fellow Muslim scholars had nothing to offer the world now, judging by the ways they approached their faith and its heritage in the late twentieth century. Whether in areas of "morality, training, or knowledge", Muslims could only lead the world backward.[69]

Some of the gathered scholars added their own examples. Hasan Ragab noted among the most "dangerous" flippant claims of the predominant Islamic discourse is the conviction that war was a means of spreading Islam.[70] The moderator, Gamal 'Attia, also offered an example: an Azhari professor believed that all *fiqh* matters had been considered and there was nothing more to research, thereby rejecting every proposal that his student presented for her doctoral dissertation.[71] Dr Fawqiyya Hasan, the only woman whose name appears in the transcript, wanted their discussions to include all of Egypt's institutions of education, not just the religious ones; so-called secular modern institutions of learning also suffered from similar serious shortcomings, Hasan said. However, their critical assessment of the Islamic scholarly heritage should not mean its total demolition, she also cautioned. Hasan proposed including home-grown Islamic themes, such as plurality, in the curricula of all Egyptian universities, regardless of discipline.[72] Nasir 'Arif argued that teaching a separate subdivision of subjects under the rubric "religious" was a brainchild of the secularists, and did not reflect Islam's worldview. He thought that the schizophrenia of religious versus non-religious in modern Egypt's educational policy left an impression among students that they had to discard either factual information or Islamic tenets. Genuine reform should end the divide between faith and other areas of knowledge, he believed.[73]

Defining Islamic sciences

Faulty terms plagued the heart of Muslim education, according to a former dean of Arabic and Islamic Studies at al-Azhar University, Shaykh al-Sayyid Rizq al-Taweel. The title of their lecture-seminar, "*Al-'ulum al-Shar'yyia*", illustrated this, he noted. If *al-'ulum al-shar'yyia* meant "the disciplines that are lawful to study", the phrase was obviously a misnomer: "according to Islam, all disciplines of knowledge are lawful", he observed. As proof, he invoked instructions of the Prophet, such as that "a believer is in constant search for wisdom [everywhere]" and "the quest for learning is an obligation on every Muslim man and woman." Al-Taweel posed the question again: "What do we mean by *al-'ulum shar'iya*?", and suggested what he thought to be alternative, more accurate titles.[74]

Like al-Ghazali, this Azhari scholar also wanted to place the study of the Arabic language at the head of a revised Islamic curriculum, in order to recover Muslims' "cut-off tongues", as he put it.[75] Al-Taweel also expressed deep apprehension of classroom texts. For the most part, contemporary Muslim institutions preferred to teach Islam using mediocre works, he observed. To illustrate, he recalled how, as Azhari students of Hanafi *fiqh*, they would gather to laugh at the silliness of works from which they learned the *maddhab*: "In the text of *Al-Ikhtiyar fi ta'lil Al-mukhtar* we read that the breath of an animal that emerges from the sea at sunrise is what produces [the morning] dew." Students of other *madhahib* also exchanged similar absurdities they had learnt with their Hanafi friends. Al-Taweel's Maliki friends studied rules that sought to regulate how a man carried a water container on his shoulder, and other "comical and irrelevant presuppositions".[76] But such fascination with juvenile, futile ideas, which peppered many works, made the task of sifting Islam's enormous literary heritage manageable, al-Taweel thought.[77] The real difficulty facing efforts to rationalize their scholarship, according to al-Taweel, lurked in misreading pluralism in *fiqh*. Casually accepting dissimilar, even contradictory, *fiqh* opinions as all equally true entrenched turmoil and irrationality, he believed. Such fuzzy perceptions of pluralism had also led many fellow Muslims to regard "every opinion recorded in a *fiqh* book as equating with Islam". It worried him that even *'aqida* (the tenets of Islam) had suffered from such shallow understanding of the variety in their uneven literary legacy. Modern casualties of this chaos included Egyptian family law, he pointed out. Experts who prepared its articles claimed to have based the law on Shari'a's sources, while in reality they had based these codes on their personal preferences from among a variety of questionable *fiqh* ideas, al-Taweel lamented.[78] Islam and *fiqh* did not always convey the same message, and he wanted Muslims to turn to only two sources to understand the tenets of their faith: the Qur'an and the genuine precedents set by their Prophet—the central message of al-Ghazali's last campaign.[79]

But unlike al-Ghazali, al-Taweel insisted that singling out al-Azhar for criticism was fair and necessary. This ancient university led other (Sunni) Islamic institutions of learning, and as such it carried great responsibility, he explained.[80] Again, al-Azhar appeared a main offender in the debacle of Muslim education. Al-Taweel questioned why it taught Sufi thought and works of Islamic philosophy as texts on *'aqida* when their contents plainly contradicted both the Qur'an and common sense. In the preparatory stages, for example, Azhari students learned that the Sufi "Shaykh al-Dusuqi had traded a piece of land in heaven [which he owned in the hereafter] for [someone's actual] garden." The assigned text even described how Shaykh al-Dusuqi "wrote a contract to delineate the northern, southern, eastern, and western borders of his [heavenly] allotment that he sold to the man", al-Taweel said.[81] In his opinion, approaches to Hadith in particular, and history in general, exposed the irrational state that now afflicted education in al-Azhar, which all other Muslim institutions mirrored. Students in Egypt's secondary schools, he explained, studied Islamic history as a list of sacrosanct names, not in terms of societies. What could these youngsters possibly learn from lessons on another Sufi, Shaykh al-Sayyid al-Badawi, except superstitious fairytales? Because the logic of a particular historical narrative posed the threat, he suggested that they had to devise a new lens for understanding the Muslim past. He wanted to teach history to Azharis in terms of civilizations, cultures, and the undisputable triumph of reason.[82]

Yes, review all, but ...

Al-Ghazali added a caution. Muslim scholars had to exercise prudence as they introduced reforms, he advised towards the end of their meeting. They ought to approach the re-assessment of their heritage thoughtfully and sensitively, or else "we will face incorrect accusations; some [fellow Muslims] could regard our deliberations hostile to Islam", he warned.[83] He should know: he suffered from accusations that he was waging war against the Prophet's Sunna because he called for re-assessing the Hadith legacy, he reminded his audience. "We must exercise vigilance in undertaking [these projects of] construction and demolition", was his counsel.[84] The gathered scholars appeared aware of the value as well as the possible damaging consequences of their critiques: "If a secular figure expressed views such as those discussed in this hall tonight, he would have been condemned for plotting to demolish Islam", Dr Saif abd al-Fattah observed.[85] Like many Muslim scholars, abd al-Fattah, who later served as an advisor to the Muslim Brotherhood president in 2012, understood that even credible leaders of Islam had to tread very carefully to make a real difference.

After al-Ghazali died, events in the region and elsewhere in the world showed that his concerns about Islamic learning in his times had been well-founded. But most of all, they confirmed his views about the toxic historical connection between Islamic scholarship and political forces, which he claimed to have never reflected the Shari'a. Many in his senior *fiqh* reformist crowd fell out when they supported different political visions and ambitions in their country. Some of them went as far as to declare each other apostates, outside the realm of Islam (*kufar*). Shaykh Yusuf al-Qaradawi and Shaykh Ali Goma are only two of them; both are world authorities on *usul al-fiqh*, leaders of Sunni Islam, and key figures in al-Ghazali's circle during his lifetime.

Notes

1. Summary of a transcript of a seminar held in early 1990 and published under the title *Nadwat Tadris al-'Ulum al-Shar'iya, Fadilat al-Shaykh Muhamad al-Ghazali: Taqdim wa Idarat Dr Gamal Eldin Attia* (Cairo: IIIT, n.d.).
2. For some of the IIIT lectures on Shari'a given by members of this scholarly "reform" circle at the time Ghazali presided over their Council of Scholars, Majlis al-Ulama, at the Cairo office, see Gamal Eldin Attia, *Al-Shari'a al-Islamiya wa al-Qanun* (Cairo: IIIT, 1988); Mohammed Salim 'Awa, *Mafhoum Tatbiq al-Shari'a al-Islamiya* (Cairo: IIIT, 1989); Ahmed Kamal Abu al-Magd, *Qadhayia Muta'liqa bi Tatbiq al-Shari'a al-Islamiya* (Cairo: IIIT, 1989).
3. Laila Bayiomi, "Tariq al-Bishri yarwi Qissat tahawuluhu min al-'Almanyia ila al-Islam", *Mufakirat al-Islam* (Mecca), 2 April, 2007 (online: http://islammemo.cc/Tahkikat/hewarat/2007/04/02/39062.html).
4. On 15 February, 2011, within days of President Mubarak's fall, the army appointed al-Bishri head of a committee for suggesting amendments to the constitution (Decree 1, 2011).
5. For years, Muslim researchers from the West sought Shaykh Goma's instructions or studied under one of his students because they held him as a foremost authority on Shari'a rule-/lawmaking. In this case too, Egyptian society's admiration of Goma had helped to support his reputation as a spokesman on Islam. However, following the army's coup against the Muslim Brotherhood government he sided with the generals and criticized

the discourse of the January 2011 Revolution. From that time, Goma lost support among significant numbers of Muslims in Egypt. These changes further illustrated the important connections between the the influence of a *faqih* and socio-political protest. His works on usul al-fiqh include *Al-Mustalah al-Usuli wa Mushkilat al-Mafahim* (Cairo: al-Ma'had al-'Alami li al-Fikr al-Islami, 1996) and *Al-Hukm al-Shari'i 'inda al-Usulyeen* (Cairo: Dar al-Salam, 2006). Goma also compiled an encyclopaedia on Hadith disciplines, *Mawsoa't Ulum al-Hadith* (Cairo: al-Majlis al-ala li al-Shoun al-Islamiya, n.d.).

6. A Master's thesis completed at al-Azhar describes Shaykh al-Taweel as having his own excellent *tafsir* school of thought which followed in the footsteps of Shaykhs Abduh, Ridha, and al-Maraghi. Ahmed Sayeed Hasan, *Sayyid Rizq al-Taweel: Manhajuhu wa Juhuduh fi al-Da'wa* (MA diss., al-Azhar, 1432 AH / 2010 CE) A summary of the thesis can be found on the *Jam'iyat Dawat al-Haq al-Islamyyia* website (online: http://www.dawatelhak.com/play-24905.html).
7. The left-leaning Egyptian writer Wael abd al-Fattah claims that before moving to the Islamist camp, 'Imara was notorious for intimidating those who disagreed with his extremist Marxist views (Wael abd al-Fattah, "Hikayat al-Doctor Mohammed 'Imara'", *Tahrir News*, 26 August, 2012).
8. In June 2012, SCAF appointed a committee to oversee religious life in Egypt, which included three regular figures in al-Ghazali's circle: Yusuf al-Qaradawi, Mohammed 'Imara, and Hasan al-Shafi'i. The rest of its members were to be elected from among the scholars of the four Sunni maddhabs, according to the army's decree ("Al-Qaradawi wa 'Imara wa al-Shafii Officially Among the Members of the Senior *'Ulama* Body", *Al-Youm*, 23 June, 2012, 7 [online: http://www1.youm7.com/News.asp?NewsID=713953&SecID=12]).
9. See Chapter 8 for further discussion on the first presidential elections.
10. Al-Ghazali, *Nadwat Tadris al-'Ulum al-Shar'iya*, 2.
11. Ibid., 1.
12. Ibid., 2; Mohammed al-Ghazali, *Al-Sunna al-Nabawiya Bayna Ahl al-Fiqh wa ahl al-Hadith*, 5th edn (no location: Sahara, 1989), 48, 55, 60–61.
13. Ibid.
14. Ibid.
15. Ibid., 9; al-Ghazali criticized Ibn Taymiya for sometimes accepting superstitions (idem, *Al-Sunna al-Nabawiya*, 98). However, he also praised him (idem, "Fiqh al Da'wa wa Mushkilat al-D'oa", *Al-Umma* [Doha], 15 Rajab, 1408 AH, 131), including for his outline for deducing rules from Shari'a (quoted by Yusuf al-Qaradawi, "Nazarat fi Tarikh al-Shaykh", *Islamiyat al-Ma'rifa* 2/3 [2007]: 25). Al-Ghazali also compared his personal circumstances to those of Ibn Taymiya (Mohammed al-Ghazali, "Qissat Haya", *Islamiyat al-Ma'rifa* 2/3 (2007): 156; idem, videotape interview #S-1).
16. Al-Ghazali, *Nadwat Tadris al-'Ulum al-Shar'iya*, 3; idem, "Fiqh al Da'wa", *Al-Umma*, 15 Rajab, 1408 AH, 138.
17. Some arguments in favour of the compatibility of Shari'a and modernity made by other Muslim scholars may initially appear similar to those of al-Ghazali. In the West these included professors Khaled Abou El Fadl, *The Great Theft: Wrestling Islam from the Extremists* (New York: HarperCollins, 2007) and Tariq Ramadan, *Radical Reform: Islamic Ethics and Liberation* (Oxford: Oxford University Press, 2008). See Chapter 8 for his views on Islam and democracy.
18. Al-Ghazali, *Nadwat Tadris al-'Ulum al-Shar'iya*, 3.
19. Ibid.
20. Ibid.
21. Ibid., 31.
22. Ibid.

23. Ibid., 4–6. Al-Ghazali believed that the only *fiqh* political ideas that could be described as dynamic could be found in early works that addressed real-life circumstances in terms of Qura'nic principles and the actual Sunna. Ibn al-Hasan al-Shaibani exemplified such rare *fiqh* instances (Ibid., 3).
24. Ibid., 30, 31.
25. Ibid., 31, 32.
26. Ibid., 2.
27. Ibid., 4.
28. Ibid. Zaynab al-Ghazali is no relation to Mohammed al-Ghazali. She is a symbol of Islamist resistance of the government of Gamal abd al-Nasser that imprisoned her. See her prison memoirs, *Aiyam min Hayati* (Cairo: Dar al-Tawz'i wa al-Nashr al-Islamiya, 1999).
29. Ibid.
30. Ibid., 10, 11, 44.
31. Ibid., 10.
32. Ibid. For sample primary texts of such discussions see Majid Fakhry, *Al-Fikr al-Akhlaqi al-Arabi. Al-Juz' al-Awal: al-Fuqaha wa al-Mutakalimoun* (Beirut: al-Ahlyia li al-Nashr wa al-Tawzi', 1978).
33. Ibid., 5–10.
34. In his article on "Ilm Al-Kalam" for the *Encyclopaedia of Islam*, 2nd edn (Leiden: Brill, 1999), Louis Gardet quotes al-Farabi describing *'ilm al-kalam* as "a science which enables a man to procure the victory of the dogmas and actions laid down by the Legislator of the religion, and to refute all opinions contradicting them."
35. Al-Ghazali, *Nadwat Tadris al-'Ulum al-Shar'iya*, 6–11.
36. Ibid., 12.
37. Ibid., 10–12.
38. Ibid., 11.
39. Ibid., 30.
40. I am indebted to Dr Mohammed Moshtahiri, who shared with the author his recorded telephone conversation with Shaykh Mohammed al-Ghazali.
41. Ibid., 6.
42. Ibid., 14.
43. Al-Ghazali told off an Arab ambassador to Egypt who claimed that Salah al-Din al-Ayyubi / Saladin (the Kurdish general who led the fight against the Crusaders and founded the Ayyubid dynasty in Egypt and Syria) was an Arab nationalist figure (idem, *Humum Da'iya* [Cairo: Nahdat Misr, 2004], 36). In the 1960s, he challenged the introduction of Arab nationalism as a required subject in the schools' curricula by authoring *Haqiqat al-Qawmiyya al-'Arabiyya wa Usturat al-Ba'th al-'Arabi* (Cairo: al-Rawda li al-Nashr wa al-Tawzi', 1993).
44. Al-Ghazali, *Nadwat Tadris al-'Ulum al-Shar'iya*, 15–16.
45. Ibid., 17.
46. Ibid. Ibn al-Hajib, Abu 'Amr b. Umar al-Dawini was a Maliki *usul al-fiqh* expert who died in Alexandria, Egypt in 1249 CE. His *Mukhtasar Muntaha al-S'ul wa al-Amal fi 'Imiyi al-Usul wa al-Jadal* serves as a standard *usul al-fiqh* text for instructions, and is a subject of numerous summaries and commentaries.
47. Al-Ghazali, *Nadwat Tadris al-'Ulum al-Shar'iya*, 16–18.
48. See Mehdi Hasan, "Why Islam Doesn't Need a Reformation" (online: http://www.theguardian.com/commentisfree/2015/may/17/islam-reformation-extremism-muslim-martin-luther-europe).
49. Al-Ghazali, *Nadwat Tadris al-'Ulum al-Shar'iya*, 24.
50. Ibid., 21.
51. Ibid., 33.

52. Ibid., 41, 44.
53. Ibid., 44.
54. Ibid., 41.
55. Ibid., 20–21.
56. Ibid., 28.
57. Ibid., 22.
58. Ibid., 24–25.
59. Ibid., 19.
60. Ibid., 29.
61. Ibid.
62. Ibid., 27.
63. Ibid.
64. Ibid., 29.
65. Ibid., 29–30.
66. Ibid., 30.
67. Ibid., 30, 32.
68. Ibid., 30, 31.
69. Ibid., 31.
70. Ibid., 33.
71. Ibid., 46.
72. Ibid., 35–37.
73. Ibid., 37–39.
74. Ibid., 41.
75. Ibid., 42–43.
76. Ibid.
77. Ibid.
78. Ibid., 42–43.
79. Ibid., 43–46.
80. Ibid., 41.
81. Ibid., 42.
82. Ibid., 45–46.
83. Ibid., 31.
84. Ibid.
85. Ibid., 39.

APPENDIX 2

Shaykh Abd Allah al-Mashad's Fatwa on the Rejection of Hadith Reports

The Arabic text of the fatwa was published in al-Ghazali's *Turathuna al-Fikri*, 176–179.

The Inquiry:

Peace be upon you, God's Mercy and his blessings.

Would a person who refused to recognize the Sunna as an independent source for making [Shari'a] rules/laws fall outside the bounds of Islam [*kafir*] or not?

Kindly inform us of your opinion as well as the evidence for it.

Signed: "A reader"

The Fatwa:

In the name of God the Most Merciful, the Most Compassionate.

The majority [of the scholars/*fuqaha*] have agreed to divide all rules into five types:

1. Mandatory: That which is evident through a clear textual evidence, which is definite historically and in substance. That [this text] has a singular import concerning which persons striving to discover rules could not differ, [and that this text is found] in the Book of God or in the extensively reported Sunna of his Prophet.
2. Forbidden: That which the [Divine] legislator wanted forsaken, as proven by a definite text, historically and in meaning, and found in the Book of God or the extensively reported Sunna of His Prophet.
3. Commendable: That which the [Divine] legislator recommended but did not make mandatory; a person could be rewarded for doing it, but would not be punished for forsaking it.
4. Repellent: That which the [Divine] legislator recommended be forsaken,

but not commanded it to be forsaken; a person would be rewarded for forsaking it, but would not be punished for committing it.

5. Permitted: That which an individual has a choice whether to perform or leave it; there is no proof for forbidding it.

As for the [nature of the Prophet's] Sunna [that comprise such textual evidence], it consists of two parts, extensively reported [Sunna] and singularly reported [Sunna], *mutawatira* and *uhadyia.*

The [Sunna] al-mutawatira is that which incalculable numbers of people have continued to report on the authority of [similarly] incalculable numbers of people such as to make it impossible, or unlikely, that all these people could concoct lying [making up] about it.

[In this regard] Al-Hazmi said in *Shurut al-a'ima al-khamsa*, page 37 that "proving *tawatir* in Hadith is extremely difficult."

And al-Shatibi said in the first part of *Al-'Itisam*, page 135, "God forbid that there exists a *mutawatir* Hadith report which originates with the Messenger of God."

Although Hadith *mutawatir* reports are rare and that the scholars of the Sunna differed about their numbers and [degrees of their] certainty, the majority of the *fuqaha* have concluded, without a doubt, that a person who refused to recognize the Sunna *al-mutawatira* as an independent source for deducing [Shari'a] rules/laws falls outside the bounds of Islam, "*qad kafar*".

The [Sunna] *al-uhadyia* are accounts that a number of people first reported the Prophet [to have said or done]; these fall short of the requirement of having immeasurable numbers of people [to have known them], *tawatir.*

The scholars have disagreed about whether this Sunna *al-uhadyia* can serve as an independent source of [Shari'a] rule-/lawmaking.

The Shafi'i *fuqaha,* and those who follow their opinion, believe that a person who refused to recognize it [the Sunna *al-uhadyia* / Hadith] as a source of rulemaking in rituals, such as prayers, fasting, Hajj, and Zakat, for example, falls outside the bounds of Islam [is *kafir*]. However, [they also believe that] a person who refused to recognize [the Sunna *al-uhadyia*] as an independent source for the tenets of Islam, in doctrinal matters such as what concerns the Day of Judgement, and the intangible Divine scheme, *ghaibyiat*, [this person] remains within the bounds of Islam. This person is not *kafir*, because knowledge of the Divine has no other proof except in the Book of God and the Sunna *al-mutawatira* of his Prophet.

The Hanafi *fuqaha*, and those who follow their opinion, believe that the Sunna *al-uhadyia* [Hadith] cannot independently give rise to a [Shari'a] rule that is mandatory or prohibitive, whether in matters of divine knowledge or in practical matters and, therefore, a person who refused to recognize [such Hadith as a source] does not fall outside the bounds of Islam. That has been the opinion of Hanafi *usul al-fiqh* scholars [rulemaking experts], hence al-Bardawi's

> To claim that an *uhadi* Hadith [report] establishes certainty must be necessarily false. An *uhadi* report is only probable, no question about it and, consequently, no certainty can be said to have been proven [by such probability]. Anyone who rejects this evident truism misleads and makes a fool of himself.

Imam Mohammed Abduh [Egypt's former mufti], Shaykh Mahmoud Shaltout [former head of al-Azhar], and Shaykh Mahmoud abou Daqiqa [former member of al-Azhar's Board of Senior *'Ulama, Hay'at kibar al-ulama*] all subscribed to this view.

In this regard, Imam Mohammed Abduh says:

> The Qur'an is the sole admissible proof for the message of Islam. Anything else, such as information reported in the Hadiths [legacy]—whether historically accurate reports, well known, or weak reports, none of them establishes certainty.

As [Shaykh Shaltut] noted in his book *al-Islam Shari'a wa 'Aqida*:

> Probability besets Sunna's origins [*sanad*] and its import [*al-ma'na*], casting doubt on its transmission and probabilities of its meaning.

And Imam al-Shatibi opines in his book *Al-Muwafaqat* that Sunna does not independently prove what [God] mandates or prohibits because its only purpose is to specify, demarcate, and clarify general Qur'anic [principles], which can only be accomplished by *mutawatir* reports, not *al-uhadi* accounts."

It is clear from the above, [therefore,] that a [Shari'a rule] to mandate or prohibit cannot be verified except through undisputable proof, that is certain in fact and in meaning, *qati al-thobout wa qati al dilala*, which, in the case of the Sunna only applies to *al-mutawatir* Hadith reports. And since these are almost unknown [to exist] in view of the disagreements among the *'ulama* about these [reports' authenticity and import], the Sunna cannot, therefore, independently [give rise to rules that either] mandate or prohibit.

Hence, that who does not accept that the Sunna can independently [give rise to a rule to] mandate or prohibit, is a person that rejects something about which there has not been an agreement among the leaders of the community and is not included in what is certain [of Islam's sources], accordingly, [this person] cannot be considered *kafir* [out of the bounds of Islam].

Signed: President of the fatwa committee of al-Azhar,
Abd Allah al-Mashad
Dated: 5 Rajab, 1410 AH [1 February, 1990 CE]

APPENDIX 3

Shaykh Abd al-Latif Mushtahiri's Letter Regarding Sunna and Hadith

Translation of letter sent to al-Ghazali by Shaykh Abd al-Latif Mushtahiri, imam of *al-Jam'iya al-Shar'iya li Ta'awun al-'Amilin bi al-Kitab wa al-Sunna* and an al-Azhar Mosque/University *dawa* official:

Cairo
11 Rajab, 1410 AH [7 February, 1990 CE]

Eminence, the great mujahid, Shaykh Mohammed al-Ghazali
Al-Salam alykum wa rahmat Allah

May God bless you for your generous character, your continued jihad in favour of the faith of Muslims, and [efforts] to awaken them from their stupor. In answer to your query about the importance of publicizing the fatwa issued by the Fatwa Committee of the honourable Azhar ruling on a person who rejects the validity of the Sunna as a source that establishes [Shari'a] commands and prohibitions, which a brother required submitted for an answer.[1]

I inform your excellency that I have contacted his eminence Shaykh Abd Allah al-Mashad, Head of the Azhar Fatwa Committee, to urge the necessity of publicizing such a fatwa in order to correct the common Muslim understanding [of their faith] and guide their scholars in what is right. [In response] His excellency informed me that the current public conditions do not allow [al-Azhar] to publicize such a fatwa and that his eminence [Ghazali] will instead include it in his book to be published shortly.

The [above] for you to note as we ask the Almighty to make us all among those who follow the best of what they hear,

And, God's Peace, His Mercy, and Blessings be upon you.

Signed:

Abd al-Latif Mushtahiri,

President and Imam of *ahl al-Sunna li al-Jam'at al-Shar'iya*, and Deputy Head of Islamic D'awa at al-Azhar

Note

1. The "brother" alluded to above is Mohammed, Abd al-Latif al-Mushtahiri's own son who kindly provided the author with a copy of this letter from his father's files.

Selected Bibliography

Works of Mohammed al-Ghazali

Al-Islam wa al-'Awda'al-Iqtisadiya. 7th edn. Cairo: Dar al-Sahwa, 1987 [first published 1947].

Al-Islam wa al-Istibdad al-Siyasi. Cairo: Dar al-Kutub al-Islamiyah, 1984 [first published c. 1951].

Al-Islam wa al-Manahij al-Ishtirakiya. Cairo: Nahdat Misr, 2007 [first published 1951].

Min Ma'alim al-Haqq fi Kifahina al-Islami al-Hadith. 2nd edn. Cairo: Dar al-Kutub al-Haditha, 1963.

Al-Islam fi Wajih al-Zahf al-Ahmar. Kuwait: Maktabat al-Amal, 1966.

Al-Janib al-'Atifi min al-Islam. Cairo: al-Dar al-Kutub al-Haditha, 1977.

Al-Da'wa al-Islamiya Tastaqbilu Qarnaha al-Khamis 'Ashr. No location: Dhat al-Salasit, 1980.

Dostur al-Wihdah al-Thaqafiyah bayn al-Muslimin. Cairo: Dar al-Ansar, 1981.

Al-Islam wa al-Taqat al-Mu'attalah. Cairo: Dar al-Kutub al-Islamiyah, 1983.

Al-Isti'mar Ahqad wa Atma'. Cairo: Dar al-Kutub al-Islamiyah, 1983.

Laysa min al-Islam. Cairo: Dar al-Kutub al-Islamiyah, 1983.

"Lima'dha al-Hugom 'ala Mohammed Abduh wa al-Afghani?" *Majalat al-Doha* (Doha) 91, 1983.

Mi'at Su'al 'an al-Islam. Cairo: Dar Thabit, 1983.

Huquq al-Insan bayna Ta'lim al-Islam wa 'Ilan al-Umam al-Motahida. Cairo: Dar al-Kutub al-Islamiyah, 1984.

'Ilal wa Adwiya. Cairo: Maktabat Akhbar al-Tum al-Islamiya, 1992 [first published in 1984].

Mustaqbalu al-Islam Kharij Ardhihi. Doha: Mo'assasat al-Sharq li al-'Alaqat al-'Ama wa al-Nashir wa al-Tarjama, 1984.

Ta'amulat fi al-Din wa al-Hayah. Cairo: Dar al-Kutub al-Islamiyah, 1984.

Sirr Ta'akhur al-'Arab wa al-Muslimeen. Cairo: Dar al-Sahwah, 1985.

Al-Ghazw al-Thaqafi Yamtaddu fi Faraghina. Cairo: Dar al-Sahwah, 1987.

Hasad al-Ghurur. Cairo: Maktabat Wahah, 1987.

Jihad al-Da'wa bayna 'Ajz al-Dakhil wa Kayd al-Kharij. Cairo: Dar al-Kutub al-Islamiyah, 1987.

Difa'a 'An al-'Aqida wa-al-Sharia Dhidd Mata'in al-Mustashriqin. Cairo: Dar al-Kutub al-Islamiyah, 1988.

Fi Shu'un al-Din wa al-Haya, vol. 2. Cairo: Dar al-'Itisam, 1988.

Fiqh al-Sira. 8th edn. Cairo: Dar al-Da'wah, 1988 [first published 1965].

Khutab al-Shaykh Mohammed al-Ghazali fi Sh'oun al-Haya wa al-Din. Cairo: Dar al-Itissam, 1988.

Muhadarat al-Shaykh Mohammed al-Ghazali. Cairo: Dar al-Bashir, 1989.

Al-Mahawir al-Khamsa li al-Qur'an. Cairo: Dar al-Sa'hwa, 1989.

Al-Sunna al-Nabawiya Bayna Ahl al-Fiqh wa ahl al-Hadith, 5th edn. No location: Sahara, 1989.

Azmat al-Shura fi al-Mujtama'at al-Arabia wa al-Islamiyia. 1st edn. Cairo: Dar al-Sharq al-Awsat, 1990.

Al-Islam wa al-Mar'a. Transcript of lecture moderated by Tariq al-Bishri, 2 December, 1990. Cairo: IIIT, 1990.

Qadhayia al-Mar'a Bayna al-Taqaleed al-Rakida wa al-Wafida. Cairo: Dar al-Shorouk, 1990.

Sayhat Tahdhir min Du'at al-Tansir. Cairo: Dar al-Sa'hwa, 1991.

Turathuna al-Fikri fi Mizan al-Shar'i wa al-'Aql. 2nd edn. Cairo: Dar al-Shorouk, 1991.

Kaifa Nat'amal ma' al-Qur'an. Ed. Umar Ubaid Hassana. Herndon, VA: IIIT, 1992 [Later Cairo editions include Nahdat Misr, 2005].

Ma'Allah Dirasat fi al-Dawa wa al-Do'a. 2 vols. Cairo: Maktabat Akhbar al-Youm, 1992.

Nahwa Tafsir Mawdui li Suwar al-Qur'an al Karim. Cairo: Dar al-Shorouk, 1992.

Haqiqat al-Qawmiyya al-'Arabiyya wa Usturat al-Ba'th al-'Arabi. Cairo: al-Rawda li al-Nashr wa al-Tawzi', 1993.

Al-Haqq al-Murr. Cairo: Markaz al-'Ilam al-'Arabi, 1993.

'Al-Hayah al-'Ula; Diwan Shir. Cairo: Dar al-Shorouk, 1998.

Kunuz Min al-Sunna. 4th edn. Ed. Mohammed Khaled Fuad. Cairo: Nahdat Misr, 2003.

'Aqidat al-Muslim. Cairo: Nahdat Misr, 2004.

Humum Da'iya. Cairo: Dar al-Bashir, 2004.

Dhalam min al-Gharb. Cairo: Nahdat Misr, 2005.

Jaddid Hayatak. Cairo: Nahdat Misr, 2005.

Kifah Din. Cairo: Nahdat Misr, 2005.

Ma'rakat al-Musfaf fi al-'Alam al-Islami. Cairo: Nahdat Misr, 2005.

Hiwarat al-Shaykh al-Ghazali; al-Sira wa al-Mu'asira. Ed. Gamal Attia, with an introduction by Taha Jabir al-Alwani. Cairo: Dar al-Salam, 2012.

Al-Islam al-Mufara 'Alayhi Bayna al-Shuyu'iyin wa al-Ra'smaliyin. Kuwait: Dar al-Bayan, n.d.

Khuluq al-Muslim. Cairo: Akhbar al-Youm, n.d. [Translated into English as *Muslim Character: An American-English Translation of Muhammad al-Ghazali's* Khuluq al-Muslim. Chicago: Kazi Publications, 2004].

Min Huna Na'lam. Cairo: Dar al-Kutub al-Haditha, n.d. [Translated into English by Ismail al-Faruqi and published as *Our Beginning in Wisdom*. Washington, DC: the Near Eastern Translation Program of the American Council of Learned Societies, 1953].

Nadwat Tadris al-'Ulum al-Shar'iya, Fadilat al-Shaykh Muhamad al-Ghazali: Taqdim wa Idarat Dr Gamal Eldin Attia. Cairo: IIIT, n.d.

Nazarat fi al-Qur'an. Cairo: Dar al-Kutub al-Haditha, n.d.

Qadhaif al-Haqq. Beirut: Manshurat al-Maktabah al-'Asriyah, n.d.

Videotape Interviews

Al-Fatwa. Interviewer: Gamal Eldin Attia. #FTW-1.

Al-Fikr al-Iqtisadi al-Mu'asir. Interviwer: Rif'at al-Awadhi. #IQTS-1.

Al-Funun. Interviewer: Gamal Eldin Attia. #FN-1.

Al-Ikhwan al-Muslimun. Interviewer: Gamal 'Atyia [2 Parts]. #IKH-1/IKH-2.

Al-Islam al-Syiasi. Interviewer: Mohammed Salim al-'Awa. #SYS-1.

Al-Islam wa al-Mar'a. Interviewer: Safinaz Kazim [2parts]. #W-1/W-2.

Al-Jami'at (universities) al-Islamiya. Interviewer: Hasan al-Shafi'i [2 parts]. #UNV-1/UNV-2.

Al-Tayyiarat wa al-Jama'at. Interviewer: Fahmy Huwaidi [2 Parts]. #TAYR-1/TAYR-2.

Mu'alafat. Interviewer: Mohammed 'Imara [2 parts]. #MUL-1/MUL-2.

Sirat Haya. Interviewer: Mohammed Kamal Imam [2 parts]. #S-1/S-2.

Tajdid al-'ulum al-Islamyia. Interviewer: Hasan al-Shafi'i. #TJD-1.

Other Works

Abd al-Rahim, Ashraf 'Abd al-Maqsud. *Jinayat al-Shaykh Mohammed al-Ghazali 'ala al-Hadith wa-Ahlih*. Cairo: Maktabat al-Imam Bukhari, 1989.

Abd al-Rahman, *'Aisha. Al-Sayyida Zaynab, Batalat Karbala'*. Cairo: al-Hilal, 1965.

———. *Nisa' al-Nabi*. Cairo: al-Hay'a al-Misriya al-'Ama li al-Kita, 2000.

Abd al-Raziq, Ali. *Al-Islam wa Usul al-Hukm*. 2nd edn. Cairo: Matba't Misr, 1925.

Abduh, Mohammed. *Mudhakirat al-Imam Mohammed Abduh*. Ed. T. Al-Tanahi. Cairo: Dar al-Hilal, n.d.

Abou el Fadl, Khaled. *And God Knows the Soldiers: The Authoritative and Authoritarian in Islamic Discourses*. Lanham, MD: University Press of America, 2001.

———. *Speaking in God's Name: Islamic Law, Authority and Women*. Oxford: Oneworld, 2001.
———. *Islam and the Challenge of Democracy*. Princeton, NJ: Princeton University Press, 2004.
———. *The Great Theft: Wrestling Islam from the Extremists*. San Francisco: HarperCollins, 2005.
———. *Reasoning with God: Reclaiming Shari'ah in the Modern Age*. Lanham, MD: Rowman and Littlefield, 2014.
Abrahamian, Ervand. *A History of Modern Iran*. Cambridge: Cambridge University Press, 2008.
Abu al-Magd, Ahmed Kamal. *Qadhayia Muta'liqa bi Tatbiq al-Shari'a al-Islamiya*. Lecture given at al-Ma'had al-'Alami li al-Fikr al-Islami, Cairo, 5 November, 1989. Cairo: IIIT, 1989.
Abu Shuqaa, Abd al-Halim. *Nadwat Tahrir al-Mar'a*. Transcript of lecture moderated by Ali Goma, 6 July, 1994. Cairo: IIIT publications, n.d.
Abu Zahra, Mohammed. *Ibn Hanbal, Hayatuh, wa 'Asruhu, wa Ara'auhu*. Cairo: Dar al-Fikr al-'Arabi, n.d. [first published 1947].
———. *Al-Jarima wa al-'Uqoba fi al-Fiqh al-Islami: al-'Uqoba*. Cairo: Dar al-Fikr al-Arabi, n.d.
———. *Tarikh al-Madhahib al-Islamiya fi al-Siyasa wa al-'Aqayid wa Tarikh al-Madhahib al-Fiqhiya*. Cairo: Dar al-Fikr al-Arabi, n.d.
———. *Usul al-Fiqh*. Cairo: Dar al-Fikr al-Arabi, n.d.
Abu-Rabi, Ibrahim M. *Contemporary Arab Thought: Studies in Post-1967 Arab Intellectual History*. London: Pluto Press, 2004.
Ahmed, Leila. *Women and Gender in Islam: Historical Roots of a Modern Debate*. New Haven, CT: Yale University Press, 1992.
Ali, Mohammed Kurd. *Rasa'el al-Bulagha*. Cairo: Dar al-Kutub al-'Arabiya, 1913.
———. *As'ilat al-Thawra*. Riyadh: Markaz Nama' li al-Bahth wa al-Dirasat, 2012.
Amin, Ahmed. *Fajr al-Islam*. Cairo: Dar al-Shorouk, 1999.
———. *Dhuha al-Islam*. Cairo: Hindawi, 2012.
Ansari, Abi Yusuf Yaqob Ibn Ibrahim al-. *Ikhtilaf Abi Hanifa wa Ibn Abi Laila*. Cairo: Matba't al-Wafa, 1357/1938 AH/CE.
'Aqqad, 'Abbas Mahmoud al-. *Al-Democratiya fi al-Islam*. Cairo: Dar al-Ma'arif, 1964.
———. *Ibrahim, Abu al-Anbiya*. Beirut: Dar al-Kitab al-Arabi, 1967.
———. *Hitler fi al-Mizan*. Beirut: Dar al-Kitab al-Arabi, 1971.
———. *Al-Tafkir Farida Islamiyya*. Beirut: Dar al-Kitab al-Arabi, 1971.
———. *Al-Abqariyiat al-Islamiyia*. 3 vols. Beirut: Dar al-Kitab al-Lubnani, 1974.
Attia, Gamal Eldin. *Al-Shari'a al-Islamiya wa al-Qanun*. Seminar given at al-Ma'had al-'Alami li al-Fikr al-Islami, Cairo, 12 October, 1988. Cairo: IIIT, 1988.
'Awa, Mohammed Salim. *Mafhoum Tatbiq al-Shari'a al-Islamiya*. Lecture given at

al-Ma'had al-'Alami li al-Fikr al-Islami, Cairo, 25 December, 1988. Cairo: IIIT, 1989.

Aziz, Abd al-Ghaffar. *Man Qatala Farag Foda?* Cairo: Dar al-'Ilam al-Dawli, 1992.

Badawi, Gamal. *The Status of Woman in Islam*. Riyadh: World Assembly of Muslim Youth, 1997.

Baghdadi, al-Khatib Ahmed Ibn Ali Ibn Thabit al-. *Tarikh Baghdad*. Cairo: Maktabat al-Khanji, 1931.

Baker, Raymond. *Islam without Fear: Egypt and the New Islamists*. Cambridge, MA: Harvard University Press, 2003.

Banna, Gamal al-. *Kala thuma Kala*. Cairo: Dar al-Fikr al-Islami, 1994.

———. *Ma Ba'd al-Ikhwan al-Muslimin*. Cairo: Dar al-Fikr al-Islami, 1996.

———. *Jinayat Qabilat "Hadathuna"*. Cairo: Dar al-Fikr al-Islami, 2008.

———. *Dhikraiyat Fawziya al-Banna*. Cairo: Dar al-Fikr al-Islami, 2009.

Banna, Hasan al-. *Mudhakirat al-Da'wa wa-l-Da'iya bi-Qalam al-Imam al-Shahid Hasan al-Banna*. Cairo: Dar al-Shihab, 1979.

———. *Majmu'at Ras'el al-Imam al-Shaheed Hasan al-Banna*. Cairo: Dar al-Dawa, 1999.

———. *Khitabat Hasan al-Banna al-Shabb ila Abih*. Ed. Gamal al-Banna. Cairo: Dar al-Fikr al-Islami, n.d.

Bassyoni, Midhat al-. *Al-Haqiqa al-Gha'iba bayna Khaled Mohammed Khaled wa Mohammed al-Ghazali*. Cairo: no publisher, 1979.

Bonaparte, Napoleon. *Napoleon on Napoleon: The Autobiography of the Emperor*. Ed. Somerset de Chair. London: Sterling Publishers, 1992.

Booth, Marilyn. *Bayram al-Tunisi's Egypt: Social Criticism and Narrative Strategies*. Exeter: Ithaca Press, 1990.

Brown, Daniel. *Rethinking Tradition in Modern Islamic Thought*. Cambridge: Cambridge University Press, 1996.

Brown, Jonathan. *The Canonization of al-Bukhari and Muslim: The Formation and Function of the Sunni Ḥadith Canon*. Leiden: Brill, 2006.

Brunton, Paul. *A Search in Secret Egypt*. London: Arrow Books, 1965 [first published London: Rider and Company, 1935].

Bulliet, Richard W. "Islamic Reformation or 'Big Crunch'? A Review Essay." *Harvard Middle Eastern and Islamic Review* 8 (2009): 7–18.

Burton, John. *The Sources of Islamic Law: Islamic Theories of Abrogation*. Edinburgh: Edinburgh University Press, 1990.

Cole, Juan. *Napoleon's Egypt: Invading the Middle East*. New York: Palgrave Macmillan, 2007.

Dallal, Ahmad. "Appropriating the Past: Twentieth-Century Reconstruction of Pre-Modern Islamic Thought". *Islamic Law and Society* 7/1 (2000): 325–358.

Deheuvels, Luc-Willy. *Islam et Pensee Contemporaine en Algerie*. Paris: CNRS, 1991.

Dhahabi, Shams al-Din Mohammed Ibn Ahmed Ibn Uthman al-. *Siyar A'lam al-Nubala'*. 3 vols. Cairo: Beit al-Afkar al-Dawliya, 2004.

Diraz, Mohammed abd Allah. *Al-Naba' al-'Azim*. Cairo: Dar al-Qalam, 2005.

Elhadj, Elie. "Arab Democracy is Fantasy: Democratic Ideology cannot Defeat Islamic Theology". *Syria Comment*, 23 February, 2010 (online: http://www.joshualandis.com/blog/arab-democracy-is-fantasy-by-elie-elhadj/).

Fakhry, Majid. *Al-Fikr al-Akhlaqi al-Arabi. Al-Juz' al-Awal: al-Fuqaha wa al-Mutakalimoun*. Beirut: al-Ahlyia li al-Nashr wa al-Tawzi', 1978.

———. *A Short Introduction to Islamic Philosophy, Theology and Mysticism*. Oxford: Oneword, 1997.

Feldman, Noah. *After Jihad: America and the Struggle for Islamic Democracy*. New York: Farrar, Straus and Giroux, 2003.

———. *The Fall and Rise of the Islamic State*. Princeton, NJ: Princeton University Press, 2008.

———. "Why Shariah?" *New York Times*, 16 March, 2008 (online: http://www.nytimes.com/2008/03/16/magazine/16Shariah-t.html).

Foda, Farag. *Al-Irhab*. Cairo: Dar Misr al-Gadida lil-Nashr wa al-Tawzi', 1988.

———. *Al-Haqiqa al-Gha'iba*. Beirut: Dar al-Ma'arif, 2003.

———. *Shahid 'ala al-'Asr*. Cairo: Dar wa Mat'abi al-Mustaqbal, 2005.

Ghazali, Abu Hamid Mohammed al-Tusi al-. *Faisal al-Tafriqa bayna al-Islam wa al-Zandaqa*. Cairo: Matbat al-Taraqi, 1901.

———. *Ayyuha 'L-Wald, Lettre au Disciple*. 2nd edn. Collection UNESCO D'oeuvre representatives. Beirut: Catholic Press, 1951.

———. *Al-Munqidh min al-Dhalal*. Cairo: Markaz al-Kitab li al-Nashr, 1991.

———. *Ihya' 'Ulum al-Din*. 4 vols. Cairo: Dar al-Salam, 2006.

———. *Al-Mustasfa min Ilm al-Usul*. Medina: Sharikat al-Madina al-Monawara li al-Tiba'a, n.d.

Ghitani, Gamal al-. *Muntaha al-Talab ila Turath al-'Arab, Dirasat fi al-Turath*. Cairo: Dar al-Shorouk, 1997.

Goma, Ali. *Al-Mustalah al-Usuli wa Mushkilat al-Mafahim*. Cairo: al-Ma'had al-'Alami li al-Fikr al-Islami, 1996.

———. *Al-Naskh 'inda al-Usuleen*. Cairo: Dar al-Nahar lil Tabi' wa al-Nashr, 1998.

———. *Al-Hukm al-Shari'i 'inda al-Usulyeen*. Cairo: Dar al-Salam, 2006.

———. *Mawsoa't Ulum al-Hadith*, Cairo: al-Majlis al-ala li al-Shoun al-Islamiya, n.d.

Green, Andrew. "Why Western Democracy Can Never Work in the Middle East". *Telegraph* (London), 16 August, 2014 (online: http://www.telegraph.co.uk/news/worldnews/middleeast/11037173/Why-Western-democracy-can-never-work-in-the-Middle-East.html).

Hajjar, Lisa. "Omar Suleiman, the CIA's Man in Cairo and Egypt's Torturer-in-Chief." *Jadaliyya* (Washington, DC), 30 January, 2011.

Hallaq, Wael. *Law and Legal Theory in Classical and Medieval Islam*. Brookfield, VT: Variorum, 1994 [first published 1986].

———. *The Impossible State: Islam, Politics, and Modernity's Moral Predicament*. New York: Columbia University Press, 2014.

Hamidullah, Mohammed. *Majmu'ah al-Watha'iq al-Siyasiyyah li al-'Ahad al-Nabawi wa al-Khilafah al-Rashidah*. Beirut: Dar al-Nafa'is, 1985.

Hanioglu, M. Sukru. *Ataturk: An Intellectual Biography*. Princeton, NJ: Princeton University Press, 2013.

Harris, Sam and Maajid Nawaz. *Islam and the Future of Tolerance: A Dialogue*. Cambridge, MA: Harvard University Press, 2015.

Hiro, Dilip. *Iran Under the Ayatollahs*. London: Routledge and Kegan Paul, 1985.

Hirsh, Michael. "Bernard Lewis Revisited: What if Islam isn't An Obstacle to Democracy in the Middle East but the Secret to Achieving It?" *Washington Monthly*, November 2004: 13–19. (online: http://www.washingtonmonthly.com/features/2004/0411.hirsh.html).

Hirsi, Ayaan Ali. *Heretic: Why Islam Needs a Reformation Now*. New York: HarperCollins, 2015.

Hopwood, Derek. "An Approach to Islamic History." *British Society for Middle Eastern Studies Bulletin*. 7/1 (1980): 24–32.

Hourani, Albert. *Arabic Thought in the Liberal Age, 1798–1939*. Cambridge: Cambridge University Press, 1983.

Hussein, Taha. *Al-Fitna al-kubra*. Cairo: al-Hay'a al-Misryia, Maktabat al-Usra, 2013.

Huwaidi, Fahmy. *Al-Islam wa al-Dimoqratyia*. Cairo: Markaz al-Ahram li al-Tarjama wa al-Nashr, 1993.

———. *Al-Qur'an wa al-Sultan*. Cairo: Dar al-Shorouk, 2002.

Ibn al-Hajib, Abu 'Amr b. Umar al-Dawini. *Mukhtasar Muntaha al-S'ul wa al-Amal fi 'Imiyi al-Usul wa al-Jadal*. Ed. Nadhir Hammadu. Beirut: Dar Ibn Hazm, 2006.

Ibn al-Jawzi, Abu al-Faraj abd al-Rahman Ibn Ali. *Al-Mawdhu'at*, vols. 1–2. Medina: Mohammed abd al-Mohsen, al-Maktaba al-Salafiya, 1966.

———. *Gharib al-Hadith*. Beirut: Dar al-Kutub al-'Ilmyia, 1985.

———. *Al-Muntazam fi Tarikh al-Muluk wa al-Umam*. Beirut, Dar al-Kutub al-'Ilmyia, 1992.

Ibn Jama'a, Badr al-Din Mohammed. *Kitab Tahrir al-Ahkam fi Tadbir ahl al-Islam*. Ed. Fouad abd al-Monem Ahmed. Doha: Ri'asat al-Mahakim al-Shariya, 1985.

Ibn Kathir, Ismail Ibn Umar al-Dimashqi. *Jami' al-Masanid wa al-Sunan al-Hadi li Aqwam Sunan*. Beirut: Dar Khidr, 1998.

———. *Al-Bidaya wa al-Nihaya*. 21 vols. Cairo: Dar al-Hadith, 2004.

Ibn Munqidh, Usama. *An Arab-Syrian Gentleman and Warrior in the Period of the Crusades* [*Kitab al-'Itibar*]. Trans. Philip Hitti. New York: Columbia University Press, 2000.

Ibn Qayyim al-Jawzia, Mohammed Ibn abi Bakr. *Ilam al-Muwaqqin 'an Rab al-'Alamin.* 4 vols. Beirut: Beirut: Dar al-Jil, 1973.

———. *Ighathat al-Lahfan Min Mas'aid al-Shaytan.* Mecca: Dar 'Alam al-Fawa'ed, 1432 AH.

———. *Jami' al-Fiqh.* 7 vols. Ed. Yusri al-Sayyid (Al-Mansoura, Egypt: Dar al-Wafa, 2001).

Ibn Qudama, Mawaffaq al-Din Abdullah Ibn Ahmed. *Al-Mughni wa Yalih al-Sharih al-Kabir.* 17 vols. Cairo: Dar al-Hadith, 1996.

Ibn Sa'd, *Kitab al-Tabaqat al-Kubra.* 11 vols. Ed. Ali M. Umar. Cairo: Maktabat al-Khanki, 2001.

Ibn al-Salam, Abu 'Amr Uthman Ibn 'Abd al-Rahamn al-Kurdi. *Muqadimat Ibn Salah.* Beirut: Dar al-Kutub al-'Ilmiya, 1978.

Ibn Taymiya, Taqi al-Din. *Al-'Aqida al-Wasittiya.* Riyadh: Adhwa' al-Salaf, 1999.

———. *Majmu'at al-Rasa'el wa al-Masa'el.* Ed. with commentary by Rashid Ridha. Beirut: Lajnat al-Turath al-'Arabi, n.d.

———. *Al-Wasita bayn al-Khalq wa al-Haq wa Rafe' al-Malama 'an al-A'imma al'Alam.* Cairo: Makaz al-Kitab li al-Nashr, n.d.

Ibrahim, Vivian. *The Copts of Egypt: The Challenges of Modernisation and Identity.* London: I.B.Tauris, 2010.

'Imara, Mohammed. *Ma'rakat al-Islam wa Usul al-Hukm.* Cairo: Dar al-Shorouk, 1989.

Islamiyat al-Ma'rifa. *'Adad khas 'an al-Shaykh Mohammed al-Ghazali.* International Institute of Islamic Thought 2/3. Cairo: IIIT, 1997.

Jabarti, abd al-Rahman al-. *Napoleon in Egypt: Al-Jabarti's Chronicle of the French Occupation, 1798.* Trans. S. Moreh. Princeton, NJ: Markus Wiener, 1993.

Jaza'iri, Abu Bakr al-. *Al-Qawl al-Karim al-Ghali fi al-Difa' 'an al-Da'iya al-Ghazali.* Mecca: Maktabat Umm al-Qura, 1991.

Jennings, Roland. *Studies on Ottoman Social History in the Sixteenth and Seventeenth Centuries: Women, Zimmis and Sharia Courts in Kayseri, Cyprus and Trabzon.* Istanbul: ISIS Press, 1999.

Johnston, David. "A Turn in the Epistemology and Hermeneutics of Twentieth Century *Usul al-Fiqh*". *Islamic Law and Society* 11/2 (2004): 233–282.

Juynboll, G.H.A. *Muslim Tradition: Studies in Chronology, Provenance, and Authorship of Early Hadith.* Cambridge: Cambridge University Press, 1983.

Katz, Marion. *Women in the Mosque: A History of Legal Thought and Social Practice.* New York: Columbia University Press, 2014.

Khaled, Mohammed Khaled. *Min Huna Nabda'.* Cairo: al-Maktaba al-Anglo Misriya, 1969.

———. *Al-Dawla fi al-Islam.* Cairo: Dar al-Thabit, 1981.

———. *Rijal Hawla al-Rasul Sala Allah wa Sallem.* Cairo: Dar al-Fikr li al-Tiba'a wa al-Nashir, 2006.

Kishk, Mohammed Galal. *Al-Shaykh Mohammed al-Ghazali bayn al-Naqd al-'Atib wa-l-Madh al-Shamit*. Cairo: Maktabat al-Turath al-Islami, 1990.

Kristof, Nicholas "Unfit for Democracy?" *New York Times*, February 26, 2011 (online: http://www.nytimes.com/2011/02/27/opinion/27kristof.html).

Lacroix, Stéphane. "Al-Albani's Revolutionary Approach to Hadith." *ISIM Review* 21 (2008): 6–7.

Lewis, Bernard. *The Emergence of Modern Turkey*. Oxford: Oxford University Press, 2002.

Lowry, Joseph. "The First Islamic Legal Theory: Ibn al-Muqaffa' on Interpretation, Authority, and the Structure of the Law." *Journal of the American Oriental Society* 128/1 (2008); 25–40.

Madkhali, Rabi' bin Hadi al-. *Kashf Mawqif al-Ghazali min al-Sunna wa Ahliha*. Medina: Maktabat Ibn al-Qayyim, 1410 AH / 1989.

Malkawi, Fathi Hasan, ed. *Al-'Ata al-Fikri li-l-Shaykh Mohammed al-Ghazali*. Amman: IIIT, 1996.

Manji, Irshad. *The Trouble with Islam Today: A Muslim's Call for Reform in Her Faith*. London: St. Martin's Griffin, 2005.

Mansour, Ismail. *Tabseer al-Umma bi Haqiqat al-Sunna*. Cairo: al-Nisr al-Dhahabi, 1995.

Marcus, Abraham. *The Middle East on the Eve of Modernity: Aleppo in the Eighteenth Century*. New York: Columbia University Press, 1992.

Masri, Abd Allah al-. *Al-Da'yia al-Shaheed al-Shaykh Mohammed al-Ghazali*. Cairo: Al-Rawafid al-Thaqafyia, 1996.

Mawardi, Abu al-Hasan al-. *Al-Ahkam al-Sultanyia*. Beirut: Dar al-Fikr al-Arabi, n.d.

Meriwether, Margaret and Judith E. Tucker. *A Social History of Women and the Family in the Middle East*. Boulder, CO: Westview Press, 1999.

Mernissi, Fatima. *The Forgotten Queens of Islam*. Minneapolis: University of Minnesota Press, 1993.

———. *The Veil and the Male Elite: A Feminist Interpretation of Women's Rights in Islam*. New York: Perseus Books, 1992.

Morrow, John. *The Covenants of the Prophet Muhammad with the Christians of the World*. Hillsdale, NY: Sophia Perennis, 2013.

Munadharat Misr Bayna al-Dawla al-Diniya wa al-Madaniya (Munathara fi Ma'radh al-Kitab) 1992. Cairo: al-Dar al-Misriya li al-Nashr wa al-Tawzi', 1992.

Mu'nis, Hussein. *Tanqiyat Usul al-Tarikh al-Islami*, Cairo: Dar al-Rashad, 1997.

Murphy, Caryle. *Passion for Islam: Shaping the Modern Middle East: The Egyptian Experience*. New York: Scribner, 2002.

Muru, Mohammed. *'Almani'yun wa Khawana*. Cairo: Dar Hira, 1996.

Nosseir, Amna, *Abu al-Faraj Ibn al-Jawzi*. Cairo: Dar al-Shrorouk, 1987.

Odah, Salman al-. *Hiwar Hadi' ma' al-Shaykh al-Ghazali*. Riyadh: al-Ri'asa al-'Ama li'Idarat al-Bohouth al-'Ilmiyya wa al-Ifta wa al-Da'wa wa al-Irshad, 1989.

Peirce, Leslie. *The Imperial Harem*. Oxford: Oxford University Press, 1993.
Qaradawi, Yusuf al-. *Al-Imam [Abu Hamid] al-Ghazali bayna Madihih wa Naqidhih*. Cairo: Dar al-Wafa', 1988 [often mistakenly identified as a discussion of Mohammed al-Ghazali].
———. *Madkhal li Dirasat al-Shari'a al-Islamiya*. Cairo: Mo'asasat al-Risala, 1993.
———. *Al-Shaykh al-Ghazali kama 'Airftuhu: Rihlat Nissf Qarn*. Cairo: Dar al-Wafa', 1995.
———. *Tarikhna al-Muftara 'Alayh*. Cairo: Dar al-Shorouk, 2006.
Rahman, Fazlur. *Islam and Modernity: Transformations of an Intellectual Tradition*. Chicago: University of Chicago Press, 1984.
Ramadan, Tariq. *Radical Reform: Islamic Ethics and Liberation*. Oxford: Oxford University Press, 2009.
Rasheed, Madawi al-. *Muted Modernists: The Struggle over Divine Politics in Saudi Arabia*, London: Hurst, 2015.
Razi-al, Abu abd Allah Mohammed Ibn Omar Fakhr al-Din al-. *Kitab M'alim Usul al-Din*. Beirut: Dar al-Fikr al-Lubnani, 1992.
Ridgeon, Lloyd, ed. *Sufi and Salafi in the Contemporary Age*. London: Bloomsbury, 2015.
Ridha, Rashid. *Tafsir al-Manar, al-Ustadh Muohammad Abduh*. 12 vols. Cairo: al-Hay'a al-Misriya al-'Ama li al-Kitab, 1990.
———, ed. and commentary. *Ibn Taymyia: Majmu'at al-Rasa'el wa al-Masa'el*. 2 vols in 5 parts. Beirut: Lajnat al-Turath al-'Arabi, n.d.
———. *Yusr al-Islam wa Usul al-Tashri' al-'Am*. Cairo: Maktabat al-Salam al-Alamiya, n.d.
Rosenthal, Franz. *A History of Muslim Historiography*. Leiden: Brill, 1968.
———. *Muslim Intellectual and Social History: A Collection of Essays*. Kettering, UK: Variorum, 1990.
Sadat, Anwar al-. *Al-Bahth 'an al-Dhat*. Cairo: al-Maktab al-Masri al-Hadith, 1978.
Saqa, Ahmed Hijazi al-. *Dafu' al-Shubuhat 'an al-Shaykh Mohammed al-Ghazali*. Cairo: Maktabat al-Kuliya al-Azhariyya, 1990.
Sha'arawi, Hoda. *Harem Years: Memoirs of an Egyptian Feminist 1879–1924*. Trans. and ed. Margot Badran. New York: Feminist Press, 1987.
Shafi'i, Mohammed Ibn Idris al-. *Al-Risala*. Ed. Ahmed Shakir. Cairo: Mustafa al-Babi al-Halabi, 1940.
Shalabi, Mohammed. *Al-Shaykh al-Ghazali wa Ma'rakat al-Mushaf fi al-'Alam al-Islami*. Cairo: Dar al-Sahwa, 1987.
Shaltut, Mahmoud. *Al-Qur'an wa al-Mar'a*. Cairo: Jamiat al-Azhar, al-Markaz al-Dawli li al-Dirasat wa al-Bohouth al-Sukkanyia, 1975.
———. *Tafsir al-Qur'an al-Kareem, al-Ajza al-'Ashr al-Ula*. Cairo: Dar al-Shorouk, 2004.
———. *Al-Islam 'Aqida wa Shari'a*. 2nd edn. Cairo: Dar al-Qalam, n.d.

Sha'rawi, Mohammed Mutawali. *Tafsir al-Sharawi: Khawatir Fadilat al-Shaykh Mohammed Mutawalli al-Sharawi hawla al-Qur'an al-karim*. Cairo: Akhbar al-Yawm, 1991.

Shatibi, Ibrahim Ibn Mosa al-Lakhmi al-Ghirnati al-. *Al-Muwafaqat*. Ed. Abu Ubaida al-Hasan Ibn Salam. Cairo: Dar Ibn 'Affan, 1997.

———. *Al-'Itisam*. 3 parts. Dammam, Saudi Arabia: Dar Ibn al-Jawzi, 2008.

Shaykh, Salih bin 'Abd al-'Aziz bin Mohammed al-. *Al-Mi'yar li-'Ilm al-Ghazali fi Kitabih al-Sunna al-Nabawiya bayn Ahl al-Fiqh wa-Ahl al-Hadith*. No location or publisher, 1410 AH / 1989.

Shukri, Ghali. *Thaqafat al-Nizam al-'Ashwa'i: Takfir al-'Aql wa 'Aql al-Takfir*. Cairo: Kitab al-Ahali, 1994.

Skovgaard-Peterson, Jakob and Bettina Gräf, eds. *Global Mufti: The Phenomenon of Yusuf al-Qaradawi*. London: Hurst, 2009.

Sonbol, Amira, ed. *Beyond the Exotic: Women's Histories in Islamic Societies*. Syracuse, NY: Syracuse University Press, 2005.

———. *Women, the Family and Divorce Laws in Islamic History*. Syracuse, NY: Syracuse University Press, 1996.

———. "Women in Shari'a Courts: A Historical and Methodological Discussion". *Kelam Araştimalari* 2:2 (2004): 25–56.

Stowasser, Barbara and Yvonne Haddad, eds. *Islamic Law and the Challenges of Modernity*, Walnut Creek, CA: Altamira Press: 2004.

Sultan, Gamal. *Azmat al-Hiwar al-Dini: Naqd Kitab al-Sunna al-Nabawiya bayn Ahl al-Fiqh wa-Ahl al-Hadith*. Cairo: Dar al-Safa, 1990.

Suyuti, Jalal al-Din al-. *Tarikh al-Khulafa*. Cairo: al-Maktaba al-Tawfiqiya, n.d.

———. *Al Radd 'ala Man Akhlada ila al-Ardh wa Jahila anna al-Ijtihad fi kul 'Asr Fard*. Alexandria, Egypt: Mu'assassat Shabab al-Jami'iah, 1985.

———. *Al-La'ali al-Masnou'a fi al-Ahadith al-Mawdhoua'*. Cairo: Dar al-Ma'rifa, 1975.

———. *Al-Mustazraf min Akhbar al-Jawari*. Cairo: Maktabat al-Turath al-Islami, 1989.

———. and Jalal al-din al-Mahalli. *Tafsir wa Bayan Kalimat al-Qur'an al-Kareem li al-Imamyin al-Jalilyin, al-Suyuti wa al-Mahalli*. Cairo: Dar al Fida al-Arabi, 1995.

Tabari, Abu Ja'far M. Ibn Jarir al-. *Tarikh al-Tabari*. Riyadh: Bait al-Afkar al-Dawlyia, n.d.

Tibi, Bassam. *The Challenge of Fundamentalism: Political Islam and the New World Disorder*. Berkeley: University of California Press, 2002.

Tucker, Judith E. *Women in Nineteenth-Century Egypt*. Cambridge: Cambridge University Press, 1985.

Tufi, Najim al-Din al-. "Risalat al-Tufi fi Ri'ayiat al-Maslaha", in Abd al-Wahab Khallaf, ed., *Masadir al-Tashr'i al-Islami fi ma Lais Fihi Nass*. Kuwait City: Dar al-Qalam, 1993.

———. *Al-Bolbul fi Usul al-Fiqh*. Cairo: Maktabat Ibn Taymiya, n.d.

Vogel, Frank and Asifa Quraishi, eds. *The Islamic Marriage Contract: Case Studies in Islamic Family Law*. Cambridge, MA: Harvard University Press, 2008.

von Grunebaum, Gustave E. *Medieval Islam: A Study in Cultural Orientation*. Chicago: University of Chicago Press, 1946.

———. *Classical Islam: A History, 600 A.D. to 1258 A.D.* London: Allen and Unwin, 1970.

———. *Theology and Law in Islam*. Wiesbaden, Germany: Harrassowitz, 1971.

Yunis, Mohammed. *Tajribat al-Shaykh Mohamed al-Ghazali fi Tajdid al-Fikr al-Islami*. Cairo: Maktabat al-Thaqafa al-Diniyya, 2013.

Zurcher, Erik J. *The Young Turk Legacy and Nation Building: From the Ottoman Empire to Atatürk's Turkey*. London: I.B.Tauris, 2010.

Index

All dates stated below are according to Common Era calendar (CE)

CPSIA information can be obtained
at www.ICGtesting.com
Printed in the USA
BVOW06*0937160517
483388BV00004B/4/P

9 781781 792957